Middle School 2-1

기말고사 완벽대비

적중 100
영어 기출 문제집

중2
비상 | 김진완

Best Collection

구성과 특징

교과서의 주요 학습 내용을 중심으로 학습 영역별 특성에 맞춰 단계별로 다양한 학습 기회를 제공하여 단원별 학습능력 평가는 물론 중간 및 기말고사 시험 등에 완벽하게 대비할 수 있도록 내용을 구성

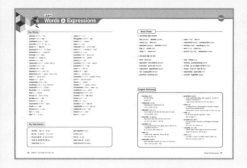

Words & Expressions

Step1 Key Words 단원별 핵심 단어 설명 및 풀이
Key Expression 단원별 핵심 숙어 및 관용어 설명
Word Power 반대 또는 비슷한 뜻 단어 배우기
English Dictionary 영어로 배우는 영어 단어

Step2 실력평가 단원별 수시평가 대비 주관식, 객관식 문제풀이

Step3 서술형 대비 학업성취도 및 수행능력평가 대비 서술형 문제풀이

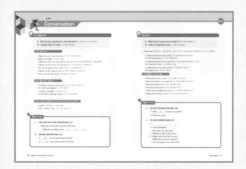

Conversation

Step1 핵심 의사소통 의사소통에 필요한 주요 표현 방법 요약
핵심 Check 기본적인 표현 방법 및 활용능력 확인

Step2 대화문 익히기 상황에 따른 대화문 활용 및 연습

Step3 기본평가 시험대비 기초 학습 능력 평가

Step4 실력평가 단원별 수시평가 대비 주관식, 객관식 문제풀이

Step5 서술형 대비 학업성취도 및 수행능력평가 대비 서술형 문제풀이

Grammar

Step1 주요 문법 단원별 주요 문법 사항과 예문을 알기 쉽게 설명
핵심 Check 기본 문법사항에 대한 이해 여부 확인

Step2 기본평가 시험대비 기초 학습 능력 평가

Step3 실력평가 단원별 수시평가 대비 주관식, 객관식 문제풀이

Step4 서술형 대비 학업성취도 및 수행능력평가 대비 서술형 문제풀이

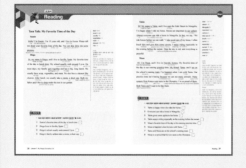

Reading

Step1 구문 분석 단원별로 제시된 문장에 대한 구문별 분석과 내용 설명
확인문제 문장에 대한 기본적인 이해와 인지능력 확인

Step2 확인학습A 빈칸 채우기를 통한 문장 완성 능력 확인

Step3 확인학습B 제시된 우리말을 영어로 완성하여 작문 능력 키우기

Step4 실력평가 단원별 수시평가 대비 주관식, 객관식 문제풀이

Step5 서술형 대비 학업성취도 및 수행능력평가 대비 서술형 문제풀이
교과서 구석구석 교과서에 나오는 기타 문장까지 완벽 학습

Composition

|영역별 핵심문제|

단어 및 어휘, 대화문, 문법, 독해 등 각 영역별 기출문제의 출제 유형을 분석하여 실전에 대비하고 연습할 수 있도록 문제를 배열

|서술형 실전 및 창의사고력 문제|

학교 시험에서 점차 늘어나는 서술형 시험에 집중 대비하고 고득점을 취득하는데 만전을 기하기 위한 학습 코너

|단원별 예상문제|

기출문제를 분석한 후 새로운 시험 출제 경향을 더하여 새롭게 출제될 수 있는 문제를 포함하여 시험에 완벽하게 대비할 수 있도록 준비

|단원별 모의고사|

영역별, 단계별 학습을 모두 마친 후 실전 연습을 위한 모의고사

on the textbook ·······················

교과서 파헤치기

- **단어Test1~2** 영어 단어 우리말 쓰기와 우리말을 영어 단어로 쓰기
- **대화문Test1~2** 대화문 빈칸 완성 및 전체 대화문 쓰기
- **본문Test1~5** 빈칸 완성, 우리말 쓰기, 문장 배열연습, 영어 작문하기 복습 등 단계별 반복 학습을 통해 교과서 지문에 대한 완벽한 습득
- **구석구석지문Test1~2** 지문 빈칸 완성 및 전문 영어로 쓰기

Contents

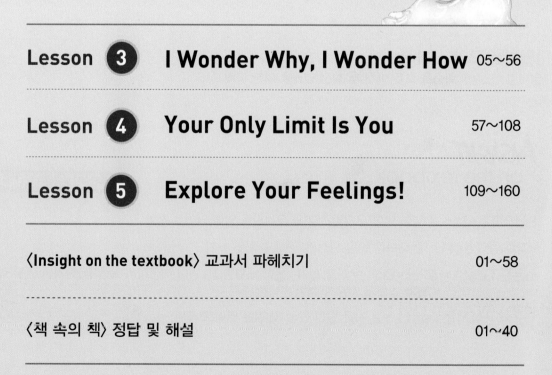

I Wonder Why, I Wonder How

 의사소통 기능

- 들어 본 적이 있는지 묻기
  A: Have you heard about the Sci-Magic show?
  B: No, I haven't.

- 설명 요청하기
  A: I made a potato clock yesterday!
  B: A potato clock? What do you mean?
  A: My clock works with potatoes, not with
     batteries.

 언어 형식

- 수동태
  The city **is powered by** the screams.

- to 부정사의 형용사적 용법
  Rapunzel has the ability **to hold** up a person.

Words & Expressions

Key Words

- **ability** [əbíləti] 명 능력
- **activity** [æktívəti] 명 활동
- **actually** [ǽktʃuəli] 부 실제로, 정말로
- **add** [æd] 동 더하다
- **advice** [ædváis] 명 충고, 조언
- **amazingly** [əméiziŋli] 부 놀랍게도
- **amount** [əmáunt] 명 양
- **amusement** [əmjúːzmənt] 명 재미, 놀이, 오락
- **appear** [əpíər] 동 나타나다
- **application** [æpləkéiʃən] 명 응용 프로그램, 적용
- **average** [ǽvəridʒ] 명 평균
- **balloon** [bəlúːn] 명 풍선
- **battery** [bǽtəri] 명 건전지, 배터리
- **bean** [biːn] 명 콩
- **car horn** 자동차 경적
- **challenge** [tʃǽlindʒ] 명 도전, 난제 동 도전하다
- **collector** [kəléktər] 명 수집가
- **drone** [droun] 명 무인 비행기, 무인 항공기
- **electricity** [ilektrísəti] 명 전기, 전류
- **entire** [intáiər] 형 전체의
- **experiment** [ikspérəmənt] 명 실험
- **explain** [ikspléin] 동 설명하다
- **fair** [fɛər] 명 박람회, 장 형 공정한
- **fold** [fould] 동 접다

- **hide** [haid] 동 숨기다, 숨다
- **however** [hauévər] 부 그러나
- **impossible** [impásəbl] 형 불가능한
- **lift** [ift] 동 들어 올리다
- **lower** [lóuər] 동 내리다, 낮추다
- **miss** [mis] 동 놓치다, 그리워하다
- **monster** [mánstər] 명 괴물, 요괴
- **normal** [nɔ́ːrməl] 형 보통의, 평범한
- **pick** [pik] 동 따다, 뜯다, 집다
- **possible** [pásəbl] 형 가능한, 있을 수 있는
- **produce** [prədjúːs] 동 생산하다, 제작하다
- **record** [rikɔ́ːrd] 동 기록하다, 녹음하다
- **ring** [riŋ] 명 반지 동 울리다
- **scare** [skɛər] 동 겁주다, 겁먹게 하다
- **scream** [skriːm] 명 비명, 외침(소리)
- **single** [síŋgl] 형 단 하나의
- **sore** [sɔːr] 형 아픈
- **string** [striŋ] 명 실
- **unbelievable** [ənbəlívəbəl] 형 믿을 수 없는
- **unlock** [ənlak] 동 자물쇠를 열다
- **useful** [júːsfəl] 형 유용한
- **vinegar** [vínəgər] 명 식초
- **weigh** [wei] 동 무게가 ~이다
- **youth** [juːθ] 동 젊은, 청춘

Key Expressions

- **a couple of** 둘의, 몇 개의
- **for example** 예를 들어
- **hold up** ~을 떠받치다
- **in front of** ~의 앞에
- **let's say that** ~라고 하자
- **light up** ~을 환하게 하다, 점등하다
- **paint over** 덧칠하다
- **pick one's brain** ~의 지혜를 빌리다

- **pump up** 주입하다, 채워 넣다
- **turn into** ~가 되다
- **take care of** ~을 돌보다
- **take away** ~을 제거하다, ~을 치우다
- **turn off** ~을 끄다
- **turn on** ~을 켜다
- **what's more** 게다가, 더구나
- **wrap ~ around** ~을 두르다, ~을 감다

Word Power

서로 반대되는 뜻을 가진 단어

□ **possible** 가능한 → **impossible** 불가능한

□ **lift** 들어 올리다 → **lower** 낮추다

□ **lock** 잠그다 → **unlock** 자물쇠를 풀다

□ **hide** 숨기다 → **reveal** 드러내다

□ **entire** 전체의 → **partial** 부분의

□ **turn on** ~을 켜다 → **turn off** ~을 끄다

□ **useful** 유용한 → **useless** 쓸모없는

□ **fair** 공정한, 공평한 → **unfair** 불공정한

□ **believable** 믿을 수 있는 → **unbelievable** 믿을 수 없는

□ **real** 현실의 → **imaginary** 상상의, 가상의

□ **normal** 보통의, 정상적인 → **abnormal** 비정상적인

□ **active** 활동적인 → **inactive** 활동하지 않은, 활발하지 않은

English Dictionary

□ **add** 더하다
→ to put something together with something else so as to increase the size, number, amount, etc.
무언가를 크기, 수, 양 등을 증가시키기 위해 다른 무언가와 함께 놓다

□ **amusement** 재미, 즐거움
→ the feeling that you have when you think that something is funny
어떤 것이 재미있다고 생각할 때 가지는 느낌

□ **average** 평균
→ calculated by adding several amounts together, finding a total, and dividing the total by the number of amounts
몇몇 합을 더해 총합을 찾은 후 합의 수로 전체를 나누어 계산한 것

□ **battery** 건전지
→ a device that is placed inside a car engine, clock, radio, etc. and that produces the electricity that makes it work
자동차 엔진, 시계, 라디오 등 안에 위치하여 그것이 작동할 수 있게 하는 전기를 만들어 내는 장치

□ **challenge** 도전
→ a new or difficult task that tests somebody's ability and skill
누군가의 능력과 기술을 시험해 보기 위한 새롭거나 어려운 과제

□ **collector** 수집가
→ a person who collects things, either as a hobby or as a job
취미나 직업으로 물건들을 모으는 사람

□ **drone** 무인 비행기
→ an aircraft without a pilot, controlled from the ground
조종사 없이 땅에서 조작되는 항공기

□ **experiment** 실험
→ a scientific test that is done in order to study what happens and to gain new knowledge
무슨 일이 일어나는지 연구해서 새로운 과학적 지식을 얻기 위해 행해지는 과학적 검사

□ **hide** 숨기다
→ to put or keep something/somebody in a place where it cannot be seen or found
어떤 물건이나 사람을 보이지 않거나 찾을 수 없는 장소에 놓거나 보관하다

□ **lift** 들어 올리다
→ to raise somebody/something or be raised to a higher position or level
누군가나 무언가를 더 높은 곳이나 수준으로 들어 올리거나 올려지다

□ **lower** 내리다, 낮추다
→ to let or make something/somebody go down
무언가나 누군가를 내려가게 만들다

□ **possible** 가능한
→ that can be done or achieved
할 수 있거나 성취될 수 있는

□ **record** 기록하다
→ to write something down so that it can be used or seen again in the future
어떤 것을 글로 적어서 나중에 다시 사용하거나 볼 수 있게 하다

□ **scare** 무서워하다
→ to become frightened
겁에 질리다

□ **scream** 비명
→ a loud high cry made by somebody who is hurt, frightened, excited, etc.
다치거나 놀라거나 흥분한 누군가에 의한 크고 높은 고함소리

□ **weigh** 무게를 재다
→ to measure how heavy somebody/something is, usually by using scales
보통 저울을 사용해서 어떤 사람이나 사물이 얼마나 무거운지 측정하다

서답형

01 다음 짝지어진 단어의 관계가 같도록 빈칸에 알맞은 말을 쓰시오.

active : inactive = possible : _____

서답형

02 다음 영영풀이에 해당하는 말을 쓰시오.

to measure how heavy somebody/ something is, usually by using scales

➡ _____

중요

03 다음 중 밑줄 친 부분의 뜻풀이가 바르지 않은 것은?

① Let's find out what happens in the experiment. 경험
② How much vinegar is used to make salad? 식초
③ My grandmother used to hide money in a cupboard. 숨기다
④ Minho is blowing up a balloon. 풍선
⑤ Many artists do their best to produce great works of art. 제작하다

04 다음 문장에 공통으로 들어갈 말을 고르시오.

• Be sure to _____ the door before you leave.
• Sue is using a _____ to protect the important document in her drawer.
• When Ann saw me, she _____(e)d me in her arms.

① move   ② lock   ③ record
④ check   ⑤ challenge

서답형

05 다음 문장의 빈칸에 들어갈 말을 〈보기〉에서 골라 쓰시오.

┤ 보기 ├
amusement / amount / challenge / add

(1) His big _____ is to win in an election.
(2) One day, my father took me to the _____ park.
(3) Would you _____ my name to the list?
(4) He gave an equal _____ of pocket money to each child.

06 다음 주어진 문장의 밑줄 친 의미와 같은 의미로 쓰인 것은?

Have you heard about the science fair?

① The referee didn't make a fair decision.
② It's important to play the fair game.
③ We are planning to visit the international IT fair.
④ That sounds like a fair deal.
⑤ It's not fair to blame others for your mistakes.

중요

07 다음 문장의 빈칸에 들어갈 말을 순서대로 쓰시오.

(1) The app tells you how to take care (A)_____ your pet.
(2) Pick (B)_____ the purse.
(3) We need candles to light (C)_____ the room.

(A)_____ (B)_____ (C)_____

01 다음 짝지어진 단어의 관계가 같도록 빈칸에 알맞은 말을 쓰시오.

> fair : unfair = lock : _____

[02~03] 다음 영영풀이에 해당하는 말을 쓰시오.

02
> a person who collects things, either as a hobby or as a job

➡ _____

03
> to put or keep something in a place where it cannot be seen or found

➡ _____

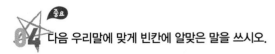

04 다음 우리말에 맞게 빈칸에 알맞은 말을 쓰시오.

(1) 당신이 부유하다고 가정해 보자.
➡ _____ _____ _____ you are rich.

(2) 너는 멀리 떠나기 전에 타이어에 바람을 넣어야 한다.
➡ You should _____ _____ the tires before going far away.

(3) 촛불을 켜 주시겠어요?
➡ Would you _____ _____ the candle?

05 다음 주어진 우리말과 일치하도록 빈칸을 완성하시오.

(1) 자동차 경적 소리가 나를 놀라게 했다.
➡ The sounds from a _____ _____ made me surprised.

(2) 그는 믿기 어려울 만큼의 많은 돈을 벌었다.
➡ He made an _____ amount of money.

(3) 야수는 미녀에게 겁을 주고 싶지 않았다.
➡ The beast didn't want to _____ the beauty.

06 다음 빈칸에 주어진 단어를 적절한 형태로 채우시오.

> (1) There is a strong _____ (possible) of snow tomorrow.
> (2) It is _____(amazing) easy to make 'Dancing Beans'.
> (3) My teacher praised my _____ (able) to speak Chinese well.

(A)_____ (B)_____ (C)_____

07 다음 우리말과 일치하도록 주어진 단어를 모두 배열하여 완성하시오.

(1) 벽을 노란색으로 고르게 칠해 보자.
(paint / let's / with / the / wall / yellow / over / evenly)
➡ _____

(2) 과학 박물관의 특별 행사에 대해 들어봤니?
(the special / have / about / you / event / at / the science / heard / museum)
➡ _____
_____

(3) 감자가 전기를 생산한다고 가정해 봅시다.
(electricity / say / produce / potatoes / that / let's)
➡ _____

Conversation

1 들어 본 적이 있는지 묻기

> **A** Have you heard about the Sci-Magic show? 과학 마술 쇼에 대해 들어 본 적 있어?
> **B** No, I haven't. 아니. 없어.

- 'Have you ever+과거분사 ~?'는 경험을 묻는 표현으로 'Have you ever heard ~?'는 들어 본 적이 있는지 묻는다. 이에 대한 대답으로 긍정일 때는 'Yes, I have.', 부정일 때는 'No, I haven't.'로 대답한다. Have you?는 상대방에게서 받은 질문을 다시 상대방에게 묻는 표현으로 반복된 부분은 생략한다.

- **경험 말하기**

  1. 현재까지의 경험을 물을 때 현재완료 시제를 사용하므로 'Have you ever+과거 분사 ~?' 형태에 유의한다.

  2. 경험하지 못한 것으로 '전혀 ~해 본 적이 없다.'라고 강조하기 위해 'No, I've never ~.'로 대답할 수 있다.

  3. 과거의 경험은 과거시제를 이용한다.

  • Did you hear the news? 과거에 뉴스를 들었는지 묻는 표현
  • Have you heard about the news? 과거부터 현재까지 뉴스를 들어 본 적이 있는지 묻는 표현

핵심 Check

1. 다음 우리말과 일치하도록 빈칸에 알맞은 말을 쓰시오.

(1) **A:** _____ _____ _____ _____ the pop song contest?
(팝송 대회에 대해 들어 본 적이 있나요?)

   B: No, I haven't. (아니요. 들어 본 적 없어요.)

(2) **A:** Have you heard about Beethoven? (베토벤에 대해 들어 본 적이 있나요?)

   B: _____, _____ _____. _____ _____? (예. 들어 보았어요. 당신은요?)

(3) **A:** Have you heard about a paper soap? (종이비누에 대해 들어 본 적이 있나요?)

   B: _____, _____ _____. (아니요. 들어 본 적 없어요.)

❷ 설명 요청하기

> **A** I made a potato clock yesterday! 나 어제 감자시계를 만들었어!
>
> **B** A potato clock? What do you mean? 감자시계? 무슨 말이야?
>
> **A** My clock works with potatoes, not with batteries. 내 시계는 건전지가 아니라 감자로 작동을 해.

■ 'What do you mean?'은 상대방이 언급한 것에 대해 명확한 설명을 요청하는 표현으로 What is it? 또는 Can you explain it specifically? 또는 Can you tell me more about it? 등으로 바꾸어 쓸 수 있다.

설명 요청하기

- What is it? 그게 무엇이니?
- Can you explain it specifically? 그것을 명확하게 설명해 줄 수 있니?
- Can you tell me more about it? 너는 내게 그것에 대해 더 이야기해 줄 수 있니?
- What do you mean? 무슨 뜻이니?
- Would you give me more information? 내게 더 정보를 주겠니?

핵심 Check

2. 다음 우리말과 일치하도록 빈칸에 알맞은 말을 쓰시오.

(1) **A:** We can make the 'Dancing Beans.' (우리는 '춤추는 콩'을 만들 수 있어.)

   B: Dancing Beans? _____ _____ _____ _____? (춤추는 콩? 무슨 뜻이야?)

(2) **A:** I made an egg ball with my brother. (남동생이랑 달걀 공을 만들었어.)

   B: An egg ball? _____ _____ _____? (달걀 공? 그게 무엇이니?)

(3) **A:** Let's make a "Mystery Card" for the science experiment.
   (과학 실험으로 '미스터리 카드'를 만들자.)

   B: "Mystery Card"? Can you _____ me _____ about it?
   (미스터리 카드? 내게 그것에 대해 더 이야기해 줄 수 있니?)

A. Listen & Talk 2-B

Minho: Anna, ❶let's make a "Mystery Card" for the science experiment.

Anna: A "Mystery Card?" ❷What do you mean?

Minho: It's a special card. It can hide your message.

Anna: How do you make ❸it?

Minho: Mix baking soda and water. Then, write a message on the card with ❹it.

Anna: How can you read the card?

Minho: ❺Paint over the card with grape juice, and then the message appears.

Minho: Anna, 우리 과학 실험으로 '미스터리 카드'를 만들자.

Anna: 미스터리 카드? 무슨 말이야?

Minho: 그건 특별한 카드야. 그 카드는 너의 메시지를 숨길 수 있어.

Anna: 어떻게 만드는데?

Minho: 베이킹 소다랑 물을 섞어. 그러고 나서 그걸로 카드 위에 메시지를 써.

Anna: 카드를 어떻게 읽을 수 있어?

Minho: 카드를 포도 주스로 칠하면 메시지가 나타나.

❶ 'let's ∼'는 '∼하자'라고 제안하는 표현이다.
❷ 'What do you mean?'은 상대방이 한 말을 잘 알아듣지 못했거나 자신이 제대로 이해했는지 다시 확인하기 위해서 사용하는 표현이다.
❸ it은 '미스터리 카드'를 가리킨다.
❹ it은 베이킹 소다와 물을 섞은 것을 가리킨다.
❺ 명령문+and ∼: ∼해라, 그러면 ∼

Check(√) True or False

(1) A "Mystery Card" can hide the message.   T ☐ F ☐

(2) Minho needs baking soda and water to read the card.   T ☐ F ☐

B. Communication

Jane: ❶Have you heard about the Smart App Contest?

Minho: Yes, I have. Are you going to enter ❷it?

Jane: Yeah, I'm going to send my idea about a Pic Gardener App.

Minho: A Pic Gardener App? ❸What do you mean?

Jane: When you take a picture of a plant, the app tells you how to ❹take care of it.

Minho: It sounds like a very useful app.

Jane: 너 스마트 앱 대회에 대해 들어 본 적 있어?

Minho: 응, 들어 봤어. 너 거기 나갈 거야?

Jane: 응, Pic Gardener 앱에 관한 내 아이디어를 보내 보려고.

Minho: Pic Gardener 앱? 무슨 말이야?

Jane: 식물의 사진을 찍으면, 그 앱이 그 식물을 가꾸는 법을 알려 주는 거야.

Minho: 그거 매우 유용한 앱 같구나.

❶ 'Have you heard about ∼?'은 상대방에게 어떤 것에 대해서 들어 본 적이 있는지 혹은 알고 있는지 여부를 묻기 위해서 사용된다.
❷ it은 스마트 앱 대회를 가리킨다.
❸ 설명을 요청하는 표현이다.
❹ take care of: ∼을 돌보다, 가꾸다

Check(√) True or False

(3) Jane is going to take part in the Smart App Contest.   T ☐ F ☐

(4) Jane is taking a picture to take care of her plant.   T ☐ F ☐

Listen & Talk 1 A-1

Mike: What show are you watching, Sally?

Sally: I'm watching the Sci-Magic show. It's a new program. Have you heard about ❶it?

Mike: No, I haven't. ❷What's it about?

Sally: The program uses science to explain magic tricks.

Mike: Oh, it sounds interesting.

❶ the Sci-Magic show를 가리킨다.
❷ the Sci-Magic show에 대한 설명을 요청하는 표현이다.

Listen & Talk A-2

Tom: Mom, ❶have you heard about the Chat Robot?

Mom: No, I haven't. What is ❷it?

Tom: It's a phone application. You can ask any questions and it will answer. ❸Let me show you. "Emily, what's the weather like today?"

Emily: "It's going to rain, so you'll need an umbrella."

Mom: Wow, ❹what a great application!

❶ Chat Robot에 관해 들어 본 적이 있는지 묻는 표현이다.
❷ Chat Robot을 가리킨다.
❸ 시범으로 보여주기 위해 쓰는 표현이다.
❹ 감탄문으로 'What+a(n)+형용사+명사!' 순서로 나타낸다.

Listen & Talk B

W: Hello, students. Have you heard about the DIY Drone Class? You can make your own drone in the class. The Youth Community Center ❶offers the class at 3 p.m. every Wednesday in May. Make your special drone and learn how to control it. Don't ❷miss this great ❸chance!

❶ offer: 제공하다, 주다
❷ miss: 놓치다
❸ chance: 기회(= opportunity)

Listen & Talk 2 A-1

Mina: ❶You know what? I made a potato clock yesterday!

Jack: A potato clock? What do you mean?

Mina: My clock works with potatoes, not with batteries. Potatoes can produce ❷electricity.

Jack: That's interesting!

❶ 상대방의 주의를 끌 때 사용하는 표현이다. ❷ electricity: 전기

Listen & Talk 2 A-2

Jimmy: Lisa, what did you do last weekend?

Lisa: I made an egg ball with my brother.

Jimmy: An egg ball? ❶What do you mean?

Lisa: We put an egg in ❷vinegar for two days. Then, the egg ❸turns into a ball.

Jimmy: Wow, I want to make ❹one, too!

❶ 달걀 공에 대한 설명을 요청하는 표현이다. ❷ vinegar: 식초 ❸ turn into ～: ～이 되다 ❹ 달걀 공을 가리킨다.

Wrap Up 1

Hojin: Hey, Katy. Have you heard about ❶the science fair?

Katy: Yeah, I'm going to go ❷there.

Hojin: ❸Me, too! I'm excited about doing different kinds of experiments.

Katy: Yeah, I'm also ❹looking forward to it!

❶ the science fair: 과학 박람회 ❷ there = to the science fair ❸ '나도 그래!'라는 의미로 'So am I.'로 바꾸어 쓸 수 있다. ❹ look forward to: ～을 기대하다

Wrap Up 2

Emma: ❶How about making "Dancing Beans" for the science project?

David: "Dancing Beans?" What do you mean?

Emma: ❷They are beans that move in the water ❸like they're dancing.

David: Sounds interesting! What do we need?

Emma: We just need some water, vinegar, baking soda, and beans.

❶ 'How about ～?'은 '～하는 게 어때?'라고 제안하는 표현이다. 'What about ～?'으로 바꾸어 쓸 수 있다. ❷ They는 Dancing Beans를 가리킨다. ❸ like: ～하는 것처럼

● 다음 우리말과 일치하도록 빈칸에 알맞은 말을 쓰시오.

Listen & Talk 1 A-1

Mike: _____ _____ are you watching, Sally?

Sally: I'm watching the Sci-Magic show. It's a new program. _____ _____ _____ _____ _____?

Mike: No, I haven't. What's it about?

Sally: The program uses _____ to explain magic tricks.

Mike: Oh, it sounds _____.

해석

Mike: Sally, 무슨 쇼 프로그램을 보고 있니?
Sally: '과학 마술 쇼'를 보고 있어. 새로 하는 프로그램이야. 너 그것에 대해 들어 본 적 있어?
Mike: 아니, 없어. 무엇에 관한 거야?
Sally: 그 프로그램에서는 마술 묘기를 설명하기 위해 과학을 이용해.
Mike: 오, 흥미로울 것 같아.

Listen & Talk 1 A-2

Tom: Mom, have you heard about the Chat Robot?

Mom: _____, _____ _____. What is it?

Tom: It's a phone application. You can ask any questions and it will answer. _____ _____ _____ _____. "Emily, what's the weather like today?"

Emily: "It's going to rain, so you'll need an umbrella."

Mom: Wow, _____ _____ _____ _____!

Tom: 엄마, Chat Robot에 관해 들어 본 적 있으세요?
Mom: 아니, 없어. 그게 뭐니?
Tom: 그건 휴대폰 앱이에요. 어떤 질문이든 물으면 그것을 대답해 줘요. 보여 드릴게요. "Emily, 오늘 날씨는 어때?"
Emily: "비가 올 예정이니까, 당신은 우산이 필요할 것입니다."
Mom: 와, 정말 멋진 앱이구나!

Listen & Talk 1 B

W: Hello, students. _____ _____ _____ _____ the DIY Drone Class? You can make your own drone in the class. The Youth Community Center _____ the class at 3 p.m. every Wednesday in May. Make your special drone and learn _____ _____ _____ _____. Don't miss this great chance!

W: 학생 여러분, 안녕하세요. DIY 무인기(드론) 수업에 관해 들어 본 적이 있나요? 그 수업에서 여러분은 자신만의 무인기를 만들 수 있어요. 청소년 지역 문화 회관에서 5월에 수요일마다 오후 3시에 수업이 있어요. 여러분의 특별한 무인기를 만들고, 조종하는 방법을 배워 보세요. 이 좋은 기회를 놓치지 마세요.

Listen & Talk 2 A-1

Mina: You know what? I made a potato clock yesterday!

Jack: A potato clock? _____ _____ _____ _____ _____?

Mina: My clock works with potatoes, not with batteries. Potatoes can produce _____.

Jack: That's interesting!

Mina: 그거 알아? 나 어제 감자 시계를 만들었어!
Jack: 감자 시계? 무슨 말이야?
Mina: 내 시계는 건전지가 아니라 감자로 작동을 해. 감자로 전기를 만들 수 있거든.
Jack: 그거 흥미롭다!

Listen & Talk 2 A-2

Jimmy: Lisa, _____ _____ _____ _____ _____ _____ _____ _____?

Lisa: I made an egg ball with my brother.

Jimmy: An egg ball? What do you mean?

Lisa: We _____ an egg _____ _____ for two days. Then, the egg _____ _____ a ball.

Jimmy: Wow, I want to make one, too!

Listen & Talk 2 B

Minho: Anna, let's make a "Mystery Card" for the science experiment.

Anna: A "Mystery Card?" _____ _____ _____ _____?

Minho: It's a special card. It can _____ your message.

Anna: How do you make it?

Minho: _____ baking soda and water. Then, write a message on the card with it.

Anna: _____ _____ _____ _____ _____ _____?

Minho: Paint over the card with grape juice, and then the message _____.

Communication

Jane: _____ _____ _____ _____ _____ the Smart App Contest?

Minho: _____, _____ _____. Are you going to enter it?

Jane: Yeah, I'm going to send my idea about a Pic Gardener App.

Minho: A Pic Gardener App? _____ _____ _____ _____?

Jane: When you take a picture of a plant, the app tells you _____ _____ _____ _____ _____ _____.

Minho: It sounds like a very _____ app.

Wrap Up 1

Hojin: Hey, Katy. Have you heard about the science fair?

Katy: Yeah, I'm going to go there.

Hojin: Me, too! I'm _____ about doing different kinds of _____.

Katy: Yeah, I'm also _____ _____ _____ it!

해석

Jimmy: Lisa, 지난 주말에 뭐 했어?
Lisa: 남동생이랑 달걀 공을 만들었어.
Jimmy: 달걀 공? 무슨 말이야?
Lisa: 우리는 달걀을 이틀 동안 식초에 담가놨어. 그러면 달걀이 공으로 변해.
Jimmy: 와, 나도 하나 만들고 싶어!

Minho: Anna, 우리 과학 실험으로 '미스터리 카드'를 만들자.
Anna: 미스터리 카드? 무슨 말이야?
Minho: 그건 특별한 카드야. 그 카드는 너의 메시지를 숨길 수 있어.
Anna: 어떻게 만드는데?
Minho: 베이킹 소다랑 물을 섞어. 그러고 나서 그걸로 카드 위에 메시지를 써.
Anna: 카드를 어떻게 읽을 수 있어?
Minho: 카드를 포도 주스로 칠하면 메시지가 나타나.

Jane: 너 스마트 앱 대회에 대해 들어 본 적 있어?
Minho: 응, 들어 봤어. 너 거기 나갈 거야?
Jane: 응, Pic Gardener 앱에 관한 내 아이디어를 보내 보려고.
Minho: Pic Gardener 앱? 무슨 말이야?
Jane: 식물의 사진을 찍으면, 그 앱이 그 식물을 가꾸는 법을 알려 주는 거야.
Minho: 매우 유용한 앱 같아.

Hojin: 저기, Katy. 너 과학 박람회에 대해 들어 본 적 있어?
Katy: 응, 나 거기에 갈 거야.
Hojin: 나도! 난 다양한 종류의 실험들을 할 생각을 하니 신나.
Katy: 맞아, 나도 그게 정말 기대돼!

01 다음 대화의 밑줄 친 (A)의 우리말을 영어로 쓰시오.

> A: I made a potato clock yesterday!
> B: A potato clock? (A)무슨 말이야?
> A: My clock works with potatoes, not with batteries.

➡ _____

02 다음 대화의 빈칸에 들어갈 말로 적절한 것은?

> A: Have you heard about the Chat Robot?
> B: _____

① Yes, I haven't.   ② Yes, I did.
③ No, I didn't.   ④ No, I have.
⑤ No, I haven't.

[03~04] 다음 대화를 읽고, 물음에 답하시오.

> Mike: What show are you watching, Sally? (A)
> Sally: I'm watching the Sci-Magic show. It's a new program. (B)
> Mike: No, I haven't. What's it about? (C)
> Sally: The program uses science to explain magic tricks. (D)
> Mike: Oh, it sounds interesting. (E)

03 위 대화의 (A)~(E) 중 주어진 문장이 들어가기에 적절한 곳은?

> Have you heard about it?

① (A)   ② (B)   ③ (C)   ④ (D)   ⑤ (E)

04 위 대화의 내용과 일치하지 않는 것은?

① Sally는 과학 마술 쇼를 보고 있다.
② 과학 마술 쇼는 새로운 프로그램이다.
③ Mike는 마술과 과학에 관심이 많다.
④ Mike는 과학 마술 쇼에 대해 들어 본 적이 없다.
⑤ 과학 마술 쇼는 마술 묘기를 설명하기 위해 과학을 사용한다.

Conversation 시험대비 실력평가

01 다음 대화가 자연스럽게 이어지도록 순서대로 배열하시오.

(A) No, I haven't. What is it?

(B) Mom, have you heard about the Chat Robot?

(C) Wow, what a great application!

(D) "It's going to rain, so you'll need an umbrella."

(E) It's a phone application. You can ask any questions and it will answer. Let me show you. "Emily, what's the weather like today?"

➡ _____

[02~04] 다음 담화문을 읽고, 물음에 답하시오.

W: Hello, students. _____(A)_____ ? You can make your own drone in the class. The Youth Community Center offers the class at 3 p.m. every Wednesday in May. Make your special drone and learn how to control it. Don't miss this great chance!

서답형

02 위 담화문의 빈칸 (A)에 들어갈 말을 〈보기〉에 주어진 어구를 모두 배열하여 완성하시오.

┌─ 보기 ├─
you / the / about / DIY Drone Class / have / heard

➡ _____

03 위 담화문의 목적으로 적절한 것은?

① to advertise
② to apologize
③ to appreciate
④ to celebrate
⑤ to protest

서답형

04 What can you do in the DIY Drone Class?

➡ _____
_____

[05~06] 다음 대화를 읽고, 물음에 답하시오.

Mike: What show are you watching, Sally?

Sally: I'm watching the Sci-Magic show. It's a new program. Have you heard about it?

Mike: (A)아니, 없어. What's it about?

Sally: The program uses science to ___(B)___ magic tricks.

Mike: Oh, it sounds interesting.

서답형

05 위 대화의 (A)의 우리말을 영어로 쓰시오.

➡ _____

06 위 대화의 빈칸 (B)에 알맞은 것은?

① explain
② produce
③ challenge
④ pump
⑤ decorate

[07~08] 다음 대화를 읽고, 물음에 답하시오.

Mina: You know what? I made a potato clock yesterday!

Jack: A potato clock? What do you mean?

Mina: My clock works with potatoes, not with batteries. Potatoes can produce electricity.

Jack: _____(A)_____

07 위 대화의 빈칸 (A)에 들어갈 말로 나머지와 의도가 <u>다른</u> 것은?

① That's interesting!

② It sounds interesting.

③ How interesting!

④ What an interesting invention!

⑤ I'm not interested in it.

08 위 대화의 내용과 일치하지 <u>않는</u> 것은?

① Mina는 어제 감자 시계를 만들었다.

② Jack은 감자 시계에 대해 잘 알지 못했다.

③ 감자 시계는 배터리가 필요하지 않다.

④ 감자 시계는 전기를 만들어 내는 데 감자를 사용한다.

⑤ Jack은 감자 시계를 만드는 데 참여했다.

[09~10] 다음 대화를 읽고, 물음에 답하시오.

Jimmy: Lisa, what did you do last weekend?
(A)

Lisa: I made an egg ball with my brother. (B)

Jimmy: An egg ball? (C)

Lisa: We put an egg in vinegar for two days.
Then, the egg turns into a ball. (D)

Jimmy: Wow, I want to make one, too! (E)

09 위 대화의 (A)~(E) 중 주어진 문장이 들어가기에 적절한 곳은?

┌─────────────────────────┐
│   What do you mean?   │
└─────────────────────────┘

① (A)   ② (B)   ③ (C)   ④ (D)   ⑤ (E)

서답형

10 Egg ball을 만드는 법을 우리말 15자 내외로 서술하시오.

➡ _____

[11~12] 다음 대화를 읽고, 물음에 답하시오.

Minho: Anna, let's make a "Mystery Card" for the science experiment.

Anna: A "Mystery Card?" What do you mean?

Minho: It's a special card. It can (A)[hide / reveal] your message.

Anna: How do you make it?

Minho: (B)[Separate / Mix] baking soda and water. Then, write a message on the card with it.

Anna: How can you read the card?

Minho: Paint over the card with grape juice, and then the message (C)[appears / disappears].

11 위 대화의 (A)~(C)에 들어갈 말이 바르게 짝지어진 것은?

① hide – Separate – appears

② hide – Mix – appears

③ hide – Separate – disappears

④ reveal – Mix – disappears

⑤ reveal – Separate – appears

12 위 대화의 내용과 일치하지 <u>않는</u> 것은?

① Minho는 과학 실험을 위해 미스터리 카드를 만들 것을 제안하였다.

② 미스터리 카드는 메시지를 숨길 수 있다.

③ 미스터리 카드를 만들기 위해 카드, 베이킹 소다, 물이 필요하다.

④ 펜으로 미스터리 카드를 쓴 후 베이킹 소다와 물을 붓는다.

⑤ 포도 주스로 미스터리 카드를 칠하면 메시지를 볼 수 있다.

01 다음 대화의 빈칸에 들어갈 말을 주어진 어구를 모두 배열하여 완성하시오.

> A: _____
>
> B: No, I haven't.

┌─ 보기 ─┐
about / heard / the / you /
Sci-Magic show / have

➡ _____

02 다음 대화의 빈칸에 들어갈 말을 주어진 단어를 사용하여 쓰시오.

> A: You are my BFF.
>
> B: BFF? _____ (mean)
>
> C: It means "Best Friends Forever."

➡ _____

[03~04] 다음 대화를 읽고, 물음에 답하시오.

> Mike: ⓐWhat show are you watching, Sally?
>
> Sally: I'm watching the Sci-Magic show. It's a new program. Have you ⓑheard about it?
>
> Mike: No, I ⓒhaven't. What's it about?
>
> Sally: The program uses science ⓓexplain magic tricks.
>
> Mike: Oh, it sounds ⓔinteresting.

03 위 대화의 ⓐ~ⓔ 중 어법상 어색한 것을 골라 바르게 고치시오.

➡ _____

04 What is the Sci-Magic show about?

➡ _____

05 다음 대화의 빈칸에 알맞은 말을 쓰시오.

> A: I made a potato clock yesterday!
>
> B: A potato clock? What do you _____?
>
> A: My clock works with potatoes, not with batteries.

➡ _____

06 다음 대화의 내용과 일치하도록 빈칸을 완성하시오.

> Tom: Mom, have you heard about the Chat Robot?
>
> Mom: No, I haven't. What is it?
>
> Tom: It's a phone application. You can ask any questions and it will answer. Let me show you. "Emily, what's the weather like today?"
>
> Emily: "It's going to rain, so you'll need an umbrella."
>
> Mom: Wow, what a great application!

> Today, my lovely son, Tom, introduced a new (A)_____, the Chat Robot. It could answer (B)_____. Tom showed me how it worked, asking about (C)_____. Surprisingly, it let us know about the weather and what we would need. I was so surprised at this application.

교과서
Grammar

> • Jack **built** this bridge. Jack은 이 다리를 건설했다. 〈능동태〉
> • This bridge **was built** by Jack. 이 다리는 Jack에 의해 건설되었다. 〈수동태〉

- 수동태는 능동태의 목적어를 주어로 만들고 동사를 'be+p.p.' 형태로 만든 후, 능동태의 주어를 'by+목적격' 형태로 하여 '주어가 ~되다'라고 해석한다. 능동태 문장의 시제에 따라 수동태 시제를 결정한다. 주체가 불분명할 경우 'by+행위자'는 생략되기도 한다.

  • Sophie **cleans** the window every day. Sophie는 매일 창문을 청소한다.

  • The window **is cleaned** by Sophie every day. 창문은 Sophie에 의해 매일 청소된다.

- 4형식 문장의 수동태는 두 가지 형태를 갖는다. 직접목적어를 주어로 한 수동태에서는 간접목적어에 특정 전치사를 붙인다. 전치사 to를 쓰는 동사는 'give, tell, teach, show, bring' 등이고, 전치사 for를 쓰는 동사는 'buy, make, cook, get' 등이며, 전치사 of를 쓰는 동사는 'ask'가 있다.

  • Math **is taught to** us by Mr. Kim. 수학은 김 선생님에 의해서 우리에게 가르쳐진다.

  • Pizza **was cooked for** her by me. 피자는 그녀를 위해 나에 의해 만들어졌다.

- 5형식 문장의 목적격보어가 원형부정사인 경우, 수동태 문장에서는 to부정사로 바꾼다. 그 외에는 모든 목적격보어를 그대로 쓸 수 있다.

  • He **is called** Zuzu by us. 그는 우리에 의해 Zuzu라고 불린다.

  • I **was made to finish** the job by him. 나는 그에 의해 그 일을 끝내도록 시켜졌다.

- 조동사의 수동태는 '조동사+be+p.p.' 형태를 취한다.

  • A new school **will be built** next year. 새로운 학교가 내년에 지어질 것이다.

  • The desks **can be replaced** with other ones. 그 책상들은 다른 것들로 교체될 수 있다.

- by 이외의 전치사를 사용하는 수동태에 유의한다.

  • I **am interested in** English. 나는 영어에 흥미가 있다.

  • Cake **is made from** flour, milk and eggs. 케이크는 밀가루, 우유, 달걀로 만들어진다.

  • John **was surprised at** seeing him. John은 그를 보고 놀랐다.

핵심 Check

1. 다음 우리말과 일치하도록 빈칸에 알맞은 말을 쓰시오.

   (1) 그의 코트는 먼지로 덮여 있다.

   ➡ His coat ＿＿＿＿ ＿＿＿＿ ＿＿＿＿ dirt.

   (2) 그 식당은 우리 이모가 운영하신다.

   ➡ The restaurant ＿＿＿＿ ＿＿＿＿ ＿＿＿＿ my aunt.

② to부정사의 형용사적 용법

> • Give the boys a chance to **introduce** themselves. 그 소년들에게 자신을 소개할 기회를 주어라.
>
> • I have a project **to finish** today. 나는 오늘 끝낼 프로젝트가 있다.

■ to부정사는 'to+동사원형'의 형태로 명사, 형용사, 부사로 사용될 수 있다.

  • **To write** a song is his favorite hobby. 작곡하는 것은 그가 가장 좋아하는 취미이다.

  • Do you have anything **to drink**? 마실 것을 가지고 있니?

  • I went to the market **to buy** some eggs. 나는 달걀을 사기 위해 시장으로 갔다.

■ to부정사가 형용사로 사용될 때는 바로 앞에 위치한 명사를 꾸며준다.

  • Click the title of the message **to read**. 읽을 메시지의 제목을 누르세요.

  • The game was something **to remember**. 그 경기는 기억할 만한 것이었다.

■ to부정사가 형용사로 사용될 때 전치사로 끝나는 경우를 주의하자. 수식하는 명사가 본래 전치사의 목적어로 사용됐으므로, 이때는 수식하는 명사를 to부정사 뒤로 넣어 전치사가 필요한지 유무를 확인하는 것이 좋다.

  • I have many friends **to rely on**. (rely on friends (○)) 나는 의지할 많은 친구들이 있다.

  • There is an issue **to deal with**. (deal with an issue (○)) 다룰 문제가 있습니다.

  ■ 형용사와 to부정사가 -thing, -body, -one으로 끝나는 부정대명사를 동시에 수식할 때는 '부정대명사+형용사+to부정사'의 어순을 따른다.

  • Can you give me anything **warm to drink**? 따뜻한 마실 것 좀 주시겠어요?

  • Jina has something **interesting to see**. Jina에게는 흥미로운 볼거리가 있다.

핵심 Check

2. 다음 우리말과 같도록 빈칸에 알맞은 말을 쓰시오.

  (1) Jason은 읽을 책을 가지고 있다.

   ➡ Jason has a book _____ _____.

  (2) 그녀는 노벨상을 탄 최초의 여성이었다.

   ➡ She was the first woman _____ _____ the Nobel Prize.

  (3) 쓸 종이를 좀 가지고 있나요?

   ➡ Do you have some paper _____ _____ _____?

01 다음 문장에서 어법상 <u>어색한</u> 부분을 바르게 고쳐 쓰시오.

(1) Can I have a book to read about?

_____ ➡ _____

(2) Kelly born in Canada in 2005.

_____ ➡ _____

(3) There are many options choose.

_____ ➡ _____

(4) A gift was given for her yesterday.

_____ ➡ _____

02 주어진 어휘를 어법에 맞게 빈칸에 쓰시오.

(1) I _____ _____ to the meeting, but I didn't go. (invite)

(2) Keep in mind the goal _____ _____. (achieve)

(3) Many accidents _____ _____ by careless driving. (cause)

(4) I don't want to do anything _____ _____ her feelings. (hurt)

(5) My keys _____ _____ in the parking lot two days ago. (find)

03 다음 우리말에 맞게 주어진 어구를 바르게 배열하시오. (필요하면 어형을 바꾸고 단어를 추가 할 것)

(1) 나는 먹을 것을 원해요. (want / eat / I / something)

➡ _____

(2) 우리에게는 계획할 여행이 있어. (We / a trip / have / plan)

➡ _____

(3) 새로운 고속도로가 지난달에 완공되었다.

(the new highway / complete / last month)

➡ _____

(4) 그 잉크는 물로 쉽게 지워진다.

(the ink / wash off / water / with / easily)

➡ _____

01 다음 빈칸에 알맞은 말이 바르게 짝지어진 것은?

> • He has twin sisters _____.
> • Actually, they have many questions _____.

① to take care – to ask about
② to take care – to ask
③ to take care of – to ask to
④ to take care of – to ask
⑤ taking care of – to ask

02 다음 중 어법상 옳은 것은?

① The glass is filled by milk.
② June is satisfied with the test result.
③ I want something to wear warm.
④ He was made do the homework first.
⑤ Some cookies were made to me by Julia.

03 다음 중 용법이 다른 하나는?

① She will buy a house to live in.
② I have a number of letters to write.
③ We need some food to buy.
④ He went out to see the scenery.
⑤ They have a problem to solve.

서답형

04 다음 빈칸에 들어갈 알맞은 말을 주어진 단어를 이용하여 쓰시오. 필요한 단어가 있으면 추가할 것.

> Her child is bored. He needs _____.
> (something / play)

➡ _____

05 다음 중 수동태로의 전환이 바르지 <u>않은</u> 것은?

① Did somebody clean my room?
　→ Was my room cleaned by somebody?
② Someone stole my backpack.
　→ My backpack was stolen by someone.
③ Jane made the dolls.
　→ The dolls were made by Jane.
④ She looked after the injured bird.
　→ The injured bird was looked after her.
⑤ Julian gave me some flowers.
　→ I was given some flowers by Julian.

06 다음 문장과 같은 의미의 문장을 <u>모두</u> 고르시오.

> A note was given to me by Amelia.

① Amelia gave a note me.
② I was given a note by Amelia.
③ A note was given for me by Amelia.
④ Amelia gave to me a note.
⑤ Amelia gave me a note.

07 다음 중 빈칸에 들어갈 동사 'make'의 형태가 <u>다른</u> 하나는?

① The fuel is _____ from corn.
② Some comments were _____ to the event.
③ These games were _____ by creative young men.
④ This floor is _____ of wood.
⑤ The girl is _____ a box now.

서답형

08 주어진 단어를 이용하여 다음 우리말을 영어로 쓰시오. 필요한 단어가 있으면 추가할 것.

> 여기에는 볼만한 것이 없다.
> (there / nothing / see / here)

➡ _____

서답형

09 다음 우리말에 맞도록 빈칸을 채우시오.

> 여행하면서 읽을 책 한 권을 빌릴 수 있을까요?
> = M a y I _____ a b o o k _____
>   _____ on my journey?

➡ _____

중요

10 다음 빈칸에 공통으로 들어갈 말로 가장 적절한 것은?

> • The bucket is filled _____ sand.
> • He was pleased _____ the news.

① by   ② at   ③ with
④ in   ⑤ from

11 다음 두 문장이 같은 의미가 되도록 빈칸에 알맞은 것은?

> Jane saw the child playing football with his friends.
> = The child _____ football with his friends by Jane.

① was seen play   ② is seen to play
③ was seen playing   ④ saw playing
⑤ is seen playing

12 다음 중 어법상 바르지 <u>않은</u> 것은?

> Kelly ①has to ②prepare ③lunch ④for serve a hundred ⑤guests.

①   ②   ③   ④   ⑤

13 다음 중 어법상 바르지 <u>않은</u> 것은?

① Jason was employed by his uncle.
② Tom was made to fix the bike by his dad.
③ Did the building designed by the brothers?
④ The pill was taken by the patient regularly.
⑤ The sweet potato was given to her by her grandmother.

서답형

14 다음 괄호 안의 단어를 어법에 맞게 고쳐 쓰시오.

> A: Is the plane going to be late?
> B: No. It (expect) to be on time.

➡ _____

중요

15 다음 빈칸에 들어갈 말이 <u>다른</u> 하나는?

① These shoes were given _____ me by John.
② Korean history is taught _____ us by Mr. Kim.
③ A package was sent _____ Kelly by someone.
④ A scarf was bought _____ my mother by us.
⑤ Paper dolls were sold _____ a lot of children at the amusement park.

16 다음 빈칸에 알맞은 것은?

> I am looking for _____ to my best friend.

① something giving
② something to give
③ something give
④ something to giving
⑤ giving something

17 다음 중 주어진 문장의 to부정사와 쓰임이 같은 것은?

> They didn't have much time to spend with my children.

① We will be glad to meet you again.
② Briana wanted to become the greatest pianist in the world.
③ It is important to be honest with your parents.
④ Do you have a friend to trust?
⑤ Ms. Greene encouraged us to do our best.

서답형

18 주어진 단어를 이용하여 다음 문장을 수동태로 쓰시오.

> Nobody saw me singing a song with my friends. (wasn't / anybody)

➡ _____
_____

서답형

19 다음 물음에 주어진 단어를 주어로 하여 답하시오.

> A: Do you know who discovered the treasure?
> B: Yes, I do. It _____ Captain Jackson.

➡ _____

20 다음 중 빈칸에 가장 적절한 것은?

> High blood pressure is a serious health problem _____.

① to deal
② to deal about
③ to deal with
④ to look
⑤ to look into

21 다음 빈칸에 들어갈 말로 적절하지 않은 것은?

> Marin has a few friends _____.

① to help her
② to play
③ to talk to
④ to trust
⑤ to meet

22 다음 밑줄 친 문장을 수동태로 바르게 전환한 것은?

> The CEO offered Robert the job, but he refused to accept it.

① The job offered to Robert by the CEO
② The job was offered to Robert by the CEO
③ Robert was offered the job by the CEO
④ The job was offered for Robert by the CEO
⑤ Robert was offered the CEO to the job

서답형

23 다음 우리말을 괄호 안의 어구들을 이용하여 영작하시오.

> 들려줄 이야기가 있나요?
> (you / a story / tell)

➡ _____

서답형

24 다음 문장을 수동태로 전환하시오.

> Mom told me to taste the food.

➡ _____

01 다음 대화의 빈칸에 알맞은 말을 쓰시오.

> A: Who wrote *Hamlet*?
> B: *Hamlet* _____ Shakespeare.

➡ _____

02 다음 빈칸에 괄호 안에 주어진 단어의 올바른 형태를 쓰시오.

(1) Give her a magazine _____ _____.
　　(read)
(2) There are many difficult subjects _____
　　_____ for this exam. (study)
(3) You have nothing _____ _____
　　_____. (worry about)

03 다음 문장을 두 가지 형태의 수동태로 쓰시오.

> My father gave me the watch a few years ago.

➡ _____
　 _____
➡ _____
　 _____

04 다음 문장을 주어진 단어로 시작하는 문장으로 다시 쓰시오.

> Helen's brother made me laugh a lot.

➡ I _____.

05 주어진 단어를 어법에 맞도록 빈칸에 쓰시오.

> invent / surround / divide / surprise / build

> • As construction cost wasn't high, a new dormitory _____ by the Hans.
> • The game of baseball _____ by Americans.
> • Our country _____ into two halves.
> • Korea _____ by water on three sides.
> • We didn't expect them to come to the meeting, but they were there. We _____ to see them.

06 주어진 단어를 이용하여 다음 우리말에 맞게 빈칸을 채우시오.

> I heard Jenny had _____.
> (something / say)
> Jenny가 네게 할 말이 있다고 들었어.

07 주어진 어구를 바르게 배열하여 다음 우리말을 영어로 쓰시오. 필요하다면 단어를 추가하시오.

> 나는 요즈음 운동할 충분한 시간이 없어.
> (these days / enough / I / work out / don't / time / have)

➡ _____

08 다음 괄호 안에 주어진 단어를 이용하여 빈칸 ⓐ, ⓑ에 알맞은 말을 쓰시오.

> A: I have so many things ⓐ_____
> _____(do).
> B: What makes you so busy?
> A: Actually, my birthday party ⓑ
> _____ _____ (throw) yesterday.
> So I put off what I had to do yesterday.

09 다음 괄호 안에 주어진 단어를 어법에 맞게 각각 쓰시오.

> Neil Armstrong was the first man ⓐ
> _____ _____(walk) on the moon.
> No one can imagine how he felt when
> Neil ⓑ_____(set) his foot on the
> moon. Some pictures of the moon ⓒ
> _____ _____(take) and they ⓓ
> _____(bring) to the earth by
> him.

10 주어진 단어를 활용하여 다음 우리말을 8 단어로 이루어진 영어 문장으로 쓰시오.

> 나는 그의 부탁을 거절할 이유가 없어.
> (have / refuse / request)

➡ _____

11 다음 각 문장을 수동태는 능동태로, 능동태는 수동태로 전환하시오.

(1) The Emperor planted a tree himself.

  ➡ _____

(2) This car was made for us by a French company.

  ➡ _____

(3) The man is looked up to by the young girls.

  ➡ _____

(4) Worker bees make honey.

  ➡ _____

12 어법상 틀린 것을 바르게 고쳐 다음 문장을 다시 쓰시오.

> Do you have any samples giving out?

➡ _____

13 다음 우리말과 뜻이 같도록 빈칸에 알맞은 말을 쓰시오.

(1) 해야 할 지겨운 일들이 많이 있어.
  ➡ There are many boring things
  _____ _____.

(2) 먹을 것을 가지고 있나요?
  ➡ Do you have something _____
  _____ ?

(3) 그녀는 그것에 대해 할 말이 많이 있다.
  ➡ She has many things _____
  _____ _____ it.

(4) 나는 탈 자전거를 샀어.
  ➡ I bought a bicycle _____ _____.

(5) 우리는 그것을 읽을 시간이 없어.
  ➡ We don't have time _____ _____
  it.

14 주어진 단어를 활용하여 다음 우리말을 능동태와 수동태로 쓰시오.

> 그 도둑은 그 용감한 젊은 남자에 의해 붙잡혔다.
> (catch)

➡ _____

➡ _____

Reading

In animation movies, amazing things are possible. But are they
현재분사형 형용사–사물을 수식   = amazing things
actually possible in real life?
현실에서

Let Down Your Hair, Rapunzel!

In the animation, Rapunzel must lower her long hair to let people in
~해야 한다   목적을 나타내는 부사적 용법의 to부정사: ~하기 위해서
her tower. But could human hair really hold up a person?
가능성을 나타내는 조동사: '~일 수도 있다'

Surprisingly, yes! A single hair can hold up 100g and an average head
문장 수식 부사   가능
has about 120,000 hairs. All those hairs could hold up a couple of
약, ~쯤
elephants! With her hair, Rapunzel has the ability to hold up a person.
~으로(수단)   the ability를 수식하는 to부정사의 형용사적 용법
But she should wrap her hair around something strong and heavy.
wrap A around B: A를 B 둘레에 감다   –thing으로 끝나는 대명사는 형용사가 뒤에서 수식
If she doesn't, she will get a very sore neck.
조건을 나타내는 부사절 접속사로 현재시제가 미래를 대신

We Scare for Energy
~을 위해

In the animation, monsters scare children to get energy from their
목적을 나타내는 to부정사의 부사적 용법: 얻기 위하여
screams. Amazingly, their city is powered by this sound! But could we
= this sound powers their city!
actually produce electricity to light up a city from sound?
electricity를 수식하는 형용사적 용법의 to부정사

animation 애니메이션
amazing 놀라운
possible 가능한
actually 실제로
let down ~을 내리다
lower ~을 내리다
let ~ in ~를 … 안으로 들이다
hold up ~을 들어 올리다
surprisingly 놀랍게도
average 평균의
about 대략, ~쯤
a couple of 둘의, 몇 개의
ability 능력
wrap ~ around ~을 …에 감다
sore 아픈
scare ~을 겁주다
get ~을 얻다
scream 비명
be powered by ~에 의하여 전기를 공급받다
produce 생산하다
light up ~을 환하게 밝히다, 환하게 하다

📎 **확인문제**

● 다음 문장이 본문의 내용과 일치하면 T, 일치하지 않으면 F를 쓰시오.

1 When she wants people to enter her tower, Rapunzel has to drop her long hair. ☐

2 It is possible to hold up a person with human hair. ☐

3 There are about 12,000 hairs on an average head. ☐

4 Rapunzel is able to hold up a person with her hair. ☐

5 Monsters' city is not powered by children's screams. ☐

Yes, sound can be changed into electricity. But it would not be
조동사가 있는 수동태   = sound

helpful in our everyday activities because the amount is too small. For
이유를 나타내는 접속사: ~이기 때문에

example, the sound from a car horn only produces 50mv. That is only
주어 the sound가 단수이므로 단수 동사

1/4400 of the average 220v of electricity in our homes. So, we would

need an unbelievable amount of screams to light up an entire city.
믿기 힘든 양의   목적을 나타내는 to부정사의 부사적 용법: 밝히기 위하여

Up, Up and Away!

The house is lifted and flown by thousands of balloons in the animation.
= Thousands of balloons lift and fly the house in the animation.
Could that actually work?
앞 문장의 내용을 받는 지시대명사

Let's say that a house weighs about 50,000kg. A normal balloon at
Let's say that+주어+동사: ~라고 가정해 보자   약, ~쯤

an amusement park can lift about 14g. So we need about 3,570,000
그래서

balloons to lift up the house. We also have to think about the weight
목적을 나타내는 to부정사의 부사적 용법: 들어 올리기 위해   = must

of the balloons themselves and the strings. Then, we need to add a few
재귀대명사로 balloons를 강조   need to+동사원형: ~할 필요가 있다

more thousand balloons. Now, the biggest challenge is pumping up all
형용사의 최상급 앞에 the

those balloons!

---

be changed into ~으로 바뀌다

helpful 유용한

activity 활동

amount 양

for example 예를 들어

horn (차량의) 경적

unbelievable 믿을 수 없는

entire 전체의

lift ~을 들어 올리다

fly(-flew-flown) ~을 날리다

work 작동하다

weigh 무게가 ~이다

normal 보통의

amusement park 놀이공원

have to ~해야만 하다

weight 무게

string 줄

add 더하다

a few 조금, 약간의

challenge 도전,

pump up (공기 등을) 주입하다

확인문제

● 다음 문장이 본문의 내용과 일치하면 T, 일치하지 않으면 F를 쓰시오.

1 Electricity changed from sound is useful in our everyday activities. ☐

2 The sound produced by a car horn is 50mv. ☐

3 We use 220v of electricity in our homes. ☐

4 Thousands of balloons are lifted by the house in the animation. ☐

5 When we plan to lift a house with balloons, the only thing that has to be considered
is the number of the balloons. ☐

6 Pumping up millions of balloons is difficult thing to do. ☐

● 우리말을 참고하여 빈칸에 알맞은 말을 쓰시오.

1 In animation movies, _____ _____ _____ _____.

2 But _____ _____ _____ _____ in real life?

3 _____ _____ Your Hair, Rapunzel!

4 In the animation, Rapunzel _____ _____ her long hair _____ _____ _____ _____ her tower.

5 But _____ human hair really _____ _____ _____ _____?

6 Surprisingly, yes! A single hair can _____ _____ 100g and an average head _____ _____ 120,000 hairs.

7 _____ _____ _____ could _____ _____ a couple of elephants!

8 With her hair, Rapunzel has _____ _____ _____ _____ _____ a person.

9 But she should _____ _____ _____ something strong and heavy.

10 If she _____, she _____ _____ a very _____ neck.

11 We _____ _____ Energy

12 In the animation, monsters _____ _____ _____ _____ energy _____ their screams.

13 Amazingly, their city _____ _____ _____ this sound!

14 But could we actually _____ _____ _____ _____ _____ a city _____ sound?

1	만화 영화에서는 놀라운 일들이 가능하다.
2	하지만 그런 일들이 실생활에서 정말 가능할까?
3	라푼젤, 네 머리카락을 내려!
4	만화 영화에서 라푼젤은 사람들이 탑에 들어오게 하기 위해서 그녀의 긴 머리카락을 내려야 한다.
5	하지만 인간의 머리카락이 정말로 사람을 들어 올릴 수 있을까?
6	놀랍게도 그렇다! 머리카락 한 가닥은 100그램의 무게를 들어 올릴 수 있고 보통 머리에는 12만 개 정도의 머리카락이 있다.
7	그 모든 머리카락은 코끼리 두 마리를 들어 올릴 수 있다!
8	라푼젤에게는 머리카락으로 사람을 들어 올릴 수 있는 능력이 있다.
9	하지만 그녀는 머리카락을 어떤 강하고 무거운 것에 감아야 한다.
10	만약 그렇게 하지 않으면 그녀는 목이 많이 아플 것이다.
11	우리는 에너지를 얻기 위해 겁을 준다
12	만화 영화에서 괴물들은 아이들의 비명에서 에너지를 얻기 위해 아이들을 겁준다.
13	놀랍게도 그들의 도시는 이 소리로 동력을 공급받는다!
14	하지만 정말 소리로부터 도시를 밝히는 전기를 만들 수 있을까?

15 Yes, sound can _____ _____ _____ electricity.

16 But it would not be _____ _____ our everyday activities _____ _____ _____ _____ too _____.

17 _____ _____, the sound _____ a car horn only _____ 50mv.

18 That is only 1/4400 _____ _____ _____ 220v of _____ in our homes.

19 So, we would need _____ _____ _____ _____ _____ to light up an _____ city.

20 Up, Up and _____!

21 The house _____ _____ _____ _____ thousands of balloons in the animation.

22 Could that _____ _____?

23 Let's say that a house _____ _____ 50,000kg.

24 A _____ balloon at _____ _____ _____ can lift about 14g.

25 So we need _____ 3,570,000 balloons _____ _____ _____ the house.

26 We also _____ _____ _____ _____ the weight of the balloons _____ and the strings.

27 Then, we need to _____ _____ _____ _____ balloons.

28 Now, the biggest _____ is _____ _____ _____ balloons!

15 그렇다, 소리는 전기로 바뀔 수 있다.

16 그렇지만 그 양이 너무 적기 때문에 그것은 우리의 일상 활동에서는 도움이 되지 않을 것이다.

17 예를 들어, 자동차 경적 소리는 겨우 50밀리볼트를 만들어 낸다.

18 그것은 우리 가정에서 사용하는 일반적인 220볼트 전기의 1/4400밖에 되지 않는다.

19 그래서 도시 전체를 밝히기 위해서는 믿기 어려운 정도로 많은 양의 비명이 필요할 것이다.

20 높이, 높이 그리고 멀리!

21 만화 영화에서 집은 수천 개의 풍선에 의해 들려 올라가고 날아간다.

22 이게 실제로 가능할까?

23 집 한 채의 무게가 5만 킬로그램 정도라고 가정해 보자.

24 놀이공원에 있는 보통의 풍선은 대략 14그램을 들어 올릴 수 있다.

25 그래서 집을 들어 올리기 위해 우리는 약 3.570.000개의 풍선이 필요하다.

26 우리는 또한 풍선 자체와 줄의 무게에 대해서도 생각해야 한다.

27 그렇게 되면, 수천 개의 풍선을 더 추가할 필요가 있다.

28 이제 가장 큰 어려움은 그 모든 풍선에 바람을 넣는 일이다!

- 우리말을 참고하여 본문을 영작하시오.

1 만화 영화에서는 놀라운 일들이 가능하다.

➡ _____

2 하지만 그런 일들이 실생활에서 정말 가능할까?

➡ _____

3 라푼젤, 네 머리카락을 내려!

➡ _____

4 만화 영화에서 라푼젤은 사람들이 탑에 들어오게 하기 위해서 그녀의 긴 머리카락을 내려야 한다.

➡ _____

5 하지만 인간의 머리카락이 정말로 사람을 들어 올릴 수 있을까?

➡ _____

6 놀랍게도 그렇다! 머리카락 한 가닥은 100그램의 무게를 들어 올릴 수 있고 보통 머리에는 12만 개 정도의 머리카락이 있다.

➡ _____

7 그 모든 머리카락은 코끼리 두 마리를 들어 올릴 수 있다!

➡ _____

8 라푼젤에게는 머리카락으로 사람을 들어 올릴 수 있는 능력이 있다.

➡ _____

9 하지만 그녀는 머리카락을 어떤 강하고 무거운 것에 감아야 한다.

➡ _____

10 만약 그렇게 하지 않으면 그녀는 목이 많이 아플 것이다.

➡ _____

11 우리는 에너지를 얻기 위해 겁을 준다

➡ _____

12 만화 영화에서 괴물들은 아이들의 비명에서 에너지를 얻기 위해 아이들을 겁준다.

➡ _____

13 놀랍게도 그들의 도시는 이 소리로 동력을 공급받는다!

➡ _____

14 하지만 정말 소리로부터 도시를 밝히는 전기를 만들 수 있을까?

➡ _____

15 그렇다. 소리는 전기로 바뀔 수 있다.

➡ _____

16 그렇지만 그 양이 너무 적기 때문에 그것은 우리의 일상 활동에서는 도움이 되지 않을 것이다.

➡ _____

17 예를 들어, 자동차 경적 소리는 겨우 50밀리볼트를 만들어 낸다.

➡ _____

18 그것은 우리 가정에서 사용하는 일반적인 220볼트 전기의 1/4400밖에 되지 않는다.

➡ _____

19 그래서 도시 전체를 밝히기 위해서는 믿기 어려운 정도로 많은 양의 비명이 필요할 것이다.

➡ _____

20 높이, 높이 그리고 멀리!

➡ _____

21 만화 영화에서 집은 수천 개의 풍선에 의해 들려 올라가고 날아간다.

➡ _____

22 이게 실제로 가능할까?

➡ _____

23 집 한 채의 무게가 5만 킬로그램 정도라고 가정해 보자.

➡ _____

24 놀이공원에 있는 보통의 풍선은 대략 14그램을 들어 올릴 수 있다.

➡ _____

25 그래서 집을 들어 올리기 위해 우리는 약 3,570,000개의 풍선이 필요하다.

➡ _____

26 우리는 또한 풍선 자체와 줄의 무게에 대해서도 생각해야 한다.

➡ _____

27 그렇게 되면, 수천 개의 풍선을 더 추가할 필요가 있다.

➡ _____

28 이제 가장 큰 어려움은 그 모든 풍선에 바람을 넣는 일이다!

➡ _____

[01~04] 다음 글을 읽고, 물음에 답하시오.

In animation movies, amazing things are possible. But are ⓐthey actually possible in real life?

Let Down Your Hair, Rapunzel!

In the animation, Rapunzel must ①lower her long hair to let people ②in her tower. But could human hair really hold up a person?

Surprisingly, yes! A single hair can hold up 100g and an average head has about 120,000 hairs. All those hairs could hold up a couple of elephants! ③Without her hair, Rapunzel has the ability to hold up a person. But she should ④wrap her hair around something ⑤strong and heavy. If she doesn't, she will get a very ⓑsore neck.

서답형

01 위 글의 밑줄 친 ⓐ가 가리키는 것을 위 글에서 찾아 쓰시오.

➡ _____

02 위 글의 내용과 일치하지 않는 것은?

① Amazing things happen in animation movies.
② Rapunzel has long hair.
③ Rapunzel has to use her hair to let people in her tower.
④ Holding up a person with human hair is not possible in real life.
⑤ Rapunzel needs to wrap her hair around something strong when she wants to hold up someone.

중요

03 위 글의 ①~⑤ 중 글의 흐름상 어색한 것은?

①   ②   ③   ④   ⑤

04 위 글의 밑줄 친 ⓑ를 대신하여 쓰기에 가장 적절한 것은?

① disappointing ② annoying
③ painful   ④ burning
⑤ excited

[05~08] 다음 글을 읽고, 물음에 답하시오.

We Scare for Energy

In the animation, monsters scare children to get energy from their screams. Amazingly, their city ____ⓐ____ (power) by this sound! But could we actually produce electricity to light up a city from sound?

Yes, sound can be changed into electricity. But it would not be ____ⓑ____ in our everyday activities because the amount is too small. ____ⓒ____, the sound from a car horn only produces 50mv. That is only 1/4400 of the average 220v of electricity in our homes. So, we would need an unbelievable amount of screams to light up an entire city.

서답형

05 위 글의 주어진 단어를 빈칸 ⓐ에 어법에 맞게 쓰시오.

➡ _____

중요

06 위 글의 흐름상 빈칸 ⓑ에 들어갈 말로 가장 적절한 것은?

① grateful   ② thankful
③ thoughtful ④ useful
⑤ wonderful

07 위 글의 빈칸 ⓒ에 들어갈 말로 가장 적절한 것은?

① As a result   ② Finally
③ For example   ④ However
⑤ On the other hand

08 다음 중 위 글의 내용과 일치하지 <u>않는</u> 것은?

① 괴물들은 에너지를 얻기 위해 아이들을 겁준다.

② 소리를 전기로 바꾸는 것이 가능하다.

③ 자동차 경적 소리는 50mv의 전기를 만들어 낼 수 있다.

④ 가정에서 사용하는 전기는 평균적으로 220v이다.

⑤ 소리를 이용해 전체 도시에 전기를 공급할 수 있는 기술을 개발 중이다.

[09~13] 다음 글을 읽고, 물음에 답하시오.

Up, Up and Away!

The house is lifted and flown ⓐ thousands of balloons in the animation. Could that actually work?

Let's say that a house weighs ⓑ 50,000kg. A normal balloon at an amusement park can lift ⓒ 14g. So we need ⓓ 3,570,000 balloons to lift up the house. We also have to think ⓔ the weight of the balloons themselves and the strings. Then, we need to add a few more thousand balloons. Now, the biggest challenge is (A)pumping up all those balloons!

서답형

09 위 글의 빈칸 ⓐ~ⓔ에 들어갈 말이 <u>다른</u> 하나는?

① ⓐ　② ⓑ　③ ⓒ　④ ⓓ　⑤ ⓔ

서답형

10 다음과 같이 풀이되는 말을 위 글에서 찾아 쓰시오.

a film in which drawings appear to move

➡ _____

11 다음 중 글의 내용과 일치하는 것의 개수는?

ⓐ Thousands of balloons are used to lift and fly the house in the animation movie.

ⓑ Lifting a house with balloons is not an easy thing to do in real life.

ⓒ Pumping up millions of balloons is a piece of cake.

ⓓ The weight of the balloons themselves and the strings should be considered when we want to lift a house with balloons.

ⓔ The animation is about pumping up balloons to fly high in the sky.

① 1개　② 2개　③ 3개

④ 4개　⑤ 5개

서답형

12 주어진 단어를 포함하여 7단어로 이루어진 문장으로 다음 물음에 답하시오.

Q: According to the passage, what is the hardest part of lifting a house with balloons? (them)

➡ _____

13 다음 중 밑줄 친 (A)와 쓰임이 같은 것은?

① She is playing the guitar.

② What is she having for lunch?

③ My goal is winning the race.

④ Jim is making fun of me.

⑤ The man is pumping up the tires.

[14~17] 다음 글을 읽고, 물음에 답하시오.

In animation movies, amazing things are possible. But are they actually possible in real life?

Let Down Your Hair, Rapunzel!

In the animation, Rapunzel must lower her long hair to let people in her tower. ① But could human hair really hold up a person?

Surprisingly, yes! ② A single hair can hold up 100g and an average head has ⓐabout 120,000 hairs. ③ With her hair, Rapunzel has the ability to hold up a person. ④ But she should wrap her hair around something strong and heavy. ⑤ If she ⓑdoesn't, she will get a very sore neck.

14 위 글의 ①～⑤ 중 주어진 문장이 들어가기에 가장 적절한 곳은?

> All those hairs could hold up a couple of elephants!

①   ②   ③   ④   ⑤

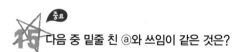

15 다음 중 밑줄 친 ⓐ와 쓰임이 같은 것은?

① This is a book about various trees.
② We wandered about the town for three hours.
③ The movie is about to begin.
④ What on earth are you talking about?
⑤ The tickets cost about 20 dollars.

서답형

16 위 글의 밑줄 친 ⓑ가 의미하는 것을 위 글에서 찾아 쓰시오.

➡ _____

17 다음 중 Rapunzel에 관한 내용으로 바르지 <u>않은</u> 것은?

① Her hair is very long.
② She is in her tower.
③ She has to use her hair to let in someone.
④ Her hair can hold up an elephant.
⑤ Her hair should be wrapped around something heavy when holding up someone.

[18~22] 다음 글을 읽고, 물음에 답하시오.

ⓐ _____

In the animation, monsters (A)[scare / are scared] children to get energy from their screams. Amazingly, (B)[its / their] city is powered by this sound! But could we actually produce electricity ___ⓑ___ a city (C)[from / into] sound?

Yes, sound can be changed into electricity. But it would not be helpful in our everyday activities because the amount is too small. For example, the sound from a car horn only produces 50mv. That is only 1/4400 of the average 220v of electricity in our homes. So, we would need ___ⓒ___ to light up an entire city.

서답형

18 주어진 단어를 바르게 배열하여 빈칸 ⓐ에 들어갈 말을 완성하시오.

> for / Scare / Energy / We

➡ _____

서답형

19 빈칸 ⓑ에 들어갈 말을 위 글에서 찾아 쓰시오.

➡ _____

20 위 글의 흐름상 빈칸 ⓒ에 들어갈 말로 가장 적절한 것은?

① a reasonable amount of car horns

② a believable amount of screams

③ an incredible amount of screams

④ a large amount of money

⑤ an unbelievable amount of monsters

21 다음 중 위 글을 읽고 답할 수 <u>없는</u> 질문은?

① What do monsters do to get energy?

② Is it possible to make electricity from sound?

③ How much electricity can a car horn make?

④ By what monsters' city is powered?

⑤ Why do we need electricity?

22 위 글의 (A)~(C)에서 어법상 옳은 것끼리 바르게 짝지어진 것은?

① scare – its – from

② are scared – their – into

③ scare – its – into

④ are scared – its – from

⑤ scare – their – from

[23~24] 다음 글을 읽고, 물음에 답하시오.

Up, Up and Away!

The house _____ⓐ_____ by thousands of balloons in the animation. Could that actually work?

Let's say that a house ①weighs about 50,000kg. A normal balloon at an amusement park can ②be lifted about 14g. So we need about 3,570,000 balloons ③to lift up the house. We also ④have to think about the weight of the balloons themselves and the strings. Then, we need ⑤to add a few more thousand balloons. Now, the biggest challenge is pumping up all those balloons!

23 위 글의 빈칸 ⓐ에 주어진 동사를 어법에 맞게 쓰시오.

lift and fly

➡ _____

24 위 글의 ①~⑤ 중 어법상 <u>틀린</u> 것을 골라 그 번호를 쓰고 바르게 고치시오.

➡ _____

25 주어진 문장에 자연스럽게 연결되도록 (A)~(C)를 바르게 나열한 것은?

In the animation, Rapunzel must lower her long hair to let people in her tower. But could human hair really hold up a person?

(A) All those hairs could hold up a couple of elephants! With her hair, Rapunzel has the ability to hold up a person.

(B) Surprisingly, yes! A single hair can hold up 100g and an average head has about 120,000 hairs.

(C) But she should wrap her hair around something strong and heavy. If she doesn't, she will get a very sore neck.

① (A) – (C) – (B) ② (B) – (A) – (C)

③ (B) – (C) – (A) ④ (C) – (A) – (B)

⑤ (C) – (B) – (A)

[01~05] 다음 글을 읽고, 물음에 답하시오.

In animation movies, amazing things are possible. But are they actually possible in real life?

Let Down Your Hair, Rapunzel!

In the animation, ⓐRapunzel must lower her long hair to let people in her tower. But could human hair really hold up a person?

Surprisingly, yes! A single hair can hold up 100g and an average head has about 120,000 hairs. ⓑAll those hairs could hold up a couple of elephants! With her hair, Rapunzel has the ability to hold up a person. But she should wrap her hair around something strong and heavy. If she doesn't, she will get a very sore neck.

01 위 글의 내용에 맞게 다음 물음에 대한 답을 완성하시오. 한 칸에 한 단어만 쓰시오.

> **Q:** According to the passage, what kind of amazing thing does Rapunzel do in the movie?
> **A:** The amazing thing that Rapunzel does in the movie is _____ _____ _____ _____ _____ _____.

02 주어진 동사를 어법에 맞게 활용하여 밑줄 친 ⓐ와 같은 의미의 문장을 완성하시오.

> Rapunzel must lower her long hair _____. (allow / enter)

03 위 글의 내용에 맞게 빈칸에 알맞은 말을 쓰시오.

> Unless Rapunzel's hair _____ _____ around something _____ _____ _____, her neck will be sore.

04 주어진 단어를 이용하여 다음 물음에 완전한 문장의 영어로 답하시오.

> **Q:** How much weight can a single hair hold up?
> **A:** _____ (it)

05 밑줄 친 ⓑ와 같은 의미의 문장이 되도록 다음 문장을 완성하시오.

> A couple of elephants could _____ _____ _____ by all those hairs!

[06~10] 다음 글을 읽고, 물음에 답하시오.

We Scare for Energy

In the animation, monsters scare children to get energy from ⓐtheir screams. Amazingly, ⓑtheir city is powered by this sound! But could we actually produce electricity to light up a city from sound?

Yes, _____ (A) _____. But it would not be helpful in our everyday activities because the amount is too small. For example, (B)the sound from a car horn only produces 50mv. That is only 1/4400 of the average 220v of electricity in our homes. So, we would need an unbelievable amount of screams to light up an entire city.

06 위 글의 밑줄 친 ⓐ와 ⓑ가 구체적으로 가리키는 것을 각각 우리말로 쓰시오.

ⓐ _____ ⓑ _____

07 (중요) 다음 문장을 수동태로 만들어 빈칸 (A)에 쓰시오.

> we can change sound into electricity

➡ _____

08 Write the reason why changing sound into electricity is not helpful in our everyday activities.

➡ _____

09 주어진 단어를 주어로 하여 밑줄 친 (B)와 같은 의미의 문장을 쓰시오.

> only 50mv _____ .

➡ _____

10 (중요) 다음은 괴물들을 본 아이의 반응이다. 위 글의 단어를 어법에 맞게 활용하여 다음 빈칸에 쓰시오.

> Mom, I am _____.

[11~13] 다음 글을 읽고, 물음에 답하시오.

Up, Up and Away!

_____(A)_____

Could that actually work?

Let's say that a house weighs about 50,000kg. A normal balloon at an amusement park can lift about 14g. So we need about 3,570,000 balloons to lift up the house. We also have to think about the weight of the balloons themselves and the strings. Then, we need to add a few more thousand balloons. Now, the biggest challenge is pumping up all those balloons!

11 (중요) 다음 문장을 수동태로 전환하여 빈칸 (A)에 쓰시오.

> Thousands of balloons lift and fly the house in the animation.

➡ _____
_____

12 적절한 대명사를 사용하여 다음 물음에 답하시오.

> Q: How many grams can a normal balloon at an amusement park lift?

➡ _____

13 (중요) 위 글의 내용에 맞게 대화의 빈칸을 채우시오.

> **Amelia:** Jason, is it possible _____ _____ _____ _____ with balloons in real life?
> **Jason:** Maybe it is. About 3,570,000 balloons _____ _____ to lift it. But can you imagine _____ _____ _____ _____ _____? I think it is the biggest challenge of all.

Grammar in Real Life

This is Jack's plan for this week. There is a lot of work to do. He needs to go
= much   needs의 목적어
to the library on Monday. He has two books to borrow from the library. Also
요일 앞에 전치사 on   two books를 수식하는 형용사적 용법
he has science homework to finish by Thursday. On Friday, he will be in the
~까지
school talent show. So, he will practice performing the songs at the talents
practice의 목적어(동명사)
show all this week.
'all+this+명사'의 어순

구문해설 • plan: 계획 • there is ~: ~이 있다 • a lot of: 많은 • library: 도서관 • borrow: 빌리다
• finish: 끝내다 • talent: 재능 • practice: 연습하다

이것은 Jack의 이번 주 계획이다. 할 일이 많이 있다. 그는 월요일에 도서관에 가야 한다. 그는 도서관에서 빌려야 할 책 두 권이 있다. 또한, 그는 목요일까지 끝내야 할 과학 숙제가 있다. 금요일에 그는 학교 장기 자랑 대회에 나갈 것이다. 그래서 그는 이번 주 내내 장기 자랑 대회에서 공연할 노래들을 연습할 것이다.

Think & Write

Hello, my name is June. Today I'd like to talk about my new wearable
would like to V: V하고 싶다
technology, SuperEye. It is helpful to take pictures and video-record. It is also
= SuperEye   형용사 helpful을 수식하는 부사적 용법
useful to show me a map. Try it out and experience a new world!
4형식 동사+간접목적어+직접목적어 동사+대명사 목적어+부사(어순 주의)

구문해설 • talk about: ~에 관하여 이야기하다 • wearable: 착용할 수 있는 • technology: 기술
• take pictures: 사진을 찍다 • helpful: 유용한 • useful: 유용한 • try out: 시도하다

안녕, 내 이름은 June이야. 오늘 나는 나의 새로운 착용 가능한 기술인 SuperEye에 관해 말하고 싶어. 그것은 사진을 찍거나 녹화를 하는 데 유용해. 또한 나에게 지도를 보여 주는 데도 유용해. 한번 사용해 보고 새로운 세계를 경험해 봐!

Wrap Up 3

Amy: Have you heard about the special event at the science museum?
Have+p.p. = 현재완료

Brian: No, I haven't. What's the event?

Amy: There are science magic shows during the weekend, but only for this
There are+복수명사   during+기간 명사   오직, 단지
month.

Brian: Oh, thank you for the information. I'll visit there this weekend.
= the science museum

구문해설 • Have you heard about ~?: ~에 대해 들어 본 적이 있니? • information: 정보

Amy: 너는 과학 박물관에서 하는 특별 이벤트에 대해 들어 본 적 있어?
Brian: 아니, 없어. 어떤 이벤트야?
Amy: 주말 동안 과학 마술 쇼가 있는데, 이번 달에만 있대.
Brian: 오, 정보 고마워. 이번 주말에 방문해야겠어.

영역별 핵심문제

Words & Expressions

01 다음 짝지어진 단어의 관계가 같도록 빈칸에 알맞은 말을 쓰시오.

> actual : actually = surprising : _____

02 다음 문장의 빈칸에 들어갈 말을 〈보기〉에서 골라 적절한 형태로 쓰시오.

> ┌─ 보기 ├─
> pump up / turn into /
> look forward to / let's say that

(1) I'm _____ _____ _____ visiting the amusement park.

(2) You should _____ _____ all the balloons for the birthday party.

(3) _____ _____ _____ you have power to lift up an elephant.

(4) Grape juice will _____ _____ wine.

03 다음 중 밑줄 친 부분의 뜻풀이가 바르지 <u>않은</u> 것은?

① I have a <u>sore</u> throat. 아픈

② I didn't realize how <u>amazing</u> his work of art was. 놀라운

③ I got <u>average</u> grades in the mid-term test. 평균

④ Why don't you <u>lower</u> the price a little? 높이다

⑤ I hate the ghosts because they <u>scare</u> me. 겁을 주다

04 다음 주어진 문장의 밑줄 친 의미와 같은 의미로 쓰인 것은?

> He must have <u>missed</u> a chance to go abroad.

① He completely <u>missed</u> the joke.

② I don't know why she didn't <u>miss</u> her mother so much.

③ What did you <u>miss</u> most when you were in Canada?

④ They don't want to <u>miss</u> a single note.

⑤ After my English teacher left, many students <u>missed</u> her.

05 다음 우리말을 주어진 단어를 이용하여 영작하시오.

(1) 제가 당신의 지혜를 빌려도 될까요?
(may, pick)

➡ _____

(2) 엄마는 내게 램프를 밝혀달라고 요청하셨다.
(ask, light, lamp)

➡ _____

(3) 나는 벤치에 앉아 있는 한 쌍의 새를 보았다.
(couple, sitting)

➡ _____

Conversation

06 다음 대화의 우리말을 알맞게 영작하시오.

> **A:** 너는 과학 축제에 대해 들어봤니?
> **B:** Yes, I have. It will be held at the science museum this weekend.

➡ _____

[07~08] 다음 대화를 읽고, 물음에 답하시오.

Tom: Mom, have you heard ⓐabout the Chat Robot?

Mom: No, I ⓑhaven't. What is it?

Tom: It's a phone application. You can ask ⓒany questions and it will answer. Let me ⓓto show you. "Emily, what's the weather like today?"

Emily: "It's going to rain, so you'll need an umbrella."

Mom: Wow, ⓔwhat a great application!

07 위 대화의 밑줄 친 ⓐ~ⓔ 중 어법상 어색한 것을 고르고 바르게 고치시오.

➡ _____

08 엄마의 마지막 말로 보아 알 수 있는 엄마의 심정으로 적절한 것은?

① nervous   ② surprised

③ disappointed   ④ upset

⑤ indifferent

[09~11] 다음 대화를 읽고, 물음에 답하시오.

Jimmy: Lisa, what did you do last weekend?

Lisa: I made an egg ball with my brother.

Jimmy: An egg ball? What do you mean?

Lisa: _____(A)_____ Then, (B)the egg turns into a ball.

Jimmy: Wow, I want to make one, too!

09 위 대화의 빈칸 (A)에 들어갈 말을 주어진 단어를 모두 배열하여 완성하시오.

┌─ 보기 ─────────────────────┐
put / vinegar / for / days / we / an egg / in / two
└────────────────────────────┘

➡ _____

10 위 대화의 밑줄 친 (B)와 의미가 같도록 change를 사용하여 다시 쓰시오.

➡ _____

11 위 대화를 읽고 알 수 없는 질문은?

① What did Lisa make last weekend?

② With whom did Lisa make an egg ball?

③ What did Lisa need to make an egg ball?

④ How long did Lisa put an egg in vinegar?

⑤ Why did an egg turn into a ball?

[12~13] 다음 대화를 읽고, 물음에 답하시오.

Minho: Anna, let's make a "Mystery Card" ⓐfor the science experiment.

Anna: A "Mystery Card?" What do you mean?

Minho: It's a special card. It can hide your message.

Anna: ⓑHow do you make it?

Minho: ⓒMix baking soda and water. Then, write a message on the card with it.

Anna: How can you read the card?

Minho: Paint ⓓover the card with grape juice, and then the message ⓔto appear.

12 위 대화의 밑줄 친 ⓐ~ⓔ 중 어법상 틀린 것을 찾아 바르게 고치시오.

➡ _____

13 위 대화를 읽고 대답할 수 없는 질문은?

① What are Minho and Anna making for the science experiment?

② What is the "Mystery Card"?

③ What should Minho and Anna prepare to make the "Mystery Card"?

④ How can Minho and Anna read a message on the "Mystery Card"?

⑤ What message do Minho and Anna want to write on the "Mystery Card"?

[14~15] 다음 대화를 읽고, 물음에 답하시오.

> Jane: Have you heard about the Smart App Contest?
>
> Minho: (A)응, 들어봤어. Are you going to enter it?
>
> Jane: Yeah, I'm going to send my idea about a Pic Gardener App.
>
> Minho: A Pic Gardener App? What do you mean?
>
> Jane: When you take a picture of a plant, the app tells you how to take care of it.
>
> Minho: It sounds like a very useful app.

14 위 대화의 밑줄 친 (A)의 우리말을 3단어를 사용하여 영어로 쓰시오.

➡ _____

15 위 대화의 내용과 일치하도록 빈칸을 완성하시오.

> Mon. Jun, 3rd. 2020.
> Today, I talked about the Smart App Contest with Jane. She said that she would enter it. I was impressed by her idea about (A)_____. It was the app that told me (B)_____, when I took a picture of a plant. I thought it was very (C)_____. I believe she will do well in the contest.

16 다음 빈칸에 알맞은 것은?

> A: Who drew the picture?
> B: The picture _____ Jin.

① was drawn to   ② was drawn by
③ is drawn to   ④ is drawn by
⑤ was drawn in

17 다음 중 어법상 옳지 <u>않은</u> 것은?

① When was the concert held?
② My camera was disappeared from my car.
③ Is there anything to drink here?
④ The music was played by the most famous pianist.
⑤ Now the lights are turned on all at once.

18 다음 중 빈칸에 들어갈 말로 가장 적절한 것은?

> A: Is there _____ in New York?
> B: You should try visiting The Metropolitan Museum of Art.

① something to see interesting
② anything interested to see
③ something interesting seeing
④ anything interesting to see
⑤ seeing anything interesting

19 다음 문장을 수동태로 전환하시오.

> Lamon didn't allow his daughter to go to the park alone.

➡ _____
  _____

20 다음 빈칸에 들어갈 말로 어법상 적절하지 <u>않은</u> 것은?

> Jenny has many friends _____.

① to see　　　② to talk to
③ to go　　　④ to call
⑤ to remember

21 다음 문장에서 어법상 옳지 <u>않은</u> 것은?

> Nothing ①was said ②about the accident ③since it ④was happened ⑤last night.

①　　②　　③　　④　　⑤

22 다음 중 밑줄 친 부분이 어법상 옳은 것은?

① Avery was made <u>clean</u> the room.
② My little sister <u>called</u> Puppy by her friends.
③ <u>Did</u> the lights in the room turned off?
④ Was the I-pad <u>borrowed</u> from Kevin?
⑤ The violin is <u>playing</u> by a famous violinist.

23 다음 우리말에 맞도록 빈칸에 알맞은 말을 쓰시오.

> 그에게 읽을 책 한 권과 마실 물, 앉을 의자 하나를 주세요.
> ➡ Please give him a book _____ _____, water _____ _____, and a chair _____ _____ _____.

24 다음 중 어법상 바르지 <u>않은</u> 것은?

① Mr. Cooper has many students to teach.
② Can I have a pen to write with?
③ They gave me a cushion to use.
④ They have many problems to discuss about.
⑤ I heard she had some work to do yesterday.

25 주어진 단어를 주어로 하여 다음 문장과 같은 의미의 문장을 쓰시오.

> If he takes care of my sisters, we will be really relieved.
> = If my sisters _____, we will be really relieved.

26 다음 우리말을 영어로 바르게 옮긴 것은?

> 주워야 할 쓰레기가 너무 많아.

① There are so many trash to pick.
② There are so much trash to pick on.
③ There is too much trash to pick on.
④ There is too much trash to pick up.
⑤ There are too many trash to pick up.

Reading

[27~29] 다음 글을 읽고, 물음에 답하시오.

In animation movies, ___ⓐ___ things are possible. But are they actually possible in real life?

Let Down Your Hair, Rapunzel!

In the animation, Rapunzel must ___ⓑ___ her long hair to ___ⓒ___ people in her tower. But could human hair really hold up a person?

Surprisingly, yes! A single hair can hold up 100g and an average head has about 120,000 hairs. All those hairs could hold up a couple of elephants! With ___(A)___, Rapunzel has the ability to hold up a person. But she should ___ⓓ___ her hair around something strong and heavy. If she doesn't, she will get a very sore neck.

27 다음 중 빈칸 ⓐ~ⓓ에 들어갈 말이 <u>아닌</u> 것은?

① wrap ② lower ③ amazing
④ hold ⑤ let

28 위 글의 빈칸 (A)에 들어갈 알맞은 말을 위 글에서 찾아 쓰시오.

➡ _____

29 다음 중 위 글을 읽고 답할 수 있는 것을 <u>모두</u> 고르면?

① How long is Rapunzel's hair?
② What made Rapunzel stay in the tower?
③ How many hairs does an average head have?
④ How much does an elephant weigh?
⑤ Why do people want to go to the tower?

[30~32] 다음 글을 읽고, 물음에 답하시오.

We Scare for Energy

In the animation, monsters scare children to get energy from their screams. ① Amazingly, their city is powered by this sound! ② But could we actually produce electricity ⓐto light up a city from sound?

Yes, sound can be changed into electricity. ③ But it would not be helpful in our everyday activities because the amount is too small. ④ For example, the sound from a car horn only produces 50mv. ⑤ So, we would need an unbelievable amount of screams to light up an entire city.

30 다음 중 주어진 문장이 들어가기에 가장 적절한 곳은?

> That is only 1/4400 of the average 220v of electricity in our homes.

①   ②   ③   ④   ⑤

31 다음 밑줄 친 ⓐ와 그 쓰임이 다른 것은?

① I want to have the ability <u>to speak</u> English well.
② Most people have a desire <u>to collect</u> things.
③ She will have a chance <u>to apply</u> for the job.
④ An attempt <u>to open</u> the jar turned out a failure.
⑤ We went to a grocery store <u>to buy</u> some milk.

32 위 글의 내용에 맞게 빈칸에 알맞은 말을 쓰시오.

> _____ would be needed to light up an entire city.

01 출제율 90%

다음 문장의 빈칸에 들어갈 말을 <보기>에서 골라 쓰시오.

┌─── 보기 ───┐
take care of / turn on /
take away / light up
└────────────┘

(1) Would you _____ _____ these empty bottles?

(2) I have the power to _____ _____ lights.

(3) Do you know how to _____ _____ this plant?

(4) Beautiful fireworks _____ _____ the sky.

02 출제율 90%

다음 영영풀이가 나타내는 말을 쓰시오.

┌────────────────────────────┐
a scientific test that is done in order to study what happens and to gain new knowledge
└────────────────────────────┘

➡ _____

03 출제율 95%

다음 우리말에 맞게 빈칸에 알맞은 말을 쓰시오.

(1) 이 로봇이 스포츠카가 될 수 있다.

➡ This robot can _____ _____ a sports car.

(2) 너는 그 천을 무릎에 감쌀 필요가 있다.

➡ You need to _____ the cloth _____ your knee.

(3) 나는 이틀 전에 그 프로젝트를 끝냈다.

➡ I finished the project _____ _____ _____ days ago.

04 출제율 100%

다음 문장에 공통으로 들어갈 말을 고르시오.

┌────────────────────────────┐
• He _____(e)d his baby in his arms.
• The _____ in this building is being fixed.
• They watched the balloons _____ up.
└────────────────────────────┘

① increase ② jump
③ repair   ④ raise
⑤ lift

05 출제율 90%

다음 대화가 자연스럽게 이어지도록 순서대로 배열하시오.

┌────────────────────────────┐
(A) Oh, it sounds interesting.
(B) No, I haven't. What's it about?
(C) What show are you watching?
(D) The program uses science to explain magic tricks.
(E) I'm watching the Sci-Magic show. It's a new program. Have you heard about it?
└────────────────────────────┘

➡ _____

[06~08] 다음 대화를 읽고, 물음에 답하시오.

Tom: Mom, _____(A)_____?
Mom: No, I haven't. What is it?
Tom: It's a phone application. You can ask any questions and it will answer. Let me show you. "Emily, what's the weather like today?"
Emily: "It's going to rain, so you'll need an umbrella."
Mom: Wow, what a great application!

출제율 95%

06 위 대화의 빈칸 (A)에 들어갈 말을 〈보기〉에 주어진 단어를 모두 배열하여 완성하시오.

┌─ 보기 ┐

you / about / Chat Robot / have / the / heard

➡ _____

출제율 90%

07 위 대화에서 다음 영영풀이가 나타내는 말을 찾아 쓰시오.

a program designed to do a particular job

➡ _____

출제율 85%

08 위 대화의 내용과 일치하지 <u>않는</u> 것은?

① Tom is explaining the Chat Robot to his mom.
② Emily, the Chat Robot, is a phone application.
③ Tom's mom hasn't heard about the Chat Robot.
④ The Chat Robot answers the question about today's weather.
⑤ Tom's mom is surprised at the rain outside.

[09~10] 다음 대화를 읽고, 물음에 답하시오.

Mina: You know what? I made a potato clock yesterday!
Jack: A potato clock? What do you mean?
Mina: My clock works with potatoes, not with batteries. Potatoes can produce electricity.
Jack: That's interesting!

출제율 95%

09 What did Mina make yesterday?

➡ _____

출제율 95%

10 How can Mina's clock work? (Use the word 'because'.)

➡ _____

출제율 100%

11 다음 괄호 안에 주어진 단어의 형태가 바르게 짝지어진 것은?

I am not good at (make) friends, so I don't have a friend (depend on).

① make – to depend on
② making – depending on
③ to make – to depend on
④ making – to depend on
⑤ to make – depending on

출제율 95%

12 다음 중 어법상 바른 문장의 개수는?

ⓐ Ann's cup was broken by Ted.
ⓑ The money I put on the table was disappeared.
ⓒ Haiti was hit by strong earthquakes a few years ago.
ⓓ Emma is married a rich and honest man.
ⓔ Steve Jobs was born in 1955.

① 1개   ② 2개   ③ 3개
④ 4개   ⑤ 5개

출제율 90%

13 다음 중 빈칸에 들어갈 말을 바르게 배열한 것은?

How about looking for _____ for dinner?

① something eat tasty
② something to eat tasty
③ something tasty eat
④ something tasty to eat
⑤ something to tasty to eat

14 다음 중 문장의 전환이 바르지 <u>않은</u> 것은?

① Two hundred people were employed by the company.
→ The company employed two hundred people.

② They didn't invite me to their party.
→ I was not invited to their party by them.

③ They canceled all flights because of the fog.
→ All flights are canceled by them because of the fog.

④ This road isn't used by us very often.
→ We don't use this road very often.

⑤ People speak English in many countries.
→ English is spoken in many countries.

15 주어진 단어를 활용하여 다음 우리말을 조건에 맞게 영어로 쓰시오.

그가 너에게 그 사진을 보여 주었니?
(shown / to you)

능동태로 ➡ _____

수동태로 ➡ _____

16 주어진 단어를 활용하여 다음 우리말을 영어로 쓰시오.

연습은 영어에 통달하는 유일한 방법이다.
(practice / mater)

➡ _____

[17~18] 다음 글을 읽고, 물음에 답하시오.

In animation movies, amazing things are possible. But are they actually possible in real life?

Let (A)[Up / Down] Your Hair, Rapunzel!

In the animation, Rapunzel must lower her long hair ⓐto let people in her tower. But could human hair really hold up a person?

Surprisingly, yes! A single hair can hold up 100g and an average head has about 120,000 hairs. All those hairs could hold up a couple of elephants! With her hair, Rapunzel has the ability (B)[hold up / to hold up] a person. But she should wrap her hair around something strong and heavy. (C)[If / Unless] she doesn't, she will get a very sore neck.

17 위 글의 (A)~(C)에서 어법상 옳은 것끼리 바르게 짝지은 것은?

① Up – hold up – If
② Up – to hold up – If
③ Down – to hold up – Unless
④ Down – hold up – If
⑤ Down – to hold up – If

18 위 글의 밑줄 친 ⓐ와 쓰임이 같은 것은?

① He hoped <u>to be</u> elected president of his class.
② Kelly encouraged me <u>to do</u> my best all the time.
③ It is possible <u>to lift</u> a person with human hair.
④ Please give me a chair <u>to sit</u> on.
⑤ Jane flew from New York <u>to see</u> me again.

[19~21] 다음 글을 읽고, 물음에 답하시오.

We ①Scare for Energy

In the animation, monsters scare children to get energy from their screams. Amazingly, their city ②is powered by this sound! But ⓐ could we actually produce electricity to light up a city from sound?

Yes, sound can ③be changed into electricity. But it would not be helpful in our everyday activities ④because the amount is too small. For example, the sound from a car horn ⑤is produced only 50mv. That is only 1/4400 of the average 220v of electricity in our homes. So, we would need an unbelievable amount of screams to light up an entire city.

출제율 90%

19 위 글의 밑줄 친 ⓐ와 같은 의미의 문장은?

① could electricity be produced by a city?

② could electricity to light up a city be changed into sound?

③ could electricity to light up a city be made from sound?

④ could a city to produce electricity be produced by us?

⑤ could we actually make electricity to light up a city into sound?

출제율 100%

20 위 글의 ①~⑤ 중 어법상 바르지 <u>않은</u> 것은?

①   ②   ③   ④   ⑤

출제율 95%

21 위 글의 내용에 맞게 다음 물음에 답하시오.

> Q: In the animation movie, what do monsters do to get energy?
>
> A: _____

[22~24] 다음 글을 읽고, 물음에 답하시오.

Up, Up and Away!

The house is lifted and flown by thousands of balloons in the animation. Could ⓐthat actually work?

Let's say that a house weighs about 50,000kg. A normal balloon at an amusement park can lift about 14g. So we need about 3,570,000 balloons to lift up the house. We also have to think about the weight of the balloons themselves and the strings. Then, we need to add a few more thousand balloons. Now, the biggest challenge is pumping up all those balloons!

출제율 90%

22 다음 중 위 글을 읽고 답할 수 있는 질문은?

① When is the house lifted in the animation?

② Who pumped up all the balloons in the animation?

③ How many people do we need to pump up millions of balloons?

④ How many balloons do we need to lift up a house?

⑤ How many grams does a balloon string weigh?

출제율 95%

23 다음 주어진 어구를 바르게 배열하여 밑줄 친 ⓐ가 의미하는 것을 쓰시오. 필요하다면 어형을 바꾸시오.

> lift / a house / with / up / thousands of balloons

➡ _____

출제율 90%

24 위 글의 내용에 맞게 빈칸에 알맞은 말을 쓰시오.

> When we plan to lift up a house, we have to consider _____ and _____.

[01~03] 다음 대화를 읽고, 물음에 답하시오.

Minho: Anna, let's make a "Mystery Card" for the science experiment.

Anna: A "Mystery Card?" What do you mean?

Minho: It's a special card. It can hide your message.

Anna: How do you make it?

Minho: Mix baking soda and water. Then, write a message on the card with it.

Anna: How can you read the card?

Minho: Paint over the card with grape juice, and then the message appears.

01 Why is a "Mystery Card" special?

➡ _____

02 What does Anna need to make a "Mystery Card"?

➡ _____

03 "Mystery Card"의 메시지를 읽을 수 있는 방법을 우리말 20자 이내로 간략히 설명하시오.

➡ _____

04 주어진 어구를 활용하여 빈칸에 알맞은 말을 쓰시오.

> A: You look very busy. What are you doing?
> B: I'm going to throw a party for my parents. So (have / many things / plan).

➡ _____

05 다음 문장을 수동태로 바꿔 쓰시오.

(1) I made some mistakes.

➡ _____

(2) My friend made me a pretty doll.

➡ _____

(3) Jason always makes us bored.

➡ _____

06 다음 중 어법상 틀린 것을 골라 바르게 고치시오.

> That hotel has a pool to swim.

_____ ➡ _____

07 다음 두 문장이 같은 의미를 가지도록 빈칸에 알맞은 말을 쓰시오.

> We didn't buy the oranges on the table.
> = The oranges on the table _____ by us.

➡ _____

08 주어진 단어를 활용하여 다음 우리말을 7 단어로 이루어진 영어 문장으로 쓰시오.

> 결정할 충분한 시간이 너에게 주어졌어.
> (be / give / decide)

➡ _____

In animation movies, amazing things are possible. But are they actually possible in real life?

Let Down Your Hair, Rapunzel!

In the animation, Rapunzel must lower her long hair to let people in her tower. ⓐ<u>But could human hair really hold up a person?</u> Surprisingly, yes! A single hair can hold up 100g and an average head has about 120,000 hairs. All those hairs could hold up a couple of elephants! With her hair, Rapunzel has the ability to hold up a person. But she should wrap her hair around something strong and heavy. If she doesn't, she will get a very sore neck.

09 According to the passage, what must be lowered so thatr people can enter Rapunzel's tower? Answer with 6 words.

➡ _____

10 위 글의 밑줄 친 ⓐ와 같은 의미가 되도록 빈칸에 알맞은 말을 쓰시오.

> But is it possible that a person _____ _____ _____ by human hair?

11 위 글의 내용에 맞게 빈칸에 알맞은 말을 쓰시오.

> **Rapunzel:** I need something _____ _____ _____ my hair in order to let a friend in my tower. I want it to be _____ and _____. Do you have something like that?

We Scare for Energy

In the animation, monsters scare children to get energy from their screams. Amazingly, their city is powered by this sound! But could we actually produce electricity to light up a city from sound?

Yes, sound can be changed into electricity. But it would not be helpful in our everyday activities because the amount is too small. For example, the sound from a car horn only produces 50mv. That is only 1/4400 of the average 220v of electricity in our homes. So, we would need an unbelievable amount of screams to light up an entire city.

12 Why do monsters scare the children in the animation movie? Answer in English with a full sentence.

➡ _____

_____

13 위 글에 나오는 단어를 이용하여 빈칸에 알맞은 말을 쓰시오.

> A: Do you know that electricity _____ _____ by a car horn?
> B: Oh, really? I didn't know that. How much amount of electricity is made?
> A: Only 50mv.

01 다음 담화문을 읽고 아래 표의 (A)~(C)를 완성하시오.

> W: Hello, students. Have you heard about the DIY Drone Class? You can make your own drone in the class. The Youth Community Center offers the class at 3 p.m. every Wednesday in May. Make your special drone and learn how to control it. Don't miss this great chance!

DIY Drone Class	
When	(A)
Where	(B)
What	You can (C)

02 〈보기〉의 동사를 활용하여 수동태로 문장을 쓰시오.

> **보기**
>
> unlock   open   take away   hit   break   pour

(1) _____

(2) _____

(3) _____

(4) _____

(5) _____

(6) _____

03 주어진 단어를 알맞게 짝지어 〈보기〉와 같은 문장을 쓰시오.

> **보기**
>
> I have no reason to give up.

> book   money   right   reason   chance   desire
> borrow   spend   speak   believe   win   have   give up   learn

(1) _____

(2) _____

(3) _____

(4) _____

(5) _____

(6) _____

단원별 모의고사

[01~02] 다음 대화를 읽고, 물음에 답하시오.

> Hojin: Hey, Katy. Have you heard about the science fair?
> Katy: Yeah, I'm going to go there.
> Hojin: Me, too! I'm excited about doing different kinds of experiments.
> Katy: Yeah, (A)I'm also looking forward to it! (wait)

01 위 대화의 밑줄 친 (A)와 의미가 같도록 주어진 단어를 사용하여 다시 쓰시오.

➡ _____

02 What can Hojin and Katy do at the science fair?

➡ _____

[03~04] 다음 대화를 읽고, 물음에 답하시오.

> Emma: _____(A)_____
> David: "Dancing Beans?" What do you mean?
> Emma: They are beans that move in the water like they're dancing.
> David: Sounds interesting! What do we need?
> Emma: We just need some water, vinegar, baking soda, and beans.

03 위 대화의 빈칸 (A)에 들어갈 말로 나머지와 의도가 다른 것은?

① Let's make "Dancing Beans" for the science project.

② Why don't we make "Dancing Beans" for the science project?

③ What about making "Dancing Beans" for the science project?

④ How about making "Dancing Beans" for the science project?

⑤ Why did you make "Dancing Beans" for the science project?

04 What David and Emma should prepare to make "Dancing Beans"?

➡ _____

_____

05 다음 담화문의 빈칸 (A)~(C)에 주어진 단어를 알맞은 형태로 쓰시오.

> W: Hello, students. Have you (A)_____(hear) about the DIY Drone Class? You can make your own drone in the class. The Youth Community Center offers the class at 3 p.m. every Wednesday in May. (B)_____(make) your special drone and learn how (C)_____(control) it. Don't miss this great chance!

[06~07] 다음 대화를 읽고, 물음에 답하시오.

> Jimmy: Lisa, what did you do last weekend?
> Lisa: I made an egg ball ___(A)___ my brother.
> Jimmy: An egg ball? What do you mean?
> Lisa: We put an egg ___(B)___ vinegar ___(C)___ two days. Then, the egg turns ___(D)___ a ball.
> Jimmy: Wow, ⓐI want to make one, too!

06 위 대화의 빈칸 (A)~(D)에 들어갈 말을 주어진 단어를 넣어 완성하시오.

┌─ 보기 ─────────────────┐
│   for / with / into / in   │
└──────────────────────────┘

(A) _____ (B) _____ (C) _____ (D) _____

07 위 대화의 밑줄 친 ⓐ와 바꾸어 쓸 수 있는 것은?

① I'm good at making one, too.
② I'd like to make one, too.
③ I'm glad to make one, too.
④ I wish I could make one, too.
⑤ I like making one, too.

08 다음 대화의 내용과 일치하도록 빈칸을 명령문을 사용하여 완성하시오.

> Minho: Anna, let's make a "Mystery Card" for the science experiment.
> Anna: A "Mystery Card?" What do you mean?
> Minho: It's a special card. It can hide your message.
> Anna: How do you make it?
> Minho: Mix baking soda and water. Then, write a message on the card with it.
> Anna: How can you read the card?
> Minho: Paint over the card with grape juice, and then the message appears.

How to Make a Mystery Card	
step 1	Mix baking soda and water.
step 2	(A)
How to Read a Mystery Card	
step 1	(B)
step 2	Then, you can read the message.

(A) _____
(B) _____

[09~10] 다음 대화를 읽고, 물음에 답하시오.

> Jane: Have you heard about the Smart App Contest?
> Minho: Yes, I have. Are you going to (A)enter it?
> Jane: Yeah, I'm going to send my idea about a Pic Gardener App.
> Minho: A Pic Gardener App? What do you mean?
> Jane: When you take a picture of a plant, the app tells you how to take care of it.
> Minho: It sounds like a very useful app.

09 위 대화의 밑줄 친 (A)와 바꾸어 쓸 수 없는 것은? (2개)

① take part in   ② share
③ join   ④ participate in
⑤ exit

10 위 대화의 내용과 일치하지 않는 것은?

① Minho와 Jane은 Smart App Contest에 대해 알고 있다.
② Jane은 Smart App Contest에 참가할 것이다.
③ Jane은 Pic Gardener App을 고안해 냈다.
④ Pic Gardener App은 식물 관리에 대한 정보를 얻을 수 있는 앱이다.
⑤ Minho는 Pic Gardener App을 유용하게 사용하고 있다.

[11~12] 다음 대화를 읽고, 물음에 답하시오.

> Hojun: Hey, Katy. (A)과학 박람회에 대해 들어보았니? (about, fair)
> Katy: Yeah, I'm going to go there.
> Hojun: (B)Me, too! I'm excited about doing different kinds of experiments.
> Katy: Yeah, I'm also looking forward to it!

11 위 대화의 밑줄 친 (A)의 우리말을 주어진 단어를 이용하여 영작하시오.

➡ _____

12 위 대화의 밑줄 친 (B)와 바꾸어 쓸 수 있는 것은?

① So do I!   ② So am I!
③ Neither do I!   ④ Neither am I!
⑤ Me, neither!

13 주어진 어구를 바르게 배열하여 다음 우리말을 영어로 쓰시오. 필요하다면 단어를 추가하시오.

> 다른 사람에게 말할 기회를 주어라.
> (talk / the other / a chance / give / person)

➡ _____

14 다음 두 문장이 같은 의미가 되도록 빈칸에 알맞은 말을 쓰시오.

> Jason laughed at me.
> ➡ I _____ .

15 다음 중 to부정사의 쓰임이 주어진 문장과 같은 것은?

> The school has strict rules to follow.

① Jim came to Korea to study Korean.
② People of the town were sad to hear the news.
③ The novelist needed something to write about.
④ His job is to make sure that everyone is safe.
⑤ I want to make more money than my friend does.

16 다음 중 어법상 바르지 않은 것은?

① My car was repaired by a mechanic.
② He has something curious to see.
③ Jason promised not to run away again.
④ I was deeply disappointed with the result.
⑤ Jessica had nothing eaten in the refrigerator.

17 다음 중 어법상 바르지 않은 것은?

① Kevin made a promise not to do it again.
② The blouse is made of silk.
③ By whom was the window shut?
④ The towels on the floor was found by Jim.
⑤ She has every reason to hate him.

[18~20] 다음 글을 읽고, 물음에 답하시오.

In animation movies, amazing things are possible. But are they actually possible ⓐ____ real life?

Let Down Your Hair, Rapunzel!

In the animation, Rapunzel must lower her long hair to let people in her tower. But could human hair really hold up a person? Surprisingly, yes! A single hair can hold up 100g and an average head has about 120,000 hairs. All those hairs could hold up a couple of elephants! With her hair, Rapunzel has the ability ⓑto hold up a person. But she should wrap her hair around something strong and heavy. If she doesn't, she will get a very sore neck.

18 위 글의 빈칸 ⓐ에 들어갈 전치사와 같은 것은?

① You don't have to worry _____ it.
② I am waiting _____ my mom.
③ Life is full _____ wonders.
④ She is interested _____ history.
⑤ Mary is well known _____ her love for animals.

19 다음 중 밑줄 친 ⓑ와 쓰임이 같은 것은?

① The subject is difficult to talk about.
② I have something to tell you.
③ The man wanted to be a doctor.
④ The river is dangerous to swim in.
⑤ It is necessary to discuss the problem.

20 위 글의 내용을 참고하여 Rapunzel에게 해 줄 조언을 완성하시오.

> _____ _____ _____ _____
> _____ _____ _____ _____ ,
> or you will get a very sore neck.

[21~24] 다음 글을 읽고, 물음에 답하시오.

We Scare for Energy

In the animation, monsters scare children to get energy from their screams. Amazingly, their city is powered by this sound! But could we actually produce electricity to light up a city from sound?

Yes, sound can be changed into electricity. But it would not be helpful in our everyday activities _____ⓐ_____ the amount is too small. For example, the sound from a car horn only produces 50mv. That is only 1/4400 of the average 220v of electricity in our homes. So, we would need an unbelievable amount of screams ⓑto light up an entire city.

21 위 글의 빈칸 ⓐ에 들어갈 말로 가장 적절한 것은?

① while   ② because   ③ if
④ before   ⑤ until

22 위 글의 내용과 일치하는 것은?

① Monsters give children scares for fun.
② With the screams of children, monsters can light up their city.
③ Seeing monsters, children scream with joy.
④ Electricity can be changed into sound.
⑤ Changing sound into electricity is not difficult.

23 위 글의 내용에 맞게 빈칸에 알맞은 말을 쓰시오.

> With the latest technology, we can actually produce _____ _____ _____. However, it is hard to say that _____ _____ _____ in our daily lives because the amount is too small.

24 위 글의 밑줄 친 ⓑ와 쓰임이 다른 하나는?

① She went to Italy to study music.
② We go to the river to catch fish.
③ He opened the door to welcome me.
④ You don't have a right to accept it.
⑤ We don't live to eat.

Your Only Limit Is You

 의사소통 기능

- 격려하기
  A: My serves were not strong enough.
  B: You're a great player. You'll do better next time.

- 상대방에게 도움 제안하기
  A: I can't wash this car alone. It's too big.
  B: Let me help you.

 언어 형식

- 관계대명사
  There are people **who** are cheering excitedly.

- 지각동사
  Max **sees** the official waving a white flag.

Words & Expressions

Key Words

- **ahead**[əhéd] 🔺 앞에, 앞선
- **amazing**[əméiziŋ] 🔶 놀랄 정도의, 굉장한
- **beat**[biːt] 🔸 뛰다, 치다, 두드리다
- **block**[blak] 🔸 막다, 방해하다
- **cheer**[tʃiər] 🔸 갈채를 보내다, 환호성을 지르다
- **close match** 아슬아슬한 승부, 접전
- **complete**[kəmplíːt] 🔸 완성하다, 달성하다 🔶 완전한
- **count**[kaunt] 🔸 중요하다, (수를) 세다
- **crowd**[kraud] 🔷 군중, 관객
- **crowded**[kráudid] 🔶 복잡한, 붐비는
- **deep**[diːp] 🔶 깊은
- **engine**[éndʒin] 🔷 엔진, 기관
- **excitedly**[iksáitidli] 🔺 흥분하여, 기를 쓰고
- **finish line** 결승선
- **fix**[fiks] 🔸 수리하다, 고정시키다
- **flag**[flæg] 🔷 기, 깃발
- **gas pedal** (자동차의) 가속 페달
- **hang**[hæŋ] 🔸 매달다, 걸다
- **hit**[hit] 🔸 부딪치다
- **kart**[kaːrt] 🔷 소형 경주용 자동차
- **kick**[kik] 🔸 차다, 걷어차다
- **lap**[læp] 🔷 (경주에서 트랙의) 한 바퀴, 무릎
- **local**[lóukəl] 🔶 지방의
- **loud**[laud] 🔶 시끄러운, (소리가) 큰
- **memorable**[mémərəbl] 🔶 기억할 만한
- **official**[əfíʃəl] 🔷 (운동 경기의) 심판 🔶 공식의
- **pitching**[pítʃiŋ] 🔷 투구
- **pitcher**[pítʃər] 🔷 투수
- **place**[pleis] 🔷 장소, (경주, 대회 등의) 등위
- **press**[pres] 🔸 누르다, 밀어붙이다
- **punch**[pʌntʃ] 🔷 타격
- **rush**[rʌʃ] 🔸 돌진하다
- **seafood**[sifud] 🔷 해산물
- **straightaway**[streitəwei] 🔶 일직선의, 즉시의
- **tear**[tiər] 🔷 눈물
- **terrible**[térəbl] 🔶 무서운, 심한
- **three-pointer** 3점슛
- **track**[træk] 🔷 경주로, 트랙
- **voice**[vɔis] 🔷 목소리
- **volleyball**[válibɔ̀ːl] 🔷 배구

Key Expressions

- **be filled with** ~로 가득 차다
- **be satisfied with** ~에 만족하다
- **cheer up** 기운을 내다
- **do one's best** 최선을 다하다
- **keep up with** ~에 뒤떨어지지 않다
- **miss a chance** 기회를 놓치다
- **out of one's reach** ~에게 닿지 않는, ~의 힘이 미치지 않는
- **role model** 역할 모델
- **sit up** 자세를 바로 하다, 바로 앉다
- **take a chance** (모험 삼아) 해보다
- **win a race** 경주에 이기다

Word Power

※ 서로 반대되는 뜻을 가진 어휘

- **official** 공식적인 ↔ **unoffical** 비공식적인
- **crowded** 혼잡한 ↔ **uncrowded** 붐비지 않는
- **thin** 얇은 ↔ **thick** 두꺼운
- **satisfied** 만족한 ↔ **dissatisfied** 만족스럽지 않은
- **deep** 깊은 ↔ **shallow** 얕은
- **comfortable** 편안한 ↔ **uncomfortable** 불편한

- **complete** 완전한 ↔ **incomplete** 불완전한
- **finish** 끝내다 ↔ **begin** 시작하다
- **straight** 곧은, 일직선의 ↔ **curved** 굽은, 곡선의
- **filled** 가득 찬 ↔ **empty** 텅 빈
- **loud** 시끄러운 ↔ **silent** 고요한, 소리 없는
- **memorable** 기억할 만한 ↔ **forgettable** 잊을 만한

English Dictionary

- **cheer** 응원하다
  → to shout loudly, to show support or praise for somebody, or to give them encouragement
  누군가를 위해 지지나 칭찬을 보여주기 위해, 또는 용기를 북돋아 주기 위해 크게 소리 지르다

- **kart** 소형 경주용 자동차
  → a small motor vehicle used for racing
  경주를 위해 사용되는 작은 자동차

- **complete** 완성하다
  → to finish making or doing something
  무언가를 만들거나 하는 것을 끝내다

- **engine** 엔진
  → the part of a vehicle that produces power to make the vehicle move
  자동차를 움직이게 만드는 힘을 만들어 내는 자동차의 한 부분

- **pitcher** 투수
  → the player who throws the ball to the batter
  타자에게 공을 던지는 선수

- **tear** 눈물
  → a drop of liquid that comes out of your eye when you cry
  당신이 울 때 눈에서부터 나오는 액체 방울

- **track** 경주로, 트랙
  → a piece of ground with a special surface for people, cars, etc. to have races on
  사람이나 자동차 등이 경주하기 위한 특별한 표면을 가진 땅의 일부

- **voice** 목소리
  → the sound or sounds produced through the mouth by a person speaking or singing
  말을 하거나 노래를 부르는 사람에 의해 입을 통해 만들어지는 소리

- **memorable** 기억할 만한
  → special, good or unusual and therefore worth remembering or easy to remember
  특별하거나 좋거나 또는 유별나서 기억할 만한 가치가 있거나 또는 기억하기 쉬운

- **kick** 차다
  → to hit somebody/something with your foot
  발로 누군가나 무언가를 치다

- **block** 막다, 방해하다
  → to stop somebody from going somewhere or seeing something by standing in front of them or in their way
  누군가의 길이나 그들 앞에 서서 어딘가로 가거나 무언가를 보게 하는 것을 막다

- **crowd** 관객, 관중
  → a large number of people gathered together in a public place, for example in the streets or at a sports game
  예를 들어 거리나 스포츠 경기를 위해 공공장소에 모인 많은 사람들

- **finish line** 결승선
  → the line across a sports track, etc. that marks the end of a race
  경주의 끝을 표시하는 스포츠 경주로를 가로지르는 선

01 다음 영영풀이에 해당하는 말을 고르시오.

> the player who throws the ball to the batter

① catcher ② coach
③ pitcher ④ hitter
⑤ outfielder

02 다음 중 밑줄 친 부분의 뜻풀이가 바르지 <u>않은</u> 것은?

① I hear the <u>voice</u> of your children. 목소리
② The stadium is filled with the <u>crowd</u>. 사람들
③ <u>Press</u> the button to open the door. 누르다
④ Mike completed the final <u>lap</u>. 무릎
⑤ The red car <u>hit</u> the bus. 부딪치다

03 다음 주어진 문장의 밑줄 친 의미와 같은 의미로 쓰인 것은?

> It is the quality that <u>counts</u>.

① Every minute <u>counts</u> in the game.
② He began to <u>count</u> the number of guests.
③ Close your eyes and <u>count</u> to the number ten.
④ I was so surprised when my little daughter was able to <u>count</u>.
⑤ Mike, <u>count</u> to ten, and open your eyes.

서답형
04 다음 짝지어진 단어의 관계가 같도록 빈칸에 알맞은 말을 쓰시오.

> deep : shallow = _____ : forgettable

중요
05 다음 문장에 공통으로 들어갈 말을 고르시오.

> • Our team won a _____ victory at the soccer match.
> • Jane will _____ the task before going out.
> • He is a _____ stranger to me.

① comfortable ② tear
③ complete ④ straight
⑤ terrible

서답형
06 다음 문장의 빈칸에 들어갈 말을 〈보기〉에서 골라 쓰시오.

> ┤ 보기 ├
> gas pedal / finish line / cheer up /
> sit up / satisfied with

(1) When Emily saw Tom, she wanted to _____ him _____.
(2) Son, _____ _____ and look at this.
(3) My father was _____ _____ my present.
(4) Don't press the _____ _____.
(5) They are running toward the _____ _____.

01 다음 짝지어진 단어의 관계가 같도록 빈칸에 알맞은 말을 쓰시오.

> possible : impossible =
> comfortable : _____

02 다음 문장의 빈칸에 들어갈 말을 <보기>에서 골라 쓰시오.

┌─ 보기 ─┐

lap / official / balance / hit

(1) As the _____ waved the flag, the race started.
(2) My car almost _____ the back of his car.
(3) Jimmy completed his tenth _____.
(4) It is important to keep the _____.

03 다음 우리말에 맞게 빈칸에 알맞은 말을 쓰시오.

(1) 우리는 경주에 우승하기 위해 최선을 다할 것이다.
➡ We will do our best to _____
_____ _____.

(2) 우리 회사의 최고 경영자를 만날 기회를 놓치지 마세요.
➡ Don't _____ _____ _____ to meet the CEO of our company.

(3) 그의 눈은 눈물로 가득 찼다.
➡ His eyes _____ _____ _____ tears.

04 다음 우리말을 주어진 어구를 이용하여 영작하시오.

(1) 나는 그의 앞에서 걸었다. (ahead)
➡ _____

(2) 나는 여동생이 2등을 했다고 들었다. (place)
➡ _____

(3) 나는 그 유명한 가수를 만날 기회를 놓치고 싶지 않았다. (miss, chance, to meet)
➡ _____
_____

05 다음 대화의 우리말을 주어진 단어를 사용하여 영작하시오.

> A: (1)왜 시무룩한 얼굴이니? (long)
> B: I couldn't block the other players.
> A: Don't worry. (2)너는 다음에는 더 잘할 거야. (better, next)

(1) _____
(2) _____

06 다음 우리말을 주어진 단어를 배열하여 완성하시오.

(1) 프로젝트가 일주일 안에 완성되어야 한다.
(the project / be / in / should / a week / completed)
➡ _____

(2) 그는 가속페달을 세게 밟았다.
(down / pressed / on / gas / the / pedal / he / hard)
➡ _____

(3) 나는 나의 투구가 만족스럽지 않았다.
(pitching / not / I / with / my / was / satisfied)
➡ _____

Conversation

① 격려하기

> **A** My serves were not strong enough. 내 서브는 충분히 강하지 않았어.
>
> **B** You're a great player. You'll do better next time.
> 오, 너는 훌륭한 선수야. 다음번에는 더 잘할 거야.

■ 'You'll do better next time.'은 상대방을 격려해 주는 표현으로 Don't worry., There's always a next time., Cheer up! 또는 You can do it! 등으로 바꾸어 쓸 수 있다.

격려하기

- There's always a next time. 항상 다음 기회가 있어.
- Cheer up! 기운 내!
- You can do it! 너는 할 수 있어!
- Don't give up! 포기하지 마!
- Don't be so hard on yourself. 너무 자책하지 마.
- Don't take it too hard. 너무 상심하지 마.
- You are a great player. 너는 훌륭한 선수야.

핵심 Check

1. 다음 우리말과 일치하도록 빈칸에 알맞은 말을 쓰시오.

   (1) **A:** I couldn't catch up with other runners today. (나는 오늘 다른 주자들을 따라잡을 수 없었어.)

   B: _____ _____ _____ _____ _____. You are a great player.

   (너무 상심하지 마. 너는 훌륭한 선수야.)

   (2) **A:** I didn't do well in the match. My punches were terrible.

   (나는 시합에서 잘하지 못했어. 내 펀치는 형편없었어.)

   B: _____ _____ _____ _____ _____ _____. (너무 자책하지 마.)

   (3) **A:** I didn't jump high enough. (나는 충분히 높게 뛰어오르지 않았어.)

   B: _____ _____! _____ _____ _____ _____! (기운 내! 너는 할 수 있어!)

② 상대방에게 도움 제안하기

> **A** I can't wash this car alone. It's too big. 내가 혼자 이 차를 세차할 수 없어. 이건 너무 커.
>
> **B** Let me help you. 내가 도와줄게.

■ 상대방에게 도움을 제안하고자 할 때 Let me help you., I'll help you. 또는 I'll give you a hand. 등으로 표현할 수 있다.

도움 요청하기

- Would you help me out? 나를 좀 도와주시겠어요?
- Could you do something for me? 좀 도와주시겠습니까?
- Would you give me a hand? 저 좀 도와주시겠어요?
- Would you mind helping me? 좀 도와주시겠습니까?

도움 제안하기

- Let me help you. 내가 도와줄게.
- Would you like me to help you? 내가 당신을 도와주길 원하나요?
- Do you need any help? 도움이 필요하세요?
- Can I give you a hand? 도와 드릴까요?
- May I help you? 제가 도와드릴까요?
- How can I help you? 무엇을 도와드릴까요?
- I'll help you. 제가 도와드릴게요.

핵심 Check

2. 다음 우리말과 일치하도록 빈칸에 알맞은 말을 쓰시오.

(1) **A:** I don't have a bottle-opener. I can't open the bottle. (나는 병따개가 없어. 병을 딸 수 없어.)

    B: Let _____ _____ _____. (제가 도와드릴게요.)

(2) **A:** _____ _____ _____ _____ _____? (도움이 필요하신가요?)

    B: Yes. I can't fix the light. It's too high. (네. 저는 전등을 고칠 수 없어요. 너무 높아요.)

(3) **A:** I can't swim here. It's too _____. (제가 여기서 수영을 못하겠어요. 너무 깊어요.)

    B: _____ _____. I'll _____ _____. (걱정 마세요. 제가 도와드릴게요.)

A. Listen & Talk B-2

Emily: I heard your baseball team, the Reds, ❶won the match. Eight to seven, right? Congratulations, John!

John: Thanks. It was a ❷close game. I'm not happy with my pitching.

Emily: Why do you say ❸that?

John: I allowed two homeruns.

Emily: Oh, you're a great pitcher. ❹You'll do better next time.

Emily: 나는 너희 the Reds 야구팀이 시합에서 이겼다고 들었어. 8대 7이 맞니? 축하해, John!

John: 고마워. 정말 접전이었어. 나는 내 투구가 만족스럽지 않아.

Emily: 왜 그렇게 말하는 거야?

John: 홈런 두 개를 허용했거든.

Emily: 오, 너는 훌륭한 투수야. 다음번에는 더 잘할 거야.

❶ win the match: 시합에 이기다
❷ close: 우열을 가리기 힘든, 막상막하의
❸ that은 John이 자신의 투구에 만족스럽지 않다고 말한 것을 가리킨다.
❹ 낙담하고 있는 상대를 격려하는 것에 그치지 않고, 특정한 근거에 기초하여 상대방이 다음에는 '더 나아질 것'이라는 믿음을 표현할 때 쓴다.

Check(√) True or False

(1) John belongs to the Reds.　　　　　　　　　　　　　　T ☐ F ☐

(2) John hit two solo homeruns.　　　　　　　　　　　　　T ☐ F ☐

B. Communication

Megan: ❶I'm worried about our next soccer match, James.

James: Why are you worried, Megan?

Megan: Well, I couldn't catch high balls in the last soccer match. I gave away too many goals.

James: I see. Here, ❷let me help you. I'll kick high balls to you.

Megan: Oh, that'll really help. I hope my skills ❸get better.

James: Don't worry. You'll do better next time.

Megan: James, 나는 다음 축구 시합이 걱정돼.

James: 왜 걱정하는 거야, Megan?

Megan: 음, 지난 축구 시합에서 나는 높은 공을 잡지 못했어. 너무 많은 골을 허용했어.

James: 알겠어. 자, 내가 도와줄게. 너에게 공을 높이 차 줄게.

Megan: 오, 그거 도움이 많이 되겠다. 내 기술이 나아지길 바라.

James: 걱정 마. 다음번에 더 잘할 거야.

❶ be worried about: ~을 걱정하다
❷ 상대방에게 도움을 제안할 때 쓰는 표현으로 Can I give you a hand?도 같은 의도로 쓰인다.
❸ get better: 좋아지다, 호전되다

Check(√) True or False

(3) Megan scored goals in the last soccer match.　　　　　　T ☐ F ☐

(4) James will kick high balls to Megan to practice for the next soccer match.　　T ☐ F ☐

Listen & Talk 1 A-1

Mom: David, how was your basketball game today?
David: We lost, Mom. I missed too many chances for a three-pointer.
Mom: Oh, ❶don't be so hard on yourself. You'll do better next time.
David: I hope so.

❶ '너무 자책하지 마.'라는 의미로 상대방을 격려하는 표현이다.

Listen & Talk 1 A-2

Jack: Did you come and watch my volleyball match yesterday?
Irene: Yeah, I did. That was a great volleyball match. You were great!
Jack: Thanks, but it was ❶a close match. My serves were not strong ❷enough.
Irene: Oh, you're a great player. You'll do better next time.

❶ a close match: 아슬아슬한 시합 ❷ enough: 충분히

Listen & Talk 2 A-1

Mike: Is it your first time riding a bike, Mina?
Mina: Yes, it is. I just can't ❶keep my balance.
Mike: Let me help you. I'll hold your bike.
Mina: Thanks, Mike. Don't ❷let go, okay?
Mike: Don't worry. Sit up and ❸look straight ahead.

❶ keep one's balance: 균형을 잡다 ❷ let go: 놓다 ❸ look straight ahead: 앞을 똑바로 보다

Listen & Talk 2 A-2

Tom: What are you doing, Sarah?
Sarah: I learned how to ❶stand on my head in PE class. So I'm trying ❷it now but it's not easy.
Tom: Let me help you. Kick your legs in the air again. I'll catch you.
Sarah: Oh, thanks. I'll try again.

❶ stand on one's head: 물구나무서다
❷ it은 물구나무 서는 것을 가리킨다.

Listen & Talk 2 B

Coach: Hey, Brain. Did you practice the *taegwondo* side kick?
Brian: Yes, Coach. But I'm still not comfortable with ❶it.
Coach: What problem are you having?
Brian: Well, I can't lift my leg high enough.
Coach: I see. Let me help you. I'll hold this kick pad for you. Show me your side kick.

❶ it은 taegwondo side kick(태권도 옆차기)을 가리킨다.

Wrap Up 1

Anna: Hi, Jake. Do you come to the ❶pool often?
Jake: Oh, hi, Anna. I ❷take a swimming class here ❸once a week.
Anna: When did you start the class?
Jake: Last month. But swimming is still not easy for me.
Anna: Oh, let me help you. I teach children how to swim in the school club.
Jake: Oh, that'll help me a lot. Thanks.

❶ pool: 수영장
❷ take a class: 수업을 듣다
❸ once a week: 일주일에 한번

Wrap Up 2

Emma: How was your soccer match last week?
Keine: We won, but ❶I'm not satisfied with our match.
Emma: Why do you say ❷that?
Keine: My passes were too short.
Emma: ❸Don't take it too hard. You're practicing a lot. You'll do better next time.

❶ be satisfied with: ~에 만족하다
❷ 이겼지만 경기에 만족하지 않는다고 말한 것을 가리킨다.
❸ Don't take it too hard.: 너무 상심하지 마.

다음 우리말과 일치하도록 빈칸에 알맞은 말을 쓰시오.

해석

Listen & Talk 1 A-1

Mom: David, how was your basketball game today?

David: We lost, Mom. I _____ too many _____ for a _____-
_____.

Mom: Oh, don't be so _____ on yourself. _____ _____ _____
next time.

David: I hope so.

Listen & Talk 1 A-2

Jack: Did you come and watch my _____ _____ yesterday?

Irene: Yeah, I did. That was a great volleyball match. You were great!

Jack: Thanks, but it was a _____ _____. My serves were not
_____ _____.

Irene: Oh, _____ _____ _____ _____. You'll do better next
time.

Listen & Talk 1 B

Emily: I heard your baseball team, the Reds, _____ _____ _____.
Eight to seven, right? _____, John!

John: Thanks. It was a close game. I'm not happy with my _____.

Emily: Why do you say that?

John: I allowed two homeruns.

Emily: Oh, _____ _____ _____ _____. You'll _____
_____ next time.

Listen & Talk 2 A-1

Mike: Is it your _____ _____ riding a bike, Mina?

Mina: Yes, it is. I just can't _____ _____ _____.

Mike: Let me help you. I'll _____ your bike.

Mina: Thanks, Mike. _____ _____ go, okay?

Mike: Don't worry. _____ _____ and _____ _____ _____ _____.

Listen & Talk 2 A-1

Tom: What are you doing, Sarah?

Sarah: I learned _____ _____ _____ _____ _____
_____ in PE class. So I'm trying it now but it's not easy.

Tom: _____ _____ _____ _____. Kick your legs in the air
again. I'll _____ _____.

Sarah: Oh, thanks. I'll try again.

Listen & Talk 2 B

Coach: Hey, Brain. Did you practice the *taegwondo* side kick?

Brian: Yes, Coach. But _____ _____ _____ _____ _____
_____.

Coach: _____ _____ are you having?

Brian: Well, I can't _____ _____ _____ _____ _____.

Coach: I see. _____ _____ help you. I'll hold this kick pad for
you. Show me your _____ _____.

Communication

Megan: I'm _____ _____ our next soccer match, James.

James: _____ _____ you worried, Megan?

Megan: Well, I couldn't _____ _____ _____ in the last soccer
match. I _____ _____ too many goals.

James: I see. Here, _____ _____ _____ _____ _____. I'll kick
high balls to you.

Megan: Oh, that'll really help. I hope _____ _____ _____
_____.

James: _____ _____. You'll do better next time.

Wrap Up 1

Anna: Hi, Jake. _____ _____ _____ to the pool often?

Jake: Oh, hi, Anna. I take a swimming class here _____ _____
_____.

Anna: When did you start the class?

Jake: Last month. But swimming is still not _____ _____ _____.

Anna: Oh, let me help you. I teach children _____ _____ _____
in the school club.

Jake: Oh, _____ _____ _____ _____ _____ _____. Thanks.

해석

Tom: Sarah, 뭐 하고 있어?

Sarah: 체육 시간에 물구나무 서는 법을 배웠거든. 그래서 지금 한번 해 보고 있는데, 쉽지 않네.

Tom: 내가 도와줄게. 다리를 공중에 차 올려봐. 내가 널 붙잡을게.

Sarah: 오, 고마워. 다시 해 볼게.

Coach: 저기, Brian. 태권도 옆 차기 연습했니?

Brian: 네, 코치님. 그런데 여전히 편하게 잘 안 돼요.

Coach: 어떤 문제가 있어?

Brian: 음, 다리를 충분히 높이 들어 올릴 수가 없어요.

Coach: 알겠다. 내가 도와줄게. 너를 위해 이 킥 패드를 잡아줄게. 너의 옆 차기를 보여주렴.

Megan: James, 나는 다음 축구 시합이 걱정돼.

James: 왜 걱정하는 거야, Megan?

Megan: 음, 지난 축구 시합에서 나는 높은 공을 잡지 못했어. 너무 많은 골을 허용했어.

James: 알겠어. 자, 내가 도와줄게. 너에게 공을 높이 차 줄게.

Megan: 오, 그거 도움이 많이 되겠다. 내 기술이 나아지길 바라.

James: 걱정 마. 다음번에는 더 잘할 거야.

Anna: 안녕, Jake. 너는 종종 수영장에 오니?

Jake: 오, 안녕, Anna. 나는 여기에서 일주일에 한 번 수영 수업을 들어.

Anna: 언제부터 수업을 시작했어?

Jake: 지난달부터. 그런데 수영은 여전히 나에게 쉽지 않아.

Anna: 오, 내가 도와줄게. 나는 학교 동아리에서 아이들에게 수영하는 법을 가르쳐 주거든.

Jake: 오, 그거 나에게 도움이 많이 되겠다. 고마워.

Conversation 시험대비 기본평가

01 다음 대화의 밑줄 친 우리말을 영작하시오.

> A: My serves were not strong enough.
> B: You're a great player. 다음번에는 더 잘할 거야.

➡ _____

02 다음 대화의 빈칸에 들어갈 말로 어색한 것은?

> A: I can't wash this car alone. It's too big.
> B: _____

① Let me help you.   ② Don't worry. I'll help you.

③ May I help you?   ④ Can I give you a hand?

⑤ It will be very grateful to me if you help me.

[03~04] 다음 대화를 읽고 물음에 답하시오.

Emily: I heard your baseball team, the Reds, won the match. Eight to seven, right? Congratulations, John!

John: Thanks. It was a close game. I'm not happy with my (A)_____ (pitch).

Emily: Why do you say that?

John: I allowed two homeruns.

Emily: Oh, you're a great (B)_____(pitch). You'll do better next time.

03 위 대화의 빈칸 (A)와 (B)에 주어진 단어를 적절한 형태로 쓰시오.

(A) _____ (B) _____

04 위 대화의 내용과 일치하지 <u>않는</u> 것은?

① John은 Reds팀의 투수이다.

② Reds팀은 8대 7로 경기에서 이겼다.

③ John은 어제 2점 홈런을 쳤다.

④ John은 자신의 투구에 만족하지 않는다.

⑤ Emily는 John이 좋은 투수라고 생각한다.

01 다음 대화의 우리말을 영작하시오.

> **A:** I can't wash this car alone. It's too big.
> **B:** 미안하지만 나는 너를 지금 도와줄 수 없어.

➡ _____

02 다음 대화의 빈칸에 들어갈 말로 어색한 것은?

> **A:** My serves were not strong enough.
> **B:** You're a great player. _____

① There's always a next time.
② You'll do better next time.
③ You can do it better.
④ Don't give up! Try it again.
⑤ Would it be possible to serve more strongly?

[03~04] 다음 대화를 읽고 물음에 답하시오.

> **Jack:** Did you come and watch my volleyball match yesterday?
> **Irene:** Yeah, I did. That was a great volleyball match. You were great!
> **Jack:** Thanks, but it was a (A)close match. My serves were not strong enough.
> **Irene:** Oh, you're a great player. You'll do better next time.

03 위 대화의 밑줄 친 (A)close와 같은 의미로 쓰인 것은?

① What time does the museum close?
② My house is close to the bus stop.
③ My team finally won in a close game.
④ Would you close the windows for me?
⑤ Emily was my close friend.

04 위 대화의 내용과 일치하지 않는 것은?

① Irene은 어제 Jack의 배구 경기를 직접 관람하였다.
② 어제 Jack의 배구 경기는 아슬아슬한 경기였다.
③ Jack은 자신의 서브가 충분히 강하지 않았다고 생각한다.
④ Irene은 Jack이 훌륭한 선수라고 격려하였다.
⑤ Irene은 경기에 져서 낙담한 Jack을 위로하였다.

[05~06] 다음 대화를 읽고, 물음에 답하시오.

> **Emily:** I heard your baseball team, the Reds, (A)[win / won] the match. Eight to seven, right? Congratulations, John!
> **John:** Thanks. It was a (B)[close / closing] game. I'm not happy with my pitching.
> **Emily:** (C)[What / Why] do you say that?
> **John:** I allowed two homeruns.
> **Emily:** Oh, you're a great pitcher. You'll do better next time.

05 What was the score of the Reds in the baseball game?

➡ _____

06 위 대화의 괄호 (A)~(C)에 들어갈 말로 바르게 짝지어진 것은?

① win – close – What
② win – closing – Why
③ won – closing – What
④ won – close – Why
⑤ won – close – What

07 다음 대화가 자연스럽게 이어지도록 순서대로 배열하시오.

> (A) Thanks, Mike. Don't let go, okay?
> (B) Is it your first time riding a bike, Mina?
> (C) Let me help you. I'll hold your bike.
> (D) Yes, it is. I just can't keep my balance.
> (E) Don't worry. Sit up and look straight ahead.

➡ _____

[08~09] 다음 대화를 읽고 물음에 답하시오.

> Megan: I'm worried about our next soccer match, James.
> James: Why are you worried, Megan?
> Megan: Well, I couldn't catch high balls in the last soccer match. (A)너무 많은 골을 허용했어. (away)
> James: I see. Here, let me help you. I'll kick high balls to you.
> Megan: Oh, that'll really help. I hope my skills get better.
> James: Don't worry. You'll do better next time.

08 위 대화의 (A)의 밑줄 친 우리말을 주어진 단어를 사용하여 영작하시오.

➡ _____

09 위 대화에서 Megan의 심정 변화로 적절한 것은?

① fearful → depressed
② anxious → hopeful
③ discouraged → upset
④ pleased → encouraged
⑤ relaxed → calm

[10~11] 다음 대화를 읽고 물음에 답하시오.

> Anna: Hi, Jake. Do you come to the pool often?
> Jake: Oh, hi, Anna. I take a swimming class here once a week.
> Anna: When did you start the class?
> Jake: Last month. But swimming is still not easy for me.
> Anna: Oh, let me help you. I teach children how to swim in the school club.
> Jake: Oh, that'll help me a lot. Thanks.

10 How many times does Jake take a swimming class a week?

➡ _____

11 What does Anna teach to children in the school club?

➡ _____

12 다음 대화의 빈칸에 들어갈 말로 어색한 것은?

> A: Why the long face?
> B: _____
> C: Don't worry. You'll do better next time.

① My serves were not strong enough.
② I couldn't keep up with other runners today.
③ I didn't do well in the match.
④ My punches were terrible.
⑤ I hit a two-run homerun.

01 다음 대화의 밑줄 친 우리말을 주어진 표현을 사용하여 영작하시오.

> A: I can't carry this bag. It's too heavy.
> B: <u>내가 도와줄까</u>? (can, hand)

➡ _____

[02~03] 다음 대화를 읽고, 물음에 답하시오.

> Tom: What are you doing, Sarah?
> Sarah: I learned how to ___(A)___ on my head in PE class. So I'm trying it now but it's not easy.
> Tom: Let me help you. ___(B)___ your legs in the air again. I'll ___(C)___ you.
> Sarah: Oh, thanks. I'll try again.

02 위 대화의 빈칸 (A)~(C)에 들어갈 말을 보기에서 골라 쓰시오.

> ┤ 보기 ├
> catch / kick / stand / sit

(A) _____ (B) _____ (C) _____

03 What is Sarah trying to do now?

> She is trying to _____ _____ _____
> _____.

[04~05] 다음 대화를 읽고, 물음에 답하시오.

> Megan: I'm worried about our next soccer match, James.
> James: Why are you worried, Megan?
> Megan: Well, I couldn't catch high balls in the last soccer match. I gave away too many goals.
> James: I see. Here, let me help you. I'll kick high balls to you.

> Megan: Oh, that'll really help. I hope my skills get better.
> James: Don't worry. You'll do better next time.

04 What problem does Megan have?

➡ _____

05 What is James going to do to improve Megan's soccer skill?

➡ _____

06 다음 대화의 내용과 일치하도록 빈칸을 완성하시오.

> Coach: Hey, Brain. Did you practice the *taegwondo* side kick?
> Brian: Yes, Coach. But I'm still not comfortable with it.
> Coach: What problem are you having?
> Brian: Well, I can't lift my leg high enough.
> Coach: I see. Let me help you. I'll hold this kick pad for you. Show me your side kick.

> Mon June 24th, 2019
> I felt disappointed when I practiced _____. Though I practiced a lot, I was not comfortable with it. Especially I couldn't _____. That was my biggest problem. Fortunately, my coach helped me, holding _____. I showed him _____ and practiced it with him a lot. I really appreciated him for helping me.

교과서 Grammar

① 관계대명사

> • I know a man **who** makes pumpkin pies well. 나는 호박파이를 잘 만드는 남자를 안다.
>
> • The book **whose** cover is blue is his. 표지가 파란색인 그 책은 그의 것이다.

■ 관계대명사는 두 개의 문장을 하나로 이어주는 접속사 역할을 하면서 동시에 대명사 역할을 한다. 본래 문장에서 주격으로 쓰인 (대)명사는 주격 관계대명사로, 소유격으로 쓰인 (대)명사는 소유격 관계대명사로, 목적격으로 쓰인 (대)명사는 목적격 관계대명사로 바꾸어 준다.

• I thanked the boys. They told me how to get there.

= I thanked the boys **who** told me how to get there.

• The glasses were under the table. My brother was looking for them.

= The glasses **which** my brother was looking for were under the table.

■ 선행사에 따라서 사용되는 관계대명사의 종류는 다음과 같으며, 목적격 관계대명사는 생략 가능하다.

	주격	소유격	목적격
사람	who	whose	whom[who]
사물	which	whose[of which]	which

• Tell me about the people **who[whom]** you invited to your party. 너의 파티에 초대했던 사람들에 관해 말해줘.

• I know a doctor **whose** first name is the same as mine. 나는 내 이름과 똑같은 이름을 가진 의사를 안다.

• The plant **which** we bought yesterday needs water. 우리가 어제 산 식물은 물을 필요로 한다.

■ 관계대명사 that은 who, whom과 which를 대신하여 사용될 수 있으며 소유격은 없다.

• The kid **that[who]** I met yesterday was active. 내가 어제 만났던 아이는 활동적이었다.

• He is the only friend **that[whom]** Jina trusts. 그는 Jina가 신뢰하는 유일한 친구이다.

핵심 Check

1. 다음 우리말과 일치하도록 빈칸에 알맞은 말을 쓰시오.

(1) 경주에서 진 그 소년은 슬펐다.

➡ The boy _____ lost the race was sad.

(2) 나는 카메라를 도난당한 그 소녀를 안다.

➡ I know the girl _____ _____ was stolen.

② 지각동사

> • I **saw** the boy **riding** a bike. 나는 그 소년이 자전거를 타는 것을 보았다.
> • They **heard** Anna **sing** a song. 그들은 Anna가 노래 부르는 것을 들었다.

■ 지각동사는 원형부정사나 현재분사를 목적격보어로 사용하는 5형식 동사이다. 따라서 '동사+목적어 +V(ing)' 구조를 취하며, 목적격보어는 목적어를 설명한다.

  • She **saw** her son **enter**(또는 **entering**) his room. 그녀는 자기 아들이 방으로 들어가는 것을 보았다.

  • The man **felt** the ground **shake**(또는 **shaking**). 그 남자는 땅이 흔들리는 것을 느꼈다.

■ 보고, 듣고, 느끼는 것과 같이 감각을 나타내는 동사들이 지각동사에 해당하며 see, watch, hear, feel 등이 있다.

  • Kelly **heard** her friend **calling** her. Kelly는 그녀의 친구가 그녀를 부르는 것을 들었다.

  • Mary **saw** me **playing** a computer game. Mary는 내가 컴퓨터 게임을 하는 것을 보았다.

■ 목적어와 목적격보어와의 관계가 수동일 경우 목적격보어로 과거분사를 쓴다.

  • I **heard** my name **called**. 나는 내 이름이 불리는 것을 들었다.

  • Jimmy **saw** the vase **broken**. Jimmy는 그 화병이 깨진 것을 보았다.

핵심 Check

2. 다음 우리말과 같도록 빈칸에 알맞은 말을 쓰시오.

(1) 그들은 그 소년이 무대 위에서 춤추는 것을 보았다.

➡ They saw the boy _____ on the stage.

(2) 나는 아버지가 면도하시는 것을 지켜보았다.

➡ I watched my dad _____.

(3) 그녀는 누군가가 그녀를 보고 있는 것을 느꼈다.

➡ She felt someone _____ her.

(4) 우리는 무언가가 땅에 떨어지는 소리를 들었다.

➡ We heard something _____ to the ground.

(5) 그녀는 엄마가 커피 한 잔을 따르는 소리를 들었다.

➡ She heard her mother _____ a cup of coffee.

Grammar 시험대비 기본평가

01 관계대명사를 이용하여 다음 두 문장을 하나의 문장으로 만드시오. (that은 쓰지 말 것.)

>> be located 위치해 있다

(1) I have a friend. He speaks English very well.

➡ _____

(2) We stayed in a hotel. It was located near the beach.

➡ _____

(3) Do you want to see the pictures? I took them.

➡ _____

(4) Jenny took care of a dog. Its tail was hurt. (whose를 이용)

➡ _____

02 다음 괄호 안의 동사를 어법에 맞게 빈칸에 쓰시오.

(1) Did you see her _____ the violin? (play)

(2) Jason heard his brother _____ a noise. (make)

(3) We heard them _____ about it. (talk)

(4) Jimmy watched us _____ the road.

03 다음 우리말에 맞게 주어진 단어를 바르게 배열하시오. (필요하면 어형을 바꿀 것.)

(1) 그녀가 너에게 사준 케이크를 먹었니?

(the cake / did / for / you / you / eat / that / she / buy)

➡ _____

(2) 보고 싶은 것이 있나요?

(see / there / to / is / you / anything / that / want)

➡ _____

(3) 그가 우는 것을 들었니?

(hear / cry / did / he / you)

➡ _____

(4) Kelly는 어떤 사람이 하얀색 깃발을 흔드는 것을 본다.

(see / wave / Kelly / a white flag / a person)

➡ _____

01 다음 빈칸에 적절한 것을 <u>모두</u> 고르시오.

> The people _____ I call most often on my cell phone are my mother and my sisters.

① which   ② who
③ that   ④ whose
⑤ whom

02 다음 빈칸에 들어갈 말이 바르게 짝지어진 것은?

> • I watched Mrs. Han _____ beside a car.
> • Julian wants his parents _____ him some money.

① stand – give
② stand – giving
③ standing – giving
④ standing – to give
⑤ to stand – to give

03 다음 우리말을 영어로 바르게 옮기지 <u>않은</u> 것은?

① 나는 그녀가 울고 있는 것을 봤어.
　→ I saw her crying.
② 너는 머리가 긴 친구가 있니?
　→ Do you have a friend who has long hair?
③ Jane에게는 달리는 것이 취미인 언니가 한 명 있다.
　→ Jane has a sister who hobby is running.
④ Tom은 어제 그가 먹은 음식을 기억할 수 없었다.
　→ Tom couldn't remember the food which he ate yesterday.
⑤ 그가 무언가를 말하는 것을 들었니?
　→ Did you hear him say something?

서답형
04 적절한 관계대명사를 이용하여 다음 두 문장을 하나의 문장으로 쓰시오.

> • I like the boy.
> • He wanted to come to the party yesterday.

➡ _____
_____

05 다음 문장의 빈칸에 알맞은 것을 <u>모두</u> 고르시오.

> We _____ the beautiful girl play the piano.

① heard   ② wanted
③ encouraged   ④ allowed
⑤ watched

06 다음 빈칸에 들어갈 말이 나머지와 <u>다른</u> 하나는?

① He is the man _____ you can depend on.
② There lived a princess _____ fell in love with a begger.
③ You can see so many people _____ live near the Han river.
④ The man _____ arrived here first was Bill.
⑤ I know the boy _____ hobby is flying a drone.

서답형
07 주어진 동사를 이용하여 다음 우리말을 영어로 쓰시오.

> 그녀는 물이 흐르는 소리를 들었다.
> (hear / run)

➡ _____

08 다음 중 빈칸에 들어갈 동사 'fly'의 형태가 다른 하나는?

① Did you see the air balloon _____ high?

② The plane is _____ the tourists home.

③ Karen watched the kite _____ away in the sky.

④ He is not allowed _____ the plane yet.

⑤ I saw a bee _____ in through the window.

09 다음 중 밑줄 친 부분의 쓰임이 적절하지 않은 것은?

① He is the man who I look up to very much.

② I apologized to the girl whose orange juice I spilled.

③ Harvard is the best university that I have ever visited.

④ Vicky made friends with a boy which is in my class.

⑤ Did the woman who stepped on your toes just walk away?

10 다음 우리말을 바르게 영작한 것을 모두 고르시오.

> 나는 금발 머리인 저 소년을 안다.

① I know the boy which has blond hair.

② I know the boy whose hair is blond.

③ I know the boy who is blond hair.

④ I know the boy that hair is blond.

⑤ I know the boy who has blond hair.

서답형

11 주어진 어구를 바르게 배열하여 다음 우리말을 영어로 쓰시오.

> 우리는 한밤중에 개 한 마리가 짖는 소리를 들었다.
> (barking / in the middle of / we / a dog / heard / the night)

➡ _____

12 다음 중 밑줄 친 부분의 어법상 쓰임이 바르지 않은 것은?

① I was listening to the music played by my friend.

② Can you hear someone singing a song?

③ Emily felt her shoulder touched by someone.

④ We watched the man climb Mount Everest.

⑤ Jessica saw a boy bully by some teenage boys.

서답형

13 관계대명사와 주어진 단어를 어법에 맞게 활용하여 다음 우리말을 영어로 쓰시오.

> 나는 수영하는 것을 정말로 즐기는 한 소녀를 안다.
> (know / enjoy / swim)

➡ _____

14 다음 문장에서 어법상 바르지 않은 것은?

> I ①saw a man ②enter the house ③who my friend ④lives ⑤in.

①   ②   ③   ④   ⑤

서답형

15 다음 빈칸에 알맞은 관계대명사를 쓰시오.

> • Robert knows a woman _____ has six daughters.
> • Everything _____ they told me was hard to believe.
> • Did you see a girl and two dogs _____ walked together the other day?

서답형

16 다음 빈칸에 알맞은 말을 쓰시오.

> I watched them _____ a new car park.
> = I watched a new car park being built by them.

➡ _____

17 다음 밑줄 친 부분의 쓰임이 <u>다른</u> 하나는?

① This is the purse <u>that</u> Kelly lost on the bus.
② Does she have the cat <u>that</u> has blue eyes?
③ Jane couldn't remember the man <u>that</u> gave her his phone number.
④ Kyle knew <u>that</u> there was nothing he could do.
⑤ Jimmy bought some plants <u>that</u> clean the air in the house.

서답형

18 주어진 단어를 바르게 배열하여 다음 문장을 완성하시오.

> August _____ September.
> (before / that / the / comes / month / is)

➡ _____

서답형

19 다음 빈칸에 공통으로 들어갈 말을 쓰시오.

> • Amelia is _____ with her friends.
> • He saw the girls _____ chess.
> • I enjoy _____ computer games.

➡ _____

20 다음 중 밑줄 친 부분을 생략할 수 <u>없는</u> 것은?

① The pants <u>that</u> you wanted to buy yesterday are sold out.
② The man <u>who</u> you wanted to meet was on vacation.
③ I don't want to hear the song <u>which</u> has a sad melody.
④ The doctor <u>who</u> you saw last week is my father.
⑤ Is this the card <u>that</u> you are looking for?

서답형

21 다음 주어진 단어를 문맥과 어법에 맞게 빈칸에 쓰시오.

> say / come / paint / climb

> • Kelly saw someone _____ close to her in the dark.
> • I saw the famous man _____ a portrait with a brush.
> • Clair heard someone _____ her name.
> • We watched him _____ through the window, and then I called the police.

01 〈보기〉와 같이 하나의 문장을 두 개의 문장으로 쓰시오.

┤ 보기 ├

The people who love romantic music are usually kind.
➡ The people love romantic music.
➡ They are usually kind.

(1) Dan lectured on a topic which was very boring.

➡ _____

➡ _____

(2) I know the woman whose necklace was stolen.

➡ _____

➡ _____

02 다음 주어진 어구를 활용하여 우리말을 영어로 쓰시오.

당신은 이른 아침에 새들이 지저귀는 소리를 들을 것입니다.
(hear / sing / in the early morning)

➡ _____

03 다음 빈칸 ⓐ와 ⓑ에 공통으로 들어갈 말을 쓰고, 빈칸 ⓒ에는 'smile'을 어법에 맞게 쓰시오.

The town ___ⓐ___ I have lived in for three years is very small. People ___ⓑ___ live in the town are very nice. If you visit there, you will see many people ___ⓒ___ brightly.

➡ _____

04 다음 중 서로 관련 있는 문장을 연결하여 하나의 문장으로 쓰시오.

- A fire fighter is someone.
- The woman is in her home now.
- The bus was the last bus.
- A train has a number of cars.
- Milk is the white liquid.

- They are all connected together.
- It is produced by cows, goats, and some other animals.
- She was in the hospital.
- It left an hour ago.
- He or she puts out fires.

➡ _____

➡ _____

➡ _____

➡ _____

➡ _____

05 주어진 단어를 활용하여 다음 우리말을 영어로 쓰시오.

그녀는 자신의 심장이 더 빠르게 뛰는 것을 느꼈다.
(feel / beat)

➡ _____

06 다음 문장을 하나의 문장으로 만드시오.

- Is the chair comfortable?
- It was made by you.

➡ _____

07 동사 steal을 어법에 맞게 빈칸에 각각 쓰시오.

> • Jimmy saw Tyler _____ a bunch of bananas.
> • Jimmy found a bunch of bananas _____ by somebody.

08 다음 주어진 두 개의 문장을 하나의 문장으로 만드시오.

(1) I don't like stories.
 They have sad endings.
 ➡ _____
 _____

(2) Jason works for a company.
 It makes cars.
 ➡ _____
 _____

(3) We live in a world.
 It is changing all the time.
 ➡ _____
 _____

(4) There are people.
 They are cheering excitedly.
 ➡ _____
 _____

09 주어진 어구를 바르게 배열하여 다음 우리말을 영어로 쓰시오. 필요하다면 어형을 변형하시오.

> 우리는 한 남자가 기차에서 내리려고 애쓰는 것을 보았다. (get off / we / watch / the train / a man / to / try)

➡ _____

10 다음 문장의 빈칸에 알맞은 관계대명사를 쓰시오.

> • This is the man _____ son I spoke to yesterday.
> • The people _____ I work with are very nice and diligent.
> • What is the name of the person _____ is very handsome?

11 주어진 단어를 활용하여 다음 우리말을 영어로 쓰시오.

> 그 창문이 잠긴 것을 보았니? (see / lock)

➡ _____

12 주어진 어구를 활용하여 다음 우리말을 영어로 쓰시오.

> 나는 너의 물고기들이 무리를 지어 헤엄치는 것을 보고 싶어.
> (want / see / swim / in a group)

➡ _____

13 관계대명사를 이용하여 다음 빈칸을 알맞게 채우시오.

> Is there anything _____ _____
> _____ _____ _____ _____ ?
> 내가 널 위해 해 줄 수 있는 것이 있니?

Reading

Seconds from Winning

At the go-kart race track, there are many people who are cheering
고카트(작은 경주용 자동차)　　　　　　　　주격 관계대명사: 불완전한 절을 이끌며 many people을 수식
excitedly. The karts that are making loud engine noises are waiting. An
주격 관계대명사: 불완전한 절을 이끌며 The karts를 수식
official waves a green flag and the race starts!

Max pushes his foot down hard on the gas pedal as he completes his
세게　　　　　　　접속사: '~하면서', '~할 때'
sixth lap on the track. On the straightaway, Max pulls right beside the
(자동차 등을) 바싹 대다, 바싹 놓다
race's leader, Simon. Last year, Simon won many races, but Max's best
└　동격
result in a race was coming in fifth place. This time, he has a chance
(경주, 대회 등의) 등위
to finish second. But he isn't going to be satisfied with second place
to부정사의 형용사적 용법: a chance를 수식　　　= won't be satisfied
today. The winner gets to meet the world famous racer L. J. Richards!
get to V: V하게 되다　　　　　　　└　동격
He doesn't want to miss the chance to meet his role model.
기회를 놓치다　　to부정사의 형용사적 용법: the chance를 수식

Max completes the tenth lap and now has five more laps to go. Max
to부정사의 형용사적 용법: laps를 수식
sees Simon's kart ahead, just out of Max's reach. Max's kart gets closer
앞에서
and closer to Simon's. It almost hits the back end of Simon's kart. They
비교급 and 비교급: 점점 더 ~한　　= Simon's kart
drive into the straightaway and Max presses harder on the gas pedal.
운전해 ~로 들어가다　　　　　　　　　더 세게

track 경주로, 트랙
cheer 환호하다, 응원하다
excitedly 흥분하여
noise 소음
official 심판
wave ~을 흔들다
push down ~을 꼭 누르다
straightaway 직선코스
right beside 바로 옆에
result 결과
fifth place 5등
be satisfied with ~에 만족하다
get to ~하게 되다
miss 놓치다
complete 끝내다, 완료하다
lap (경주에서 트랙의) 한 바퀴
out of one's reach ~에게 닿지 않는
비교급 and 비교급: 점점 더 ~한
press on ~을 누르다

확인문제

● 다음 문장이 본문의 내용과 일치하면 T, 일치하지 <u>않으면</u> F를 쓰시오.

1 People are cheering at the go-kart race track. ☐

2 The karts are waiting without making noises. ☐

3 A green flag means that the race starts. ☐

4 Simon is the leader of the race until the sixth lap. ☐

5 Max won many races last year. ☐

6 Anyone can get a chance to meet L. J. Richards ☐

7 L. J. Richards is Simon's role model. ☐

"I can catch up," says Max.
= catch up (with Simon)

Max sees the official waving a white flag which means the last lap.
지각동사+목적어+Ving: 목적어가 V하는 것을 보다 / 주격 관계대명사(= that)

Max is right behind Simon. The finish line is getting closer, and the
바로 / close의 비교급

cheering from the crowd is getting louder.
get+비교급: 점점 더 ~해지다

"I can do it!" Max says loudly. He can feel his heart beating hard. The
지각동사+목적어+Ving

karts rush across the finish line. Who is the winner?

Max's eyes are filled with tears as he finds out that he came in second.
접속사: '~할 때' / 명사절을 이끄는 접속사

"No need for tears, kid," says a man's voice. Max can't believe his
= There is no need for tears / 동사+주어: 도치 구문

eyes. The man who is standing in front of him is L. J. Richards! "Thank
주격 관계대명사(= that) / ~ 앞에

you, but I'm not the winner," says Max.

"It was a real close race. Even though you didn't win the race, you did
우열을 가릴 수 없는 / '비록 ~이지만' (양보의 부사절을 이끎)

your best. That's the thing that counts!" says L. J. Richards.
주격 관계대명사: the thing을 수식하는 형용사절

'Did I do my best?' thinks Max. After a moment, he smiles. "Yeah, I
잠시 후에

guess I did."
= did my best

---

catch up 따라잡다
mean 의미하다
last 마지막의
behind ~ 뒤에
finish line 결승선
cheering 환호
beat 뛰다
be filled with ~으로 가득 차다
find out ~을 알게 되다
need 필요
voice 목소리
believe 믿다
stand 서 있다
close 막상막하의
even though 비록 ~일지라도
count 중요하다
do one's best 최선을 다하다
guess 추측하다, 생각하다

📎 **확인문제**

● 다음 문장이 본문의 내용과 일치하면 T, 일치하지 않으면 F를 쓰시오.

1   When a white flag is waved, racers know that it is the last lap. ☐

2   Simon is right in front of Max. ☐

3   As the finish line is getting closer, the sound of cheering is getting quieter. ☐

4   Max feels calm when he rushes across the finish line. ☐

5   L. J. Richards comes to Max to cheer him up. ☐

6   Max thinks that he did his best. ☐

● 우리말을 참고하여 빈칸에 알맞은 말을 쓰시오.

1 _____ the go-kart race _____, _____ _____ many people _____ _____ _____ excitedly.

2 The karts _____ _____ making loud engine noises _____ _____.

3 An official _____ a green _____ and the race _____!

4 Max _____ his foot _____ _____ on the gas pedal _____ he _____ his sixth lap on the track.

5 _____ the straightaway, Max _____ _____ _____ the race's leader, Simon.

6 Last year, Simon _____ _____ _____, but Max's best result in a race _____ _____ fifth place.

7 This time, he has a _____ _____ _____ _____ _____.

8 But he isn't going to _____ _____ _____ second _____ today.

9 The winner _____ _____ _____ the world famous racer L. J. Richards!

10 He doesn't want _____ _____ the chance _____ _____ his role model.

11 Max _____ the tenth lap and now has five more laps _____ _____.

12 Max _____ Simon's kart _____, just _____ _____ Max's reach.

13 Max's kart gets _____ _____ _____ to Simon's.

14 It almost _____ _____ _____ _____ of Simon's kart.

15 They _____ _____ the straightaway and Max _____ _____ _____ the gas pedal.

16 "I can _____ _____," says Max.

17 Max sees the official _____ _____ _____ _____ which _____ the last lap.

1 고카트 경기 트랙에 신이 나서 응원하고 있는 많은 사람들이 있다.

2 시끄러운 엔진 소음을 내고 있는 카트들이 기다리고 있다.

3 심판이 초록 깃발을 흔들고, 경기가 시작된다!

4 Max는 트랙을 여섯 바퀴 돌았을 때, 발로 가속 페달을 힘껏 누른다.

5 직선 구간에서 Max는 경기에서 선두를 달리고 있는 Simon의 바로 옆까지 다가간다.

6 작년에 Simon은 경기에서 여러 번 이겼지만 Max의 최고 경기 성적은 5등으로 들어온 것이었다.

7 이번에 그는 2등으로 끝낼 수 있는 기회를 잡았다.

8 그러나 그는 오늘 2등으로 만족하지 않을 것이다.

9 우승자는 세계적으로 유명한 경주 선수인 L.J. Richards를 만나게 된다!

10 그는 그의 역할 모델을 만날 수 있는 기회를 놓치길 원하지 않는다.

11 Max는 10바퀴를 다 돌고 이제 5바퀴를 더 돌아야 한다.

12 Max는 앞에 바로 닿을 듯한 거리에 있는 Simon의 카트를 본다.

13 Max의 카트는 Simon의 카트에 점점 더 가까워진다.

14 Max의 카트는 Simon의 카트의 뒷부분에 거의 닿을 것 같다.

15 그들은 직선 구간을 운전해가고, Max는 가속 페달을 더 세게 밟는다.

16 "나는 따라잡을 수 있어." Max가 말한다.

17 Max는 심판이 마지막 바퀴라는 것을 알려주는 흰색 깃발을 흔드는 것을 본다.

18 Max is _____ _____ Simon.

19 The finish line is _____ _____, and the cheering _____ _____ _____ is _____ _____.

20 "I _____ _____ _____!" Max says loudly.

21 He can _____ his heart _____ _____.

22 The karts _____ _____ the finish line.

23 _____ is the winner?

24 Max's eyes are _____ _____ _____ as he _____ _____ _____ he came in second.

25 "_____ _____ _____ _____, kid," says a man's voice.

26 Max _____ _____ his eyes.

27 The man _____ _____ _____ in front of him _____ L. J. Richards!

28 "Thank you, but I'm _____ _____ _____," says Max.

29 "It was _____ _____ _____ _____.

30 Even though you _____ _____ _____ _____, you _____ your best.

31 That's the thing _____ _____!" says L. J. Richards.

32 '_____ I _____ _____ _____?' thinks Max.

33 _____ a moment, he _____.

34 "Yeah, I _____ I _____."

18 Max는 Simon 바로 뒤에 있다.

19 결승점이 점점 가까워지고, 관중으로부터 들리는 환호성이 점점 커진다.

20 "나는 할 수 있어!" Max는 큰 소리로 말한다.

21 그는 그의 심장이 세게 뛰는 것을 느낄 수 있다.

22 카트들이 돌진해 결승점을 지난다.

23 누가 승자인가?

24 Max는 자신이 2등으로 들어왔다는 것을 알았을 때, 눈에 눈물이 가득 찬다.

25 "울 필요 없단다, 얘야." 어떤 남자의 목소리가 말한다.

26 Max는 그의 눈을 믿을 수 없다.

27 그 앞에 서 있는 남자는 L.J. Richards이다!

28 "고마워요, 하지만 저는 일등이 아니에요." Max가 말한다.

29 "정말 아슬아슬한 경기였어.

30 네가 비록 경기를 이기지 못했지만, 너는 최선을 다했어.

31 중요한 것은 바로 그거란다!" L.J. Richards가 말한다.

32 '나는 최선을 다했을까?' Max는 생각한다.

33 잠시 후에, 그는 미소를 짓는다.

34 "네, 저는 최선을 다한 것 같아요."

● 우리말을 참고하여 본문을 영작하시오.

1 고카트 경기 트랙에 신이 나서 응원하고 있는 많은 사람들이 있다.

➡ _____

2 시끄러운 엔진 소음을 내고 있는 카트들이 기다리고 있다.

➡ _____

3 심판이 초록 깃발을 흔들고, 경기가 시작된다!

➡ _____

4 Max는 트랙을 여섯 바퀴 돌았을 때, 발로 가속 페달을 힘껏 누른다.

➡ _____

5 직선 구간에서 Max는 경기에서 선두를 달리고 있는 Simon의 바로 옆까지 다가간다.

➡ _____

6 작년에 Simon은 경기에서 여러 번 이겼지만 Max의 최고 경기 성적은 5등으로 들어온 것이었다.

➡ _____

7 이번에 그는 2등으로 끝낼 수 있는 기회를 잡았다.

➡ _____

8 그러나 그는 오늘 2등으로 만족하지 않을 것이다.

➡ _____

9 우승자는 세계적으로 유명한 경주 선수인 L. J. Richards를 만나게 된다!

➡ _____

10 그는 그의 역할 모델을 만날 수 있는 기회를 놓치길 원하지 않는다.

➡ _____

11 Max는 10바퀴를 다 돌고 이제 5바퀴를 더 돌아야 한다.

➡ _____

12 Max는 앞에 바로 닿을 듯한 거리에 있는 Simon의 카트를 본다.

➡ _____

13 Max의 카트는 Simon의 카트에 점점 더 가까워진다.

➡ _____

14 Max의 카트는 Simon의 카트의 뒷부분에 거의 닿을 것 같다.

➡ _____

15 그들은 직선 구간을 운전해가고, Max는 가속 페달을 더 세게 밟는다.

➡ _____

16 "나는 따라잡을 수 있어." Max가 말한다.

➡ _____

17 Max는 심판이 마지막 바퀴라는 것을 알려주는 흰색 깃발을 흔드는 것을 본다.

➡ _____

18 Max는 Simon 바로 뒤에 있다.

➡ _____

19 결승점이 점점 가까워지고, 관중으로부터 들리는 환호성이 점점 커진다.

➡ _____

20 "나는 할 수 있어!" Max는 큰 소리로 말한다.

➡ _____

21 그는 그의 심장이 세게 뛰는 것을 느낄 수 있다.

➡ _____

22 카트들이 돌진해 결승점을 지난다.

➡ _____

23 누가 승자인가?

➡ _____

24 Max는 자신이 2등으로 들어왔다는 것을 알았을 때, 눈에 눈물이 가득 찬다.

➡ _____

25 "울 필요 없단다, 얘야." 어떤 남자의 목소리가 말한다.

➡ _____

26 Max는 그의 눈을 믿을 수 없다.

➡ _____

27 그 앞에 서 있는 남자는 L. J. Richards이다!

➡ _____

28 "고마워요, 하지만 저는 일등이 아니에요." Max가 말한다.

➡ _____

29 "정말 아슬아슬한 경기였어.

➡ _____

30 네가 비록 경기를 이기지 못했지만, 너는 최선을 다했어.

➡ _____

31 중요한 것은 바로 그거란다!" L. J. Richards가 말한다.

➡ _____

32 '나는 최선을 다했을까?'' Max는 생각한다.

➡ _____

33 잠시 후에, 그는 미소를 짓는다.

➡ _____

34 "네, 저는 최선을 다한 것 같아요."

➡ _____

[01~04] 다음 글을 읽고, 물음에 답하시오.

At the go-kart race track, (A)[there is / there are] many people ___ⓐ___ are cheering excitedly. The karts ___ⓑ___ are making loud engine noises (B)[is / are] waiting. An official (C)[waves / waving] a green flag and the race starts!

01 위 글의 (A)~(C)에서 어법상 옳은 것끼리 바르게 짝지은 것은?

① there is – is – waves
② there are – is – waves
③ there is – are – waving
④ there are – are – waving
⑤ there are – are – waves

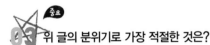

02 위 글의 빈칸 ⓐ와 ⓑ에 공통으로 들어갈 말을 쓰시오.

➡ _____

03 위 글의 분위기로 가장 적절한 것은?

① disappointing   ② boring
③ pleasing   ④ exciting
⑤ scaring

04 위 글의 내용과 일치하지 <u>않는</u> 것은?

① The passage is about a kart racing.
② A lot of people are there to watch the kart racing.
③ The engine noises are loud.
④ All the karts are running a race now.
⑤ There is a flag that gives a signal to start.

[05~08] 다음 글을 읽고, 물음에 답하시오.

Max pushes his foot down hard on the gas pedal ⓐas he completes his sixth lap on the track. ① On the straightaway, Max pulls right beside the race's leader, Simon. ② Last year, Simon won many races, but Max's best result in a race was coming in fifth place. ③ This time, he has a chance to finish second. ④ The winner gets to meet the world famous racer L. J. Richards! ⑤ He doesn't want to miss the chance to meet his role model.

05 위 글의 ①~⑤ 중 주어진 문장이 들어가기에 가장 적절한 곳은?

> But he isn't going to be satisfied with second place today.

①   ②   ③   ④   ⑤

06 다음 중 밑줄 친 ⓐ를 대신하여 쓸 수 있는 것은?

① but   ② because
③ when   ④ since
⑤ if

07 위 글을 읽고 답할 수 <u>없는</u> 것은?

① What does Max do on the straightaway?
② What is the name of the leader?
③ What was the best result of Max last year?
④ How many races did Simon win?
⑤ Who is L. J. Richards?

08 다음 중 위 글에서 유의어를 찾을 수 없는 것은?

① opportunity   ② next to
③ well-known   ④ press
⑤ lose

[09~14] 다음 글을 읽고, 물음에 답하시오.

> Max completes the tenth lap and now has five more laps ①to go. Max sees Simon's kart ahead, just ②out of Max's reach. Max's kart gets closer and closer to Simon's. It almost ③hit the back end of Simon's kart. They drive ④into the straightaway and Max presses harder ⑤on the gas pedal.
> "I can catch up," says Max.
> Max sees the official waving a white flag which means the last lap. Max is right behind Simon. The finish line is _____(A)_____, and the cheering from the crowd is _____(B)_____.
> "I can do it!" Max says loudly. He can feel his heart ____(C)____ (D)hard. The karts rush across the finish line. Who is the winner?

서답형

09 주어진 단어를 문맥과 어법에 맞게 활용하여 빈칸 (A)와 (B)에 쓰시오.

get / close / loud

(A)_____ (B)_____

서답형

10 다음 주어진 동사를 어법에 맞게 빈칸 (C)에 쓰시오.

beat

➡ _____

11 위 글의 밑줄 친 ①~⑤ 중 어법상 바르지 않은 것은?

①   ②   ③   ④   ⑤

서답형

12 위 글의 내용에 맞게 빈칸에 알맞은 말을 쓰시오.

> People _____ _____ cheering see Max's cart _____ _____ _____ _____ to the kart which is right in front of his cart.

13 다음 중 밑줄 친 (D)와 쓰임이 같은 것은?

① How about buying a hard mattress this time?
② It is hard to believe that she is only seven.
③ I heard that shoveling snow is a hard work.
④ Something cold and hard pressed into the back of my neck.
⑤ She kicked the door very hard and broke her toe.

14 다음 중 위 글의 내용과 일치하지 않는 것은?

① The total number of laps that racers have to finish is fifteen laps.
② It is not easy for Max to catch up with Simon.
③ Max presses harder on the gas pedal on the straightaway.
④ A white flag means that there is no lap left.
⑤ Max comes in second place in the race.

[15~18] 다음 글을 읽고, 물음에 답하시오.

> Max's eyes are filled with tears as he finds out ⓐthat he came in second.
>
> "No need for tears, kid," says a man's voice. Max can't believe his eyes. _____ (A)
>
> "Thank you, but I'm not the winner," says Max.
>
> "It was a real close race. Even though you didn't win the race, you did your best. That's the thing that ⓑcounts!" says L. J. Richards. 'Did I do my best?' thinks Max. After a moment, he smiles. "Yeah, I guess ⓒI did."

서답형

15 다음 두 문장을 하나의 문장으로 만들어 빈칸 (A)에 쓰시오.

> The man is L. J. Richards! He is standing in front of him.

➡ _____

_____

중요

16 다음 중 밑줄 친 ⓐ와 쓰임이 다른 것은?

① The fact that he has the data can be denied.

② I can see that he is crying with happiness.

③ Can I see the ticket that you bought online?

④ She thinks that he stole the money in her bag.

⑤ They said that Kelvin had to take part in the race.

17 다음 중 밑줄 친 ⓑ를 대신하여 쓸 수 있는 것은?

① adds   ② numbers   ③ matters

④ considers   ⑤ believes

서답형

18 위 글의 밑줄 친 ⓒ를 생략되지 않은 문장으로 쓰시오.

➡ _____

[19~22] 다음 글을 읽고, 물음에 답하시오.

> Max pushes his foot down hard on the gas pedal as ⓐhe completes his sixth lap on the track. On the straightaway, Max pulls right beside the race's leader, Simon. Last year, ⓑhe won many races, but Max's best result in a race was coming in fifth place. This time, ⓒhe has a chance to finish second. But ⓓhe isn't going to be satisfied with second place today. The winner gets to meet the world famous racer L. J. Richards! He doesn't want to miss the chance (A)to meet ⓔhis role model.

중요

19 위 글의 밑줄 친 ⓐ~ⓔ 중 지칭하는 사람이 다른 하나는?

① ⓐ   ② ⓑ   ③ ⓒ   ④ ⓓ   ⑤ ⓔ

서답형

20 주어진 어구를 바르게 배열하여 다음 물음에 답하시오. 필요하다면 단어를 추가하거나 변형하시오.

> **Q:** Why does Max want to win the race?
> **B:** Because _____.
> (the winner / the chance / have / meet / L. J. Richards)

➡ _____

서답형

21 위 글의 내용에 맞게 다음 빈칸에 알맞은 말을 쓰시오.

> L. J. Richards _____ Max admires is
> ___ ___ ___ ___.

22 다음 중 밑줄 친 (A)와 쓰임이 같은 것은?

① Brad allowed his friend to use his USB.

② Did you go out to buy some flowers?

③ It is not easy to forgive you.

④ I have the ability to speak English well.

⑤ David hoped to become a dentist.

[23~25] 다음 글을 읽고, 물음에 답하시오.

Max completes the tenth lap and now has five more laps to go. Max sees Simon's kart ahead, just out of Max's reach. Max's kart gets closer and closer to Simon's. ⓐIt almost hits the back end of Simon's kart. They drive into the straightaway and Max presses harder on the gas pedal.

"I can catch up," says Max.

Max sees the official waving a white flag which means the last lap. Max is right behind Simon. The finish line is getting closer, and the cheering from the crowd is getting louder.

"I can do it!" Max says loudly. He can feel his heart beating hard. The karts rush across the finish line. Who is the winner?

23 위 글의 밑줄 친 문장 ⓐ의 의미로 가장 적절한 것은?

① Max's kart crashes Simon's kart.

② Max's kart is really close to Simon's kart.

③ Max's kart is right in front of Simon's kart.

④ Max wants to hit Simon's kart.

⑤ Max can barely see Simon's kart.

서답형

24 위 글의 내용에 맞게 빈칸에 알맞은 말을 쓰시오.

When they are in the final lap, Simon is right _____ _____ _____ Max.

서답형

25 다음과 같이 풀이되는 말을 위 글에서 찾아 쓰시오.

the place on the track or course where the race officially ends

➡ _____

26 다음 주어진 문장과 자연스럽게 이어지도록 (A)~(C)를 바르게 나열한 것은?

An official waves a green flag and the race starts!

(A) But he isn't going to be satisfied with second place today. The winner gets to meet the world famous racer L. J. Richards! He doesn't want to miss the chance to meet his role model.

(B) Last year, he won many races, but Max's best result in a race was coming in fifth place. This time, he has a chance to finish second.

(C) Max pushes his foot down hard on the gas pedal as he completes his sixth lap on the track. On the straightaway, Max pulls right beside the race's leader, Simon.

① (A) – (C) – (B)　　② (B) – (A) – (C)

③ (B) – (C) – (A)　　④ (C) – (A) – (B)

⑤ (C) – (B) – (A)

[01~02] 다음 글을 읽고 물음에 답하시오.

At the go-kart race track, _____(A)_____.
The karts that are making loud engine noises are waiting. An official waves a green flag and the race starts!

01 다음 두 문장을 하나의 문장으로 만들어 빈칸 (A)에 쓰시오.

There are many people. They are cheering excitedly.

➡ _____

02 When does the race starts? Answer in Korean.

➡ _____

[03~08] 다음 글을 읽고, 물음에 답하시오.

Max pushes his foot down hard on the gas pedal as he completes his sixth lap on the track. On the straightaway, Max pulls right beside the race's leader, Simon. Last year, Simon ___ⓐ___ many races, but Max's best result in a race was coming in fifth place. This time, he has a chance to finish second. But he isn't going to ___(A)___ with second place today. The winner gets ___ⓑ___ the world famous racer L. J. Richards! He doesn't want ___ⓒ___ the chance to meet his role model.

03 주어진 동사를 문맥과 어법에 맞게 빈칸 ⓐ~ⓒ에 쓰시오.

meet / miss / win

ⓐ_____ ⓑ_____ ⓒ_____

04 다음은 Simon에 관한 설명이다. 관계대명사를 이용하여 빈칸에 알맞은 말을 쓰시오.

Simon _____ last year is the race's leader.

05 주어진 동사를 어법에 맞게 빈칸 (A)에 쓰시오.

satisfy

➡ _____

06 위 글의 내용에 맞게 빈칸에 알맞은 말을 쓰시오.

Last year, when Max finished _____ _____ _____ in a race, it was Max's best result.

07 What does Max do on the straightaway? Answer in English with five words.

➡ _____

08 다음 빈칸에 들어갈 말을 위 글에서 찾아 쓰시오.

A _____ is the situation that exists at the end of a contest.

➡ _____

[09~11] 다음 글을 읽고, 물음에 답하시오.

Max completes the tenth lap and now has five more laps to go. (A)Max sees Simon's kart ahead,(see, go) just out of Max's reach. Max's kart gets closer and closer to Simon's. It almost hits the back end of Simon's kart. They drive into the straightaway and Max presses harder on the gas pedal. "I can catch up," says Max. Max sees the official waving a white flag which means the last lap. Max is right behind Simon. The finish line is getting closer, and the cheering from the crowd is getting louder. "I can do it!" Max says loudly. He can feel his heart beating hard. The karts rush across the finish line. Who is the winner?

09 주어진 단어를 활용하여 밑줄 친 (A)와 같은 의미의 문장을 쓰시오.

➡ _____

10 다음은 관중의 대화이다. 글의 내용에 맞게 빈칸에 알맞은 말을 쓰시오.

> A: Do you see the official _____ _____ _____ _____? I don't know what it means.
> B: _____ _____ that it is _____ _____.

11 다음은 경기가 끝난 후 Max가 쓴 일기의 일부이다. 빈칸에 알맞은 말을 쓰시오.

> When I got _____ to the finish line, I could hear the crowd _____. Also I started to feel my heart _____ very hard.

[12~14] 다음 글을 읽고, 물음에 답하시오.

The karts rush across the finish line. Who is the winner?
Max's eyes are filled with tears as he finds out that he came in second.
"No need for tears, kid." says a man's voice. Max can't believe his eyes. The man who is standing in front of him is L. J. Richards!
"Thank you, but I'm not the winner," says Max.
"It was a real close race. Even though you didn't win the race, you did your best. That's the thing that counts!" says L. J. Richards.
'Did I do my best?' thinks Max. After a moment, he smiles. "Yeah, I guess I did."

12 다음은 관중의 대화이다. 위 글의 내용에 맞게 빈칸에 알맞은 말을 쓰시오.

> A: Can you see the man _____ _____ _____ _____ Max? Who is he?
> B: Oh, he is L. J. Richards. I heard that Max looks up to him.

13 In what place did Max finish the race? Answer in English with a full sentence.

➡ _____

14 주어진 단어를 바르게 배열하여 위 글이 주는 교훈을 쓰시오.

> the best / important / our best / than / being / doing / is / more

➡ _____
_____

Listen & Talk C

Amy: Michael, why the long face?

Michael: I couldn't block the other player.
막다

Amy: Don't worry, Michael. You'll do better next time.
낙담하거나 실망한 사람을 격려하기 위해서 사용하는 표현이다.

구문해설 · long face: 시무룩한 얼굴

해석

Amy: Michael, 왜 시무룩한 얼굴이니?

Michael: 나는 다른 선수를 막지 못했어.

Amy: 걱정 마. Michael. 다음번에는 더 잘할 거야.

Grammar in Real Life

Ms. Green is a good cook who cooks delicious Italian food. She always goes
주격 관계대명사(= that)   빈도부사(일반동사 앞)

to the local store which has many fresh vegetables. Her restaurant is always
사물 선행사에 쓰이는 주격 관계대명사(= that)   빈도부사

crowded with people who like to eat her food. I want you to try her seafood
주격 관계대명사(= that)   want+목적어+to부정사

pizza which is the most popular.
사물 선행사에 쓰이는 주격 관계대명사(= that)

구문해설 · cook: 요리사 · delicious: 맛있는 · fresh: 신선한 · vegetables: 야채

· be crowded with: ~으로 붐비다

Green씨는 맛있는 이탈리아 음식을 만드는 훌륭한 요리사이다. 그녀는 항상 신선한 채소가 많이 있는 지역 상점에 간다. 그녀의 레스토랑은 그녀의 음식을 좋아하는 많은 사람들로 항상 붐빈다. 나는 네가 가장 인기 있는 그녀의 해산물 피자를 먹어 보기를 원한다.

Think & Write

A basketball match between Class 1 and Class 2 was held at school on Friday.
(둘) 사이의   수동태   요일 앞에 전치사 on

Class 1 won the game by a score. There are some memorable players. One
1점 차이로

of them was Sarah. She was the player who made a basket one second before
One에 수의 일치   주격 관계대명사   = before

the end of the game. It was a great match. We are looking forward to the next
the game ended   인칭대명사 It   전치사 to

match.

구문해설 · match: 경기 · be held: 개최되다 · by: ~ 차이로 · memorable: 기억에 남는

· make a basket: 득점을 올리다 · look forward to: ~을 기대하다

금요일에 학교에서 1반과 2반 사이의 농구 경기가 열렸습니다. 1반은 1점 차이로 그 경기에서 이겼습니다. 기억에 남는 몇 명의 선수가 있습니다. 그 중 한 명은 Sarah입니다. 그녀는 경기가 끝나기 1초 전에 득점을 올린 선수였습니다. 그것은 훌륭한 경기였습니다. 우리는 다음 경기를 기대하고 있습니다.

영역별 핵심문제

01 다음 영영풀이에 해당하는 말을 고르시오.

> to shout loudly, to show support or praise for somebody, or to give them encouragement

① cheer   ② rush
③ press   ④ block
⑤ kick

02 다음 중 밑줄 친 부분의 뜻풀이가 바르지 <u>않은</u> 것은?

① John and Tom met at the <u>race track</u>.
경마장
② Many people cheered for him <u>excitedly</u>.
흥분하여
③ I stood at the starting line, waving the <u>flag</u>. 깃발
④ Suddenly, she burst into <u>tears</u>. 눈물
⑤ I watched your <u>volleyball</u> match yesterday.
피구

03 다음 주어진 문장의 밑줄 친 의미와 같은 의미로 쓰인 것은?

> As an <u>official</u> waved the green flag, the race started.

① The <u>official</u> record cannot be changed.
② The <u>official</u> asked me to fill up the bottle with water.
③ Canada has two <u>official</u> languages.
④ I haven't written any <u>official</u> documents.
⑤ This is the President's <u>official</u> visit to Vietnam.

04 다음 문장의 빈칸에 공통으로 들어갈 말을 고르시오.

> • He won first _____ at the contest.
> • Ann, _____ the dishes on the table.
> • People gathered into a market _____.

① voice   ② place   ③ rush
④ press   ⑤ count

05 다음 우리말과 일치하도록 주어진 말을 이용하여 완성하시오.

(1) Jake는 젊은 세대에게 뒤떨어지지 않기 위해 노력하고 있다. (keep)
➡ Jake is trying to _____ _____ _____ the younger generation.

(2) 최선을 다하는 사람은 기회를 잡을 수 있다. (chance)
➡ Those who _____ _____ are able to _____ _____ _____.

(3) 이 상자는 많은 초콜릿과 사탕들로 채워져 있다. (fill)
➡ This box _____ _____ _____ lots of chocolate and candies.

[06~07] 다음 대화를 읽고, 물음에 답하시오.

Mike: Is it your first time riding a bike, Mina?
Mina: Yes, it is. I just can't keep my balance.
Mike: (A)<u>Let me help you.</u> (hand) I'll hold your bike.
Mina: Thanks, Mike. Don't let go, okay?
Mike: Don't worry. Sit up and look straight ahead.

06 위 대화의 밑줄 친 (A)와 의미가 같도록 주어진 표현을 사용하여 다시 쓰시오.

➡ _____

07 위 대화의 내용과 일치하지 <u>않는</u> 것은?

① Mina는 자전거를 처음 타본다.
② Mina는 균형을 잡기 어려워한다.
③ Mike가 Mina의 자전거를 잡아 주려고 한다.
④ Mina는 Mike에게 자전거를 잡지 말라고 부탁하였다.
⑤ Mike는 Mina에게 똑바로 앉아 앞을 보라고 하였다.

[08~09] 다음 대화를 읽고, 물음에 답하시오.

Tom: What are you doing, Sarah?
Sarah: (A)나는 체육 시간에 물구나무 서는 법을 배웠거든. So I'm trying it now but it's not easy.
Tom: Let me help you. Kick your legs in the air again. I'll catch you.
Sarah: Oh, thanks. _____(B)

08 위 대화의 밑줄 친 (A)의 우리말과 일치하도록 〈보기〉에 주어진 모든 단어를 배열하여 완성하시오.

┌─ 보기 ┤
stand / head / in / I / how / learned / PE class / my / to / on
└─

➡ _____

09 위 대화의 빈칸 (B)에 들어갈 말로 <u>어색한</u> 것은?

① Let me try it one more time.
② I'll do it again.
③ I'll give it a try.
④ I'll try again.
⑤ Don't give up!

[10~11] 다음 대화를 읽고, 물음에 답하시오.

Coach: Hey, Brain. Did you practice the *taegwondo* side kick?
Brian: Yes, Coach. But I'm still (A) [comfortable / uncomfortable] with it.
Coach: What problem are you having?
Brian: Well, I can't (B)[lift / drop] my leg high enough.
Coach: I see. Let me help you. I'll (C)[lose / hold] this kick pad for you. Show me your side kick.

10 다음 영영풀이가 나타내는 말을 위 대화에서 찾아 쓰시오.

┌─────────────────────────┐
to hit somebody/something with your foot
└─────────────────────────┘

➡ _____

11 위 대화의 (A)~(C)에 들어갈 말로 바르게 짝지어진 것은?

① comfortable – lift – lose
② comfortable – drop – hold
③ uncomfortable – lift – hold
④ uncomfortable – drop – lose
⑤ uncomfortable – lift – lose

[12~13] 다음 대화를 읽고, 물음에 답하시오.

Anna: Hi, Jake. Do you come to the pool often?
Jake: Oh, hi, Anna. I take a swimming class here once a week.
Anna: When did you start the class?
Jake: Last month. But swimming is still not easy for me.
Anna: Oh, let me help you. _____(A)
Jake: Oh, that'll help me a lot. Thanks.

12 위 대화의 빈칸 (A)에 들어갈 말을 주어진 단어를 모두 배열하여 완성하시오.

> ┤ 보기 ├
> swim / to / how / in / the / club /
> teach / children / I / school

➡ _____

13 위 대화의 내용과 일치하지 <u>않는</u> 것은?

① Jake는 일주일에 한 번씩 수영 수업을 듣는다.
② Jake는 지난달에 수영 수업을 듣기 시작했다.
③ Jake는 여전히 수영이 쉽지 않다.
④ Anna는 학교 동아리에서 아이들에게 수영을 가르친다.
⑤ Jake는 수영 수업이 만족스럽지 않다.

[14~15] 다음 대화를 읽고, 물음에 답하시오.

Jack: Did you come and ⓐ<u>watch</u> my volleyball match yesterday?

Irene: Yeah, I ⓑ<u>have</u>. That was a great volleyball match. You were great!

Jack: Thanks, but it was a ⓒ<u>close</u> match. My serves were not strong ⓓ<u>enough</u>.

Irene: Oh, you're a great player. You'll do ⓔ <u>better</u> next time.

14 위 대화의 ⓐ~ⓔ 중 어법상 <u>어색한</u> 것을 찾아 바르게 고치시오.

➡ _____

15 What was Jack not satisfied with?

➡ _____

Grammar

16 다음 빈칸에 공통으로 들어갈 말은?

> • The picture _____ my dad hang on the wall yesterday is painted by me.
> • This is a picture of a girl and dogs _____ are playing together in the garden.

① who   ② whose   ③ which
④ what   ⑤ that

17 다음 중 어법상 바르지 <u>않은</u> 것은?

① I saw my father washing his car.
② Did you hear about the woman that took part in the war?
③ She will hear the boys yelled at each other.
④ Julia saw her friend taking a selfie.
⑤ I met a man whose sister worked with you.

18 다음 우리말을 영어로 바르게 옮긴 것은?

> 나는 누군가가 우리를 따라오는 것을 느꼈다.

① I heard us following someone.
② I heard us following him well.
③ I felt someone following us.
④ I felt me followed by somebody.
⑤ I felt myself following by someone.

19 주어진 단어를 이용하여 다음 우리말을 영어로 쓰시오.

> 네 전화기가 울리는 것을 들었니?
> (phone / ring)

➡ _____

20 다음 중 주어진 문장의 빈칸에 들어갈 말과 <u>다른</u> 하나는?

> There were many children _____ were eating cotton candies.

① Did you see the movie _____ was about a woman's life?

② Many pictures _____ were painted by Vincent van Gogh are now very expensive.

③ I have twin babies _____ I should take care of.

④ Look at the house _____ fence is broken.

⑤ The man and the dog _____ are running together live next door to me.

21 다음 문장의 빈칸에 들어갈 말을 바르게 짝지은 것은?

> • We _____ some girls talking gladly.
> • I _____ my brothers to calm down.

① made – encouraged
② wanted – forced
③ heard – would like
④ saw – watched
⑤ listened to – finished

22 주어진 단어를 바르게 배열하여 문장을 완성하시오.

> A myth _____ .
> (traditional / is / a / expresses / story / beliefs / which)

➡ _____

23 다음 중 어법상 옳은 것을 바르게 묶은 것은?

> ⓐ In our town, there are people aren't interested in other people at all.
> ⓑ The dress my friend is wearing is very expensive.
> ⓒ Thank you for the tip which is helpful.
> ⓓ Bradley enjoyed the show that I didn't like it.
> ⓔ Mr. Jang wanted to talk about the subject that was hard to understand.

① ⓐ, ⓑ, ⓓ   ② ⓑ, ⓒ, ⓓ   ③ ⓑ, ⓒ, ⓔ
④ ⓒ, ⓓ, ⓔ   ⑤ ⓐ, ⓓ, ⓔ

24 다음 우리말에 맞게 빈칸 ⓐ~ⓒ에 알맞은 말을 쓰시오.

> • Did you see _____ ?
> 그 비행기가 이륙하는 것을 보았니?
> • He heard _____ .
> 그는 우리가 싸우는 소리를 들었어.
> • I watched _____ .
> 나는 Jinna가 줄넘기를 하는 걸 보았어.

Reading

[25~28] 다음 글을 읽고, 물음에 답하시오.

> An official waves a green flag and the race starts! Max pushes his foot ①<u>down</u> hard ____ⓐ____ the gas pedal as he ②<u>completes</u> his sixth lap ____ⓑ____ the track. On the straightaway, Max pulls right beside the race's leader, Simon. Last year, Simon ③<u>won</u> many races, but Max's best result in a race was coming in fifth place. This time, he has a chance to ④<u>start</u> second. But he isn't going to be satisfied ____ⓒ____ second place today. The

winner gets to ⑤meet the world famous racer L. J. Richards! He doesn't want to miss ⓓ그의 역할 모델을 만날 그 기회.

25 위 글의 빈칸 ⓐ와 ⓑ에 공통으로 들어갈 말은?

① in ② over ③ about

④ on ⑤ up

26 다음 중 빈칸 ⓒ에 들어갈 말과 같은 말이 들어가는 것은?

① Tom had to take care _____ his mother.

② I am afraid my idea is different _____ yours.

③ Are you interested _____ writing a poem?

④ Soon she got used _____ my smell.

⑤ The glass is filled _____ milk.

27 위 글의 ①~⑤ 중 글의 흐름상 어색한 것은?

① ② ③ ④ ⑤

28 주어진 단어를 활용하여 밑줄 친 우리말 ⓓ를 영어로 쓰시오.

chance / meet

➡ _____

[29~31] 다음 글을 읽고, 물음에 답하시오.

"I can do it!" Max says loudly. He can feel his heart beating hard. The karts rush across the finish line. Who is the winner?
Max's eyes are filled with tears as he finds out that he came in second.

"No need for tears, kid," says a man's voice. Max can't believe his eyes. The man who is standing in front of him is L. J. Richards!
"Thank you, but I'm not the winner," says Max.
"It was a real close race. ____ⓐ____ you didn't win the race, you did your best. That's the thing that counts!" says L. J. Richards.
'Did I do my best?' thinks Max. After a moment, he smiles. "Yeah, I guess I did."

29 위 글의 빈칸 ⓐ에 들어갈 말로 가장 적절한 것은?

① Because ② When
③ If ④ Even though
⑤ While

30 다음 물음에 완전한 문장의 영어로 답하시오.

Q: What does Max feel when he gets near the finish line?

A: _____

➡ _____

31 다음 중 글의 내용과 일치하지 않는 것은?

① Max says that he can win the race.
② Max finishes the race in the second place.
③ Max talks with L. J. Richards.
④ Max is happy to know that he came in second.
⑤ Max thinks he did his best.

01 다음 영영풀이에 해당하는 말을 고르시오. 출제율 90%

> a piece of ground with a special surface for people, cars, etc. to have races on

① engine   ② track
③ flag   ④ tear
⑤ kart

02 다음 우리말에 맞게 빈칸에 알맞은 말을 쓰시오. 출제율 95%

(1) 기운 내! 너는 할 수 있어!

➡ _____ _____! You can do it!

(2) 모든 약은 아기의 손에 닿지 않는 곳에 보관하세요.

➡ Keep all the medicines _____

_____ _____ _____.

(3) 비록 접전이었지만 우리 팀은 경기에 우승하였다.

➡ Although it was a _____ _____, my team won the game.

03 다음 주어진 문장의 밑줄 친 의미와 다른 의미로 쓰인 것은? 출제율 100%

> Amy is wiping tears from her eyes.

① The sad story made her shed tears.
② Her eyes were filled with tears, listening to music.
③ Tears rolled down in my face.
④ Have you heard about the benefits of tears?
⑤ Be careful! This material tears easily.

[04~06] 다음 대화를 읽고, 물음에 답하시오.

Mom: David, how was your basketball game today?
David: We lost, Mom. I missed too many chances for a three-pointer.
Mom: Oh, don't be so hard on yourself. You'll do better next time.
David: _____

04 위 대화의 빈칸에 들어갈 말로 알맞은 것은? 출제율 90%

① No, thanks.
② I hope so.
③ Don't blame me.
④ It's all your fault.
⑤ Not at all.

05 위 대화에서 David의 기분으로 적절한 것은? 출제율 95%

① upset   ② discouraged
③ pleased   ④ nervous
⑤ lonely

06 위 대화의 내용과 일치하지 않는 것은? 출제율 100%

① David played the basketball game today.
② David's team lost the basketball game.
③ David blamed himself for his mistakes.
④ David's mom encouraged David to do better next time.
⑤ David's mom wanted to be so hard on herself.

[07~08] 다음 대화를 읽고, 물음에 답하시오.

Mike: (A) Is it your first time riding a bike, Mina?

Mina: (B) Yes, it is. I just can't keep my balance.

Mike: (C) I'll hold your bike.

Mina: (D) Thanks, Mike. Don't let go, okay?

Mike: (E) Don't worry. Sit up and look straight ahead.

07 위 대화의 (A)~(E) 중 주어진 문장이 들어가기에 적절한 곳은?

Let me help you.

① (A)　② (B)　③ (C)　④ (D)　⑤ (E)

08 위 대화의 내용과 일치하도록 빈칸을 완성하시오.

A: What is Mina doing now?

B: She is learning how to _____ _____ _____.

[09~10] 다음 대화를 읽고, 물음에 답하시오.

Coach: (A) Hey, Brain. Did you practice the *taegwondo* side kick?

Brian: (B) Yes, Coach. But I'm still not comfortable with it.

Coach: (C) What problem are you having?

Brian: (D) Well, I can't lift my leg high enough.

Coach: (E) I'll hold this kick pad for you. Show me your side kick.

09 위 대화의 (A)~(E) 중 주어진 문장이 들어가기에 적절한 곳은?

I see. Let me help you.

① (A)　② (B)　③ (C)　④ (D)　⑤ (E)

10 위 대화의 내용과 일치하지 <u>않는</u> 것은?

① Brain practiced the *taegwondo* side kick.

② Brain didn't feel comfortable with the *taegwondo* side kick.

③ Brain was not good at lifting his leg high enough.

④ The coach helped Brain practice the *taegwondo* side kick.

⑤ The coach showed the *taegwondo* side kick to Brain.

11 다음 빈칸에 들어갈 말이 바르게 짝지어진 것은?

- There was a boy _____ dream was to be a pilot.
- I don't want to eat the bread _____ tastes sour.

① who – which　② whom – that

③ whose – that　④ whose – who

⑤ who – whose

12 다음 중 빈칸에 들어갈 'play'의 형태가 <u>다른</u> 하나는?

① We saw the people in the park _____ catch.

② I heard the boys _____ cards in the living room.

③ Did you watch them _____ together last week?

④ I heard the music _____ by someone.

⑤ Have you seen the team _____ football in the stadium?

13 적절한 관계대명사를 이용하여 다음 두 문장을 하나의 문장으로 쓰시오.
출제율 90%

> • Unfortunately we couldn't go to the wedding.
> • We were invited to the wedding.

➡ _____
_____

14 다음 중 빈칸에 들어갈 말이 바르게 짝지어진 것은?
출제율 100%

> • Mrs. Brown heard someone _____ downstairs.
> • We watched a woman _____ behind the counter.

① come – to serve   ② to come – to serve

③ coming – serve   ④ comes – serving

⑤ to come – served

15 다음 중 밑줄 친 부분의 쓰임이 <u>다른</u> 하나는?
출제율 95%

① Do you know <u>that</u> Jason threw a ball to Kelly?

② I thought <u>that</u> telling the truth was important then.

③ He was the man <u>that</u> you mentioned about.

④ I know <u>that</u> you did your best on the test.

⑤ She believes <u>that</u> he will make her happy.

16 주어진 동사를 활용하여 다음 우리말을 영어로 쓰시오.
출제율 90%

> 우리는 한 B-boy가 무대 위에서 공연하는 것을 보았다. (watch / perform)

➡ _____

[17~19] 다음 글을 읽고, 물음에 답하시오.

> At the go-kart race track, there are many people ___ⓐ___ are cheering excitedly. The karts that are making loud engine noises are waiting. An official waves a green flag and the race starts!

17 다음 중 빈칸 ⓐ에 들어갈 말과 <u>다른</u> 하나는?
출제율 95%

① Do you know the woman _____ hair is curly and blond?

② Tom's dog _____ is walking with Tom looks happy.

③ He is not the man _____ always tells a lie.

④ This is the watch _____ Jenny bought last month.

⑤ Kelly will take part in the race _____ will be held next week.

18 위 글을 읽고 답할 수 있는 것은?
출제율 95%

① How many racers are there at the go-kart race?

② How many people are cheering?

③ What color of flag does an official wave?

④ Where is the go-kart track?

⑤ How long do the karts race?

19 위 글의 내용에 맞게 빈칸에 알맞은 말을 쓰시오.
출제율 95%

You will hear the kart _____ _____ _____ _____ in the go-kart race track.

[20~22] 다음 글을 읽고, 물음에 답하시오.

Max completes the tenth lap and now has five more laps to go. Max sees Simon's kart ahead, just out of Max's reach. Max's kart gets closer and closer to Simon's. It almost hits the back end of Simon's kart. They drive into the straightaway and Max presses harder on the gas pedal. "I can catch up," says Max. _____ (A) _____.
Max is right behind Simon. The finish line is getting closer, and the cheering from the crowd is getting louder.
"I can do it!" Max says loudly. He can feel his heart beating hard. The karts rush across the finish line. Who is the winner?

20 위 글의 빈칸 (A)에 다음 두 문장을 하나의 문장으로 바꿔 써 넣으시오.
출제율 85%

Max sees the official waving a white flag. It means the last lap.

➡ _____

_____

21 다음과 같이 풀이되는 단어를 위 글에서 찾아 쓰시오.
출제율 90%

a large group of people who have gathered together

➡ _____

22 위 글의 내용과 일치하는 문장의 개수를 고르시오.
출제율 90%

ⓐ After finishing the tenth lap, there are still ten laps left.
ⓑ Max can't see Simon's kart all the time.
ⓒ Max's cart hits the back end of Simon's kart.
ⓓ Max is at the back of Simon when the finish line is getting closer.
ⓔ The crowd is holding their breath while watching the racing game.

① 1개 ② 2개 ③ 3개
④ 4개 ⑤ 5개

[23~24] 다음 글을 읽고, 물음에 답하시오.

Max's eyes are filled with tears as he finds out that he came in second.
"No need for tears, kid," says a man's voice. Max can't believe his eyes. The man __ ⓐ __ is standing in front of him is L. J. Richards!
"Thank you, but I'm not the ⓑwin," says Max.
"It was a real close race. Even though you didn't win the race, you did your best. That's the thing that counts!" says L. J. Richards.
'Did I do my best?' thinks Max. After a moment, he smiles. "Yeah, I guess I did."

23 위 글의 빈칸 ⓐ에 들어갈 말로 적절한 것을 <u>모두</u> 고르시오.
출제율 100%

① whom ② who ③ whose
④ which ⑤ that

24 위 글의 밑줄 친 ⓑ를 알맞은 어형으로 고치시오.
출제율 95%

➡ _____

[01~03] 다음 대화를 읽고 물음에 답하시오.

> Emily: I heard your baseball team, the Reds, won the match. Eight to seven, right? Congratulations, John!
>
> John: Thanks. (A)그것은 접전이었어. I'm not happy with my pitching.
>
> Emily: Why do you say that?
>
> John: I allowed two homeruns.
>
> Emily: Oh, you're a great pitcher. You'll do better next time.

01 위 대화의 밑줄 친 (A)를 영작하시오.

➡ _____

02 위 대화에서 주어진 영영 풀이가 가리키는 말을 찾아 쓰시오.

> a sport event where people or teams compete against each other

➡ _____

03 Why was John unhappy with his pitching?

➡ _____

04 다음 우리말과 같은 뜻이 되도록 빈칸에 알맞은 말을 쓰시오.

(1) 나는 빠르게 결정하고 행동하는 사람을 좋아해.
➡ I like the person _____ _____ and _____ quickly.

(2) 그들은 꼬리를 가진 인형을 찾는 중이다.
➡ They are looking for _____ _____ _____ tails.

(3) 우리는 눈이 아름다운 소녀와 함께 이야기를 나누었다.
➡ We had a conversation with a girl _____ _____ _____ beautiful.

05 주어진 동사를 활용하여 다음 우리말을 영어로 쓰시오.

> 당신은 꽃들이 바람 속에서 춤추는 것을 볼 수 있습니다. (see / dance)

➡ _____
_____

06 다음 동사 'make'를 어법에 맞게 빈칸에 각각 쓰시오.

> • We saw Mom _____ cookies.
> • We ate cookies _____ by Mom.

07 적절한 관계대명사를 이용하여 다음 두 문장을 하나의 문장으로 쓰시오.

> • Where is the cheese?
> • I put it in the refrigerator.

➡ _____
_____

08 〈보기〉의 문장과 관계대명사를 이용하여 빈칸을 알맞게 채우시오.

> ┤ 보기 ├
> • You saw him driving a car.
> • They don't feel sorry for other people.
> • It has existed for a long time.

(1) A tradition is a custom _____
_____.

(2) What happened to the person _____
_____?

(3) I don't like people _____
_____.

At the go-kart race track, there are many people who are cheering excitedly. ⓐThe karts that are making loud engine noises are waiting. An official waves a green flag and the race starts!

09 위 글의 내용에 맞게 빈칸에 알맞은 말을 쓰시오.

When you are at the go-kart race track, you can see many people _____ _____.

10 위 글의 밑줄 친 문장 ⓐ를 두 개의 문장으로 나누어 쓰시오.

➡ _____

_____

11 위 글의 내용에 맞게 빈칸에 알맞은 말을 쓰시오.

We will see the karts _____ on the track, making loud engine noises. As an official _____ _____ _____ _____, the go-kart race _____.

Max's eyes are filled with tears as he finds out that he came in second.
"No need for tears, kid," says a man's voice. Max can't believe his eyes. The man who is standing in front of him is L. J. Richards!
"Thank you, but I'm not the winner," says Max.
"It was a real close race. Even though you didn't win the race, you did your best. That's the thing that counts!" says L. J. Richards.
'Did I do my best?' thinks Max. After a moment, he smiles. "Yeah, I guess I did."

12 위 글의 내용에 맞게 빈칸에 알맞은 말을 쓰시오.

At first, Max was not _____ with the result of the race _____ _____ he came in second.

13 위 글의 내용에 맞게 다음 물음에 완전한 문장의 영어로 답하시오.

Q: According to L. J. Richards, what is important to Max in the race?

A: _____

➡ _____

01 다음 대화의 내용과 일치하도록 빈칸을 완성하시오.

> **Megan:** I'm worried about our next soccer match, James.
>
> **James:** Why are you worried, Megan?
>
> **Megan:** Well, I couldn't catch high balls in the last soccer match. I gave away too many goals.
>
> **James:** I see. Here, let me help you. I'll kick high balls to you.
>
> **Megan:** Oh, that'll really help. I hope my skills get better.
>
> **James:** Don't worry. You'll do better next time.

> Mon June 24th, 2019
>
> Today, I met Megan. She was worried about (A)_____ because she gave away too many goals in the last soccer match. She said she had trouble (B)_____. So, I decided to give (C)_____ to her. I (D)_____ for practice. She was satisfied with my help and wanted to improve her skills. I believe that she can do well next time.

02 〈보기〉와 같이 관계대명사를 이용하여 문장을 완성하시오.

> ┌ 보기 ┐
>
> A soldier is a person who works in an army.

(1) Math teachers are people _____.

(2) Architects are people _____.

(3) Coffee is a drink _____.

(4) A car is a vehicle _____.

(5) King Sejong is the person _____.

03 주어진 동사의 동사원형이나 현재분사형을 써서 다양한 문장을 만드시오.

> ┌ 보기 ┐
>
> see   hear   watch   listen to   feel

(1) _____

(2) _____

(3) _____

(4) _____

(5) _____

(6) _____

단원별 모의고사

01 다음 문장의 빈칸에 들어갈 말을 보기에서 골라 적절한 형태로 쓰시오.

> ┤ 보기 ├
> be satisfied with / be filled with /
> keep up with / do one's best

(1) I'll _____ to win this match.

(2) The street _____ cherry blossom now.

(3) I can't _____ you.

(4) He _____ his student's answer.

[02~03] 다음 대화를 읽고, 물음에 답하시오.

> Emma: (A) How was your soccer match last week?
> Keine: (B) We won, but I'm not ⓐsatisfying with our match.
> Emma: (C) Why do you say ⓑthat?
> Keine: (D) My passes were too ⓒshort.
> Emma: (E) You're ⓓpracticing a lot. You'll do ⓔbetter next time.

02 위 대화의 (A)~(E) 중 주어진 문장이 들어가기에 적절한 곳은?

> Don't take it too hard.

① (A) ② (B) ③ (C) ④ (D) ⑤ (E)

03 위 대화의 ⓐ~ⓔ 중 어법상 어색한 것을 골라 바르게 고치시오.

➡ _____

[04~05] 다음 대화를 읽고, 물음에 답하시오.

> Megan: I'm (A)worried about our next soccer match, James.
> James: Why are you worried, Megan?
> Megan: Well, I couldn't catch high balls in the last soccer match. I gave away too many goals.
> James: I see. Here, let me help you. I'll kick high balls to you.
> Megan: Oh, that'll really help. I hope my skills get better.
> James: Don't worry. You'll do better next time.

04 위 대화의 밑줄 친 (A)worried와 바꾸어 쓸 수 있는 것을 모두 고르시오.

① concerned ② comforted
③ anxious ④ satisfied
⑤ alarmed

05 위 대화의 내용과 일치하지 않는 것은?

① Megan은 다음 축구 시합을 걱정하고 있다.
② Megan은 지난 축구 시합 때 많은 골을 내주었다.
③ James는 Megan에게 높은 공을 차 줄 것이다.
④ Megan은 자신의 실력이 점차 나아지길 바란다.
⑤ Megan은 James에게 공을 잡는 법을 알려줄 것이다.

[06~07] 다음 대화를 읽고, 물음에 답하시오.

> Tom: What are you doing, Sarah?
> Sarah: I learned how to stand on my head in PE class. So I'm trying it now but it's not easy.
> Tom: Let me help you. Kick your legs in the air again. I'll catch you.
> Sarah: Oh, thanks. I'll try again.

06 What did Sarah learn in PE class?

➡ _____

07 What did Tom tell Sarah to do to help her?

➡ _____

[08~09] 다음 대화를 읽고, 물음에 답하시오.

Mom: David, how was your basketball game today?

David: We lost, Mom. I missed too many chances for a three-pointer.

Mom: Oh, _____. You'll do better next time.

David: I hope so.

08 위 대화의 빈칸에 들어갈 말을 주어진 단어를 모두 배열하여 완성하시오.

┌─ 보기 ─┐
so / on / don't / hard / yourself / be
└──────┘

➡ _____

09 Why was David depressed after playing the basketball game?

➡ _____

_____

10 다음 대화의 (A)~(E) 중 주어진 문장이 들어가기에 알맞은 곳은?

┌────────────────────────────────┐
│ You'll do better next time. │
└────────────────────────────────┘

┌────────────────────────────────┐
│ Emily: I heard your baseball team, the Reds, won the match. Eight to seven, right? Congratulations, John! (A) │
│ John: Thanks. It was a close game. I'm not happy with my pitching. (B) │
│ Emily: Why do you say that? (C) │
│ John: I allowed two homeruns. (D) │
│ Emily: Oh, you're a great pitcher. (E) │
└────────────────────────────────┘

① (A)　② (B)　③ (C)　④ (D)　⑤ (E)

11 다음 빈칸에 공통으로 들어갈 말은?

┌────────────────────────────────┐
│ • What is the name of the woman _____ legs are really long? │
│ • I became friends with a girl _____ first language is the same as mine. │
└────────────────────────────────┘

① who　　② that　　③ which
④ whose　⑤ whom

12 다음 빈칸에 알맞은 것을 모두 고르시오.

┌────────────────────────────────┐
│ 나는 누군가가 내 이름을 부르는 소리를 들었다. │
│ ➡ I heard _____. │
└────────────────────────────────┘

① someone to call me

② someone call my name

③ my name calling me

④ someone calling me

⑤ my name called

13 다음 중 빈칸에 들어갈 말이 바르게 짝지어진 것은?

> • Have you heard of a man _____ wallet was stolen?
> • Maybe Jefferson is the person _____ is respected by every student.

① that – that   ② who – whose
③ whose – whom   ④ whom – that
⑤ whose – who

14 주어진 단어를 활용하여 다음 우리말을 영어로 쓰시오.

> 나는 Jason과 Helen이 함께 자전거를 타는 것을 봤어. (see / ride)

➡ _____

_____

15 다음 두 개의 문장을 하나의 문장으로 쓰시오.

> • There are a girl and a goat.
> • They are resting on the hill.

➡ _____

_____

[16~19] 다음 글을 읽고, 물음에 답하시오.

> Max pushes his foot down @hardly on the gas pedal as he completes his sixth lap on the track. On the straightaway, Max pulls ⓑright beside the race's leader, Simon. Last year, Simon won many races, but Max's best result in a race was (A)coming in fifth place. This time, he has a chance to finish ⓒsecond. But he isn't going to be satisfied with second place today. The winner ⓓgets to meet the world famous racer L. J. Richards! He doesn't want ⓔto miss the chance to meet his role model.

16 위 글의 @~ⓔ 중 어법상 바르지 <u>않은</u> 것은?

① @   ② ⓑ   ③ ⓒ   ④ ⓓ   ⑤ ⓔ

17 다음 중 위 글을 읽고 답할 수 <u>없는</u> 것은?

① What does Max do when he completes his sixth lap?
② What does Max do on the straightaway?
③ How many races did Simon win last year?
④ Why isn't Max going to be satisfied with second place today?
⑤ Who is Max's role model?

18 다음 중 밑줄 친 (A)와 쓰임이 <u>다른</u> 것은?

① Do you mind <u>closing</u> the door?
② His hobby is <u>riding</u> a bike alone.
③ <u>Eating</u> regularly is important.
④ We saw them <u>jumping</u> a rope.
⑤ The writer didn't finish <u>writing</u> a book.

19 다음은 Max와 엄마의 대화이다. 빈칸에 알맞은 말을 쓰시오.

> **Mom:** Max, why do you want to win this race?
> **Max:** Because only the winner gets the chance to meet L. J. Richards. If I win, you will see me _____
> _____ .

[20~23] 다음 글을 읽고, 물음에 답하시오.

"I can do it!" Max says loudly. He can feel his heart ⓐbeating hard. The karts rush across the finish line. Who is the winner?

Max's eyes _____ (A) _____ tears as he finds out ⓑthat he came in second.

"No need for tears, kid." says a man's voice. Max can't believe his eyes. The man ⓒwho is standing in front of him is L. J. Richards!

"Thank you, but I'm not the winner," says Max.

"It was a real ⓓclose race. Even though you didn't win the race, you did your best. That's the thing ⓔthat counts!" says L. J. Richards.

'Did I do my best?' thinks Max. After a moment, he smiles. "Yeah, I guess I did."

20 동사 fill을 이용해 빈칸 (A)를 완성하시오. (3 words)

➡ _____

21 다음 중 밑줄 친 ⓐ~ⓔ에 대한 설명으로 바르지 <u>않은</u> 것은?

① ⓐ: 'beat'와 바꿔 쓸 수 있다.
② ⓑ: 목적어가 되는 명사절을 이끄는 접속사로 생략 가능하다.
③ ⓒ: 'that'을 대신 쓸 수 있다.
④ ⓓ: '가까운'이라는 의미이다.
⑤ ⓔ: 'which is important'와 같은 의미이다.

22 다음 중 글의 내용과 일치하는 것은?

① Max feels nothing when he rushes across the finish line.
② Max doesn't know who L. J. Richards is.
③ L. J. Richards wants Max to cry out loud.
④ Max regrets that he didn't do his best.
⑤ L. J. Richards cheers up Max.

23 위 글의 내용에 맞게 빈칸에 알맞은 말을 쓰시오.

L. J. Richards saw Max's kart _____ in second. He thought that Max _____ _____ _____. So he wanted to tell Max not to cry.

24 다음 대화가 자연스럽게 이어지도록 순서대로 배열하시오.

(A) Oh, thanks. I'll try again.
(B) What are you doing, Sarah?
(C) Let me help you. Kick your legs in the air again. I'll catch you.
(D) I learned how to stand on my head in PE class. So I'm trying it now but it's not easy.

➡ _____

25 주어진 문장과 자연스럽게 연결되도록 (A)~(C)를 바르게 나열하시오.

Max completes the tenth lap and now has five more laps to go.

(A) It almost hits the back end of Simon's kart. They drive into the straightaway and Max presses harder on the gas pedal. "I can catch up," says Max.
(B) Max sees Simon's kart ahead, just out of Max's reach. Max's kart gets closer and closer to Simon's.
(C) Max sees the official waving a white flag which means the last lap. Max is right behind Simon. The finish line is getting closer, and the cheering from the crowd is getting louder.

➡ _____

Explore Your Feelings!

🎤 의사소통 기능

- 좋지 않은 감정을 느끼게 된 원인 묻기

  A: You look down today. What's the matter?

  B: I got a haircut but it's too short.

- 고민을 해결할 방법 제안하기

  A: I've gained weight lately.

  B: I think you should exercise regularly.

🎤 언어 형식

- 현재완료

  They **have been** best friends since childhood.

- 목적격 관계대명사

  I'm sure there is a reason **that** we don't know about.

Words & Expressions

Key Words

- **advice** [ədváis] 몡 조언
- **advise** [ədváiz] 동 조언하다, 충고하다
- **alone** [əlóun] 뷔 홀로, 혼자
- **avoid** [əvɔ́id] 동 피하다
- **bar** [bɑːr] 몡 (특정 음식이나 음료를 파는) 전문점
- **contact** [kántækt] 몡 접촉, 닿음
- **difficult** [dífikʌlt] 혱 어려운
- **elementary** [èləméntəri] 혱 초보의, 초급의
- **explain** [ikspéin] 동 설명하다
- **fear** [fiər] 몡 두려움, 공포
- **fight** [fait] 동 싸우다
- **forgive** [fərgív] 동 용서하다
- **haircut** [héərkʌt] 몡 이발, 머리 깎기
- **hate** [heit] 동 싫어하다
- **hurt** [həːrt] 동 다치게 하다, 아프게 하다
- **limit** [límit] 몡 한계, 제한
- **line** [lain] 몡 (연극, 영화의) 대사
- **matter** [mǽtər] 몡 문제
- **mean** [miːn] 동 의도하다, 작정하다

- **messy** [mési] 혱 어질러진, 더러운
- **mirror** [mírər] 몡 거울
- **pack** [pæk] 동 싸다, 꾸리다
- **reason** [ríːzn] 몡 이유, 까닭
- **repeat** [ripíːt] 동 반복하다
- **share** [ʃɛər] 동 공유하다, 나누다
- **since** [sins] 전 ~부터, ~ 이후
- **snack** [snæk] 몡 간식
- **solve** [sɑlv] 동 풀다, 해결하다
- **stand** [stænd] 동 참다, 견디다
- **stuff** [stʌf] 몡 물건
- **suggestion** [səgdʒéstʃən] 몡 제안
- **toothache** [túːθeik] 몡 치통
- **upset** [ʌ́pset] 혱 속상한, 마음이 상한
- **wise** [waiz] 혱 현명한
- **worry** [wə́ːri] 동 걱정하다 몡 걱정
- **yell** [jel] 동 소리치다, 소리 지르다
- **yet** [jet] 뷔 아직

Key Expressions

- **face a problem** 문제에 직면하다
- **focus on** ~에 집중하다
- **gain weight** 체중이 늘다
- **in the end** 결국, 마침내
- **let it go** 그쯤 해 두다, 내버려 두다
- **lunch break** 점심시간
- **make a mistake** 실수하다
- **on purpose** 고의로, 일부러

- **point out** 지적하다
- **put ~ down** ~을 깎아내리다
- **set an alarm** 자명종을 맞추다
- **shut down** (기계가) 멈추다, 정지하다
- **stay up late** 늦게까지 자지 않고 있다
- **up and down** 좋다가 나쁘다가 하는
- **wake up** 잠에서 깨다
- **work out** 해결하다

Word Power

※ 서로 반대되는 뜻을 가진 어휘

- easy 쉬운 ↔ difficult 어려운
- hate 싫어하다 ↔ like 좋아하다
- wise 현명한 ↔ stupid 어리석은
- upset 속상한, 마음이 상한 ↔ relieved 안도하는
- messy 어질러진, 더러운 ↔ clean 깔끔한
- avoid 피하다 ↔ face 맞서다

- pack 싸다, 꾸리다 ↔ unpack (꾸러미, 짐을) 풀다
- alone 혼자 ↔ together 함께
- limited 한정된 ↔ limitless 무한의, 무제한의
- on purpose 고의로 ↔ by accident 우연히
- elementary 초급의, 초보의 ↔ advanced 상급의, 고등의
- gain weight 체중이 늘다 ↔ lose weight 체중이 줄다

English Dictionary

- **advice** 조언
  → an opinion or a suggestion about what somebody should do in a particular situation
  누군가가 특정한 상황에서 해야 하는 것에 대한 의견 또는 제안

- **avoid** 피하다
  → to keep away from somebody/something; to try not to do something
  누군가 또는 무언가로부터 멀리하다; 무언가를 하지 않으려고 하다

- **contact** 접촉
  → the state of touching something
  무언가를 만지는 상태

- **elementary** 초급의
  → in or connected with the first stages of a course of study
  학업 과정에서 첫 번째 단계에 관련된

- **forgive** 용서하다
  → to stop feeling angry with somebody who has done something to harm, annoy or upset you
  당신에게 해롭게 하거나 화나게 하거나 또는 불안하게 하는 무언가를 한 사람에게 화내는 감정을 그만두다

- **hate** 싫어하다
  → to dislike something very much
  무언가를 매우 싫어하다

- **hurt** 다치게 하다
  → to cause physical pain to somebody/yourself; to injure somebody/yourself
  누군가 또는 당신 자신에게 신체적 고통을 야기하다; 누군가 또는 당신 자신을 부상을 입히다

- **line** 대사
  → the words spoken by an actor in a play or film/movie
  연극 또는 영화에서 배우에 의해 이야기되는 말

- **messy** 어질러진, 더러운
  → dirty and/or untidy
  더러운, 그리고[또는] 정돈되지 않은

- **repeat** 반복하다
  → to say or write something again or more than once
  무언가를 다시 또는 한번 이상 말하거나 쓰다

- **share** 공유하다
  → to have or use something at the same time as somebody else
  다른 누군가와 동시에 무언가를 갖거나 사용하다

- **suggestion** 제안
  → an idea or a plan that you mention for somebody else to think about
  다른 누군가가 그것에 관해 생각하도록 당신이 언급한 의견 또는 계획

- **toothache** 치통
  → a pain in one of your teeth
  치아의 아픔

- **yell** 소리 지르다
  → to shout loudly, for example because you are angry, excited, frightened or in pain
  예를 들어 당신이 화가 나거나, 흥분하거나, 깜짝 놀라거나 고통을 당하고 있기 때문에 크게 소리 지르다

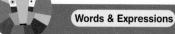

서답형

01 다음 짝지어진 단어의 관계가 같도록 빈칸에 알맞은 말을 쓰시오.

> easy : difficult = like : h_____

중요

02 다음 중 밑줄 친 부분의 뜻풀이가 바르지 않은 것은?

① I didn't want to go there alone. 혼자, 홀로
② The sport is dangerous because there is a lot of body contact. 접촉
③ You can overcome your fear of water. 두려움
④ Susan will forgive the rude boy. 용서하다
⑤ I can't memorize my lines at all. 선

서답형

03 다음 우리말에 맞게 빈칸에 알맞은 말을 쓰시오.

(1) 밤에 혼자 다니지 마세요.
  ➡ Don't walk round _____ at night.
(2) 내가 무대에 섰을 때, 나는 대사를 잊어버렸다.
  ➡ When I was on the stage, I forgot my
  _____.
(3) 여기 제한 속도는 60km/h이다.
  ➡ The speed _____ is 60km/h here.
(4) 저는 여섯 살 때 이후부터 여기에 살고 있습니다.
  ➡ I've lived here _____ I was six years old.

04 다음 영영풀이가 가리키는 것을 고르시오.

> an opinion or a suggestion about what somebody should do in a particular situation

① matter
② fear
③ mirror
④ stuff
⑤ advice

서답형

05 다음 우리말에 맞게 주어진 단어를 사용하여 영작하시오.

(1) 나는 추위를 별로 잘 참지 못한다. (very, stand)
  ➡ _____
(2) 그들은 그 문제에 대해 이야기했다. (matter)
  ➡ _____
(3) 제게 조언 좀 주세요. (some, please)
  ➡ _____
(4) 그녀가 내게 먼저 물어보지 않고 내 물건을 사용해서 나는 화가 났다. (stuff, upset)
  ➡ _____
  _____

중요

06 다음 주어진 문장의 밑줄 친 stand와 같은 의미로 쓰인 것은?

> I can't stand his arrogant attitude.

① You don't have to stand. Just sit down.
② Let's stand up and talk about it now.
③ The old buildings stand in front of the library.
④ Can you stand the pain?
⑤ Tall trees stand on the riverside.

01 다음 빈칸에 들어갈 말을 〈보기〉에서 찾아 쓰시오.

| a pain in one of your teeth |

➡ _____

02 다음 우리말에 맞게 빈칸에 알맞은 말을 쓰시오.

(1) 우리의 점심시간은 12시부터 1시까지이다.
  ➡ Our _____ is from twelve to one.
(2) 나는 너의 조언을 받아들여 집에 일찍 들어갔다.
  ➡ I took your _____ and went home early.
(3) 난 그녀의 마음을 아프게 하고 싶지 않다.
  ➡ I don't want to _____ her feelings.

03 다음 문장의 빈칸에 들어갈 말을 〈보기〉에서 골라 쓰시오.

┌ 보기 ┐
gain weight / in the end / focus on / on purpose

(1) He broke his glasses _____.
(2) You can _____ because of lack of sleep.
(3) We should _____ the changes in the global market.
(4) _____, I accepted his suggestion.

04 다음 우리말을 주어진 단어를 이용하여 영작하시오.

(1) 그는 때때로 사람들을 깎아내린다. (puts)
  ➡ _____
(2) 그녀는 항상 내 실수들을 지적한다. (points)
  ➡ _____
(3) 잠자리에 들기 전에 자명종을 맞춰라. (set)
  ➡ _____

05 다음 우리말과 일치하도록 주어진 어구를 배열하여 완성하시오.

(1) 내 보고서의 몇몇 실수들을 지적해 주어 고마워요.
  (you / mistakes / my / in / report / out / pointing / thank / for / some)
  ➡ _____
(2) 여기 여러분의 대본이 있으니 대사를 연습하세요.
  (your / practice / so / your / here / scripts / are / lines)
  ➡ _____
(3) 내가 전화한 이유는 토요일 계획에 대해 묻기 위해서였다.
  (for / the reason / to / the plans / ask / called / I / Saturday / was / about)
  ➡ _____
  _____
(4) 화재의 위험을 피하기 위해 조치를 취하는 것은 중요하다.
  (avoid / is / to / it / important / to / take / the risk / fire / measures / of)
  ➡ _____
  _____

Conversation

1 좋지 않은 감정을 느끼게 된 원인 묻기

> **A** You look down today. What's the matter? (너 오늘 침울해 보여. 무슨 일 있어?)
>
> **B** I got a haircut but it's too short. (머리를 잘랐는데 너무 짧아.)

■ "What's the matter?"는 상대방의 기분이 언짢아 보일 때 무슨 일이 있는지 혹은 좋지 않은 기분의 원인을 묻고자 할 때 사용된다. 예를 들어, 상대방의 기분이 안 좋아 보일 때 "What's the matter? You look upset."과 같이 말한다.

좋지 않은 감정을 느끼게 된 원인 묻기

- What's wrong? (무슨 일이에요?)
- Is something the matter? (무슨 문제가 있나요?)
- Is there something wrong? (무슨 일이에요?)
- Why do you look so sad[mad]? (왜 그렇게 슬퍼[화나] 보이니?)
- What's the problem with you? (무슨 일이야?)

핵심 Check

1. 다음 우리말과 일치하도록 빈칸에 알맞은 말을 쓰시오.

(1) **A:** You look so _____. _____? (매우 초조해 보여. 무슨 일이야?)

　B: I dropped my mom's new glasses and broke them. (내가 엄마의 새 안경을 떨어뜨렸는데 그게 깨졌어.)

(2) **A:** _____? (왜 그렇게 슬퍼 보이니?)

　B: I didn't pass the test. I don't know what to do. (시험을 통과하지 못했어. 나는 무엇을 해야 할지 모르겠어.)

(3) **A:** You don't look good today. Is there something _____? (너 오늘 좋아 보이지 않아. 무슨 일이야?)

　B: I can't sleep well at night. _____? (밤에 잠을 잘 잘 수 없어. 내가 무엇을 해야 할까?)

② 고민을 해결할 방법 제안하기

> **A** I've gained weight lately. (나는 최근에 체중이 늘었어.)
>
> **B** I think you should exercise regularly. (내 생각에 네가 규칙적으로 운동을 해야 할 것 같아.)

■ "I think you should ~."는 뭔가 고민하고 있거나 어려움을 겪고 있는 사람에게 그 문제에 대한 해결책을 제안할 때 사용된다. 예를 들어, 친구와 말다툼을 한 후 고민하고 있는 친구에게 문제를 해결할 방안을 제시하고 싶다면 "I think you should talk to your friend first."와 같이 말할 수 있다.

고민을 해결할 방법 제안하기

- Why don't you talk to your father first? (먼저 아빠와 이야기해 보는 게 어때?)
- How about playing a video game? (비디오 게임을 하는 것이 어때?)
- If I were you, I'd go to bed first and think about it later. (내가 너라면 나는 먼저 잠자리에 들고 나중에 생각할래.)
- What about setting an alarm before you go to bed? (잠자리에 들기 전에 알람을 맞추는 게 어때?)
- I recommend writing a letter to your friend. (나는 네 친구에게 편지 쓰는 걸 추천해.)
- I advise you to meet her personally. (나는 네가 개인적으로 그녀를 만나보는 것을 권해.)

핵심 Check

2. 다음 우리말과 일치하도록 빈칸에 알맞은 말을 쓰시오.

(1) **A:** My face turns red when I'm in front of many people. (저는 많은 사람들 앞에 서면 얼굴이 빨개져요.)

   B: ＿＿＿＿＿＿＿＿＿ take a deep breath first. (내 생각에 네가 먼저 깊게 숨을 쉬어야 할 것 같아.)

(2) **A:** I'm really bad at making eye contact. (저는 정말로 눈을 마주치는 것을 잘 못해요.)

   B: I ＿＿＿＿ you to practice looking into your own eyes in the mirror. (나는 네가 거울에서 네 눈을 보는 것을 연습하길 충고해.)

(3) **A:** I want a better style. (나는 더 나은 스타일을 원해요.)

   B: ＿＿＿＿＿＿＿＿＿ look for magazines with fashion tips? (패션 정보가 있는 잡지를 찾아보는 게 어때?)

Listen & Talk 1-B

Jane: You look tired. ❶What's the matter?

Mike: I didn't have breakfast this morning. I'm so hungry.

Jane: Oh, ❷that's too bad. We still have two more hours ❸until lunch break.

Mike: Our school should have a snack bar. Then, we could have a quick breakfast or snacks.

Jane: I think so, too. How can we ❹make that suggestion?

Mike: We can post it on the suggestion board.

Jane: 너 피곤해 보인다. 무슨 일 있어?

Mike: 오늘 아침에 밥을 못 먹었어. 너무 배가 고파.

Jane: 오, 안됐다. 점심시간까지 아직 두 시간도 더 남았는데.

Mike: 우리 학교도 매점이 있어야 돼. 그러면 간단히 아침이나 간식을 먹을 수 있잖아.

Jane: 내 생각도 그래. 어떻게 하면 우리가 그 제안을 할 수 있을까?

Mike: 우리는 이걸 제안 게시판에 올릴 수 있어.

❶ 상대방의 기분이 언짢아 보일 때 무슨 일이 있는지 혹은 좋지 않은 기분의 원인을 묻고자 한다. What's the problem with you? 등으로 바꾸어 쓸 수 있다.

❷ 유감을 나타내는 표현으로 I'm sorry to hear that. 등으로 바꾸어 쓸 수 있다.

❸ until: ~까지, ~이 되기까지

❹ make a suggestion: 제안을 하다

Check(√) True or False

(1) There isn't a snack bar in Jane's school.　　T ☐ F ☐

(2) Mike is going to have lunch with Jane soon.　　T ☐ F ☐

Communication

Solomon: Hello, you're ❶on the air.

Amy: Hi, Solomon. I'm Amy.

Solomon: Hi, Amy. What's the matter?

Amy: I ❷hate sharing my room with my little sister. She uses my ❸stuff without asking me first. What should I do?

Solomon: Hmm.... I think you should tell her your feelings. And you should also make some rules with your sister.

Amy: Oh, I'll try ❹that. Thanks for the advice.

Solomon: 안녕하세요. (방송에) 연결되었습니다.

Amy: 안녕하세요, Solomon. 전 Amy라고 해요.

Solomon: 안녕하세요, Amy. 무슨 일 있어요?

Amy: 전 여동생이랑 제 방을 같이 쓰는 게 싫어요. 그 애는 제게 먼저 물어보지도 않고 제 물건을 쓰거든요. 제가 어떻게 해야 할까요?

Solomon: 흠.... 제 생각엔 당신의 기분을 여동생에게 말해야 할 것 같아요. 그리고 여동생과 몇 가지 규칙을 만들어 봐요.

Amy: 오, 그렇게 할게요. 조언 감사해요.

❶ on the air: 방송 중에

❷ hate은 to부정사와 동명사 모두를 목적어로 취할 수 있다.

❸ stuff: 물건

❹ that은 Solomon의 조언으로 제시된 여동생에게 기분을 이야기하는 것과 여동생과 몇 가지 규칙을 만들어 보는 것을 가리킨다.

Check(√) True or False

(3) Amy is upset because of her little sister.　　T ☐ F ☐

(4) Solomon thinks that Amy should share her stuff with her little sister.　　T ☐ F ☐

Listen & Talk 1-A-1

M: You don't look so happy today. What's the matter?

W: I wore my sister's favorite T-shirt. But I got grape juice on ❶it.

M: Oh, no. Did you tell your sister?

W: No, ❷not yet. I don't know ❸what to do.

❶ it은 her sister's favorite T-shirt를 가리킨다.
❷ not yet: 아직 (~ 않다)
❸ what to do = what I should do

Listen & Talk 1-A-2

Sora: David, you look ❶down today. What's the matter?

David: I got a haircut but it's too short. I look ❷funny.

Sora: ❸Take off your hat and let me see. (*pause*) Oh, it looks fine.

David: Really? I guess ❹I'm just not used to it yet.

❶ down: 우울한(= depressed, gloomy)
❷ funny: 우스꽝스러운, 우스운, cf. fun: 즐거운, 재미있는
❸ take off: ~을 벗다
❹ be used to ~: ~에 익숙하다

Listen & Talk 2 A-1

Sujin: I don't know how to do better in math. Can you give me some ❶advice?

Jake: How do you study for tests?

Sujin: I just solve a lot of problems.

Jake: Well, don't solve everything. I think you should ❷focus on the ❸ones you got wrong.

❶ advice: 조언, cf. advise: 조언하다
❷ focus on: ~에 집중하다
❸ ones는 problems를 가리킨다.

Listen & Talk 2 A-2

Emily: I was late for class again. I just can't ❶wake up in the morning.

Tom: Do you ❷set an alarm?

Emily: Yeah, but I ❸turn ❹it off and go back to sleep.

Tom: I think you should put ❹it far from your bed. That way, you'll have to ❺get out of bed.

❶ wake up: 잠에서 깨다
❷ set an alarm: 자명종을 맞추다
❸ turn off: ~을 끄다 (↔ turn on: ~을 켜다)
❹ it은 alarm을 가리킨다.
❺ get out of ~: ~에서 나오다

Listen & Talk 2 B

Eric: Ms. Morris, I just can't ❶stop playing computer games. What should I do?

Ms. Morris: Well, ❷why don't you use a special program? When you set a time limit, the computer ❸shuts down at that time.

Eric: Oh, that's a good idea.

Ms. Morris: And I think you should move the computer out of your room and into the living room.

Eric: I think I should. Thank you for the advice, Ms. Morris.

❶ stop+동명사: ~하던 것을 멈추다, cf. stop+to부정사: ~하기 위해 멈추다
❷ why don't you ~?: ~하는 게 어때?
❸ shut down: (기계가) 멈추다, 정지하다

● 다음 우리말과 일치하도록 빈칸에 알맞은 말을 쓰시오.

Listen & Talk 1-A-1

M: You _____ _____ so happy today. What's the _____?

W: I _____ my sister's favorite T-shirt. But I _____ grape juice on it.

M: Oh, no. Did you tell your sister?

W: No, not yet. I don't know _____ _____ _____.

Listen & Talk 1-A-2

Sora: David, you _____ _____ today. _____ _____?

David: I got a _____ but it's too short. I look _____.

Sora: _____ _____ your hat and let me see. (*pause*) Oh, it looks fine.

David: Really? I guess I'm just not _____ _____ it yet.

Listen & Talk 1-B

Jane: You look _____. What's the matter?

Mike: _____ _____ _____ _____ _____ _____ _____. I'm so hungry.

Jane: Oh, that's _____ _____. We still have two more hours until _____ _____.

Mike: Our school should have a _____ _____. Then, we could have a quick breakfast or snacks.

Jane: I think so, too. How can we _____ that _____?

Mike: We can _____ it on the suggestion board.

Listen & Talk 2 A-1

Sujin: I don't know _____ _____ _____ better in math. Can you give me some _____?

Jake: How do you study for tests?

Sujin: I just _____ a lot of problems.

Jake: Well, don't _____ everything. I think you should _____ _____ the _____ you _____ wrong.

해석

M: 너 오늘은 별로 행복해 보이지가 않네. 무슨 일 있어?
W: 언니가 가장 좋아하는 티셔츠를 입었어. 그런데 거기에 포도 주스를 쏟았지 뭐야.
M: 오, 저런. 너희 언니에게 말했어?
W: 아니, 아직. 내가 뭘 해야 할지 모르겠어.

Sora: David, 너 오늘 침울해 보여. 무슨 일 있어?
David: 머리를 잘랐는데 너무 짧아. 우스꽝스럽게 보여.
Sora: 모자를 벗으면 내가 한 번 볼게. 오, 괜찮아 보이는데.
David: 정말? 난 아직 익숙해지지 않은 것 같아.

Jane: 너 피곤해 보인다. 무슨 일 있어?
Mike: 오늘 아침에 밥을 못 먹었어. 너무 배가 고파.
Jane: 오, 안됐다. 점심시간까지 아직 두 시간도 더 남았는데.
Mike: 우리 학교도 매점이 있어야 돼. 그러면 간단히 아침이나 간식을 먹을 수 있잖아.
Jane: 내 생각도 그래. 어떻게 하면 우리가 그 제안을 할 수 있을까?
Mike: 우리는 이걸 제안 게시판에 올릴 수 있어.

Sujin: 수학을 더 잘하는 방법을 모르겠어. 나에게 조언을 좀 해 줄래?
Jake: 시험을 목표로 어떻게 공부해?
Sujin: 난 그냥 많은 문제를 풀어 봐.
Jake: 글쎄, 전부 풀지 마. 내 생각엔 네가 틀린 문제들에 집중해야 할 것 같아.

Listen & Talk 2 A-2

Emily: I was _____ _____ class again. I just can't _____ _____ in the morning.

Tom: Do you _____ _____ _____?

Emily: Yeah, but I _____ _____ _____ and go back to sleep.

Tom: I think you should put it _____ _____ your bed. _____ _____, you'll have to get out of bed.

해석

Emily: 나 또 수업에 늦었어. 난 정말 아침에 못 일어나겠어.
Tom: 자명종은 맞춰 두는 거야?
Emily: 응, 그렇지만 자명종을 끄고 다시 잠들게 돼.
Tom: 내 생각엔 자명종을 침대에서 멀리 떨어진 곳에 두어야 할 것 같아. 그러면 침대에서 일어날 수밖에 없을 거야.

Listen & Talk 2 B

Eric: Ms. Morris, I just can't _____ _____ _____ _____. _____ _____ _____ _____?

Ms. Morris: Well, why don't you use a special program? When you _____ a time _____, the computer _____ _____ at that time.

Eric: Oh, that's a good idea.

Ms. Morris: And _____ _____ _____ _____ move the computer _____ _____ your room and _____ the living room.

Eric: I think I should. Thank you for the _____, Ms. Morris.

Eric: Morris 선생님, 저 컴퓨터 게임하는 것을 멈출 수가 없어요. 제가 어떻게 해야 할까요?
Mr. Morris: 음, 특별한 프로그램을 써보는 게 어떨까? 네가 시간 제한을 정해 두면 컴퓨터가 그 시간에 맞춰 종료돼.
Eric: 오, 좋은 생각이네요.
Mr. Morris: 그리고 내 생각엔 컴퓨터를 네 방에서 거실로 옮겨 두어야 할 것 같아.
Eric: 제 생각에도 그래야 할 것 같아요. Morris 선생님, 조언해 주셔서 감사합니다.

Communication

Solomon: Hello, you're _____ _____ _____.

Amy: Hi, Solomon. I'm Amy.

Solomon: Hi, Amy. What's the _____?

Amy: I hate _____ my room _____ my little sister. She uses my _____ without asking me first. What should I do?

Solomon: Hmm.... I think you should tell her your _____. And you should also _____ _____ _____ with your sister.

Amy: Oh, _____ _____ _____. Thanks for the advice.

Solomon: 안녕하세요. (방송에) 연결되었습니다.
Amy: 안녕하세요, Solomon. 전 Amy라고 해요.
Solomon: 안녕하세요, Amy. 무슨 일 있어요?
Amy: 전 여동생이랑 제 방을 같이 쓰는 게 싫어요. 그 애는 제게 먼저 물어보지도 않고 제 물건을 쓰거든요. 제가 어떻게 해야 할까요?
Solomon: 흠.... 제 생각엔 당신의 기분을 여동생에게 말해야 할 것 같아요. 그리고 여동생과 몇 가지 규칙을 만들어 봐요.
Amy: 오, 그렇게 할게요. 조언 감사해요.

Conversation 시험대비 기본평가

01 다음 대화가 자연스럽게 이어지도록 순서대로 배열하시오.

> (A) Do you set an alarm?
> (B) I think you should put it far from your bed. That way, you'll have to get out of bed.
> (C) Yeah, but I turn it off and go back to sleep.
> (D) I was late for class again. I just can't wake up in the morning.

➡ _____

[02~04] 다음 대화를 읽고 물음에 답하시오.

> Jane: You look tired. What's the matter?
> Mike: (A) I didn't have breakfast this morning. I'm so hungry.
> Jane: (B) Oh, that's too bad. We still have two more hours until lunch break.
> Mike: (C) Then, we could have a quick breakfast or snacks.
> Jane: (D) ⓐI think so, too. How can we make that suggestion?
> Mike: (E) We can post it on the suggestion board.

02 위 대화의 (A)~(E) 중 주어진 문장이 들어가기에 적절한 곳은?

> Our school should have a snack bar.

① (A)　　② (B)　　③ (C)　　④ (D)　　⑤ (E)

03 위 대화의 밑줄 친 ⓐ와 바꾸어 쓸 수 있는 것을 <u>모두</u> 고르시오.

① I'm against it.　　② I'm with you in what you say.
③ That's not right.　　④ I agree with you.
⑤ This won't work.

04 위 대화의 내용과 일치하지 <u>않는</u> 것은?
① Mike는 아침을 먹지 않아 피곤해 보인다.
② Jane과 Mike는 곧 점심을 먹을 예정이다.
③ 학교에 매점이 없다.
④ Mike는 매점이 있다면 간단히 아침이나 간식을 먹을 수 있을 것이라고 생각한다.
⑤ Jane과 Mike는 제안 게시판에 매점 설치 제안을 할 수 있다.

[01~03] 다음 대화를 읽고 물음에 답하시오.

Tom: You don't look so happy today. (A) <u>What's the matter?</u>

Sue: I wore my sister's favorite T-shirt. But I got grape juice on it.

Tom: Oh, no. Did you tell your sister?

Sue: No, not yet. I don't know what to do.

01 위 대화의 밑줄 친 (A)와 바꾸어 쓰기에 <u>어색한</u> 것은?

① What's the problem with you?

② What's wrong?

③ Is there something wrong?

④ Is something the matter?

⑤ What do you do?

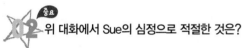

02 위 대화에서 Sue의 심정으로 적절한 것은?

① worried　　② joyful　　③ lonely

④ happy　　⑤ pleased

03 위 대화의 내용과 일치하도록 빈칸을 완성하시오.

Sue looked so worried because she got grape juice on _____.

[04~06] 다음 대화를 읽고 물음에 답하시오.

Jane: You look tired. What's the matter?

Mike: I didn't have breakfast this morning. I'm so hungry.

Jane: Oh, (A)<u>that's too bad.</u> We still have two more hours until lunch break.

Mike: Our school should have a snack bar. Then, we could have a quick breakfast or snacks.

Jane: I think so, too. How can we make that suggestion?

Mike: We can post it on the suggestion board.

04 위 대화에서 주어진 영영풀이가 나타내는 말을 찾아 쓰시오. [서답형]

an idea or a plan that you mention for somebody else to think about

➡ _____

05 How can Jane and Mike make the suggestion? [서답형]

➡ _____

06 위 대화의 밑줄 친 (A)와 바꾸어 쓸 수 있는 것을 <u>모두</u> 고르시오.

① I'm sorry to hear that.

② but I'm afraid I can't.

③ what a pity!

④ no problem.

⑤ don't mention it.

07 다음 대화가 자연스럽게 이어지도록 순서대로 배열하시오. [서답형]

(A) Take off your hat and let me see. (*pause*) Oh, it looks fine.

(B) I got a haircut but it's too short. I look funny.

(C) You look down today. What's the matter?

(D) Really? I guess I'm just not used to it yet.

➡ _____

[08~09] 다음 대화를 읽고 물음에 답하시오.

Sujin: I don't know how to do better in math. (a)Can you give me some advice?

Jake: How do you study for tests?

Sujin: I just solve a lot of problems.

Jake: Well, don't solve everything. (A)_____
_____

서답형

08 위 대화의 빈칸 (A)에 들어갈 말을 보기에 주어진 단어를 모두 배열하여 완성하시오.

┌─── 보기 ───┐
you / should / ones / you / got / the / wrong / think / focus / I / on
└──────────┘

➡ _____

중요
09 위 대화의 밑줄 친 (a)와 바꾸어 쓸 수 없는 것은?

① What should I do?

② Would you give me some tips?

③ Would you advise me?

④ Will you give me a hint as to what I should do?

⑤ What can I do for you?

[10~12] 다음 대화를 읽고 물음에 답하시오.

Eric: Ms. Morris, I just can't stop ⓐto play computer games. What should I do?

Ms. Morris: Well, (A)why don't you use a special program?(how) When you set a time ⓑlimit, the computer ⓒ shuts down at that time.

Eric: Oh, that's a good idea.

Ms. Morris: And I think you should move the computer ⓓout of your room and ⓔinto the living room.

Eric: I think I should. I'll try that. Thank you for the advice, Ms. Morris.

서답형
10 위 대화의 밑줄 친 ⓐ~ⓔ 중 대화의 흐름상 어색한 것을 찾아 바르게 고치시오.

➡ _____

서답형
11 위 대화의 밑줄 친 (A)와 의미가 같도록 주어진 단어를 사용하여 다시 쓰시오.

➡ _____

12 위 대화의 내용과 일치하지 않는 것은?

① Eric은 컴퓨터 게임을 멈추지 못해 고민이다.

② Ms. Morris는 Eric에게 특별한 프로그램을 사용해 볼 것을 추천한다.

③ 특별한 프로그램은 시간을 정해 두면 컴퓨터가 그 시간에 맞춰 종료된다.

④ Ms. Morris는 Eric이 컴퓨터를 거실에서 그의 방으로 옮길 것을 조언한다.

⑤ Eric은 Ms. Morris의 조언을 실행해 볼 것이다.

[13~14] 다음 대화를 읽고 물음에 답하시오.

Emily: I was late for class again. I just can't wake up in the morning.

Tom: Do you set an alarm?

Emily: Yeah, but I turn it off and go back to sleep.

Tom: I think you should put it far from your bed. That way, you'll have to get out of bed.

서답형
13 Why was Emily late for class?

➡ _____

서답형
14 Why does Tom advise Emily to put an alarm far from the bed?

➡ _____

[01~03] 다음 대화를 읽고 물음에 답하시오.

Solomon: Hello, (A)you're on the air.

Amy: Hi, Solomon. I'm Amy.

Solomon: Hi, Amy. What's the matter?

Amy: I hate sharing my room with my little sister. She uses my stuff without asking me first. What should I do?

Solomon: Hmm.... I think you should tell her your feelings. And you should also make some rules with your sister.

Amy: Oh, I'll try that. Thanks for the advice.

01 위 대화의 밑줄 친 (A)의 의미를 우리말로 쓰시오.

➡ _____

02 Why doesn't Amy like sharing her room with her little sister?

➡ _____

_____

 03 위 대화의 내용과 일치하도록 빈칸을 완성하시오.

> Amy: I'm so upset with my sister who uses my stuff without asking me first. I hate sharing my room with her.
>
> Solomon: If I were you, I'd _____
> _____.

[04~05] 다음 대화를 읽고 물음에 답하시오.

Sujin: I don't know how to do better in math. Can you give me some advice?

Jake: How do you study for tests?

Sujin: I just solve a lot of problems.

Jake: Well, don't solve everything. I think you should focus on the ones you got wrong.

04 What's the matter with Sujin?

➡ _____

05 What is Jake's advice to do better in math?

➡ _____

06 다음 대화를 읽고 대화의 내용과 일치하도록 다음 표를 완성하시오.

Eric: Ms. Morris, I just can't stop playing computer games. What should I do?

Ms. Morris: Well, why don't you use a special program? When you set a time limit, the computer shuts down at that time.

Eric: Oh, that's a good idea.

Ms. Morris: And I think you should move the computer out of your room and into the living room.

Eric: I think I should. Thank you for the advice, Ms. Morris.

⬇

Student Name	Eric
Date	August 24th
Problem	(A) _____.
Advice	(1) Use a special program to (B) _____. (2) Move the computer from (C) _____ to (D) _____.

Grammar

교과서

1 현재완료

> • I **have read** 500 books since I was six. 여섯 살 이후로 나는 책을 500권 읽었다.
> • My father **has never** been to a grocery store. 나의 아버지는 식료품점에 가 본 적이 없다.

■ 현재완료는 과거의 사건이 현재까지 영향을 미칠 때 사용한다. 'have[has]+p.p.'의 형태로, 부정형은 'have[has] not+p.p.'이며, 의문형은 'Have[Has]+주어+p.p. ~?'로 나타낸다.

   • The man **has worked** for the company since 2010. 그 남자는 2010년 이래로 그 회사를 위해 일해 왔다.

   • **Have** you ever **been** to China? 너는 중국에 가 본 적 있니?

■ 현재완료는 '완료, 경험, 계속, 결과'의 네 가지 용법으로 쓰인다. 완료 용법은 'just, already, yet'과 같은 부사와 주로 함께 쓰이며, 경험은 'ever, never, once, before' 등과 같은 부사와 함께 쓰인다. 'How long ~?'으로 묻는 질문이나 'for+기간', 'since+특정 시점'은 현재완료의 계속 용법에 속한다. 결과 용법은 특별한 부사와 어울리지 않고 과거에 발생한 사건으로 인하여 현재까지 영향을 미치고 있는 상태를 나타낼 때 결과 용법으로 본다.

   • The boy **has drunk** the milk already. 그 소년은 벌써 우유를 마셨다. 〈완료〉

   • David **has played** ping-pong for an hour. David는 한 시간 동안 탁구를 쳤다. 〈계속〉

   • We **have seen** the program several times. 우리는 그 프로그램을 몇 번 본 적이 있다. 〈경험〉

   • The girls **have gone** to Busan. 그 소녀들은 부산에 가고 없다. 〈결과〉

   *have[has] been to와 have[has] gone to의 사용에 유의하자. '~에 가 본 적이 있다'는 경험은 have[has] been to로 표현하고, '~에 가고 없다'는 결과는 have[has] gone to로 표현한다.

■ 현재완료는 과거의 일이 현재까지 영향을 미칠 때 쓰는 시제이므로 과거를 나타내는 어구인 yesterday, last year, ~ ago 등과 함께 쓸 수 없다.

   • Jane has met Tom yesterday. (✗)

   • Jane met Tom yesterday.　　(○)

핵심 Check

1. 다음 우리말과 일치하도록 빈칸에 알맞은 말을 쓰시오.

   (1) Jason은 세 시간 동안 공부하고 있다.

   ➡ Jason _____ _____ for three hours.

   (2) 그 비행기는 막 도착했다.

   ➡ The plane _____ just _____.

   (3) 나는 어제 이후로 아무것도 하지 않았다.

   ➡ I _____ _____ nothing since yesterday.

② 목적격 관계대명사

> • There is a man **whom** my sister likes. 내 여동생이 좋아하는 남자가 있어.
>
> • The flowers **which** you take care of are beautiful. 네가 돌보는 꽃들은 아름다워.

■ 관계대명사는 두 개의 문장을 하나로 이어주는 접속사 역할을 하면서 동시에 (대)명사 역할을 한다. 전치사의 목적어 혹은 동사의 목적어였던 (대)명사를 목적격 관계대명사로 만들어 문장을 하나로 이어준다.

• This is the book **that** Ms. Han recommended. 〈동사의 목적어〉
이것이 한 선생님이 추천하신 책이다.

• He is the only friend **that** I can rely on. 〈전치사의 목적어〉
그는 내가 의지할 수 있는 유일한 친구이다.

■ 목적격 관계대명사 who(m), which는 that으로 대체할 수 있으며, 생략 가능하다. 관계대명사가 전치사의 목적어로 사용된 경우 전치사는 동사 뒤에 그대로 두거나, 전치사를 관계대명사 앞으로 보낼 수 있다. 단, 전치사를 관계대명사 앞으로 보낸 경우 관계대명사 that을 쓸 수 없고 관계대명사를 생략할 수 없음에 유의한다.

• Do you know the woman (**who/whom/that**) Maria is talking to? 너는 Maria가 대화하고 있는 여자를 아니?

• The bag (**which/that**) he brought the other day smells bad. 그가 지난번에 가져온 가방에서 나쁜 냄새가 난다.

• I have the wallet (**which/that**) Tom was looking **for**. Tom이 찾던 지갑을 내가 가지고 있어.
= I have the wallet **for which** Tom was looking.

• The subject (**which/that**) I am interested **in** is English. 내가 흥미를 느끼는 과목은 영어이다.
= The subject **in which** I am interested is English.

핵심 Check

2. 다음 우리말과 일치하도록 빈칸에 알맞은 말을 쓰시오.

(1) 네가 만든 그 샌드위치는 맛있어 보인다.
➡ The sandwich _____ _____ _____ looks delicious.

(2) 이것은 그가 나에게 사 준 목걸이야.
➡ This is the necklace _____ _____ _____ for me.

(3) Helen이 함께 온 저 남자를 아니?
➡ Do you know the man _____ _____ _____ _____?

Grammar 시험대비 기본평가

01 다음 문장에서 어법상 <u>어색한</u> 부분을 바르게 고쳐 쓰시오.

(1) When have you left the place?

_____ ➡ _____

(2) Mr. Pang who the children love teach how to swim to them.

_____ ➡ _____

(3) I did this work for a long time until now. So I know about the work well.

_____ ➡ _____

(4) The knife whom you used is very sharp.

_____ ➡ _____

02 적절한 관계사를 이용하여 다음 두 문장을 하나의 문장으로 쓰시오.

(1) Have you found the pen? You lost it.

➡ _____

(2) Did she take the class? James taught the class.

➡ _____

(3) I want to meet the boy. You speak highly of him.

➡ _____

(4) Molly likes the movie. Tom Cruise starred in the movie.

➡ _____

star in: ~에서 주연을 맡다

03 주어진 어구를 바르게 배열하여 다음 우리말을 영어로 쓰시오. 필요하다면 단어를 추가하거나 변형하시오.

(1) 나는 아직 점심을 다 먹지 않았다. (yet / finished / lunch / I / my / haven't)

➡ _____

(2) 그녀는 그 교회에 두 번 가봤어. (two / she / times / been / has / the church)

➡ _____

(3) 나는 내가 가지고 있던 모든 돈을 그녀에게 주었다. (that / I / I / had / all the money / her / gave)

➡ _____

(4) 우리가 제출한 보고서는 어디에 있나요? (in / where / hand / is / which / we / the report)

➡ _____

01 다음 중 빈칸에 들어갈 말로 가장 적절한 것은?

> A: Have you seen her lately?
> B: _____

① Yes, I do.　　② No, I don't.
③ Yes, I saw.　　④ Yes, I have.
⑤ No, I have.

02 다음 우리말을 영어로 바르게 옮긴 것은?

> 너는 Jamie가 쓴 책을 읽고 싶니?

① Have you wanted to read the book which Jamie has written?
② Do you want to the book that Jamie was writing?
③ Did you wrote the book that Jamie read?
④ Did you read the book that Jamie wrote?
⑤ Do you want to read the book which Jamie wrote?

03 다음 중 빈칸에 들어갈 말로 가장 적절한 것은?

> Tyler has studied Economy _____.

① last year　　② the other day
③ since yesterday　　④ last week
⑤ a year ago

서답형

04 다음 두 문장을 한 문장으로 쓸 때 빈칸을 완성하시오.

> • I like the dress.
> • You want to buy the dress.

➡ I _____.

05 다음 우리말을 영어로 바르게 옮기지 <u>않은</u> 것은?

① 네가 악수한 그 소년은 누구니?
→ Who is the boy that you shook hands with?
② 나는 그녀를 한 번 만난 적 있어.
→ I have met her once.
③ 그는 그녀를 3년 동안 알아왔습니다.
→ He has known her for three years.
④ 그들은 네가 만든 기계를 좋아해.
→ They like the machine that you made.
⑤ 너는 서울에 가 본 적이 있니?
→ Have you ever gone to Seoul?

06 다음 중 어법상 바르지 <u>않은</u> 것은?

① Katherine likes the music which her friends don't like.
② Kelly has met Julian a few minutes ago.
③ Can you tell me the story that Tom told you?
④ Have you eaten the food before?
⑤ Did you buy the pants that you wanted to buy?

07 다음 중 빈칸에 들어갈 말로 가장 적절한 것은?

> Jina has paid the bill _____ five years.

① since　　② already　　③ for
④ just　　⑤ almost

서답형
08 다음 우리말을 영어로 쓸 때 빈칸에 알맞은 말을 세 단어로 쓰시오.

> 그들은 네가 파티에 초대한 사람들이니?
> ➡ Are they the people _____
>   to the party?

중요
09 다음 빈칸에 들어갈 말이 바르게 짝지어진 것은?

> • _____ you ever met a famous person like Justin Bieber?
> • Brad _____ to Italy. He is enjoying his vacation.

① Have – was   ② Have – has gone
③ Did – have been   ④ Did – went
⑤ Did – want to go

10 다음 두 문장을 하나의 문장으로 바르게 표현한 것은?

> They began to talk about the subject two hours ago. They still talk about it.

① They talked about the subject two hours ago.
② They talked about the subject until now.
③ They have talked about the subject since two hours.
④ They have talked about the subject for two hours.
⑤ They have just talked about the subject.

서답형
11 다음 두 문장을 하나의 문장으로 쓰시오.

> • Tell me about the people.
> • You met them in the hospital.

➡ _____
  _____

12 다음 중 현재완료의 용법이 다른 하나는?

① They have just finished their work.
② He has already signed up for the class.
③ Jena has seen the menu for 20 minutes.
④ Melissa has not passed the test yet.
⑤ Brad has checked the schedule already.

중요
13 다음 중 밑줄 친 부분을 생략할 수 없는 것은?

① The boys that you are looking at are my children.
② The cat that is resting on the chair looks so cute.
③ My car was made in the company that Paul works for.
④ The candy that the girl is eating was made by me.
⑤ The cup that Amelia likes to use is on the shelf.

14 다음 빈칸에 가장 적절한 말을 고르시오.

> Look at the man and the dog _____ are walking together.

① which   ② who   ③ what
④ that   ⑤ whom

서답형
15 주어진 어구를 바르게 배열하여 다음 우리말을 영어로 쓰시오.

> 네가 나에게 보낸 그 편지는 아직 도착하지 않았어.
> (yet / the letter / has / that / not / to me / arrived / sent / you)

➡ _____

16 (A)~(C)에서 어법상 옳은 것끼리 바르게 짝지어진 것은?

> • Ted has used the computer (A)[for / since] he was a high school student.
> • What (B)[did you do / have you done] last weekend?
> • Clara (C)[has painted / painted] the wall twice until now.

① for – did you do – has painted
② for – did you do – painted
③ for – have you done – has painted
④ since – did you do – has painted
⑤ since – have you done – painted

17 다음 중 밑줄 친 부분의 쓰임이 <u>다른</u> 하나는?

① Do you know the girl <u>that</u> is making something with clay?
② The fact <u>that</u> is well known to us is that she is a great cook.
③ I don't know about the party <u>that</u> was planned by Jane.
④ The man likes to see the movie <u>that</u> was filmed at Sydney.
⑤ I don't care about the information <u>that</u> Sarah told us.

18 다음 중 빈칸에 들어갈 말이 바르게 짝지어진 것은?

> The company considers publishing a book _____ David _____ three years ago.

① who – has written
② whose – wrote
③ which – wrote
④ that – has wrote
⑤ that – is writing

19 서답형 다음 주어진 단어를 활용하여 우리말을 영어로 쓰시오.

> 전에 인도에 가 본 적이 있나요? (ever)

➡ _____

20 다음 중 어법상 바르지 <u>않은</u> 것은?

① Maria has learned math for three years.
② Can you give me back the pen that you borrowed from me?
③ Mina has had lunch a few minutes ago.
④ I have made my own jacket once.
⑤ The plants that you have just watered look beautiful.

21 서답형 다음 두 문장을 하나의 문장으로 쓰시오.

> I lost my cap. And I still don't have it.

➡ _____

22 서답형 다음 두 문장을 하나의 문장으로 쓰시오.

> • The I-pad was my birthday present.
> • I got it from my father.

➡ _____
_____

23 서답형 주어진 단어를 바르게 배열하여 문장을 완성하시오.

> The toys (with / that / play / the children) look dirty.

➡ _____

01 주어진 단어를 이용하여 다음 두 문장을 하나의 문장으로 표현하시오.

> It was sunny yesterday. It is still sunny today. (since)

➡ _____

02 다음 우리말에 맞도록 빈칸에 알맞은 말을 써서 문장을 완성하시오.

> 네가 마시고 있는 그 차 어때?
> ➡ How do you like the tea _____
> _____ _____ _____?

 주어진 단어를 어법에 맞게 빈칸에 각각 쓰시오.

> ago　　for　　since

> • Julia has known Karl _____ 2015.
> • We have discussed the problem _____ a couple of hours.
> • Tom and Jane got married sixteen years _____.
> • We have known each other _____ we were young.

04 주어진 어구를 바르게 배열하여 다음 우리말을 영어로 쓰시오.

> 사람들이 찾던 그 실종 소년이 어젯밤 집으로 왔습니다.
> (were / the missing boy / whom / looking / people / for / last night / home / came)

➡ _____

_____

 다음 대화의 빈칸에 알맞은 말을 쓰시오.

> A: How long _____ _____ _____ in this house?
> B: We moved into this house two years _____. So we _____ _____ in this house _____ two years.

06 자연스러운 문장이 되도록 관계대명사를 이용하여 하나의 문장으로 연결하시오. that은 사용하지 마시오.

> • What is the name of the man?
> • This is the car.
> • Where is the red sweater?

> • My friend hopes to buy it someday.
> • I put it in my drawer.
> • You want to meet him.

➡ (1) _____

_____

(2) _____

_____

(3) _____

_____

07 다음 우리말을 영어로 쓰시오.

> A: 너는 전에 코끼리를 본 적이 있니?
> B: 아니, 본 적 없어.

➡ _____

➡ _____

08 다음 문장에서 어법상 **틀린** 것을 고쳐 문장을 다시 쓰시오.

(1) Have you thrown a party for her yesterday?

➡ _____

(2) I have gone to Boston many times.

➡ _____

(3) The sandwich who he made for us is very delicious.

➡ _____

_____

09 다음 상황을 읽고 한 문장으로 표현하시오.

> Yesterday Kevin lost his umbrella. So he doesn't have it now.

➡ _____

10 적절한 관계사를 이용하여 다음 두 문장을 한 문장으로 쓸 때 빈칸을 완성하시오.

(1) There isn't much information. You can get it.

➡ There _____ .

(2) I gave Tim the pants. He always liked them.

➡ I _____ .

(3) Is he the man? You respect him very much.

➡ Is _____ ?

11 다음 우리말을 8 단어로 이루어진 영어 문장으로 쓰시오.

> 이것은 우리 아빠가 만드신 책상이야.

➡ _____

12 다음 문장에서 생략 가능한 것을 생략하여 문장을 다시 쓰시오.

(1) The tennis game that he played yesterday was great.

➡ _____

(2) Do you know the boy who is talking with your sister?

➡ _____

(3) The subject which Jane is interested in is history and Korean.

➡ _____

13 다음 빈칸에 알맞은 말을 4 단어로 쓰시오.

> 그녀는 좋아하지 않는 음식에는 손도 대지 않는다.
> ➡ She never touches the food _____
> _____ .

14 다음 상황을 읽고 빈칸에 알맞은 말을 쓰시오.

> I lost my shoes last week. I still don't have them. In other words, I _____ _____ my shoes.

15 우리말에 맞게 빈칸에 알맞은 말을 세 단어로 쓰시오.

> 네가 참석한 파티에 얼마나 많은 사람들이 있었니?
> = How many people were there at the party _____ _____ _____ ?

Voices in Our Mind

Bella is 15 years old this year and <u>these days</u> her feelings are going up
　　　　　　　　　　　　　　　　　요즘에
and down. Today, she looks <u>down</u>. Let's listen to Bella's feelings and
　　　　　　　　　　　　　우울한
find out <u>why</u>.
　　　= why she looks down today

Day 1

Anger: <u>What a day!</u> I can't believe Jenny yelled at Bella after the
　　　정말 끔찍한 날이야!
school play.

Sadness: Well, <u>that's because</u> Bella forgot her lines on stage.
　　　　that's because+원인: 그것은 ~이기 때문이다

Anger: Jenny pointed out the mistake <u>that</u> Bella made. How could she
　　　　　　　　　　　　　　목적격 관계대명사 (which로 대체 가능)
do <u>that</u> in front of everyone?
　'Jenny pointed out the mistake that Bella made'를 가리킴

Joy: But I'm sure Jenny did not <u>mean to hurt</u> Bella. They <u>have been</u>
　　　　　　　　　　　　　mean to V: V하는 것을 의도하다　　Jenny와 Bella가 초등학교 때부터 지금까지 쭉 가장 친한 친구였다는 의미
best friends <u>since</u> elementary school. Remember?

Anger: That's <u>what</u> I'm saying. A true friend <u>would</u> never put Bella
　　　관계대명사(~하는 것)　　　　If가 없는 가정문에서 주어가 if절을 대신하고 있다.(= If she were a true friend, she)
down <u>like that</u>.
　　　그렇게
Fear: I'm worried that they are <u>not</u> going to be friends <u>anymore</u>.
　　　　　　　　　　　　not ~ anymore: 더 이상 ~ 않다(= no longer)
Joy: Come on, Fear. Don't <u>go too far</u>. We'll <u>see</u>.
　　　　　　　　　　도를 넘다　　　　　알다

📎 **확인문제**

● 다음 문장이 본문의 내용과 일치하면 T, 일치하지 <u>않으면</u> F를 쓰시오.

1　Bella's feelings are going up and down lately. ☐

2　Jenny yelled at Bella during the school play. ☐

3　Bella couldn't remember her lines on stage. ☐

4　Bella shouted at Jenny in front of others. ☐

5　Bella has known Jenny since elementary school. ☐

Day 2

Anger: I can't forgive Jenny. She didn't say a word to Bella.

Fear: Jenny didn't even look at her. Jenny has never been this cold
before.

Sadness: Bella ate alone during lunch today. Poor Bella!

Joy: Jenny is Bella's best friend. I'm sure there is a reason that we
don't know about.

Anger: I can't stand this any longer. Bella should just go and tell her
about her feelings.

Fear: I don't want Bella to be hurt again. She should let it go.

Joy: They are good friends. They will work it out.

Day 3

Joy: Whew! I'm so happy that they are talking again.

Anger: Yeah, Bella went to Jenny and talked to her first.

Joy: Jenny didn't avoid Bella on purpose.

Sadness: Yeah, Jenny didn't know a way to say sorry.

Fear: I hope Bella doesn't have any more problems like this.

Joy: Me, too. But problems are part of growing up. Just like this
time, Bella will face the problems, solve them, and become wiser
in the end.

forgive: 용서하다
alone: 홀로, 혼자
reason: 이유, 까닭
stand: 참다, 견디다
let it go: 그쯤 해 두다, 내버려 두다
work out: 해결하다
avoid: 피하다
on purpose: 고의로, 일부러
grow up: 성장하다
face a problem: 문제에 직면하다
in the end: 결국, 마침내

확인문제

● 다음 문장이 본문의 내용과 일치하면 T, 일치하지 <u>않으면</u> F를 쓰시오.

1 Jenny said nothing to Bella on the second day. ☐

2 Jenny was cold towards Bella several times. ☐

3 Anger wants Bella to go to Jenny to talk about her feelings. ☐

4 Fear thinks Bella needs to be hurt. ☐

5 Bella and Jenny finally made up. ☐

6 Fear wants Bella not to have any more problems. ☐

● 우리말을 참고하여 빈칸에 알맞은 말을 쓰시오.

1 Bella is 15 _____ _____ this year and _____ _____
her feelings are _____ _____ _____ _____.

2 Today, she _____ _____.

3 Let's listen to Bella's _____ and _____ _____.

Day 1

4 Anger: _____ _____ _____! I can't believe Jenny
_____ _____ Bella _____ the school play.

5 Sadness: Well, that's _____ Bella _____ her _____ on
stage.

6 Anger: Jenny pointed out the mistake _____ _____
_____.

7 How _____ she do that _____ _____ _____ everyone?

8 Joy: But I'm sure Jenny _____ _____ _____
_____ Bella.

9 They _____ _____ best friends _____ elementary
school. Remember?

10 Anger: That's _____ I'm _____.

11 A true friend _____ _____ _____ Bella down like that.

12 Fear: I'm worried _____ they are _____ _____
_____ _____ _____ anymore.

13 Joy: Come on, Fear. Don't go _____ _____. We'll
_____.

Day 2

14 Anger: I can't _____ Jenny. She didn't _____ _____
_____ to Bella.

15 Fear: Jenny didn't _____ _____ _____ her.

1 Bella는 올해 15세이고 요즘 그 애의 기분은 좋다가 안 좋다가 한다.

2 오늘 그 애는 우울해 보인다.

3 Bella의 감정에 귀 기울여 보고 그 이유를 알아보자.

Day 1

4 Anger: 정말 끔찍한 하루야! 학교 연극이 끝난 후 Jenny가 Bella에게 소리를 지르다니 믿을 수가 없어.

5 Sadness: 글쎄, 그건 Bella가 무대에서 그녀의 대사를 잊어버렸기 때문이잖아.

6 Anger: Jenny는 Bella가 저지른 실수를 지적했잖아.

7 어떻게 모든 사람 앞에서 그렇게 할 수가 있니?

8 Joy: 하지만 난 Jenny가 Bella에게 상처를 주려고 했던 건 아니었다고 확신해.

9 그들은 초등학교 때부터 가장 친한 친구였잖아. 기억하지?

10 Anger: 내 말이 바로 그거야.

11 진정한 친구라면 절대로 그런 식으로 Bella를 깎아내리지 않을 거야.

12 Fear: 나는 그들이 더 이상 친구로 지내지 않을까봐 걱정돼.

13 Joy: 자, Fear. 너무 극단적으로 생각하지 마. 곧 알게 되겠지.

Day 2

14 Anger: 난 Jenny를 용서할 수 없어. 그 애는 Bella에게 한마디도 말을 안 했어.

15 Fear: Jenny는 심지어 Bella를 쳐다 보지도 않았어.

16 Jenny _____ _____ _____ this cold before.

17 Sadness: Bella _____ _____ _____ lunch today. Poor Bella!

18 Joy: Jenny is Bella's _____ _____.

19 I'm sure there is a reason _____ _____ _____ _____ _____.

20 Anger: I can't _____ this _____ _____.

21 Bella should just _____ and _____ her _____ her feelings.

22 Fear: I don't want Bella _____ _____ _____ again.

23 She should _____ _____ _____.

24 Joy: They are good friends. They will _____ _____.

Day 3

25 Joy: Whew! I'm so happy _____ they _____ _____ again.

26 Anger: Yeah, Bella went to Jenny and _____ _____ _____ first.

27 Joy: Jenny didn't _____ Bella _____ _____.

28 Sadness: Yeah, Jenny didn't know _____ _____ _____ sorry.

29 Fear: I hope Bella doesn't have _____ _____ _____ like this.

30 Joy: Me, too. But problems are _____ _____ _____ _____.

31 _____ _____ this time, Bella will _____ the problems, _____ _____, and become _____ in the end.

16	Jenny가 전에 이렇게 차가웠던 적이 없었어.
17	Sadness: Bella는 오늘 점심시간에 혼자 밥을 먹었잖아. 가엾은 Bella!
18	Joy: Jenny는 Bella의 가장 친한 친구야.
19	나는 우리가 모르는 어떤 이유가 있다고 확신해.
20	Anger: 나는 더 이상 이 상황을 못 참아.
21	Bella는 일단 가서 Jenny에게 자신의 감정을 말해야 해.
22	Fear: 나는 Bella가 또다시 상처 받는 걸 원하지 않아.
23	그 애는 그냥 내버려 두어야 해.
24	Joy: 그 애들은 좋은 친구야. 그 애들이 잘 해낼 거야.

Day 3

25	Joy: 휴! 나는 그 애들이 다시 이야기하게 되어 무척 기뻐.
26	Anger: 그래, Bella가 Jenny에게 가서 그 애에게 먼저 말을 걸었지.
27	Joy: Jenny는 일부러 Bella를 피한 게 아니었어.
28	Sadness: 맞아, Jenny는 사과하는 방법을 몰랐던 거야.
29	Fear: 나는 Bella에게 이번과 같은 문제가 더 이상 없기를 바라.
30	Joy: 나도 그래. 하지만 문제들은 성장의 일부야.
31	이번과 꼭 마찬가지로 Bella는 문제들에 직면하게 될 거고, 그것들을 해결할 거고, 그리고 결국 더 현명해질 거야.

● 우리말을 참고하여 본문을 영작하시오.

1 Bella는 올해 15세이고 요즘 그 애의 기분은 좋다가 안 좋다가 한다.

➡ _____

2 오늘 그 애는 우울해 보인다.

➡ _____

3 Bella의 감정에 귀 기울여 보고 그 이유를 알아보자.

➡ _____

Day 1

4 Anger: 정말 끔찍한 하루야! 학교 연극이 끝난 후 Jenny가 Bella에게 소리를 지르다니 믿을 수가 없어.

➡ _____

5 Sadness: 글쎄, 그건 Bella가 무대에서 그녀의 대사를 잊어버렸기 때문이잖아.

➡ _____

6 Anger: Jenny는 Bella가 저지른 실수를 지적했잖아.

➡ _____

7 어떻게 모든 사람 앞에서 그렇게 할 수가 있니?

➡ _____

8 Joy: 하지만 난 Jenny가 Bella에게 상처를 주려고 했던 건 아니었다고 확신해.

➡ _____

9 그들은 초등학교 때부터 가장 친한 친구였잖아. 기억하지?

➡ _____

10 Anger: 내 말이 바로 그거야.

➡ _____

11 진정한 친구라면 절대로 그런 식으로 Bella를 깎아내리지 않을 거야.

➡ _____

12 Fear: 나는 그들이 더 이상 친구로 지내지 않을까봐 걱정돼.

➡ _____

13 Joy: 자, Fear. 너무 극단적으로 생각하지 마. 곧 알게 되겠지.

➡ _____

Day 2

14 Anger: 난 Jenny를 용서할 수 없어. 그 애는 Bella에게 한마디도 말을 안 했어.

➡ _____

15 Fear: Jenny는 심지어 Bella를 쳐다보지도 않았어.

➡ _____

16 Jenny가 전에 이렇게 차가웠던 적이 없었어.

➡ _____

17 Sadness: Bella는 오늘 점심시간에 혼자 밥을 먹었잖아. 가엾은 Bella!

➡ _____

18 Joy: Jenny는 Bella의 가장 친한 친구야.

➡ _____

19 나는 우리가 모르는 어떤 이유가 있다고 확신해.

➡ _____

20 Anger: 나는 더 이상 이 상황을 못 참아.

➡ _____

21 Bella는 일단 가서 Jenny에게 자신의 감정을 말해야 해.

➡ _____

22 Fear: 나는 Bella가 또다시 상처받는 걸 원하지 않아.

➡ _____

23 그 애는 그냥 내버려 두어야 해.

➡ _____

24 Joy: 그 애들은 좋은 친구야. 그 애들이 잘 해낼 거야.

➡ _____

Day 3

25 Joy: 휴! 나는 그 애들이 다시 이야기하게 되어 무척 기뻐.

➡ _____

26 Anger: 그래, Bella가 Jenny에게 가서 그 애에게 먼저 말을 걸었지.

➡ _____

27 Joy: Jenny는 일부러 Bella를 피한 게 아니었어.

➡ _____

28 Sadness: 맞아, Jenny는 사과하는 방법을 몰랐던 거야.

➡ _____

29 Fear: 나는 Bella에게 이번과 같은 문제가 더 이상 없기를 바라.

➡ _____

30 Joy: 나도 그래. 하지만 문제들은 성장의 일부야.

➡ _____

31 이번과 꼭 마찬가지로 Bella는 문제들에 직면하게 될 거고, 그것들을 해결할 거고, 그리고 결국 더 현명해질 거야.

➡ _____

[01~06] 다음 글을 읽고 물음에 답하시오.

Bella is 15 years old this year and these days her feelings are going up and down. Today, she looks (A)_____. Let's listen to Bella's feelings and find out why.

Day 1

Anger: What a day! I can't believe Jenny yelled at Bella after the school play.

Sadness: Well, that's because Bella forgot her lines on stage.

Anger: Jenny pointed out the mistake (B)_____ Bella made. How could she do (C)that in front of everyone?

Joy: But I'm sure Jenny did not mean to hurt Bella. They have been best friends (D)____ elementary school. Remember?

Anger: That's what I'm saying. A true friend would never put Bella down like that.

Fear: I'm worried that they are not going to be friends anymore.

Joy: Come on, Fear. Don't go too far. We'll see.

서답형

01 빈칸 (A)에 알맞은 말을 위 글에서 찾아 쓰시오.

➡ _____

02 다음 중 빈칸 (B)에 들어갈 말로 적절한 것을 모두 고르시오.

① which   ② that   ③ who
④ what   ⑤ whose

서답형

03 밑줄 친 (C)가 의미하는 것을 우리말로 쓰시오.

➡ _____

중요
04 다음 중 빈칸 (D)에 들어갈 말과 다른 말이 들어가는 것은?

① We have known you _____ you were a baby.
② I have studied English _____ 2010.
③ You have sung the same song _____ an hour.
④ They have played the computer game _____ 5 o'clock.
⑤ He has exercised regularly _____ he was in college.

05 다음 중 위 글을 읽고 답할 수 없는 것은?

① How old is Bella?
② How are Bella's feelings these days?
③ What did Jenny do to Bella today?
④ Why did Bella forget her lines on stage?
⑤ What is Joy sure about?

서답형
06 다음 질문의 답을 위 글에서 찾아 쓰시오.

> **Q:** Why did Jenny yell at Bella after the school play?

➡ _____

[07~10] 다음 글을 읽고 물음에 답하시오.

Anger: I can't forgive Jenny. She didn't say a word to Bella.

Fear: Jenny didn't even look at ⓐher. (A)Jenny has never been this cold before.

Sadness: Bella ate alone during lunch today. Poor Bella!

Joy: Jenny is ⓑher best friend. I'm sure there is a reason that we don't know about.

Anger: I can't stand this any longer. Bella should just go and tell ⓒher about ⓓ her feelings.

Fear: I don't want ⓔher to be hurt again. She should let it go.

Joy: They are good friends. They will work it out.

07 다음 중 밑줄 친 (A)에서 쓰인 현재완료와 그 쓰임이 같은 것은?

① We have just left the restaurant.
② How long have you been here?
③ Helen has never met the mailman.
④ I have lost it, so I don't know where it is.
⑤ Has he finished his project yet?

08 밑줄 친 ⓐ~ⓔ에서 지칭하는 바가 다른 하나는?

① ⓐ   ② ⓑ   ③ ⓒ   ④ ⓓ   ⑤ ⓔ

09 다음 중 위 글의 내용과 일치하지 않는 것은?

① Jenny said nothing to Bella.
② Jenny didn't look at Bella even once.
③ Anger doesn't want to bear the situation.
④ Fear thinks Bella should let Jenny go.
⑤ Joy is hopeful about Jenny and Bella.

서답형
10 다음과 같이 풀이되는 말을 위 글에서 찾아 쓰시오.

to stop being angry with someone and stop blaming

➡ _____

[11~14] 다음 글을 읽고 물음에 답하시오.

Joy: Whew! I'm so happy that they are talking again.

Anger: Yeah, Bella went to Jenny and talked to her first.

Joy: Jenny didn't avoid Bella (A)___ purpose.

Sadness: Yeah, Jenny didn't know a way to say sorry.

Fear: I hope Bella doesn't have any more problems like this.

Joy: Me, too. But problems are (B)성장의 일부. Just like this time, Bella will face the problems, solve them, and become wiser (C)in the end.

11 다음 중 빈칸 (A)에 들어갈 말과 같은 말이 들어가는 것은?

① She is not satisfied _____ the result.
② Don't give _____. You can do it.
③ She will take part _____ the race.
④ He came up _____ a great idea.
⑤ I'm cold. Can you turn _____ the heater?

서답형
12 밑줄 친 우리말 (B)를 영어로 쓰시오. (4단어)

➡ _____

13 다음 중 밑줄 친 (C)를 대신할 수 있는 것은?

① at last   ② suddenly
③ fortunately   ④ lastly
⑤ lately

서답형
14 Write the reason why Joy is so happy. Fill in the blank with six words.

➡ Joy is happy because _____
_____ .

[15~19] 다음 글을 읽고 물음에 답하시오.

Bella is 15 years old this year and these days her feelings are going up and down. Today, she looks down. Let's (A)[listen / listen to] Bella's feelings and find out why.

Day 1

Anger: What a day! I can't believe Jenny yelled at Bella after the school play.

Sadness: Well, (B)[that's because / that's why] Bella forgot her ⓐlines on stage.

Anger: Jenny pointed out the mistake that Bella made. How could she do that in front of everyone?

Joy: But I'm sure Jenny did not mean to hurt Bella. They (C)[were / have been] best friends since elementary school. Remember?

Anger: That's what I'm saying. A true friend would never put Bella down like that.

Fear: I'm worried that they are not going to be friends anymore.

Joy: Come on, Fear. Don't go too far. We'll see.

15 (A)~(C)에서 어법상 옳은 것끼리 바르게 짝지은 것은?

① listen – that's because - were
② listen – that's why – were
③ listen – that's because – have been
④ listen to – that's because – have been
⑤ listen to – that's why – have been

서답형
16 According to the passage, how does Bella feel these days?

➡ _____

서답형
17 What is Fear worried about? Answer in English with a full sentence.

➡ _____
_____

18 다음 중 밑줄 친 ⓐ를 풀이한 말로 가장 적절한 것은?

① a long thin mark which is drawn on a surface
② a line of written words, for example in a play or film
③ a long thin mark that appears on someone's skin as they grow older
④ the edge, outline, or shape of something
⑤ a row of people or things next to each other or behind each other

19 다음 중 위 글의 내용과 일치하지 않는 것은?

① Bella feels depressed today.
② Jenny shouted at Bella.
③ Joy is sure that Jenny intended to hurt Bella.
④ Jenny pointed out Bella's mistake in front of everyone.
⑤ Bella made a mistake on stage.

[20~23] 다음 글을 읽고 물음에 답하시오.

Anger: I can't forgive Jenny. She didn't say a word to Bella.

Fear: Jenny didn't even look at her. Jenny has never been this cold before.

Sadness: Bella ate alone during lunch today. Poor Bella!

Joy: Jenny is Bella's best friend. I'm sure there is a reason (A)that we don't know about.

Anger: I can't stand this any longer. Bella should just go and tell her about her feelings.

Fear: I don't want Bella to be hurt again. She should let it go.

Joy: They are good friends. They will work it out.

20 다음 중 밑줄 친 (A)와 쓰임이 <u>다른</u> 하나는?

① The cheese <u>that</u> you ate is not mine.

② People <u>that</u> participate in the game look happy.

③ The car <u>that</u> he wants to sell is a little old.

④ I will pay you back the money <u>that</u> you lent to me.

⑤ The news <u>that</u> he won first prize is true.

서답형
21 글의 내용에 맞게 빈칸에 알맞은 말을 쓰시오.

> Sadness feels sorry for Bella because
> _____ .

서답형
22 What does Anger want Bella to do about her problem? Answer in English with a full sentence.

➡ _____

_____

23 다음 중 글의 내용과 일치하는 것은?

① Fear doesn't want to bear the situation.

② Fear is afraid that Bella will be hurt again.

③ Joy thinks Bella has to find another good friend.

④ Anger is upset by the fact that Bella ate alone.

⑤ Sadness wants Bella to tell her feelings.

[24~27] 다음 글을 읽고 물음에 답하시오.

> Day 3
> Joy: Whew! I'm so ⓐhappy that they are talking again.
> Anger: Yeah, Bella went to Jenny and talked to her first.
> Joy: Jenny didn't ⓑavoid Bella on purpose.
> Sadness: Yeah, Jenny didn't know a way to say ⓒsorry.
> Fear: I hope Bella doesn't have any more problems like (A)this.
> Joy: Me, too. But problems are part of growing up. Just like this time, Bella will ⓓavoid the problems, ⓔsolve them, and become wiser in the end.

24 밑줄 친 ⓐ~ⓔ 중 글의 흐름상 <u>어색한</u> 것은?

① ⓐ　② ⓑ　③ ⓒ　④ ⓓ　⑤ ⓔ

중요
25 밑줄 친 (A)가 의미하는 것으로 가장 적절한 것은?

① Bella가 Jenny에게 화를 낸 것

② Jenny와 Bella가 서로 이야기하지 않는 것

③ Jenny가 Bella에게 사과하지 않은 것

④ Bella가 Jenny에게 먼저 다가간 것

⑤ Bella가 Jenny를 일부러 피한 것

서답형
26 글의 내용에 맞게 다음 빈칸에 알맞은 말을 쓰시오.

> According to Joy, Bella will become
> _____ by solving problems with Jenny.

서답형
27 다음은 Jenny에게 Bella가 한 말이다. 빈칸에 알맞은 말을 쓰시오.

> We _____ _____ _____ to each other for two days. Now I want to solve the problem between us.

[01~05] 다음 글을 읽고, 물음에 답하시오.

Bella is 15 years old this year and these days her feelings are going up and down. Today, she looks down. Let's listen to Bella's feelings and find out (A)why.

Day 1

Anger: What a day! I can't believe Jenny yelled at Bella after the school play.

Sadness: Well, that's because Bella forgot her lines on stage.

Anger: (B)Jenny pointed out the mistake that Bella made. How could she do that in front of everyone?

Joy: But I'm sure Jenny did not mean to hurt Bella. (C)They became best friends in elementary school. They are still best friends. Remember?

Anger: That's what I'm saying. A true friend would never put Bella down like that.

Fear: I'm worried that they are not going to be friends anymore.

Joy: Come on, Fear. Don't go too far. We'll see.

01 밑줄 친 (A)가 의미하는 것을 완전한 문장으로 쓰시오.

➡ _____

02 밑줄 친 (B)를 두 문장으로 나누어 쓰시오.

➡ _____
➡ _____

03 밑줄 친 문장 (C)를 하나의 문장으로 쓰시오.

➡ _____

04 What mistake did Bella make? Answer in English with a full sentence.

➡ _____

05 다음 물음에 완전한 문장의 영어로 답하시오.

Q: What did Jenny do to Bella after the school play?

➡ _____

[06~08] 다음 글을 읽고 물음에 답하시오.

Day 2

Anger: I can't forgive Jenny. She didn't say a word to Bella.

Fear: Jenny didn't even look at her. Jenny has never been this cold before.

Sadness: Bella ate alone during lunch today. Poor Bella!

Joy: Jenny is Bella's best friend. I'm sure there is a reason that we don't know about.

Anger: I can't stand this any longer. Bella should just go and tell her about her feelings.

Fear: I don't want Bella to be hurt again. She should let it go.

Joy: They are good friends. They will work it out.

06 What did Jenny do to Bella on the second day? Answer in English with a full sentence.

➡ _____

07 위 글의 표현을 이용하여 다음 우리말을 영어로 쓰시오.

> 나는 전에 나의 가장 친한 친구를 용서해 본 적이
> 있다.

➡ _____

08 다음 물음에 'It's because'를 사용하여 답하시오.

> Q: Why does Sadness say "Poor Bella"?

➡ _____

[09~11] 다음 글을 읽고 물음에 답하시오.

> Day 3
> Joy: Whew! I'm so happy that they are talking again.
> Anger: Yeah, Bella went to Jenny and talked to her first.
> Joy: Jenny didn't avoid Bella on purpose.
> Sadness: Yeah, Jenny didn't know a way to say sorry.
> Fear: I hope Bella doesn't have any more problems like this.
> Joy: Me, too. But problems are part of growing up. Just like this time, Bella will face the problems, solve them, and become wiser in the end.

09 다음 질문에 대한 답을 위 글의 내용에 맞게 완성하시오.

> Q: How did Bella make up with Jenny?
> A: _____,
> so they cleared up the misunderstanding.

10 다음 빈칸에 알맞은 말을 쓰시오.

> According to Joy, the problems _____
> _____ _____ help us to become
> wiser.

 11 Fill in the blank with the reason why Jenny avoided Bella.

> Jenny avoided Belly because _____
> _____.

[12~15] 다음 글을 읽고 물음에 답하시오.

> Dear Worry Doll,
> (A)_____ I'm worried about
> my terrible math grades. I (B)(have) this
> problem since last year. I want to do better in
> math. But when I try to study math, I just can't
> focus on it. (C)무엇을 해야 할지 모르겠어. I have
> not had a good night's sleep because of (D)this
> worry. Can you take my worries away?

 12 다음 두 문장을 하나의 문장으로 바꿔 빈칸 (A)에 쓰시오.

> • I want to tell you a problem.
> • I have a problem.

➡ _____

13 (B)에 주어진 동사를 어법에 맞게 고쳐 쓰시오.

➡ _____

14 to부정사를 이용하여 밑줄 친 우리말 (C)를 영어로 쓰시오.

➡ _____

15 밑줄 친 (D)가 의미하는 것을 위 글에서 찾아 쓰시오.

➡ _____

구석구석

Wrap up 1

Mr. Jones: Daisy, you're late again.

Daisy: I'm really sorry, Mr. Jones. I stayed up late again last night.

Mr. Jones: Well, I think you should try to go to bed earlier.
<u>try to</u>+동사원형: ～하려고 노력하다, cf. try ～ing: (시험 삼아) ～해 보다

You should also pack your bag the night before, so you can <u>save time in</u>
시간을 절약하다

the morning.

Daisy: Okay, Mr. Jones. I'll try your advice.

구문해설 • stay up late: 늦게까지 자지 않고 깨어 있다 • pack: (짐을) 싸다 • advice: 조언

Read & Think

Bella: Jenny, I was upset <u>when</u> you pointed out my mistake in front of <u>others</u>.
때를 나타내는 부사절 접속사   other people

But I'm sure you didn't mean to hurt my feelings.

Jenny: I'm so sorry, Bella. Thanks for <u>coming</u> up to me first.
전치사의 목적어(동명사)

구문해설 • upset: 화난 • point out: 지적하다 • mistake: 실수 • in front of: ～ 앞에서
• others: 다른 사람들 • mean to V: V을 의도하다

Think and Write

Dear Worry Doll,

I want to tell you a problem <u>that</u> I have. I'm worried about my terrible math
목적격 관계대명사

grades. I <u>have had</u> this problem <u>since</u> last year. I <u>want to</u> do better in math.
현재완료(계속)   since+특정 시점   to부정사를 목적어로 취하는 동사

But when I try to study math, I just can't focus on it. I don't know <u>what to do</u>.
무엇을 해야 할지(= what I should do)

I <u>have not had</u> a good night's sleep because of this worry. Can you take my
현재완료 부정문

worries away?

구문해설 • terrible: 끔찍한, 형편없는 • grade: 성적, 점수 • better: 더 나은 • because of: ～ 때문에
• take A away: A를 없애 주다

해석

Mr. Jones: Daisy, 너 또 지각이구나.

Daisy: Jones 선생님, 정말 죄송해요. 어젯밤에 또 늦게까지 자지 않고 깨어 있었어요.

Mr. Jones: 음, 내 생각엔 넌 더 일찍 잠자리에 들려고 노력해야 할 것 같구나. 또 전날 밤에 가방을 싸 둔다면 아침에 시간을 절약할 수 있어.

Daisy: 알겠어요, Jones 선생님. 조언해 주신 것을 해 볼게요.

Bella: Jenny야, 네가 다른 사람들 앞에서 내 잘못을 지적했을 때 화가 났었어. 그렇지만 난 네가 내게 상처를 주려고 일부러 그런 게 아니라고 믿어.

Jenny: Bella야, 미안해. 먼저 내게 와 줘서 고마워.

걱정 인형에게,

나는 너에게 내가 가진 문제를 말하고 싶어. 나는 나의 끔찍한 수학 성적이 걱정 돼. 나는 작년부터 이 문제를 가지고 있어. 나는 수학을 더 잘하고 싶어. 하지만 내가 수학을 공부하려고 하면, 나는 그것에 집중할 수 없어. 무엇을 해야 할지 모르겠어. 이 걱정 때문에 밤에 잠도 잘 못 자. 내 걱정을 없애 줄 수 있겠니?

영역별 핵심문제

01 다음 영영풀이가 가리키는 것을 고르시오.

> to stop feeling angry with somebody who has done something to harm, annoy or upset you

① give   ② forgive
③ receive   ④ fight
⑤ share

02 다음 중 밑줄 친 부분의 뜻풀이가 바르지 않은 것은?

① A bear can grow up to two meters in height. 성장하다
② I usually gain weight in winter. 체중이 늘다
③ They won the Olympic medal in the end. 결국
④ John pushed me hard on purpose. 실수로
⑤ I'll let it go this time. 내버려두다

03 다음 우리말을 주어진 단어를 이용하여 영작하시오.

(1) 너는 가까이에 있는 문제에 집중해야 한다. (hand, problem, on)

➡ _____

(2) 우리는 또 다시 문제에 직면할 수 있다. (face)

➡ _____

(3) 아이들이 요즘은 아주 빠르게 성장한다. (so, these, up, fast)

➡ _____

04 다음 짝지어진 단어의 관계가 같도록 빈칸에 알맞은 말을 쓰시오.

> wise : stupid = advanced : _____

05 다음 주어진 문장의 밑줄 친 lines와 같은 의미로 쓰인 것은?

> It is difficult for me to memorize the lines perfectly.

① The red lines refer to the main roads on the map.
② I was embarrassed when I forgot my lines.
③ I'm not good at drawing lines without a ruler.
④ I think the cable lines seem to be damaged.
⑤ I found out just dots and lines on this picture.

06 다음 문장에 공통으로 들어갈 말을 고르시오.

> • I'm sorry, but I didn't _____ it.
> • I hate the man who is _____ about money.
> • Are there any _____ s of contacting Mike?

① stand   ② mean
③ check   ④ fight
⑤ point

Conversation

[07~08] 다음 대화를 읽고 물음에 답하시오.

> Emily: I was (A)[late / lately] for class again. I just can't wake up in the morning.
>
> Tom: Do you set an alarm?
>
> Emily: Yeah, but I turn it (B)[on / off] and go back to sleep.
>
> Tom: I think you should put it (C)[close to / far from] your bed. That way, you'll have to get out of bed.

07 위 대화의 빈칸 (A)~(C)에 알맞은 말로 짝지어진 것은?

	(A)	(B)	(C)
①	late	on	close to
②	late	off	far from
③	late	off	close to
④	lately	off	far from
⑤	lately	on	close to

08 위 대화의 내용과 일치하지 <u>않는</u> 것은?

① Emily는 전에도 수업에 늦은 적이 있다.
② Emily는 아침에 일어나는 데 어려움을 겪고 있다.
③ Emily는 자명종을 잘못 맞추어 놓는다.
④ Emily는 자명종을 끄고 다시 잠든다.
⑤ Tom은 Emily에게 자명종을 침대에서 멀리 둘 것을 조언한다.

09 다음 대화의 내용과 일치하도록 Amy의 일기를 완성하시오.

> Solomon: Hello, you're on the air.
>
> Amy: Hi, Solomon. I'm Amy.
>
> Solomon: Hi, Amy. What's the matter?
>
> Amy: I hate sharing my room with my little sister. She uses my stuff without asking me first. What should I do?
>
> Solomon: Hmm.... I think you should tell her your feelings. And you should also make some rules with your sister.
>
> Amy: Oh, I'll try that. Thanks for the advice.

> Mon, 26th Aug, 2019
>
> I was upset again because my little sister used my stuff without asking me first. I didn't want to (A)_____ anymore. To solve this problem, I called Solomon and asked him to give me his (B)_____. He advised me to (C)_____.
> It was a great advice for me and I decided to try that.

10 다음 대화가 자연스럽게 이어지도록 순서대로 배열하시오.

> (A) No, not yet. I don't know what to do.
> (B) Oh, no. Did you tell your sister?
> (C) You don't look so happy today. What's the matter?
> (D) I wore my sister's favorite T-shirt. But I got grape juice on it.

➡ _____

[11~12] 다음 대화를 읽고 물음에 답하시오.

> Eric: (A) Ms. Morris, I just can't stop playing computer games. What should I do?
>
> Ms. Morris: (B) When you set a time limit, the computer shuts down at that time.
>
> Eric: (C) Oh, that's a good idea.
>
> Ms. Morris: (D) And I think you should move the computer out of your room and into the living room.
>
> Eric: (E) I think I should. Thank you for the advice, Ms. Morris.

11 위 대화의 (A)~(E) 중 주어진 문장이 들어가기에 적절한 곳은?

> Well, why don't you use a special program?

① (A)　② (B)　③ (C)　④ (D)　⑤ (E)

12 위 대화를 읽고 대답할 수 <u>없는</u> 것은?

① What's the matter with Eric?
② Why can't Eric stop playing computer games?
③ Why does Ms. Morris recommend using a special program?
④ Where will Eric move his computer?
⑤ Where does Eric use his computer?

[13~14] 다음 대화를 읽고 물음에 답하시오.

Sora: David, you look down today. What's the matter?
David: I got a haircut but it's too short. I look funny.
Sora: Take off your hat and let me see. (*pause*) Oh, it looks fine.
David: Really? I guess I'm just not used to it yet.

13 Why did David feel down?

➡ _____

14 What did Sora think about David's haircut?

➡ _____

Grammar

15 다음 중 that이 들어가기에 가장 적절한 곳은?

> The watch (①) you are looking for (②) is (③) on the table (④) in your room (⑤).

①　　②　　③　　④　　⑤

16 다음 우리말을 영어로 바르게 옮기지 <u>않은</u> 것은?

> 그들은 김 선생님이 영어를 가르친 학생들이다.

① They are the students who Mr. Kim taught English.
② They are the students to whom Mr. Kim taught English.
③ They are the students Mr. Kim taught English.
④ They are the students whom Mr. Kim taught English.
⑤ They are the students who taught Mr. Kim English.

17 다음 빈칸에 들어갈 말로 적절한 것을 <u>모두</u> 고르시오.

> The suitcase _____ she brought into this room is similar to mine.

① who　　② which　　③ that
④ whose　　⑤ whom

18 괄호 안의 단어를 바르게 배열하여 문장을 완성하시오.

> The person (about / I / most / whom / care) is not her but you.

➡ _____

19 다음 문장을 읽고 알 수 있는 것을 <u>모두</u> 고르시오.

> Jason has just come back home from his journey.

① Jason has gone on his journey.
② Jason went on a journey.
③ Jason wants to go on his journey.
④ Jason has not arrived at his home yet.
⑤ Jason is at his home now.

20 다음 중 서로 의미가 같지 <u>않은</u> 것은?

① I didn't see her. I still don't know where she is.
   → I have not seen her lately.
② Paul is the man. I work with him.
   → Paul is the man I work with.
③ I lost my umbrella. But I have it now.
   → I have lost my umbrella.
④ The coffee is too hot. June is drinking it.
   → The coffee which June is drinking is too hot.
⑤ Where is the jacket? You have had it since 2010.
   → Where is the jacket you have had since 2010?

21 다음 중 주어진 문장의 현재완료와 쓰임이 같은 것은?

> Mike <u>has visited</u> this place many times.

① Yumi <u>has</u> just <u>read</u> the book.
② He <u>has written</u> many books since 1990.
③ They <u>have watched</u> the movie for an hour.
④ Tom <u>has cleaned</u> his room already.
⑤ We <u>have been</u> to Washington.

22 다음 대화의 빈칸에 알맞은 말을 네 단어로 쓰시오.

> A: Where is Sally?
> B: Oh, _____ her home.
> A: Do you mean she is not here now?
> A: Yes.

23 다음 중 어법상 바르지 <u>않은</u> 것은?

① The bread Susan is baking smells good.
② They have noticed it more than twice until now.
③ How long have you waited for her yesterday?
④ Where are all the guests whom you invited?
⑤ Can you tell me the secret which Katherine told you?

24 다음 두 문장을 하나의 문장으로 쓰시오.

> • I will read the book.
> • I borrowed it from the library.

➡ _____

Reading

[25~28] 다음 글을 읽고 물음에 답하시오.

Bella is 15 years old this year and these days her feelings are going up and down. Today, she looks down. Let's listen to Bella's feelings and find out why.
Day 1
Anger: What a day! I can't believe Jenny yelled at Bella after the school play.
Sadness: Well, that's because Bella forgot her lines on stage.

Anger: Jenny pointed out the mistake (A)that Bella made. How could she do that in front of everyone?

Joy: But I'm sure Jenny did not mean to hurt Bella. They have been best friends since elementary school. Remember?

Anger: That's what I'm saying. A true friend would never put Bella down like that.

Fear: I'm worried that they are not going to be friends anymore.

Joy: Come on, Fear. (B)Don't go too far. We'll see.

25 다음 중 밑줄 친 (A)와 쓰임이 같은 것은?

① Do you think that he is honest?
② Jimmy believes that she stole the bag.
③ This is the man that I admire very much.
④ The fact that she is older than me doesn't matter.
⑤ How do you know that he came back?

26 다음 중 밑줄 친 (B)의 의미로 가장 적절한 것은?

① Don't go farther than I expected.
② Don't think that you can go as far as you want.
③ Bella should run away as far as possible.
④ Don't think that they are not going to be friends anymore.
⑤ Try to be nice to the friends in need.

27 According to the conversation, what did Bella forget on stage? Answer in English with a full sentence.

➡ _____

28 다음 중 위 글을 읽고 답할 수 없는 것은?

① How does Bella look today?
② Who yelled at Bella today?
③ Who pointed out Bella's mistake?
④ Who is Bella's best friend?
⑤ What is the name of the school play?

[29~31] 다음 글을 읽고 물음에 답하시오.

Joy: Whew! I'm so happy that they are talking again.

Anger: Yeah, Bella went to Jenny and talked to her first.

Joy: Jenny didn't avoid Bella (A)on purpose.

Sadness: Yeah, Jenny didn't know a way to say sorry.

Fear: I hope Bella doesn't have any more problems like this.

Joy: Me, too. But problems are part of growing up. Just like this time, Bella will face the problems, solve them, and become wiser in the end.

29 다음 중 밑줄 친 (A)를 대신하여 쓸 수 있는 것은?

① all of sudden   ② by accident
③ intentionally   ④ by mistake
⑤ immediately

30 주어진 어구를 바르게 배열하여 Bella와 Jenny가 처해 있던 문제의 결과를 쓰시오.

> Bella and Jenny / each other / with / up / finally / made

➡ _____

31 위 글의 내용과 일치하지 <u>않는</u> 것은?

① Joy feels happy because Bella is talking with Jenny again.
② It was Bella that went to Jenny and talked to her first.
③ Jenny didn't know how to say sorry.
④ Bella doesn't want to face problems like this.
⑤ Problems are part of growth.

[01~02] 다음 대화를 읽고 물음에 답하시오.

> Sujin: I don't know how to do better in math.
>   (A)_____
> Jake: How do you study for tests?
> Sujin: I just solve a lot of problems.
> Jake: Well, don't solve everything. (B)I think you should focus on the ones you got wrong.

✏️ 출제율 90%

01 위 대화의 빈칸 (A)에 들어가기에 어색한 것은?

① What should I do to improve my math?
② Would you give me some tips for me?
③ Could you tell me what to do?
④ How can I help you?
⑤ Can you give me some advice?

✏️ 출제율 95%

02 위 대화의 밑줄 친 (B)와 바꾸어 쓰기가 어색한 것은?

① Why don't you focus on the ones you got wrong?
② How about focusing on the ones you got wrong?
③ You had better focus on the ones you got wrong.
④ You need to focus on the ones you got wrong.
⑤ You don't have to focus on the ones you got wrong.

[03~05] 다음 대화를 읽고 물음에 답하시오.

> Jane: You look tired. What's the matter?
> Mike: I didn't have breakfast this morning. I'm so hungry.
> Jane: Oh, that's too bad. We still have two more hours until lunch break.
> Mike: Our school should have a snack bar. Then, we could have a quick breakfast or snacks.

> Jane: I think so, too. How can we make that suggestion?
> Mike: We can post it on the suggestion board.

✏️ 출제율 90%

03 Why doesn't Mike look good?

➡ _____

✏️ 출제율 85%

04 How long should Jane and Mike wait for lunch break?

➡ _____

✏️ 출제율 90%

05 What can Jane and Mike do if there is a snack bar in school?

➡ _____

[06~07] 다음 대화를 읽고 물음에 답하시오.

> Solomon: Hello, you're on the air.
> Amy: Hi, Solomon. I'm Amy.
> Solomon: Hi, Amy. What's the matter?
> Amy: I hate sharing my room with my little sister. She uses my stuff without asking me first. What should I do?
> Solomon: Hmm.... _____ And you should also make some rules with your sister.
> Amy: Oh, I'll try that. Thanks for the advice.

✏️ 출제율 95%

06 위 대화의 빈칸에 들어갈 말을 주어진 단어를 배열하여 완성하시오.

┌─ 보기 ─┐
feelings / you / tell / your / her / I / think / should

➡ _____

07 위 대화를 읽고 알 수 <u>없는</u> 것은?

① Why did Amy call Solomon?
② What's wrong with Amy?
③ Why didn't Amy like sharing her room with her little sister?
④ What is Solomon's advice?
⑤ How will Amy make up with her little sister?

[08~09] 다음 대화를 읽고 물음에 답하시오.

Julia: Kevin, you look so nervous. What's the matter?
Kevin: I dropped my mom's new glasses and broke them.
Julia: (A)_____ So, your mom also knows about it?
Kevin: Not yet. I can't tell her about it. What should I do?
Julia: Just tell her first before she finds out about it.

출제율 95%

08 위 대화에서 나타난 Kevin의 심경으로 적절한 것은?

① relieved   ② lonely
③ worried   ④ surprised
⑤ angry

출제율 85%

09 위 대화의 빈칸 (A)에 들어갈 말로 적절한 것을 <u>모두</u> 고르시오.

① I'm very disappointed.
② I'm sorry to hear that.
③ I can't stand it.
④ Oh, that's terrible.
⑤ What a relief!

출제율 90%

10 다음 대화가 자연스럽게 이어지도록 순서대로 배열하시오.

(A) Okay, Mr. Jones. I'll try your advice.
(B) Daisy, you're late again.
(C) Well, I think you should try to go to bed earlier. You should also pack your bag the night before, so you can save time in the morning.
(D) I'm really sorry, Mr. Jones. I stayed up late again last night.

➡ _____

출제율 100%

11 다음 중 주어진 문장에 쓰인 현재완료와 쓰임이 <u>다른</u> 것은?

They <u>have</u> not <u>passed</u> the test yet.

① There <u>has</u> just <u>been</u> a car accident.
② Nick <u>has</u> already <u>heard</u> about the news.
③ Karl <u>has</u> just <u>parked</u> his car in the parking lot.
④ Lora <u>has</u> <u>traveled</u> alone many times.
⑤ We <u>have</u> not <u>decided</u> what to do yet.

출제율 95%

12 〈보기〉와 같이 하나의 문장을 둘로 나누어 쓰시오.

┤ 보기 ├
Who is the woman whom your sister wants to talk to?
➡ Who is the woman? Your sister wants to talk to her.

(1) Where is the man who you cheered for?
➡ _____

(2) The car that Tony Stark drives in the movie is very expensive.
➡ _____
_____

13 다음 빈칸에 공통으로 들어갈 말로 가장 적절한 것은? (출제율 90%)

- This is the key _____ Christine gave to me.
- I know the boy _____ you met at a dance party.

① who   ② which   ③ whom
④ whose   ⑤ that

14 다음 중 어법상 바르지 <u>않은</u> 것은? (출제율 95%)

① The train has left already.
② That is the famous building which Antonio Gaudi built.
③ Do you know about the book that Joe is reading it?
④ When did you get the phone call?
⑤ I have not had dinner with her for a month.

15 다음 밑줄 친 부분 중 생략할 수 <u>없는</u> 것은? (출제율 95%)

① Everything <u>that</u> he told you is true.
② It is not easy to find the money <u>that</u> someone stole from you.
③ Where is the milk <u>that</u> Mom put in the refrigerator?
④ The information <u>that</u> you found is very valuable to us.
⑤ She wants me to buy a jacket <u>that</u> has many pockets.

16 다음 두 문장을 여섯 단어로 이루어진 하나의 문장으로 표현하시오. (출제율 90%)

I lost my cell phone. I still can't find it until now.

➡ _____

17 주어진 문장과 같은 의미가 되도록 빈칸에 알맞은 말을 쓰시오. (출제율 85%)

We began to see this movie two hours ago. And we still see it.
= We _____ _____ this movie _____ two hours.

[18~21] 다음 글을 읽고, 물음에 답하시오.

Day 2
Anger: I can't forgive Jenny. She didn't say a word to Bella.
Fear: Jenny didn't even look (A)[at / after] her. Jenny has never been this cold before.
Sadness: Bella ate alone (B)[while / during] lunch today. Poor Bella!
Joy: Jenny is Bella's best friend. ⓐI'm sure there is a reason that we don't know about.
Anger: I can't stand this any longer. Bella should just go and tell her about her feelings.
Fear: I don't want Bella to be hurt again. She should let it go.
Joy: They are good friends. They will (C)[work it out / work out it].

18 (A)~(C)에서 어법상 옳은 것끼리 바르게 짝지은 것은? (출제율 100%)

① at – while – work it out
② at – during – work out it
③ at – during – work it out
④ after – during – work out it
⑤ after – while – work it out

19 밑줄 친 문장 ⓐ를 두 문장으로 나누어 쓰시오. (출제율 90%)

➡ _____

➡ _____

20 다음 중 위 글의 내용과 일치하지 <u>않는</u> 것은?

① Jenny said nothing to Bella on the second day.

② Jenny has not been this cold to Bella before.

③ Bella didn't have lunch today.

④ Anger wants Bella to tell her feelings to Jenny.

⑤ Joy thinks Bella and Jenny are good friends.

21 위 글의 내용에 맞게 다음 물음에 완전한 문장의 영어로 답하시오.

Q: What does Fear want for Bella?

➡ _____

[22~24] 다음 글을 읽고 물음에 답하시오.

Day 3

Joy: Whew! I'm so happy that they are talking again.

Anger: Yeah, Bella went to Jenny and talked to her first.

Joy: Jenny didn't avoid Bella on purpose.

Sadness: Yeah, Jenny didn't know a way (A)<u>to say</u> sorry.

Fear: I hope Bella doesn't have any more problems like this.

Joy: Me, too. But problems are part of growing up. Just like this time, Bella will face the problems, solve them, and become wiser in the end.

22 다음 중 밑줄 친 (A)와 쓰임이 같은 것은?

① Tom went to the office <u>to get</u> the job.

② I want you <u>to make</u> up your mind.

③ David decided <u>to finish</u> the project.

④ I am so happy <u>to see</u> you again.

⑤ I have something <u>to talk</u> to you.

23 What does Fear hope? Answer in English with a full sentence.

➡ _____

_____

24 다음 중 위 글의 내용과 일치하지 <u>않는</u> 것은?

①Thanks to Bella's effort, Bella and Jenny were back to being friends. ② Bella told Jenny about her feelings first. ③Owing to Bella's courage, she found out that Jenny avoided her on purpose. ④She just didn't know a good way to say sorry. ⑤Bella will become wiser by solving problems like this.

①　　②　　③　　④　　⑤

[25~26] 다음 글을 읽고 물음에 답하시오.

Dear Worry Doll,

I want to tell you a problem (A)_____ I have. I'm worried about my terrible math grades. (B)_____ I want to do better in math. But when I try to study math, I just can't focus on it. I don't know what to do. I have not had a good night's sleep because of this worry. Can you take my worries away?

25 다음 중 빈칸 (A)에 들어갈 말로 적절한 것을 <u>모두</u> 고르시오.

① that　　② what　　③ who

④ which　　⑤ whom

26 다음 두 문장을 하나의 문장으로 바꿔 빈칸 (B)에 쓰시오.

I had this problem last year. I still have it.

➡ _____

[01~03] 다음 대화를 읽고 물음에 답하시오.

> Eric: Ms. Morris, I just can't stop playing computer games. (A)제가 어떻게 해야 할까요?(should)
>
> Ms. Morris: Well, why don't you use a special program? When you set a time limit, the computer shuts down at that time.
>
> Eric: Oh, that's a good idea.
>
> Ms. Morris: And I think you should move the computer out of your room and into the living room.
>
> Eric: I thinks I should. Thank you for the advice, Ms. Morris.

01 위 대화의 밑줄 친 (A)의 우리말을 주어진 단어를 사용하여 영작하시오.

➡ _____

02 What happens if Eric sets a time limit using the special program?

➡ _____

03 Where does Ms. Morris advise Eric to move the computer?

➡ _____

_____

04 다음 우리말을 영어로 각각 쓰시오.

> (1) 너는 부산에 가 본 적이 있니?
> (2) 그녀는 부산에 가고 없습니다.

➡ (1) _____

(2) _____

05 자연스러운 문장이 되도록 관계대명사를 이용하여 하나의 문장으로 바꿔 쓰시오.

> • The box is not that heavy.
> • The restaurant is crowded with people.
> • The children are very noisy.

> • Paul runs it.
> • She is lifting it.
> • I take care of them.

➡ _____

➡ _____

➡ _____

06 알맞은 질문으로 대화를 완성하시오.

> A: _____
>
> B: We have known each other for 10 years.

➡ _____

07 주어진 어구를 바르게 배열하여 다음 우리말을 영어로 쓰시오.

> Tom이 바라보고 있는 그 소녀는 Danny의 친구이다.
> (Danny's friend / is / is / looking / whom / the girl / at / Tom)

➡ _____

08 다음 우리말에 맞도록 빈칸에 알맞은 말을 네 단어로 쓰시오.

> Jimmy가 쓰고 있는 헬멧은 나의 것과 비슷해.
> = The helmet _____
>   is similar to mine.

09 다음 대화의 빈칸에 알맞은 말을 쓰시오.

> A: How long _____ your brother
>   _____ golf?
> B: He learned golf _____ he was seven
>   years old. So he _____ _____
>   golf _____ five years.

[10~14] 다음 글을 읽고 물음에 답하시오.

Bella is 15 years old this year and these days her feelings are going up and down. Today, she looks down. Let's listen to Bella's feelings and find out why.

Day 1

Anger: What a day! I can't believe Jenny yelled at Bella after the school play.

Sadness: Well, (A)that's because Bella forgot her lines on stage.

Anger: Jenny pointed out the mistake that Bella made. How could she do that in front of everyone?

Joy: But I'm sure Jenny did not mean to hurt Bella. They have been best friends since elementary school. Remember?

Anger: That's what I'm saying. (B)_____

_____

Fear: I'm worried that they are not going to be friends anymore.

Joy: Come on, Fear. Don't go too far. We'll see.

10 밑줄 친 (A)가 의미하는 것을 위 글에서 찾아 쓰시오.

➡ _____

11 주어진 어구를 바르게 배열하여 빈칸 (B)에 들어갈 말을 쓰시오.

> (that / would / down / Bella / like / never / put / a true friend)

➡ _____

12 주어진 어구를 바르게 배열하여 다음 대화를 완성하시오.

> A: Bella, why are you so upset?
> B: I am upset because _____
>   _____.
>   And she even shouted loudly.
>   (everyone / Jenny / my mistake / out / in / of / front / pointed)

13 위 글을 읽고 사건의 순서를 바르게 나열하시오.

> ⓐ Jenny yelled at Bella.
> ⓑ Bella was sad because of it.
> ⓒ Bella forgot her lines during the play.

➡ _____

14 다음 우리말에 맞게 빈칸에 알맞은 말을 7 단어로 쓰시오.

> 초등학교 때부터 알아온 Jenny는 나의 가장 친한 친구이다.
> ➡ Jenny _____
>   is my best friend.

01 다음 대화의 내용과 일치하도록 Mike의 일기를 완성하시오.

> **Jane:** You look tired. What's the matter?
>
> **Mike:** I didn't have breakfast this morning. I'm so hungry.
>
> **Jane:** Oh, that's too bad. We still have two more hours until lunch break.
>
> **Mike:** Our school should have a snack bar. Then, we could have a quick breakfast or snacks.
>
> **Jane:** I think so, too. How can we make that suggestion?
>
> **Mike:** We can post it on the suggestion board.

Mon, Sep 23rd, Sunny

I got up late and almost missed the bus. Fortunately, I wasn't late for school. But I felt so tired and hungry because (A)_____ in the morning. Even worse, I had to wait for (B)_____ for lunch break. I thought (C)_____ for hungry students. When I talked about it with Jane, she agreed with my idea. I made a plan to post my idea on (D)_____ soon.

02 주어진 어구와 현재완료 시제를 이용하여 자신과 친구에 관한 여러 가지 이야기를 써 보시오.

argue with a friend	visit one's house	have a snow fight
know him or her since	be to a concert before	

(1) _____

(2) _____

(3) _____

(4) _____

(5) _____

03 다음 Ryan의 글을 읽고 주어진 어휘를 이용하여 빈칸을 채우시오.

> Hi. I'm Ryan. My family moved to New York in 2008 and we still live in New York. I took trip to Spain in 2011 and 2012 with my family. And Cooper, our dog, became a member of our family in 2013. He likes to play with a ball. Also, I became friends with John in 2016. He is my best friend.

(1) Ryan _____ for more than ten years. (live)

(2) Ryan _____ twice. (be)

(3) Ryan _____ 2013. (raise)

(4) Ryan _____ 2016. (know each other)

단원별 모의고사

01 다음 우리말에 맞게 빈칸에 알맞은 말을 쓰시오.

(1) 저는 제안을 하고 싶습니다.
➡ I'd like to make a _____.

(2) 결코 같은 실수를 반복하지 마라.
➡ Never _____ the same mistake.

(3) 약속을 지키지 못한 걸 용서해 주세요.
➡ Please _____ me for breaking my promise.

02 다음 문장에 공통으로 들어갈 말을 고르시오. (대·소문자 무시)

- I've been busy _____ I came here.
- _____ I'm driving my car, I'll drop by your office.
- _____ when are you a member of the dance club?

① for
② at
③ because
④ from
⑤ since

03 다음 문장의 빈칸에 들어갈 말을 〈보기〉에서 골라 쓰시오.

┌─ 보기 ┤
up and down / work out / stay up late / wake up
└─

(1) Did you _____ last night?
(2) Life goes _____.
(3) I _____ early in the morning.
(4) We can _____ any problem.

04 다음 문장의 빈칸에 들어갈 말을 〈보기〉에서 골라 쓰시오.

┌─ 보기 ┤
pack / explain / fight / worry / yell
└─

(1) I'll _____ the details of this product.
(2) You should not _____ or run in the museum.
(3) You don't have to _____ about this matter. Everything will be fine.
(4) I have to _____ for my business trip.
(5) My brother and I used to _____ like cat and dog.

[05~06] 다음 대화를 읽고 물음에 답하시오.

Sora: David, you look ⓐdown today. What's the matter?

David: I got a haircut but it's too short. I look funny.

Sora: Take off your hat and let me see. (*pause*) Oh, it looks fine.

David: Really? I guess I'm just not used to it yet.

05 위 대화의 밑줄 친 ⓐdown과 같은 의미로 쓰인 것은?

① Don't look down on me.
② When I feel down, I usually listen to music.
③ You don't need to write it down.
④ I jumped down off the second floor.
⑤ Would you turn the music down?

06 위 대화의 내용과 일치하는 것은?

① Sora needed a haircut.
② The boy really likes his haircut.
③ Sora takes off her hat to show her haircut to David.
④ David doesn't feel good because of his new hairstyle.
⑤ Sora used to have a short haircut.

[07~08] 다음 대화를 읽고 물음에 답하시오.

Solomon: Hello, you're on the air.
Amy: (A) Hi, Solomon. I'm Amy.
Solomon: (B) Hi, Amy. What's the matter?
Amy: (C) She uses my stuff without asking me first. What should I do?
Solomon: (D) Hmm.... I think you should tell her your feelings. And you should also make some rules with your sister.
Amy: (E) Oh, I'll try that. Thanks for the advice.

07 위 대화의 (A)~(E) 중 주어진 문장이 들어가기에 적절한 곳은?

I hate sharing my room with my little sister.

① (A)　② (B)　③ (C)　④ (D)　⑤ (E)

08 위 대화의 내용과 일치하지 않는 것은?

① Amy is talking to Solomon face to face.
② Amy has difficulty sharing her room with her little sister.
③ Amy's sister used Amy's stuff without asking her first.
④ Solomon advises Amy to tell her feelings to her sister.
⑤ Solomon recommends making some rules with her sister to Amy.

09 다음 대화의 내용과 일치하도록 다음 표의 빈칸을 완성하시오.

Jane: You look tired. What's the matter?
Mike: I didn't have breakfast this morning. I'm so hungry.
Jane: Oh, that's too bad. We still have two more hours until lunch break.
Mike: Our school should have a snack bar. Then, we could have a quick breakfast or snacks.
Jane: I think so, too. How can we make that suggestion?
Mike: We can post it on the suggestion board.

⬇

Let's Make a Better School	
Title	Many students are hungry!
Name	Mike, Jane
Suggestion	Some students don't have (A)_____, so they get (B)_____ in the morning. We should (C)_____ _____.

[10~11] 다음 대화를 읽고 물음에 답하시오.

Mr. Jones: Daisy, you're late again.
Daisy: I'm really sorry, Mr. Jones. I stayed up late again last night.
Mr. Jones: Well, I think you should try to go to bed earlier. You should also pack your bag the night before, so you can save time in the morning.
Daisy: Okay, Mr. Jones. I'll try your advice.

10 Why is Daisy late again?

➡ _____

11 According to Mr. Jones, what should Daisy do to save time in the morning?

➡ _____

12 다음 주어진 우리말과 일치하도록 주어진 단어를 모두 배열하여 영작하시오.

(1) 나는 더 이상 그와 일하는 것을 견딜 수 없다.
(stand / him / more / working / any / I / with / can't)

➡ _____

(2) Minho는 영어로 된 대사를 외워야 한다.
(English / lines / memorize / Minho / his / to / in / has)

➡ _____

(3) 나는 그가 내 실수들을 지적했을 때 당황스러웠다.
(mistakes / he / pointed / I / my / was / when / embarrassed / out)

➡ _____

13 다음 빈칸에 알맞은 말이 바르게 짝지어진 것은?

• I have known Chris _____ I was in college.
• They have made the video _____ about three hours.

① for – for
② since – already
③ since – for
④ already – for
⑤ just – since

14 다음 우리말을 영어로 바르게 옮기지 <u>않은</u> 것은?

① 네가 어제 입은 외투는 멋져 보였어.
→ The jacket you wore yesterday looked fancy.
② 이곳에 얼마나 오랫동안 있었던 거야?
→ How long have you been here?
③ 네가 찾던 책이 여기에 있어.
→ The book you were looking for is here.
④ Tina는 그녀의 고향으로 가고 없습니다.
→ Tina has gone to her hometown.
⑤ 나는 네가 말하고 있는 사람을 알지 못해.
→ I don't know the person whom you are talking.

15 다음 중 어법상 바르지 <u>않은</u> 것은?

① There are some rules you have to keep.
② The apple juice which you drank this morning was made by my mom.
③ Ann has never worn the scarf.
④ I ate nothing since yesterday.
⑤ The music that I often listen to is very sad.

16 주어진 어구를 바르게 배열하여 다음 우리말을 영어로 쓰시오.

네가 나에게 사 주었던 그 케이크를 나는 방금 먹었어.
(me / I / for / have / bought / you / just / that / eaten / the cake)

➡ _____

17 주어진 단어를 이용하여 다음 문장을 하나의 문장으로 표현하시오.

I lost my gold necklace. I can't find it. (yet)

➡ _____

[18~20] 다음 글을 읽고 물음에 답하시오.

Bella is 15 years old this year and these days her feelings are going up and down. Today, she looks down. Let's listen to Bella's feelings and find out why.
Day 1
Anger: What a day! I can't believe Jenny yelled at Bella after the school play.
Sadness: Well, that's because Bella forgot her lines on stage.
Anger: Jenny pointed out the mistake that Bella made. How could she do that in front of everyone?

Joy: But I'm sure Jenny did not mean to hurt Bella. They have been best friends since elementary school. Remember?

Anger: That's what I'm saying. A true friend would never put Bella down like that.

Fear: I'm worried that they are not going to be friends anymore.

Joy: Come on, Fear. Don't go too far. We'll see.

18 다음은 Bella의 일기이다. 위 글의 내용과 일치하지 <u>않는</u> 것은?

①I was upset today. ②It was because of Jenny. ③She pointed out the mistake I made during the school play. ④And she even yelled at me during the play. ⑤ There were other people around us. I was so embarrassed.

①   ②   ③   ④   ⑤

19 위 글의 내용에 맞게 대화의 빈칸에 알맞은 말을 쓰시오.

A: Bella, did Jenny point out your mistake in a quiet place?

B: _____, _____. _____
_____.

20 다음 중 위 글의 내용과 일치하지 <u>않는</u> 것은?

① Bella forgot her lines on stage.

② It was Jenny that pointed out the mistake Bella made.

③ Joy believes that Jenny didn't intend to hurt Bella.

④ Jenny looks gloomy because of Bella.

⑤ Anger thinks Jenny is not Bella's true friend.

[21~23] 다음 글을 읽고 물음에 답하시오.

Day 2

Anger: I can't forgive Jenny. She didn't say a word to Bella.

Fear: Jenny didn't even look at her. Jenny has never been this cold before.

Sadness: Bella ate alone during lunch today. Poor Bella!

Joy: Jenny is Bella's best friend. I'm sure there is a reason that we don't know about.

Anger: I can't (A)_____ this any longer. Bella should just go and tell her about her feelings.

Fear: I don't want Bella to be hurt again. She should let it go.

Joy: They are good friends. They will work it out.

21 주어진 영영풀이를 참고하여 빈칸 (A)에 철자 s로 시작하는 단어를 쓰시오.

to be able to accept or deal well with a difficult situation

➡ _____

22 다음 중 둘째 날 일어난 일과 관련이 <u>없는</u> 것은?

① Jenny didn't say a word to Bella.

② Bella was cold toward Jenny.

③ Bella talked to Jenny first.

④ Bella ate lunch alone.

⑤ Jenny didn't look at Bella at all.

23 위 글의 내용에 맞게 다음 물음에 대한 답을 완성하시오.

Q: Why does Joy think Bella and Jenny will work it out?

A: Joy thinks that way because _____
_____.

INSIGHT
on the textbook

교과서 파헤치기

※ 다음 영어를 우리말로 쓰시오.

01 produce _____

02 useful _____

03 vinegar _____

04 appear _____

05 balloon _____

06 bean _____

07 car horn _____

08 drone _____

09 entire _____

10 experiment _____

11 average _____

12 hide _____

13 unbelievable _____

14 impossible _____

15 lower _____

16 application _____

17 ability _____

18 monster _____

19 record _____

20 normal _____

21 collector _____

22 scare _____

23 single _____

24 scream _____

25 electricity _____

26 amusement _____

27 explain _____

28 unlock _____

29 entire _____

30 miss _____

31 fold _____

32 activity _____

33 sore _____

34 string _____

35 a couple of _____

36 hold up _____

37 let's say that _____

38 paint over _____

39 pump up _____

40 take care of _____

41 take away _____

42 what's more _____

43 wrap ~ around _____

※ 다음 우리말을 영어로 쓰시오.

01 놀랍게도 _____

02 전체의 _____

03 무게가 ∼이다 _____

04 양 _____

05 풍선 _____

06 전기, 전류 _____

07 평균 _____

08 활동 _____

09 박람회; 공정한 _____

10 재미, 놀이 _____

11 접다 _____

12 그러나 _____

13 충고, 조언 _____

14 들어 올리다 _____

15 놓치다, 그리워하다 _____

16 아픈 _____

17 설명하다 _____

18 가능한, 있을 수 있는 _____

19 건전지, 배터리 _____

20 실 _____

21 더하다 _____

22 따다, 집다 _____

23 도전; 도전하다 _____

24 자물쇠를 열다 _____

25 반지; 울리다 _____

26 믿을 수 없는 _____

27 나타나다 _____

28 내리다, 낮추다 _____

29 기록하다 _____

30 보통의, 평범한 _____

31 괴물, 요괴 _____

32 능력 _____

33 유용한 _____

34 비명, 외침(소리) _____

35 ∼을 제거하다 _____

36 예를 들어 _____

37 ∼을 끄다 _____

38 ∼을 환하게 하다 _____

39 주입하다, 채워 넣다 _____

40 ∼의 지혜를 빌리다 _____

41 ∼가 되다 _____

42 ∼의 앞에 _____

43 ∼을 돌보다 _____

※ 다음 영영풀이에 알맞은 단어를 <보기>에서 골라 쓴 후, 우리말 뜻을 쓰시오.

1 _____ : to measure how heavy somebody/something is, usually by using scales: _____

2 _____ : a person who collects things, either as a hobby or as a job: _____

3 _____ : calculated by adding several amounts together, finding a total, and dividing the total by the number of amounts: _____

4 _____ : a new or difficult task that tests somebody's ability and skill: _____

5 _____ : that can be done or achieved: _____

6 _____ : to become frightened: _____

7 _____ : to put something together with something else so as to increase the size, number, amount, etc.: _____

8 _____ : a scientific test that is done in order to study what happens and to gain new knowledge: _____

9 _____ : a loud high cry made by somebody who is hurt, frightened, excited, etc.: _____

10 _____ : to put or keep something/somebody in a place where it cannot be seen or found: _____

11 _____ : an aircraft without a pilot, controlled from the ground: _____

12 _____ : a device that is placed inside a car engine, clock, radio, etc. and that produces the electricity that makes it work: _____

13 _____ : to raise somebody/something or be raised to a higher position or level: _____

14 _____ : to let or make something/somebody go down: _____

15 _____ : the feeling that you have when you think that something is funny: _____

16 _____ : an event at which many people gather to buy things or to get information about a product or activity: _____

보기			
amusement	lower	drone	collector
fair	scare	scream	lift
experiment	challenge	add	average
possible	weigh	battery	hide

※ 다음 우리말과 일치하도록 빈칸에 알맞은 말을 쓰시오.

Listen and Talk 1 A-1

Mike: _____ _____ are you _____, Sally?

Sally: I'm _____ the Sci-Magic show. It's a new program. _____ _____ _____ _____ _____?

Mike: No, I _____. What's it _____?

Sally: The program uses _____ _____ _____ magic tricks.

Mike: Oh, it _____ _____.

Mike: Sally, 무슨 쇼 프로그램을 보고 있니?
Sally: '과학 마술 쇼'를 보고 있어. 새로 하는 프로그램이야. 너 그것에 대해 들어 본 적 있어?
Mike: 아니, 없어. 무엇에 관한 거야?
Sally: 그 프로그램에서는 마술 묘기를 설명하기 위해 과학을 이용해.
Mike: 오, 흥미로울 것 같아.

Listen and Talk 1 A-2

Tom: Mom, _____ you _____ _____ the Chat Robot?

Mom: _____, _____ _____. What is it?

Tom: It's a _____ _____. You _____ _____ any questions and it will answer. _____ _____ _____ _____. "Emily, _____ the weather _____ today?"

Emily: "It's _____ _____ _____, so you'll _____ an umbrella."

Mom: Wow, _____ _____ _____ _____!

Tom: 엄마, Chat Robot에 관해 들어 본 적 있으세요?
Mom: 아니, 없어. 그게 뭐니?
Tom: 그건 휴대폰 앱이에요. 어떤 질문이든 물으면 그것을 대답해 줘요. 보여 드릴게요. "Emily, 오늘 날씨는 어때?"
Emily: "비가 올 예정이니까, 당신은 우산이 필요할 것입니다."
Mom: 와, 정말 멋진 앱이구나!

Listen and Talk 1 B

W: Hello, students. _____ _____ _____ _____ the DIY Drone Class? You can make your _____ _____ in the _____. The Youth Community Center _____ the class at 3 p.m. _____ _____ in May. _____ your _____ _____ and learn _____ _____ _____ _____. _____ _____ this great chance!

W: 학생 여러분, 안녕하세요. DIY 무인기(드론) 수업에 관해 들어 본 적이 있나요? 그 수업에서 여러분은 자신만의 무인기를 만들 수 있어요. 청소년 지역 문화 회관에서 5월에 수요일마다 오후 3시에 수업이 있어요. 여러분의 특별한 무인기를 만들고, 조종하는 방법을 배워 보세요. 이 좋은 기회를 놓치지 마세요.

Listen and Talk 2 A-1

Mina: You know _____? I _____ a potato clock yesterday!

Jack: A potato clock? _____ _____ _____ _____ _____?

Mina: My clock _____ _____ potatoes, _____ _____ batteries. Potatoes can produce _____.

Jack: That's _____!

Mina: 그거 알아? 나 어제 감자 시계를 만들었어!
Jack: 감자 시계? 무슨 말이야?
Mina: 내 시계는 건전지가 아니라 감자로 작동을 해. 감자로 전기를 만들 수 있거든.
Jack: 그거 흥미롭다!

Listen and Talk 2 A-2

Jimmy: Lisa, _____ _____ _____ _____ _____ _____ _____ _____ _____?

Lisa: I _____ an egg ball _____ my brother.

Jimmy: An egg ball? _____ do you _____?

Lisa: We _____ an egg _____ _____ _____ two days. Then, the egg _____ _____ a ball.

Jimmy: Wow, I _____ _____ make one, _____!

Jimmy: Lisa, 지난 주말에 뭐 했어?
Lisa: 남동생이랑 달걀 공을 만들었어.
Jimmy: 달걀 공? 무슨 말이야?
Lisa: 우리는 달걀을 이틀 동안 식초에 담가놨어. 그러면 달걀이 공으로 변해.
Jimmy: 와, 나도 하나 만들고 싶어!

Listen and Talk 2 B

Minho: Anna, _____ make a "Mystery Card" for the _____ _____.

Anna: A "Mystery Card?" _____ _____ _____ _____ _____?

Minho: It's a _____ card. It can _____ _____ _____ _____.

Anna: _____ do you _____ it?

Minho: _____ baking soda and water. Then, write a message _____ _____ _____ _____ it.

Anna: _____ _____ _____ _____ _____ _____ _____?

Minho: _____ _____ the card _____ grape juice, _____ _____ the message _____.

Minho: Anna, 우리 과학 실험으로 '미스터리 카드'를 만들자.
Anna: 미스터리 카드? 무슨 말이야?
Minho: 그건 특별한 카드야. 그 카드는 너의 메시지를 숨길 수 있어.
Anna: 어떻게 만드는데?
Minho: 베이킹 소다랑 물을 섞어. 그러고 나서 그걸로 카드 위에 메시지를 써.
Anna: 카드를 어떻게 읽을 수 있어?
Minho: 카드를 포도 주스로 칠하면 메시지가 나타나.

Communication

Jane: _____ _____ _____ _____ the Smart App Contest?

Minho: _____, _____ _____. Are you _____ _____ enter it?

Jane: Yeah, I'm _____ _____ _____ my idea _____ a Pic Gardener App.

Minho: A Pic Gardener App? _____ _____ _____ _____?

Jane: When you _____ _____ _____ _____ a plant, the app _____ you _____ _____ _____ _____ _____ _____.

Minho: It _____ _____ a very _____ app.

Jane: 너 스마트 앱 대회에 대해 들어본 적 있어?
Minho: 응, 들어 봤어. 너 거기 나갈 거야?
Jane: 응, Pic Gardener 앱에 관한 내 아이디어를 보내 보려고.
Minho: Pic Gardener 앱? 무슨 말이야?
Jane: 식물의 사진을 찍으면, 그 앱이 그 식물을 가꾸는 법을 알려 주는 거야.
Minho: 매우 유용한 앱 같아.

Wrap Up 1

Hojin: Hey, Katy. _____ you _____ _____ the science fair?

Katy: Yeah, I'm _____ _____ there.

Hojin: Me, _____! I'm _____ about doing different _____ _____.

Katy: Yeah, I'm also _____ _____ _____ it!

Hojin: 저기, Katy. 너 과학 박람회에 대해 들어 본 적 있어?
Katy: 응, 나 거기에 갈 거야.
Hojin: 나도! 난 다양한 종류의 실험들을 할 생각을 하니 신나.
Katy: 맞아, 나도 그게 정말 기대돼!

※ 다음 우리말에 맞도록 대화를 영어로 쓰시오.

Listen and Talk 1 A-1

Mike: _____

Sally: _____

_____

Mike: _____

Sally: _____

Mike: _____

Mike: Sally, 무슨 쇼 프로그램을 보고 있니?
Sally: '과학 마술 쇼'를 보고 있어. 새로 하는 프로그램이야. 너 그것에 대해 들어 본 적 있어?
Mike: 아니, 없어. 무엇에 관한 거야?
Sally: 그 프로그램에서는 마술 묘기를 설명하기 위해 과학을 이용해.
Mike: 오, 흥미로울 것 같아.

Listen and Talk 1 A-2

Tom: _____

Mom: _____

Tom: _____

_____

Emily: _____

Mom: _____

Tom: 엄마, Chat Robot에 관해 들어 본 적 있으세요?
Mom: 아니, 없어. 그게 뭐니?
Tom: 그건 휴대폰 앱이에요. 어떤 질문이든 물으면 그것을 대답해 줘요. 보여 드릴게요. "Emily, 오늘 날씨는 어때?"
Emily: "비가 올 예정이니까, 당신은 우산이 필요할 것입니다."
Mom: 와, 정말 멋진 앱이구나!

Listen and Talk 1 B

W: _____

_____

_____

_____

W: 학생 여러분, 안녕하세요. DIY 무인기(드론) 수업에 관해 들어 본 적이 있나요? 그 수업에서 여러분은 자신만의 무인기를 만들 수 있어요. 청소년 지역 문화 회관에서 5월에 수요일마다 오후 3시에 수업이 있어요. 여러분의 특별한 무인기를 만들고, 조종하는 방법을 배워 보세요. 이 좋은 기회를 놓치지 마세요.

Listen and Talk 2 A-1

Mina: _____

Jack: _____

Mina: _____

_____

Jack: _____

Mina: 그거 알아? 나 어제 감자 시계를 만들었어!
Jack: 감자 시계? 무슨 말이야?
Mina: 내 시계는 건전지가 아니라 감자로 작동을 해. 감자로 전기를 만들 수 있거든.
Jack: 그거 흥미롭다!

Listen and Talk 2 A-2

Jimmy: _____

Lisa: _____

Jimmy: _____

Lisa: _____

Jimmy: _____

Jimmy: Lisa, 지난 주말에 뭐 했어?
Lisa: 남동생이랑 달걀 공을 만들었어.
Jimmy: 달걀 공? 무슨 말이야?
Lisa: 우리는 달걀을 이틀 동안 식초에 담가놨어. 그러면 달걀이 공으로 변해.
Jimmy: 와, 나도 하나 만들고 싶어!

Listen and Talk 2 B

Minho: _____

Anna: _____

Minho: _____

Anna: _____

Minho: _____

Anna: _____

Minho: _____

Minho: Anna, 우리 과학 실험으로 '미스터리 카드'를 만들자.
Anna: 미스터리 카드? 무슨 말이야?
Minho: 그건 특별한 카드야. 그 카드는 너의 메시지를 숨길 수 있어.
Anna: 어떻게 만드는데?
Minho: 베이킹 소다랑 물을 섞어. 그러고 나서 그걸로 카드 위에 메시지를 써.
Anna: 카드를 어떻게 읽을 수 있어?
Minho: 카드를 포도 주스로 칠하면 메시지가 나타나.

Communication

Jane: _____

Minho: _____

Jane: _____

Minho: _____

Jane: _____

Minho: _____

Jane: 너 스마트 앱 대회에 대해 들어 본 적 있어?
Minho: 응, 들어 봤어. 너 거기 나갈 거야?
Jane: 응, Pic Gardener 앱에 관한 내 아이디어를 보내 보려고.
Minho: Pic Gardener 앱? 무슨 말이야?
Jane: 식물의 사진을 찍으면, 그 앱이 그 식물을 가꾸는 법을 알려 주는 거야.
Minho: 매우 유용한 앱 같아.

Wrap Up 1

Hojin: _____

Katy: _____

Hojin: _____

Katy: _____

Hojin: 저기, Katy. 너 과학 박람회에 대해 들어 본 적 있어?
Katy: 응, 나 거기에 갈 거야.
Hojin: 나도! 난 다양한 종류의 실험들을 할 생각을 하니 신나.
Katy: 맞아, 나도 그게 정말 기대돼!

※ 다음 우리말과 일치하도록 빈칸에 알맞은 것을 골라 쓰시오.

1 In _____ movies, _____ things are _____ .
A. possible   B. amazing   C. animation

2 But are they _____ possible in _____ life?
A. real   B. actually

3 _____ _____ Your Hair, Rapunzel!
A. Down   B. Let

4 In the animation, Rapunzel _____ _____ her long hair to _____ people _____ her tower.
A. in   B. let   C. lower   D. must

5 But could _____ hair really _____ up a _____ ?
A. person   B. hold   C. human

6 Surprisingly, yes! A _____ hair can hold up 100g and an _____ head has _____ 120,000 hairs.
A. about   B. average   C. single

7 _____ _____ hairs could hold up a _____ _____ elephants!
A. of   B. couple   C. those   D. all

8 _____ her hair, Rapunzel has the _____ to hold _____ a person.
A. up   B. ability   C. with

9 But she should _____ her hair _____ something strong and _____ .
A. heavy   B. around   C. wrap

10 If she _____ , she _____ get a very _____ neck.
A. sore   B. will   C. doesn't

11 We _____ _____ Energy
A. for   B. scare

12 In the animation, monsters _____ children _____ _____ energy _____ their screams.
A. from   B. to   C. scare   D. get

13 _____ , their city is _____ _____ this sound!
A. by   B. amazingly   C. powered

14 But could we actually _____ electricity to _____ _____ a city _____ sound?
A. from   B. light   C. produce   D. up

1 만화 영화에서는 놀라운 일들이 가능하다.

2 하지만 그런 일들이 실생활에서 정말 가능할까?

3 라푼젤, 네 머리카락을 내려!

4 만화 영화에서 라푼젤은 사람들이 탑에 들어오게 하기 위해서 그녀의 긴 머리카락을 내려야 한다.

5 하지만 인간의 머리카락이 정말로 사람을 들어 올릴 수 있을까?

6 놀랍게도 그렇다! 머리카락 한 가닥은 100그램의 무게를 들어 올릴 수 있고 보통 머리에는 12만 개 정도의 머리카락이 있다.

7 그 모든 머리카락은 코끼리 두 마리를 들어 올릴 수 있다!

8 라푼젤에게는 머리카락으로 사람을 들어 올릴 수 있는 능력이 있다.

9 하지만 그녀는 머리카락을 어떤 강하고 무거운 것에 감아야 한다.

10 만약 그렇게 하지 않으면 그녀는 목이 많이 아플 것이다.

11 우리는 에너지를 얻기 위해 겁을 준다

12 만화 영화에서 괴물들은 아이들의 비명에서 에너지를 얻기 위해 아이들을 겁준다.

13 놀랍게도 그들의 도시는 이 소리로 동력을 공급받는다!

14 하지만 정말 소리로부터 도시를 밝히는 전기를 만들 수 있을까?

15 Yes, sound can _____ _____ _____ electricity.

A. into　　　　B. changed　　　C. be

16 But it would not be _____ in our everyday activities _____ the _____ is too _____ .

A. small　　　B. because　　　C. helpful　　　D. amount

17 _____ _____ , the sound _____ a car horn only _____ 50mv.

A. produces　　B. for　　　　C. from　　　D. example

18 That is _____ 1/4400 of the _____ 220v of _____ in our homes.

A. electricity　　B. average　　　C. only

19 So, we would need an _____ amount of _____ to light up an _____ city.

A. entire　　　B. screams　　　C. unbelievable

20 Up, _____ and _____ !

A. Away　　　B. Up

21 The house is _____ and _____ by _____ of balloons in the animation.

A. thousands　　B. flown　　　C. lifted

22 _____ that _____ work?

A. actually　　B. could

23 _____ say that a house _____ _____ 50,000kg.

A. about　　　B. weighs　　　C. let's

24 A _____ balloon at an _____ park can _____ about 14g.

A. lift　　　　B. amusement　　C. normal

25 So we need _____ 3,570,000 balloons _____ _____ _____ the house.

A. up　　　　B. lift　　　C. to　　　D. about

26 We also _____ to think _____ the weight of the balloons _____ and the _____ .

A. themselves　B. about　　　C. strings　　　D. have

27 Then, we _____ to _____ a _____ more thousand balloons.

A. few　　　　B. add　　　C. need

28 Now, the biggest _____ is _____ up _____ _____ balloons!

A. those　　　B. pumping　　　C. all　　　D. challenge

15 그렇다. 소리는 전기로 바뀔 수 있다.

16 그렇지만 그 양이 너무 적기 때문에 그것은 우리의 일상 활동에서는 도움이 되지 않을 것이다.

17 예를 들어, 자동차 경적 소리는 겨우 50밀리볼트를 만들어 낸다.

18 그것은 우리 가정에서 사용하는 일반적인 220볼트 전기의 1/4400밖에 되지 않는다.

19 그래서 도시 전체를 밝히기 위해서는 믿기 어려운 정도로 많은 양의 비명이 필요할 것이다.

20 높이, 높이 그리고 멀리!

21 만화 영화에서 집은 수천 개의 풍선에 의해 들려 올라가고 날아간다.

22 이게 실제로 가능할까?

23 집 한 채의 무게가 5만 킬로그램 정도라고 가정해 보자.

24 놀이공원에 있는 보통의 풍선은 대략 14그램을 들어 올릴 수 있다.

25 그래서 집을 들어 올리기 위해 우리는 약 3.570.000개의 풍선이 필요하다.

26 우리는 또한 풍선 자체와 줄의 무게에 대해서도 생각해야 한다.

27 그렇게 되면. 수천 개의 풍선을 더 추가할 필요가 있다.

28 이제 가장 큰 어려움은 그 모든 풍선에 바람을 넣는 일이다!

※ 다음 우리말과 일치하도록 빈칸에 알맞은 말을 쓰시오.

1 In _____ movies, _____ _____ _____ _____ .

2 But are they _____ _____ in _____ _____ ?

3 _____ _____ Your Hair, Rapunzel!

4 _____ the animation, Rapunzel _____ _____ her long hair _____ _____ _____ _____ her tower.

5 But _____ human hair really _____ _____ _____ _____ ?

6 _____ , yes! A _____ hair can _____ _____ 100g and an _____ head _____ _____ 120,000 hairs.

7 _____ _____ could _____ _____ a couple of elephants!

8 _____ _____ _____ , Rapunzel has _____ _____ _____ _____ _____ a person.

9 But she should _____ _____ _____ _____ something _____ and _____ .

10 If she _____ , she _____ _____ a very _____ _____ .

11 We _____ _____ Energy

12 In the animation, monsters _____ _____ _____ _____ energy _____ _____ _____ .

13 _____ , their city _____ _____ _____ this sound!

14 But _____ we actually _____ _____ _____ _____ _____ a city _____ sound?

1 만화 영화에서는 놀라운 일들이 가능하다.

2 하지만 그런 일들이 실생활에서 정말 가능할까?

3 라푼젤, 네 머리카락을 내려!

4 만화 영화에서 라푼젤은 사람들이 탑에 들어오게 하기 위해서 그녀의 긴 머리카락을 내려야 한다.

5 하지만 인간의 머리카락이 정말로 사람을 들어 올릴 수 있을까?

6 놀랍게도 그렇다! 머리카락 한 가닥은 100그램의 무게를 들어 올릴 수 있고 보통 머리에는 12만 개 정도의 머리카락이 있다.

7 그 모든 머리카락은 코끼리 두 마리를 들어 올릴 수 있다!

8 라푼젤에게는 머리카락으로 사람을 들어 올릴 수 있는 능력이 있다.

9 하지만 그녀는 머리카락을 어떤 강하고 무거운 것에 감아야 한다.

10 만약 그렇게 하지 않으면 그녀는 목이 많이 아플 것이다.

11 우리는 에너지를 얻기 위해 겁을 준다

12 만화 영화에서 괴물들은 아이들의 비명에서 에너지를 얻기 위해 아이들을 겁준다.

13 놀랍게도 그들의 도시는 이 소리로 동력을 공급받는다!

14 하지만 정말 소리로부터 도시를 밝히는 전기를 만들 수 있을까?

15 Yes, sound can _____ _____ _____ _____ .

16 But it _____ _____ be _____ _____ our everyday activities _____ _____ _____ _____ too _____ .

17 _____ _____ , the sound _____ a _____ _____ only _____ 50mv.

18 That is only 1/4400 _____ _____ 220v of _____ _____ _____ _____ .

19 So, we would need _____ _____ _____ _____ to _____ _____ an _____ city.

20 _____ , _____ and _____ !

21 The house _____ _____ _____ _____ by _____ _____ _____ in the animation.

22 _____ that _____ _____ ?

23 _____ _____ that a house _____ _____ 50,000kg.

24 A _____ balloon at _____ _____ _____ can _____ _____ 14g.

25 So we _____ _____ 3,570,000 balloons _____ _____ _____ the house.

26 We also _____ _____ _____ _____ the _____ of the balloons _____ and the _____ .

27 Then, we need to _____ _____ _____ _____ balloons.

28 Now, the _____ _____ is _____ _____ _____ _____ balloons!

15 그렇다. 소리는 전기로 바뀔 수 있다.

16 그렇지만 그 양이 너무 적기 때문에 그것은 우리의 일상 활동에서는 도움이 되지 않을 것이다.

17 예를 들어. 자동차 경적 소리는 겨우 50밀리볼트를 만들어 낸다.

18 그것은 우리 가정에서 사용하는 일반적인 220볼트 전기의 1/4400밖에 되지 않는다.

19 그래서 도시 전체를 밝히기 위해서는 믿기 어려운 정도로 많은 양의 비명이 필요할 것이다.

20 높이, 높이 그리고 멀리!

21 만화 영화에서 집은 수천 개의 풍선에 의해 들려 올라가고 날아간다.

22 이게 실제로 가능할까?

23 집 한 채의 무게가 5만 킬로그램 정도라고 가정해 보자.

24 놀이공원에 있는 보통의 풍선은 대략 14그램을 들어 올릴 수 있다.

25 그래서 집을 들어 올리기 위해 우리는 약 3,570,000개의 풍선이 필요하다.

26 우리는 또한 풍선 자체와 줄의 무게에 대해서도 생각해야 한다.

27 그렇게 되면, 수천 개의 풍선을 더 추가할 필요가 있다.

28 이제 가장 큰 어려움은 그 모든 풍선에 바람을 넣는 일이다!

※ 다음 문장을 우리말로 쓰시오.

1 In animation movies, amazing things are possible.

➡ _____

2 But are they actually possible in real life?

➡ _____

3 Let Down Your Hair, Rapunzel!

➡ _____

4 In the animation, Rapunzel must lower her long hair to let people in her tower.

➡ _____

5 But could human hair really hold up a person?

➡ _____

6 Surprisingly, yes! A single hair can hold up 100g and an average head has about 120,000 hairs.

➡ _____

7 All those hairs could hold up a couple of elephants!

➡ _____

8 With her hair, Rapunzel has the ability to hold up a person.

➡ _____

9 But she should wrap her hair around something strong and heavy.

➡ _____

10 If she doesn't, she will get a very sore neck.

➡ _____

11 We Scare for Energy

➡ _____

12 In the animation, monsters scare children to get energy from their screams.

➡ _____

13 Amazingly, their city is powered by this sound!

➡ _____

14 But could we actually produce electricity to light up a city from sound?

➡ _____

15 ► Yes, sound can be changed into electricity.

➡ _____

16 ► But it would not be helpful in our everyday activities because the amount is too small.

➡ _____

17 ► For example, the sound from a car horn only produces 50mv.

➡ _____

18 ► That is only 1/4400 of the average 220v of electricity in our homes.

➡ _____

19 ► So, we would need an unbelievable amount of screams to light up an entire city.

➡ _____

20 ► Up, Up and Away!

➡ _____

21 ► The house is lifted and flown by thousands of balloons in the animation.

➡ _____

22 ► Could that actually work?

➡ _____

23 ► Let's say that a house weighs about 50,000kg.

➡ _____

24 ► A normal balloon at an amusement park can lift about 14g.

➡ _____

25 ► So we need about 3,570,000 balloons to lift up the house.

➡ _____

26 ► We also have to think about the weight of the balloons themselves and the strings.

➡ _____

27 ► Then, we need to add a few more thousand balloons.

➡ _____

28 ► Now, the biggest challenge is pumping up all those balloons!

➡ _____

Step4

※ 다음 괄호 안의 단어들을 우리말에 맞도록 바르게 배열하시오.

1 (movies, / animation / in / things / are / possible. / amazing)

➡ _____

2 (are / but / actually / they / in / possible / life? / real)

➡ _____

3 (Down / Let / Hair, / Your / Rapunzel!)

➡ _____

4 (the / animation, / in / Rapunzel / lower / must / long / her / hair / people / let / to / tower. / her / in)

➡ _____

5 (but / human / could / really / hair / up / hold / person? / a)

➡ _____

6 (surprisingly, / yes! / a / hair / single / hold / can / 100g / up / and / an / head / average / has / hairs. / 120,000 / about)

➡ _____

7 (those / all / hairs / hold / could / up / couple / a / elephants! / of)

➡ _____

8 (hair, / with / her / Rapunzel / the / has / a / ability / hold / to / person. / up)

➡ _____

9 (but / she / wrap / should / hair / her / something / around / heavy. / and / strong)

➡ _____

10 (she / doesn't, / if / she / get / will / sore / a / neck. / very)

➡ _____

11 (for / Scare / we / Energy)

➡ _____

12 (the / in / animation, / scare / monsters / to / children / energy / got / screams. / their / from)

➡ _____

13 (amazingly, / city / their / powered / this / is / sound! / by)

➡ _____

14 (but / we / could / produce / actually / to / electricity / up / light / sound? / from / a / city)

➡ _____

---

1 만화 영화에서는 놀라운 일들이 가능하다.

2 하지만 그런 일들이 실생활에서 정말 가능할까?

3 라푼젤. 네 머리카락을 내려!

4 만화 영화에서 라푼젤은 사람들이 탑에 들어오게 하기 위해서 그녀의 긴 머리카락을 내려야 한다.

5 하지만 인간의 머리카락이 정말로 사람을 들어 올릴 수 있을까?

6 놀랍게도 그렇다! 머리카락 한 가닥은 100그램의 무게를 들어 올릴 수 있고 보통 머리에는 12만 개 정도의 머리카락이 있다.

7 그 모든 머리카락은 코끼리 두 마리를 들어 올릴 수 있다!

8 라푼젤에게는 머리카락으로 사람을 들어 올릴 수 있는 능력이 있다.

9 하지만 그녀는 머리카락을 어떤 강하고 무거운 것에 감아야 한다.

10 만약 그렇게 하지 않으면 그녀는 목이 많이 아플 것이다.

11 우리는 에너지를 얻기 위해 겁을 준다

12 만화 영화에서 괴물들은 아이들의 비명에서 에너지를 얻기 위해 아이들을 겁준다.

13 놀랍게도 그들의 도시는 이 소리로 동력을 공급받는다!

14 하지만 정말 소리로부터 도시를 밝히는 전기를 만들 수 있을까?

15 (yes, / can / sound / be / electricity. / into / changed)
➡ _____

16 (but / it / be / not / would / helpful / our / in / everyday / activities / the / because / amount / too / small. / is)
➡ _____
_____

17 (example, / for / sound / the / from / car / a / horn / 50mv. / produces / only)
➡ _____

18 (is / that / 1/4400 / only / of / average / the / 220v / electricity / of / homes. / in / our)
➡ _____

19 (so, / we / need / would / an / amount / unbelievable / screams / of / light / up / to / city. / entire / an)
➡ _____

20 (Away! / Up / and / Up,)
➡ _____

21 (house / the / lifted / is / and / flown / thousands / by / balloons / of / the / animation. / in)
➡ _____

22 (that / could / work? / actually)
➡ _____

23 (say / let's / that / house / a / weighs / 50,000kg. / about)
➡ _____

24 (normal / a / balloon / at / amusement / an / park / lift / can / 14g. / about)
➡ _____

25 (so / need / we / 3,570,000 / about / balloons / lift / to / up / house. / the)
➡ _____

26 (we / have / also / think / to / the / about / weight / of / balloons / the / themselves / strings. / the / and)
➡ _____
_____

27 (then, / need / we / add / to / a / more / few / balloons. / thousand)
➡ _____

28 (now, / biggest / the / challenge / is / up / pumping / balloons! / those / all)
➡ _____

15 그렇다. 소리는 전기로 바뀔 수 있다.

16 그렇지만 그 양이 너무 적기 때문에 그것은 우리의 일상 활동에서는 도움이 되지 않을 것이다.

17 예를 들어, 자동차 경적 소리는 겨우 50밀리볼트를 만들어 낸다.

18 그것은 우리 가정에서 사용하는 일반적인 220볼트 전기의 1/4400밖에 되지 않는다.

19 그래서 도시 전체를 밝히기 위해서는 믿기 어려운 정도로 많은 양의 비명이 필요할 것이다.

20 높이, 높이 그리고 멀리!

21 만화 영화에서 집은 수천 개의 풍선에 의해 들려 올라가고 날아간다.

22 이게 실제로 가능할까?

23 집 한 채의 무게가 5만 킬로그램 정도라고 가정해 보자.

24 놀이공원에 있는 보통의 풍선은 대략 14그램을 들어 올릴 수 있다.

25 그래서 집을 들어 올리기 위해 우리는 약 3.570.000개의 풍선이 필요하다.

26 우리는 또한 풍선 자체와 줄의 무게에 대해서도 생각해야 한다.

27 그렇게 되면, 수천 개의 풍선을 더 추가할 필요가 있다.

28 이제 가장 큰 어려움은 그 모든 풍선에 바람을 넣는 일이다!

※ 다음 우리말을 영어로 쓰시오.

1 만화 영화에서는 놀라운 일들이 가능하다.

➡ _____

2 하지만 그런 일들이 실생활에서 정말 가능할까?

➡ _____

3 라푼젤, 네 머리카락을 내려!

➡ _____

4 만화 영화에서 라푼젤은 사람들이 탑에 들어오게 하기 위해서 그녀의 긴 머리카락을 내려야 한다.

➡ _____

5 하지만 인간의 머리카락이 정말로 사람을 들어 올릴 수 있을까?

➡ _____

6 놀랍게도 그렇다! 머리카락 한 가닥은 100그램의 무게를 들어 올릴 수 있고 보통 머리에는 12만 개 정도의 머리카락이 있다.

➡ _____

7 그 모든 머리카락은 코끼리 두 마리를 들어 올릴 수 있다!

➡ _____

8 라푼젤에게는 머리카락으로 사람을 들어 올릴 수 있는 능력이 있다.

➡ _____

9 하지만 그녀는 머리카락을 어떤 강하고 무거운 것에 감아야 한다.

➡ _____

10 만약 그렇게 하지 않으면 그녀는 목이 많이 아플 것이다.

➡ _____

11 우리는 에너지를 얻기 위해 겁을 준다

➡ _____

12 만화 영화에서 괴물들은 아이들의 비명에서 에너지를 얻기 위해 아이들을 겁준다.

➡ _____

13 놀랍게도 그들의 도시는 이 소리로 동력을 공급받는다!

➡ _____

14 하지만 정말 소리로부터 도시를 밝히는 전기를 만들 수 있을까?

➡ _____

15 그렇다. 소리는 전기로 바뀔 수 있다.

➡ _____

16 그렇지만 그 양이 너무 적기 때문에 그것은 우리의 일상 활동에서는 도움이 되지 않을 것이다.

➡ _____

17 예를 들어, 자동차 경적 소리는 겨우 50밀리볼트를 만들어 낸다.

➡ _____

18 그것은 우리 가정에서 사용하는 일반적인 220볼트 전기의 1/4400밖에 되지 않는다.

➡ _____

19 그래서 도시 전체를 밝히기 위해서는 믿기 어려운 정도로 많은 양의 비명이 필요할 것이다.

➡ _____

20 높이, 높이 그리고 멀리!

➡ _____

21 만화 영화에서 집은 수천 개의 풍선에 의해 들려 올라가고 날아간다.

➡ _____

22 이게 실제로 가능할까?

➡ _____

23 집 한 채의 무게가 5만 킬로그램 정도라고 가정해 보자.

➡ _____

24 놀이공원에 있는 보통의 풍선은 대략 14그램을 들어 올릴 수 있다.

➡ _____

25 그래서 집을 들어 올리기 위해 우리는 약 3,570,000개의 풍선이 필요하다.

➡ _____

26 우리는 또한 풍선 자체와 줄의 무게에 대해서도 생각해야 한다.

➡ _____

27 그렇게 되면, 수천 개의 풍선을 더 추가할 필요가 있다.

➡ _____

28 이제 가장 큰 어려움은 그 모든 풍선에 바람을 넣는 일이다!

➡ _____

※ 다음 우리말과 일치하도록 빈칸에 알맞은 말을 쓰시오.

Grammar in Real Life

1. This is Jack's _____ _____ this week.

2. There is _____ _____ _____ work to do.

3. He needs _____ _____ to the library _____ Monday.

4. He has two books _____ _____ from the library.

5. Also he has _____ _____ to finish _____ Thursday.

6. _____ Friday, he will be in the school _____ _____.

7. So, he will _____ _____ the songs at the _____ _____ all this week.

1. 이것은 Jack의 이번 주 계획이다.
2. 할 일이 많이 있다.
3. 그는 월요일에 도서관에 가야 한다.
4. 그는 도서관에서 빌려야 할 책 두 권이 있다.
5. 또한, 그는 목요일까지 끝내야 할 과학 숙제가 있다.
6. 금요일에 그는 학교 장기 자랑 대회에 나갈 것이다.
7. 그래서 그는 이번 주 내내 장기 자랑 대회에서 공연할 노래들을 연습할 것이다.

Think & Write

1. Hello, _____ _____ is June.

2. Today _____ _____ to _____ _____ my new _____ technology, SuperEye.

3. It is _____ _____ _____ pictures and video-record.

4. It is also useful to _____ _____ _____ _____.

5. _____ _____ _____ and experience a new world!

1. 안녕, 내 이름은 June이야.
2. 오늘 나는 나의 새로운 착용 가능한 기술인 SuperEye에 관해 말하고 싶어.
3. 그것은 사진을 찍거나 녹화를 하는 데 유용해.
4. 또한 나에게 지도를 보여 주는 데도 유용해.
5. 한 번 사용해 보고 새로운 세계를 경험해 봐!

Wrap Up 3

1. Amy: _____ _____ _____ about the _____ event at the _____ _____?

2. Brian: No, I _____. What's the event?

3. Amy: _____ _____ science magic shows _____ the weekend, but _____ _____ this month.

4. Brian: Oh, _____ you _____ the information. I'll visit _____ this weekend.

1. Amy: 너는 과학 박물관에서 하는 특별 이벤트에 대해 들어 본 적 있어?
2. Brian: 아니, 없어. 어떤 이벤트야?
3. Amy: 주말 동안 과학 마술쇼가 있는데, 이번 달에만 있대.
4. Brian: 오, 정보 고마워. 이번 주말에 방문해야겠어.

※ 다음 우리말을 영어로 쓰시오.

Grammar in Real Life

1. 이것은 Jack의 이번 주 계획이다.
   ➡ _____

2. 할 일이 많이 있다.
   ➡ _____

3. 그는 월요일에 도서관에 가야 한다.
   ➡ _____

4. 그는 도서관에서 빌려야 할 책 두 권이 있다.
   ➡ _____

5. 또한, 그는 목요일까지 끝내야 할 과학 숙제가 있다.
   ➡ _____

6. 금요일에 그는 학교 장기 자랑 대회에 나갈 것이다.
   ➡ _____

7. 그래서 그는 이번 주 내내 장기 자랑 대회에서 공연할 노래들을 연습할 것이다.
   ➡ _____

Think & Write

1. 안녕, 내 이름은 June이야.
   ➡ _____

2. 오늘 나는 나의 새로운 착용 가능한 기술인 SuperEye에 관해 말하고 싶어.
   ➡ _____

3. 그것은 사진을 찍거나 녹화를 하는 데 유용해.
   ➡ _____

4. 또한 나에게 지도를 보여 주는 데도 유용해.
   ➡ _____

5. 한 번 사용해 보고 새로운 세계를 경험해 봐!
   ➡ _____

Wrap Up 3

1. Amy: 너는 과학 박물관에서 하는 특별 이벤트에 대해 들어 본 적 있어?
   ➡ _____

2. Brian: 아니, 없어. 어떤 이벤트야?
   ➡ _____

3. Amy: 주말 동안 과학 마술쇼가 있는데, 이번 달에만 있대.
   ➡ _____

4. Brian: 오, 정보 고마워. 이번 주말에 방문해야겠어.
   ➡ _____

※ 다음 영어를 우리말로 쓰시오.

01	amazing		22	deep
02	terrible		23	crowded
03	voice		24	memorable
04	place		25	seafood
05	engine		26	rush
06	block		27	beat
07	excitedly		28	complete
08	cheer		29	finish line
09	close match		30	crowd
10	local		31	pitcher
11	gas pedal		32	fix
12	hit		33	ahead
13	lap		34	press
14	loud		35	take a chance
15	official		36	sit up
16	punch		37	miss a chance
17	hang		38	be satisfied with
18	straightaway		39	cheer up
19	three-pointer		40	be filled with
20	kick		41	do one's best
21	count		42	keep up with
			43	out of one's reach

※ 다음 우리말을 영어로 쓰시오.

01 뛰다, 치다 _____

02 중요하다, (수를) 세다 _____

03 앞에, 앞선 _____

04 배구 _____

05 경주로, 트랙 _____

06 투구 _____

07 결승선 _____

08 기, 깃발 _____

09 해산물 _____

10 깊은 _____

11 완성하다; 완전한 _____

12 수리하다, 고정시키다 _____

13 복잡한, 붐비는 _____

14 기억할 만한 _____

15 소형 경주용 자동차 _____

16 군중, 관객 _____

17 돌진하다 _____

18 투수 _____

19 눈물 _____

20 누르다, 밀어붙이다 _____

21 무서운, 심한 _____

22 갈채를 보내다 _____

23 흥분하여, 기를 쓰고 _____

24 목소리 _____

25 아슬아슬한 승부, 접전 _____

26 막다, 방해하다 _____

27 3점슛 _____

28 매달다, 걸다 _____

29 타격 _____

30 시끄러운, (소리가) 큰 _____

31 놀랄 정도의, 굉장한 _____

32 일직선의, 즉시의 _____

33 지방의 _____

34 (경주, 대회 등의) 등위 _____

35 ~에 만족하다 _____

36 기운을 내다 _____

37 최선을 다하다 _____

38 경주에 이기다 _____

39 ~로 가득 차다 _____

40 ~에 뒤떨어지지 않다 _____

41 기회를 놓치다 _____

42 자세를 바로 하다, 바로 앉다 _____

43 (모험 삼아) 해 보다 _____

※ 다음 영영풀이에 알맞은 단어를 <보기>에서 골라 쓴 후, 우리말 뜻을 쓰시오.

1 _____ : a small motor vehicle used for racing: _____

2 _____ : to have value or importance: _____

3 _____ : to finish making or doing something: _____

4 _____ : to hit somebody/something with your foot: _____

5 _____ : the player who throws the ball to the batter: _____

6 _____ : a drop of liquid that comes out of your eye when you cry: _____

7 _____ : a piece of ground with a special surface for people, cars, etc. to have races on: _____

8 _____ : fish and shellfish that live in the ocean and are used for food: _____

9 _____ : the sound or sounds produced through the mouth by a person speaking or singing: _____

10 _____ : the part of a vehicle that produces power to make the vehicle move: _____

11 _____ : a game in which two teams of players hit a large ball back and forth over a high net: _____

12 _____ : special, good or unusual and therefore worth remembering or easy to remember: _____

13 _____ : to shout loudly, to show support or praise for somebody, or to give them encouragement: _____

14 _____ : to stop somebody from going somewhere or seeing something by standing in front of them or in their way: _____

15 _____ : a large number of people gathered together in a public place, for example in the streets or at a sports game: _____

16 _____ : the line across a sports track, etc. that marks the end of a race: _____

보기

crowd	count	finish line	track
cheer	tear	pitcher	seafood
voice	memorable	complete	kart
block	kick	volleyball	engine

※ 다음 우리말과 일치하도록 빈칸에 알맞은 말을 쓰시오.

Listen & Talk 1 A-1

Mom: David, _____ was your _____ _____ today?

David: We _____, Mom. I _____ too many _____ for a _____ - _____.

Mom: Oh, _____ _____ _____ _____ on yourself. _____ _____ _____ next time.

David: I _____ _____.

Mom: David, 오늘 너희 농구 경기는 어땠니?
David: 저희가 졌어요, 엄마. 제가 3점 슛을 할 기회를 너무 많이 놓쳤어요.
Mom: 오, 너무 자책하지 마. 다음번에는 더 잘할 거야.
David: 저도 그러길 바라요.

Listen & Talk 1 A-2

Jack: Did you come and watch my _____ _____ yesterday?

Irene: Yeah, I did. That was a great volleyball match. _____ _____!

Jack: Thanks, _____ it was a _____ _____. My serves _____ _____ _____ _____.

Irene: Oh, _____ _____ _____ _____. You'll _____ _____ next time.

Jack: 어제 내 배구 시합 보러 왔어?
Irene: 응, 그랬어. 정말 멋진 배구 시합이었어. 너 정말 잘했어!
Jack: 고마워. 하지만 아슬아슬한 시합이었어. 내 서브는 충분히 강하지 않았어.
Irene: 오, 너는 훌륭한 선수야. 다음번에는 더 잘할 거야.

Listen & Talk 1 B

Emily: I _____ your baseball team, the Reds, _____ _____ _____. _____ _____ _____, right? _____, John!

John: Thanks. It was _____ _____ _____. I'm _____ _____ _____ my _____.

Emily: _____ do you _____ that?

John: I _____ _____ _____.

Emily: Oh, _____ _____ _____ _____. You'll _____ _____ next time.

Emily: 나는 너희 the Reds 야구팀이 시합에서 이겼다고 들었어. 8 대 7이 맞니? 축하해, John!
John: 고마워. 정말 접전이었어. 나는 내 투구에 만족스럽지 않아.
Emily: 왜 그렇게 말하는 거야?
John: 홈런 두 개를 허용했거든.
Emily: 오, 너는 훌륭한 투수야. 다음번에는 더 잘할 거야.

Listen & Talk 2 A-1

Mike: Is it your _____ _____ _____ a bike, Mina?

Mina: Yes, it is. I just _____ _____ _____ _____.

Mike: _____ _____ _____ you. I'll _____ your bike.

Mina: Thanks, Mike. _____ _____ go, okay?

Mike: Don't worry. _____ _____ and _____ _____ _____.

Mike: 미나야, 자전거 처음 타는 거야?
Mina: 응. 균형을 잘 못 잡겠어.
Mike: 내가 도와줄게. 네 자전거를 잡아 줄게.
Mina: 고마워, Mike. 놓으면 안 돼, 알았지?
Mike: 걱정 마. 앉아서 앞을 똑바로 봐.

Listen & Talk 2 A-1

Tom: What _____ you _____, Sarah?

Sarah: I learned _____ _____ _____ _____ _____

_____ in PE class. So I'm _____ it now but it's _____ _____.

Tom: _____ _____ _____ _____. _____ your legs in the

air again. I'll _____ _____.

Sarah: Oh, thanks. I'll _____ _____.

Tom: Sarah, 뭐 하고 있어?
Sarah: 체육 시간에 물구나무 서는 법을 배웠거든. 그래서 지금 한번 해 보고 있는데, 쉽지 않네.
Tom: 내가 도와줄게. 다리를 공중에 차 올려봐. 내가 널 붙잡을게.
Sarah: 오, 고마워. 다시 해 볼게.

Listen & Talk 2 B

Coach: Hey, Brian. _____ you _____ the *taegwondo* side kick?

Brian: Yes, Coach. But _____ _____ _____ _____ _____

_____.

Coach: _____ _____ are you _____?

Brian: Well, I _____ _____ _____ _____ _____ _____.

Coach: I see. _____ _____ help you. I'll _____ this kick pad

for you. _____ me your _____ _____.

Coach: 저기, Brian. 태권도 옆 차기 연습했니?
Brian: 네, 코치님. 그런데 여전히 편하게 잘 안 돼요.
Coach: 어떤 문제가 있어?
Brian: 음, 다리를 충분히 높이 들어 올릴 수가 없어요.
Coach: 알겠다. 내가 도와줄게. 너를 위해 이 킥 패드를 잡아줄게. 너의 옆 차기를 보여주렴.

Communication

Megan: I'm _____ _____ _____ next soccer match, James.

James: _____ _____ you _____, Megan?

Megan: Well, I _____ _____ _____ _____ in the last soccer

match. I _____ _____ too many goals.

James: I see. Here, _____ _____ _____ _____. I'll _____

_____ _____ to you.

Megan: Oh, that'll really help. I hope _____ _____

_____.

James: _____ _____. You'll _____ _____ next time.

Megan: James, 나는 다음 축구 시합이 걱정돼.
James: 왜 걱정하는 거야, Megan?
Megan: 음, 지난 축구 시합에서 나는 높은 공을 잡지 못했어. 너무 많은 골을 허용했어.
James: 알겠어. 자, 내가 도와줄게. 너에게 공을 높이 차 줄게.
Megan: 오, 그거 도움이 많이 되겠다. 내 기술이 나아지길 바라.
James: 걱정 마. 다음번에는 더 잘할 거야.

Wrap Up 1

Anna: Hi, Jake. _____ _____ _____ _____ the pool often?

Jake: Oh, hi, Anna. I _____ _____ _____ _____ here _____

_____ _____.

Anna: _____ did you _____ _____ _____ _____?

Jake: _____ _____. But swimming is still not _____ _____

_____.

Anna: Oh, _____ _____ _____ you. I teach children _____

_____ _____ in the school club.

Jake: Oh, _____ _____ _____ _____ _____. Thanks.

Anna: 안녕, Jake. 너는 종종 수영장에 오니?
Jake: 오, 안녕, Anna. 나는 여기에서 일주일에 한 번 수영 수업을 들어.
Anna: 언제부터 수업을 시작했어?
Jake: 지난달부터. 그런데 수영은 여전히 나에게 쉽지 않아.
Anna: 오, 내가 도와줄게. 나는 학교 동아리에서 아이들에게 수영하는 법을 가르쳐 주거든.
Jake: 오, 그거 나에게 도움이 많이 되겠다. 고마워.

※ 다음 우리말에 맞도록 대화를 영어로 쓰시오.

Listen & Talk 1 A-1

Mom: _____

David: _____

Mom: _____

David: _____

Mom: David, 오늘 너희 농구 경기는 어땠니?
David: 저희가 졌어요, 엄마. 제가 3점 숏을 할 기회를 너무 많이 놓쳤어요.
Mom: 오, 너무 자책하지 마. 다음번에는 더 잘할 거야.
David: 저도 그러길 바라요.

Listen & Talk 1 A-2

Jack: _____

Irene: _____

Jack: _____

Irene: _____

Jack: 어제 내 배구 시합 보러 왔어?
Irene: 응, 그랬어. 정말 멋진 배구 시합이었어. 너 정말 잘했어!
Jack: 고마워. 하지만 아슬아슬한 시합이었어. 내 서브는 충분히 강하지 않았어.
Irene: 오, 너는 훌륭한 선수야. 다음번에는 더 잘할 거야.

Listen & Talk 1 B

Emily: _____

_____

John: _____

Emily: _____

John: _____

Emily: _____

Emily: 나는 너희 the Reds 야구팀이 시합에서 이겼다고 들었어. 8 대 7이 맞니? 축하해, John!
John: 고마워. 정말 접전이었어. 나는 내 투구에 만족스럽지 않아.
Emily: 왜 그렇게 말하는 거야?
John: 홈런 두 개를 허용했거든.
Emily: 오, 너는 훌륭한 투수야. 다음번에는 더 잘할 거야.

Listen & Talk 2 A-1

Mike: _____

Mina: _____

Mike: _____

Mina: _____

Mike: _____

Mike: 미나야, 자전거 처음 타는 거야?
Mina: 응. 균형을 잘 못 잡겠어.
Mike: 내가 도와줄게. 네 자전거를 잡아 줄게.
Mina: 고마워, Mike. 놓으면 안 돼, 알았지?
Mike: 걱정 마. 앉아서 앞을 똑바로 봐.

Listen & Talk 2 A-1

Tom: _____

Sarah: _____

_____

Tom: _____

Sarah: _____

Tom: Sarah, 뭐 하고 있어?

Sarah: 체육 시간에 물구나무 서는 법을 배웠거든. 그래서 지금 한번 해 보고 있는데, 쉽지 않네.

Tom: 내가 도와줄게. 다리를 공중에 차 올려봐. 내가 널 붙잡을게.

Sarah: 오, 고마워. 다시 해 볼게.

Listen & Talk 2 B

Coach: _____

Brian: _____

Coach: _____

Brian: _____

Coach: _____

_____

Coach: 저기, Brian. 태권도 옆 차기 연습했니?

Brian: 네, 코치님. 그런데 여전히 편하게 잘 안 돼요.

Coach: 어떤 문제가 있어?

Brian: 음, 다리를 충분히 높이 들어 올릴 수가 없어요.

Coach: 알겠다. 내가 도와줄게. 너를 위해 이 킥 패드를 잡아줄게. 너의 옆 차기를 보여주렴.

Communication

Megan: _____

James: _____

Megan: _____

_____

James: _____

Megan: _____

James: _____

Megan: James, 나는 다음 축구 시합이 걱정돼.

James: 왜 걱정하는 거야, Megan?

Megan: 음, 지난 축구 시합에서 나는 높은 공을 잡지 못했어. 너무 많은 골을 허용했어.

James: 알겠어. 자, 내가 도와줄게. 너에게 공을 높이 차 줄게.

Megan: 오, 그거 도움이 많이 되겠다. 내 기술이 나아지길 바라.

James: 걱정 마. 다음번에는 더 잘할 거야.

Wrap Up 1

Anna: _____

Jake: _____

Anna: _____

Jake: _____

Anna: _____

Jake: _____

Anna: 안녕, Jake. 너는 종종 수영장에 오니?

Jake: 오, 안녕, Anna. 나는 여기에서 일주일에 한 번 수영 수업을 들어.

Anna: 언제부터 수업을 시작했어?

Jake: 지난달부터. 그런데 수영은 여전히 나에게 쉽지 않아.

Anna: 오, 내가 도와줄게. 나는 학교 동아리에서 아이들에게 수영하는 법을 가르쳐 주거든.

Jake: 오, 그거 나에게 도움이 많이 되겠다. 고마워.

※ 다음 우리말과 일치하도록 빈칸에 알맞은 것을 골라 쓰시오.

1 _____ the go-kart race track, _____ are many people _____ are _____ excitedly.
   A. there   B. cheering   C. who   D. at

2 The karts _____ are _____ loud engine noises _____ _____.
   A. waiting   B. making   C. are   D. that

3 An official _____ a green _____ and the race _____!
   A. starts   B. flag   C. waves

4 Max _____ his foot _____ hard on the gas pedal _____ he _____ his sixth lap on the track.
   A. completes   B. down   C. as   D. pushes

5 _____ the straightaway, Max _____ right _____ the race's leader, Simon.
   A. pulls   B. beside   C. on

6 Last year, Simon _____ many races, but Max's best _____ in a race was _____ in fifth _____.
   A. place   B. result   C. won   D. coming

7 This time, he has a _____ to _____ _____.
   A. second   B. chance   C. finish

8 But he isn't _____ to be _____ with second _____ today.
   A. satisfied   B. place   C. going

9 The winner _____ to _____ the world _____ racer L. J. Richards!
   A. gets   B. famous   C. meet

10 He doesn't want to _____ the _____ to meet his _____ model.
   A. role   B. chance   C. miss

11 Max _____ the _____ lap and now has five more _____ to go.
   A. tenth   B. laps   C. completes

12 Max sees Simon's kart _____, just _____ of Max's _____.
   A. ahead   B. reach   C. out

13 Max's kart _____ closer and _____ to Simon's.
   A. closer   B. gets

14 It _____ _____ the back _____ of Simon's kart.
   A. almost   B. end   C. hits

15 They _____ _____ the straightaway and Max _____ _____ on the gas pedal.
   A. into   B. presses   C. drive   D. harder

16 "I can _____ _____," says Max.
   A. up   B. catch

17 Max sees the _____ _____ a white flag which _____ the last lap.
   A. waving   B. means   C. official

1 고카트 경기 트랙에 신이 나서 응원하고 있는 많은 사람들이 있다.

2 시끄러운 엔진 소음을 내고 있는 카트들이 기다리고 있다.

3 심판이 초록 깃발을 흔들고, 경기가 시작된다!

4 Max는 트랙을 여섯 바퀴 돌았을 때, 발로 가속 페달을 힘껏 누른다.

5 직선 구간에서 Max는 경기에서 선두를 달리고 있는 Simon의 바로 옆까지 다가간다.

6 작년에 Simon은 경기에서 여러 번 이겼지만 Max의 최고 경기 성적은 5등으로 들어온 것이었다.

7 이번에 그는 2등으로 끝낼 수 있는 기회를 잡았다.

8 그러나 그는 오늘 2등으로 만족하지 않을 것이다.

9 우승자는 세계적으로 유명한 경주 선수인 L.J. Richards를 만나게 된다!

10 그는 그의 역할 모델을 만날 수 있는 기회를 놓치길 원하지 않는다.

11 Max는 10바퀴를 다 돌고 이제 5바퀴를 더 돌아야 한다.

12 Max는 앞에 바로 닿을 듯한 거리에 있는 Simon의 카트를 본다.

13 Max의 카트는 Simon의 카트에 점점 더 가까워진다.

14 Max의 카트는 Simon의 카트의 뒷부분에 거의 닿을 것 같다.

15 그들은 직선 구간을 운전해가고, Max는 가속 페달을 더 세게 밟는다.

16 "나는 따라잡을 수 있어." Max가 말한다.

17 Max는 심판이 마지막 바퀴라는 것을 알려주는 흰색 깃발을 흔드는 것을 본다.

18 Max is _____ _____ Simon.
    A. behind   B. right

19 The finish line is _____ closer, and the _____ from the _____ is getting _____.
    A. louder   B. getting   C. crowd   D. cheering

20 "I _____ _____ it!" Max says _____.
    A. loudly   B. do   C. can

21 He can _____ his heart _____ _____.
    A. hard   B. beating   C. feel

22 The karts _____ _____ the _____ line.
    A. across   B. rush   C. finish

23 _____ is the _____?
    A. winner   B. who

24 Max's eyes are _____ _____ tears as he finds _____ that he came in second.
    A. filled   B. out   C. with

25 "No _____ for _____, kid," says a man's _____.
    A. need   B. voice   C. tears

26 Max _____ _____ his eyes.
    A. believe   B. can't

27 The man who is _____ in _____ of him _____ L. J. Richards!
    A. standing   B. is   C. front

28 "Thank you, _____ I'm _____ the _____," says Max.
    A. winner   B. not   C. but

29 "It was a _____ _____ _____.
    A. close   B. race   C. real

30 _____ though you didn't _____ the race, you did your _____.
    A. win   B. best   C. even

31 That's the thing _____ _____!" says L. J. Richards.
    A. counts   B. that

32 '_____ I do my _____?' thinks Max.
    A. best   B. did

33 _____ a moment, he _____.
    A. smiles   B. after

34 "Yeah, I _____ I _____."
    A. did   B. guess

---

18 Max는 Simon 바로 뒤에 있다.

19 결승점이 점점 가까워지고, 관중으로부터 들리는 환호성이 점점 커진다.

20 "나는 할 수 있어!" Max는 큰 소리로 말한다.

21 그는 그의 심장이 세게 뛰는 것을 느낄 수 있다.

22 카트들이 돌진해 결승점을 지난다.

23 누가 승자인가?

24 Max는 자신이 2등으로 들어왔다는 것을 알았을 때, 눈에 눈물이 가득 찬다.

25 "울 필요 없단다, 얘야." 어떤 남자의 목소리가 말한다.

26 Max는 그의 눈을 믿을 수 없다.

27 그 앞에 서 있는 남자는 L.J. Richards이다!

28 "고마워요, 하지만 저는 일등이 아니에요." Max가 말한다.

29 "정말 아슬아슬한 경기였어.

30 네가 비록 경기를 이기지 못했지만, 너는 최선을 다했어.

31 중요한 것은 바로 그거란다!" L.J. Richards가 말한다.

32 '나는 최선을 다했을까?' Max는 생각한다.

33 잠시 후에, 그는 미소를 짓는다.

34 "네, 저는 최선을 다한 것 같아요."

※ 다음 우리말과 일치하도록 빈칸에 알맞은 말을 쓰시오.

1 _____ the go-kart race _____, _____ _____ many people _____ _____ _____ _____.

2 The karts _____ _____ _____ _____ engine noises _____ _____.

3 An _____ _____ a green _____ and the race _____!

4 Max _____ his foot _____ _____ on the gas pedal _____ he _____ his _____ _____ on the track.

5 _____ _____ _____, Max _____ _____ _____ the race's leader, Simon.

6 Last year, Simon _____ _____ _____, but Max's best result in a race _____ _____ _____ _____ _____ _____.

7 This time, he has a _____ _____ _____ _____ _____.

8 But he isn't going to _____ _____ _____ _____ _____ today.

9 The winner _____ _____ _____ the world famous racer L. J. Richards!

10 He doesn't want _____ _____ the chance _____ _____ _____ _____ _____.

11 Max _____ _____ _____ _____ and now has five more laps _____ _____.

12 Max _____ Simon's kart _____, just _____ _____ Max's reach.

13 Max's kart _____ _____ _____ _____ to Simon's.

14 It almost _____ _____ _____ _____ of Simon's kart.

15 They _____ _____ the straightaway and Max _____ _____ _____ _____ _____ _____ _____.

16 "I _____ _____ _____," says Max.

17 Max sees the official _____ _____ _____ _____ which _____ _____ _____.

1 고카트 경기 트랙에 신이 나서 응원하고 있는 많은 사람들이 있다.

2 시끄러운 엔진 소음을 내고 있는 카트들이 기다리고 있다.

3 심판이 초록 깃발을 흔들고, 경기가 시작된다!

4 Max는 트랙을 여섯 바퀴 돌았을 때, 발로 가속 페달을 힘껏 누른다.

5 직선 구간에서 Max는 경기에서 선두를 달리고 있는 Simon의 바로 옆까지 다가간다.

6 작년에 Simon은 경기에서 여러 번 이겼지만 Max의 최고 경기 성적은 5등으로 들어온 것이었다.

7 이번에 그는 2등으로 끝낼 수 있는 기회를 잡았다.

8 그러나 그는 오늘 2등으로 만족하지 않을 것이다.

9 우승자는 세계적으로 유명한 경주 선수인 L.J. Richards를 만나게 된다!

10 그는 그의 역할 모델을 만날 수 있는 기회를 놓치길 원하지 않는다.

11 Max는 10바퀴를 다 돌고 이제 5바퀴를 더 돌아야 한다.

12 Max는 앞에 바로 닿을 듯한 거리에 있는 Simon의 카트를 본다.

13 Max의 카트는 Simon의 카트에 점점 더 가까워진다.

14 Max의 카트는 Simon의 카트의 뒷부분에 거의 닿을 것 같다.

15 그들은 직선 구간을 운전해가고, Max는 가속 페달을 더 세게 밟는다.

16 "나는 따라잡을 수 있어." Max가 말한다.

17 Max는 심판이 마지막 바퀴라는 것을 알려주는 흰색 깃발을 흔드는 것을 본다.

18 Max is _____ _____ Simon.

19 The finish line is _____ _____, and the _____ _____ _____ _____ is _____ _____.

20 "I _____ _____ _____!" Max _____ _____.

21 He _____ _____ his heart _____ _____.

22 The karts _____ _____ _____ _____.

23 _____ is the _____?

24 Max's eyes are _____ _____ _____ as he _____ _____ _____ he came _____ _____.

25 "_____ _____ _____ _____, kid," says a man's voice.

26 Max _____ _____ _____ _____.

27 The man _____ _____ _____ _____ _____ him _____ L. J. Richards!

28 "Thank you, but I'm _____ _____ _____," says Max.

29 "It was _____ _____ _____ _____.

30 _____ _____ you _____ _____ _____ _____ _____, you _____ your best.

31 That's the thing _____ _____!" says L. J. Richards.

32 '_____ I _____ _____ _____ _____?' _____ Max.

33 _____ _____ _____, he _____.

34 "Yeah, I _____ I _____."

---

18 Max는 Simon 바로 뒤에 있다.

19 결승점이 점점 가까워지고, 관중으로부터 들리는 환호성이 점점 커진다.

20 "나는 할 수 있어!" Max는 큰 소리로 말한다.

21 그는 그의 심장이 세게 뛰는 것을 느낄 수 있다.

22 카트들이 돌진해 결승점을 지난다.

23 누가 승자인가?

24 Max는 자신이 2등으로 들어왔다는 것을 알았을 때, 눈에 눈물이 가득 찬다.

25 "울 필요 없단다. 얘야." 어떤 남자의 목소리가 말한다.

26 Max는 그의 눈을 믿을 수 없다.

27 그 앞에 서 있는 남자는 L.J. Richards이다!

28 "고마워요, 하지만 저는 일등이 아니에요." Max가 말한다.

29 "정말 아슬아슬한 경기였어.

30 네가 비록 경기를 이기지 못했지만, 너는 최선을 다했어.

31 중요한 것은 바로 그거란다!" L.J. Richards가 말한다.

32 '나는 최선을 다했을까?' Max는 생각한다.

33 잠시 후에, 그는 미소를 짓는다.

34 "네, 저는 최선을 다한 것 같아요."

※ 다음 문장을 우리말로 쓰시오.

1 At the go-kart race track, there are many people who are cheering excitedly.
➡ _____

2 The karts that are making loud engine noises are waiting.
➡ _____

3 An official waves a green flag and the race starts!
➡ _____

4 Max pushes his foot down hard on the gas pedal as he completes his sixth lap on the track.
➡ _____

5 On the straightaway, Max pulls right beside the race's leader, Simon.
➡ _____

6 Last year, Simon won many races, but Max's best result in a race was coming in fifth place.
➡ _____

7 This time, he has a chance to finish second.
➡ _____

8 But he isn't going to be satisfied with second place today.
➡ _____

9 The winner gets to meet the world famous racer L. J. Richards!
➡ _____

10 He doesn't want to miss the chance to meet his role model.
➡ _____

11 Max completes the tenth lap and now has five more laps to go.
➡ _____

12 Max sees Simon's kart ahead, just out of Max's reach.
➡ _____

13 Max's kart gets closer and closer to Simon's.
➡ _____

14 It almost hits the back end of Simon's kart.
➡ _____

15 They drive into the straightaway and Max presses harder on the gas pedal.
➡ _____

16 "I can catch up," says Max.
➡ _____

17 Max sees the official waving a white flag which means the last lap.
➡ _____

18 ➤ Max is right behind Simon.

➡ _____

19 ➤ The finish line is getting closer, and the cheering from the crowd is getting louder.

➡ _____

20 ➤ "I can do it!" Max says loudly.

➡ _____

21 ➤ He can feel his heart beating hard.

➡ _____

22 ➤ The karts rush across the finish line.

➡ _____

23 ➤ Who is the winner?

➡ _____

24 ➤ Max's eyes are filled with tears as he finds out that he came in second.

➡ _____

25 ➤ "No need for tears, kid," says a man's voice.

➡ _____

26 ➤ Max can't believe his eyes.

➡ _____

27 ➤ The man who is standing in front of him is L. J. Richards!

➡ _____

28 ➤ "Thank you, but I'm not the winner," says Max.

➡ _____

29 ➤ "It was a real close race.

➡ _____

30 ➤ Even though you didn't win the race, you did your best.

➡ _____

31 ➤ That's the thing that counts!" says L. J. Richards.

➡ _____

32 ➤ 'Did I do my best?' thinks Max.

➡ _____

33 ➤ After a moment, he smiles.

➡ _____

34 ➤ "Yeah, I guess I did."

➡ _____

※ 다음 괄호 안의 단어들을 우리말에 맞도록 바르게 배열하시오.

1 (the / at / race / go-kart / track, / are / there / people / many / are / who / excitedly. / cheering)
➡ _____

2 (karts / the / that / making / are / engine / loud / waiting. / are / noises)
➡ _____

3 (official / an / waves / green / a / flag / the / and / starts! / race)
➡ _____

4 (pushes / Max / foot / his / hard / down / the / on / pedal / gas / as / he / his / completes / sixth / on / track. / the / lap)
➡ _____
_____

5 (the / on / straightaway, / pulls / Max / beside / right / race's / the / Simon. / leader,)
➡ _____

6 (year, / last / won / Simon / races, / many / but / best / Max's / result / a / in / race / coming / was / place. / fifth / in)
➡ _____

7 (time, / this / has / he / chance / a / second. / finish / to)
➡ _____

8 (he / but / going / isn't / be / to / satisfied / second / with / today. / place)
➡ _____

9 (winner / the / gets / meet / to / world / the / racer / Richards! / L. / famous / J.)
➡ _____

10 (doesn't / he / to / want / miss / chance / the / meet / to / model. / role / his)
➡ _____

11 (Max / the / completes / tenth / and / lap / now / five / has / laps / go. / more / to)
➡ _____

12 (sees / Max / kart / Simon's / ahead, / out / just / reach. / of / Max's)
➡ _____

13 (kart / Max's / closer / gets / and / Simon's. / to / closer)
➡ _____

14 (almost / it / hits / back / the / of / end / kart. / Simon's)
➡ _____

15 (drive / they / into / straightaway / the / and / presses / Max / on / harder / pedal. / gas / the)
➡ _____

16 (can / "I / up," / catch / Max. / says)
➡ _____

17 (sees / Max / official / the / waving / white / a / flag / means / which / lap. / last / the)
➡ _____

1 고카트 경기 트랙에 신이 나서 응원하고 있는 많은 사람들이 있다.

2 시끄러운 엔진 소음을 내고 있는 카트들이 기다리고 있다.

3 심판이 초록 깃발을 흔들고, 경기가 시작된다!

4 Max는 트랙을 여섯 바퀴 돌았을 때, 발로 가속 페달을 힘껏 누른다.

5 직선 구간에서 Max는 경기에서 선두를 달리고 있는 Simon의 바로 옆까지 다가간다.

6 작년에 Simon은 경기에서 여러 번 이겼지만 Max의 최고 경기 성적은 5등으로 들어온 것이었다.

7 이번에 그는 2등으로 끝낼 수 있는 기회를 잡았다.

8 그러나 그는 오늘 2등으로 만족하지 않을 것이다.

9 우승자는 세계적으로 유명한 경주 선수인 L.J. Richards를 만나게 된다!

10 그는 그의 역할 모델을 만날 수 있는 기회를 놓치길 원하지 않는다.

11 Max는 10바퀴를 다 돌고 이제 5바퀴를 더 돌아야 한다.

12 Max는 앞에 바로 닿을 듯한 거리에 있는 Simon의 카트를 본다.

13 Max의 카트는 Simon의 카트에 점점 더 가까워진다.

14 Max의 카트는 Simon의 카트의 뒷부분에 거의 닿을 것 같다.

15 그들은 직선 구간을 운전해가고, Max는 가속 페달을 더 세게 밟는다.

16 "나는 따라잡을 수 있어." Max가 말한다.

17 Max는 심판이 마지막 바퀴라는 것을 알려주는 흰색 깃발을 흔드는 것을 본다.

18 (is / Max / behind / right / Simon.)
➡ _____

19 (finish / the / line / getting / is / closer, / and / cheering / the / from / crowd / louder. / getting / is)
➡ _____
_____

20 (can / "I / do / it!" / loudly. / says / Max)
➡ _____

21 (can / he / feel / heart / his / hard. / beating)
➡ _____

22 (karts / the / rush / across / line. / finish / the)
➡ _____

23 (is / who / winner? / the)
➡ _____

24 (eyes / Max's / filled / are / tears / with / as / finds / he / that / out / came / he / second. / in)
➡ _____
_____

25 (need / "no / tears, / for / kid," / a / voice. / man's / says)
➡ _____

26 (can't / Max / eyes. / his / believe)
➡ _____

27 (man / the / is / who / standing / front / in / of / Richards! / him / L. / J. / is)
➡ _____

28 (you, / "thank / I'm / but / not / winner," / Max. / says)
➡ _____

29 ("it / a / was / real / race. / close)
➡ _____

30 (though / even / didn't / you / the / win / race, / did / you / best. / your)
➡ _____
_____

31 (the / that's / thing / counts!" / that / Richards. / L. / J. / says)
➡ _____

32 (I / 'did / my / do / best?' / Max. / thinks)
➡ _____

33 (a / after / moment, / smiles. / he)
➡ _____

34 ("yeah, / guess / I / did." / I)
➡ _____

18 Max는 Simon 바로 뒤에 있다.

19 결승점이 점점 가까워지고, 관중으로부터 들리는 환호성이 점점 커진다.

20 "나는 할 수 있어!" Max는 큰 소리로 말한다.

21 그는 그의 심장이 세게 뛰는 것을 느낄 수 있다.

22 카트들이 돌진해 결승점을 지난다.

23 누가 승자인가?

24 Max는 자신이 2등으로 들어왔다는 것을 알았을 때, 눈에 눈물이 가득 찬다.

25 "울 필요 없단다, 얘야." 어떤 남자의 목소리가 말한다.

26 Max는 그의 눈을 믿을 수 없다.

27 그 앞에 서 있는 남자는 L.J. Richards이다!

28 "고마워요, 하지만 저는 일등이 아니에요." Max가 말한다.

29 "정말 아슬아슬한 경기였어.

30 네가 비록 경기를 이기지 못했지만, 너는 최선을 다했어.

31 중요한 것은 바로 그거란다!" L.J. Richards가 말한다.

32 '나는 최선을 다했을까?' Max는 생각한다.

33 잠시 후에, 그는 미소를 짓는다.

34 "네, 저는 최선을 다한 것 같아요."

※ 다음 우리말을 영어로 쓰시오.

1 고카트 경기 트랙에 신이 나서 응원하고 있는 많은 사람들이 있다.
➡ _____

2 시끄러운 엔진 소음을 내고 있는 카트들이 기다리고 있다.
➡ _____

3 심판이 초록 깃발을 흔들고, 경기가 시작된다!
➡ _____

4 Max는 트랙을 여섯 바퀴 돌았을 때, 발로 가속 페달을 힘껏 누른다.
➡ _____

5 직선 구간에서 Max는 경기에서 선두를 달리고 있는 Simon의 바로 옆까지 다가간다.
➡ _____

6 작년에 Simon은 경기에서 여러 번 이겼지만 Max의 최고 경기 성적은 5등으로 들어온 것이었다.
➡ _____

7 이번에 그는 2등으로 끝낼 수 있는 기회를 잡았다.
➡ _____

8 그러나 그는 오늘 2등으로 만족하지 않을 것이다.
➡ _____

9 우승자는 세계적으로 유명한 경주 선수인 L. J. Richards를 만나게 된다!
➡ _____

10 그는 그의 역할 모델을 만날 수 있는 기회를 놓치길 원하지 않는다.
➡ _____

11 Max는 10바퀴를 다 돌고 이제 5바퀴를 더 돌아야 한다.
➡ _____

12 Max는 앞에 바로 닿을 듯한 거리에 있는 Simon의 카트를 본다.
➡ _____

13 Max의 카트는 Simon의 카트에 점점 더 가까워진다.
➡ _____

14 Max의 카트는 Simon의 카트의 뒷부분에 거의 닿을 것 같다.
➡ _____

15 그들은 직선 구간을 운전해가고, Max는 가속 페달을 더 세게 밟는다.
➡ _____

16 "나는 따라잡을 수 있어." Max가 말한다.
➡ _____

17 Max는 심판이 마지막 바퀴라는 것을 알려주는 흰색 깃발을 흔드는 것을 본다.
➡ _____

18 Max는 Simon 바로 뒤에 있다.

➡ _____

19 결승점이 점점 가까워지고, 관중으로부터 들리는 환호성이 점점 커진다.

➡ _____

20 "나는 할 수 있어!" Max는 큰 소리로 말한다.

➡ _____

21 그는 그의 심장이 세게 뛰는 것을 느낄 수 있다.

➡ _____

22 카트들이 돌진해 결승점을 지난다.

➡ _____

23 누가 승자인가?

➡ _____

24 Max는 자신이 2등으로 들어왔다는 것을 알았을 때, 눈에 눈물이 가득 찬다.

➡ _____

25 "울 필요 없단다, 얘야." 어떤 남자의 목소리가 말한다.

➡ _____

26 Max는 그의 눈을 믿을 수 없다.

➡ _____

27 그 앞에 서 있는 남자는 L. J. Richards이다!

➡ _____

28 "고마워요, 하지만 저는 일등이 아니에요." Max가 말한다.

➡ _____

29 "정말 아슬아슬한 경기였어.

➡ _____

30 네가 비록 경기를 이기지 못했지만, 너는 최선을 다했어.

➡ _____

31 중요한 것은 바로 그거란다!" L. J. Richards가 말한다.

➡ _____

32 '나는 최선을 다했을까?'' Max는 생각한다.

➡ _____

33 잠시 후에, 그는 미소를 짓는다.

➡ _____

34 "네, 저는 최선을 다한 것 같아요."

➡ _____

※ 다음 우리말과 일치하도록 빈칸에 알맞은 말을 쓰시오.

Listen & Talk C

1. Amy: Michael, _____ _____ _____ _____?

2. Michael: I _____ _____ the _____ _____.

3. Amy: _____ _____, Michael. You'll _____ _____ next time.

1. Amy: Michael, 왜 시무룩한 얼굴이니?
2. Michael: 나는 다른 선수를 막지 못했어.
3. Amy: 걱정 마. Michael. 다음번에는 더 잘할 거야.

Grammar in Real Life

1. Ms. Green is a good _____ _____ _____ _____ Italian food.

2. She _____ _____ to the local store _____ has many _____ vegetables.

3. Her restaurant _____ _____ _____ _____ people _____ like to eat her food.

4. I _____ _____ _____ _____ her seafood pizza which is the _____ _____.

1. Green씨는 맛있는 이탈리아 음식을 만드는 훌륭한 요리사이다.
2. 그녀는 항상 신선한 채소가 많이 있는 지역 상점에 간다.
3. 그녀의 레스토랑은 그녀의 음식을 좋아하는 많은 사람들로 항상 붐빈다.
4. 나는 네가 가장 인기 있는 그녀의 해산물 피자를 먹어 보기를 원한다.

Think & Write

1. A basketball match _____ Class 1 _____ Class 2 _____ _____ at school _____ Friday.

2. Class 1 _____ the game _____ _____ _____.

3. There are some _____ _____.

4. _____ _____ them _____ Sarah.

5. She was the player who _____ _____ _____ one second before _____ _____ _____ the game.

6. It was a _____ _____.

7. We _____ _____ _____ to the next match.

1. 금요일에 학교에서 1반과 2반 사이의 농구 경기가 열렸습니다.
2. 1반은 1점 차이로 그 경기에서 이겼습니다.
3. 기억에 남는 몇 명의 선수가 있습니다.
4. 그 중 한 명은 Sarah입니다.
5. 그녀는 경기가 끝나기 1초 전에 득점을 올린 선수였습니다.
6. 그것은 훌륭한 경기였습니다.
7. 우리는 다음 경기를 기대하고 있습니다.

구석구석 지문 Test Step2

※ 다음 우리말을 영어로 쓰시오.

Listen & Talk C

1. Amy: Michael, 왜 시무룩한 얼굴이니?

   ➡ _____

2. Michael: 나는 다른 선수를 막지 못했어.

   ➡ _____

3. Amy: 걱정 마. Michael. 다음번에는 더 잘할 거야.

   ➡ _____

Grammar in Real Life

1. Green씨는 맛있는 이탈리아 음식을 만드는 훌륭한 요리사이다.

   ➡ _____

2. 그녀는 항상 신선한 채소가 많이 있는 지역 상점에 간다.

   ➡ _____

3. 그녀의 레스토랑은 그녀의 음식을 좋아하는 많은 사람들로 항상 붐빈다.

   ➡ _____

4. 나는 네가 가장 인기 있는 그녀의 해산물 피자를 먹어 보기를 원한다.

   ➡ _____

Think & Write

1. 금요일에 학교에서 1반과 2반 사이의 농구 경기가 열렸습니다.

   ➡ _____

2. 1반은 1점 차이로 그 경기에서 이겼습니다.

   ➡ _____

3. 기억에 남는 몇 명의 선수가 있습니다.

   ➡ _____

4. 그 중 한 명은 Sarah입니다.

   ➡ _____

5. 그녀는 경기가 끝나기 1초 전에 득점을 올린 선수였습니다.

   ➡ _____

6. 그것은 훌륭한 경기였습니다.

   ➡ _____

7. 우리는 다음 경기를 기대하고 있습니다.

   ➡ _____

※ 다음 영어를 우리말로 쓰시오.

01 avoid   22 stand

02 suggestion   23 limit

03 upset   24 explain

04 worry   25 advise

05 contact   26 yet

06 advice   27 pack

07 fight   28 difficult

08 haircut   29 forgive

09 alone   30 elementary

10 stuff   31 fear

11 hurt   32 reason

12 messy   33 solve

13 wise   34 line

14 share   35 focus on

15 lunch break   36 wake up

16 repeat   37 stay up late

17 matter   38 gain weight

18 yell   39 on purpose

19 since   40 shut down

20 mean   41 work out

21 hate   42 in the end

     43 point out

※ 다음 우리말을 영어로 쓰시오.

01 거울 _____

02 초보의, 초급의 _____

03 공유하다, 나누다 _____

04 어려운 _____

05 반복하다 _____

06 소리치다 _____

07 접촉, 닿음 _____

08 조언하다, 충고하다 _____

09 문제 _____

10 싸다, 꾸리다 _____

11 싸우다 _____

12 점심시간 _____

13 이발, 머리 깎기 _____

14 물건 _____

15 다치게 하다 _____

16 참다, 견디다 _____

17 피하다 _____

18 한계, 제한 _____

19 아직 _____

20 치통 _____

21 제안 _____

22 홀로, 혼자 _____

23 걱정하다; 걱정 _____

24 어질러진, 더러운 _____

25 속상한, 마음이 상한 _____

26 이유, 까닭 _____

27 싫어하다 _____

28 (연극, 영화의) 대사 _____

29 조언 _____

30 용서하다 _____

31 설명하다 _____

32 두려움, 공포 _____

33 현명한 _____

34 풀다, 해결하다 _____

35 결국, 마침내 _____

36 ~에 집중하다 _____

37 (기계가) 멈추다 _____

38 체중이 늘다 _____

39 좋다가 나쁘다가 하는 _____

40 늦게까지 자지 않고 있다 _____

41 고의로 _____

42 자명종을 맞추다 _____

43 잠에서 깨다 _____

※ 다음 영영풀이에 알맞은 단어를 <보기>에서 골라 쓴 후, 우리말 뜻을 쓰시오.

1 _____ : dirty and/or untidy: _____

2 _____ : to dislike something very much: _____

3 _____ : a pain in one of your teeth: _____

4 _____ : the state of touching something: _____

5 _____ : the act of someone cutting your hair: _____

6 _____ : the words spoken by an actor in a play or film/movie: _____

7 _____ : to say or write something again or more than once: _____

8 _____ : to have or use something at the same time as somebody else: _____

9 _____ : an idea or a plan that you mention for somebody else to think about: _____

10 _____ : the bad feeling that you have when you are in danger: _____

11 _____ : to keep away from somebody/something; to try not to do something: _____

12 _____ : in or connected with the first stages of a course of study: _____

13 _____ : to cause physical pain to somebody/yourself; to injure somebody/yourself: _____

14 _____ : to shout loudly, for example because you are angry, excited, frightened or in pain: _____

15 _____ : an opinion or a suggestion about what somebody should do in a particular situation: _____

16 _____ : to stop feeling angry with somebody who has done something to harm, annoy or upset you: _____

보기			
forgive	advice	toothache	contact
line	messy	hurt	elementary
hate	yell	repeat	share
fear	suggestion	avoid	haircut

※ 다음 우리말과 일치하도록 빈칸에 알맞은 말을 쓰시오.

Listen & Talk 1-A-1

M: You don't _____ so _____ today. What's the _____?

W: I _____ my _____ _____ T-shirt. But I _____ grape juice on it.

M: Oh, no. _____ you _____ your sister?

W: No, _____ _____. I don't know _____ _____ _____.

M: 너 오늘은 별로 행복해 보이지가 않네. 무슨 일 있어?
W: 언니가 가장 좋아하는 티셔츠를 입었어. 그런데 거기에 포도 주스를 쏟았지 뭐야.
M: 오, 저런. 너희 언니에게 말했어?
W: 아니, 아직. 내가 뭘 해야 할지 모르겠어.

Listen & Talk 1-A-2

Sora: David, you _____ _____ today. _____ _____ _____?

David: I _____ _____ _____ but it's too short. I look _____.

Sora: _____ _____ your hat and _____ _____ _____. (*pause*) Oh, it _____ _____.

David: Really? I guess I'm just _____ _____ _____ it yet.

Sora: David, 너 오늘 침울해 보여. 무슨 일 있어?
David: 머리를 잘랐는데 너무 짧아. 우스꽝스럽게 보여.
Sora: 모자를 벗으면 내가 한 번 볼게. 오, 괜찮아 보이는데.
David: 정말? 난 아직 익숙해지지 않은 것 같아.

Listen & Talk 1-B

Jane: You _____ _____. What's _____ _____?

Mike: _____ _____ _____ _____ _____. I'm so hungry.

Jane: Oh, that's _____ _____. We still have two more hours _____ _____ _____.

Mike: Our school should have a _____ _____. Then, we _____ _____ a quick breakfast or snacks.

Jane: I _____ _____, _____. _____ can we _____ that _____?

Mike: We _____ _____ it on the _____ board.

Jane: 너 피곤해 보인다. 무슨 일 있어?
Mike: 오늘 아침에 밥을 못 먹었어. 너무 배가 고파.
Jane: 오, 안됐다. 점심시간까지 아직 두 시간도 더 남았는데.
Mike: 우리 학교도 매점이 있어야 돼. 그러면 간단히 아침이나 간식을 먹을 수 있잖아.
Jane: 내 생각도 그래. 어떻게 하면 우리가 그 제안을 할 수 있을까?
Mike: 우리는 이걸 제안 게시판에 올릴 수 있어.

Listen & Talk 2 A-1

Sujin: I don't know _____ _____ _____ in math. Can you _____ _____ _____ _____?

Jake: _____ do you _____ for tests?

Sujin: I just _____ _____ _____ _____ problems.

Jake: Well, don't _____ everything. I think you _____ _____ the _____ you _____ _____.

Sujin: 수학을 더 잘하는 방법을 모르겠어. 나에게 조언을 좀 해 줄래?
Jake: 시험을 목표로 어떻게 공부해?
Sujin: 난 그냥 많은 문제를 풀어 봐.
Jake: 글쎄, 전부 풀지 마. 내 생각엔 네가 틀린 문제들에 집중해야 할 것 같아.

Listen & Talk 2 A-2

Emily: I _____ _____ _____ _____ again. I just can't _____
_____ in the morning.

Tom: Do you _____ _____ _____?

Emily: Yeah, but I _____ _____ _____ and go back to sleep.

Tom: I _____ _____ _____ put it _____ _____ your bed.
_____ _____, you'll have to _____ _____ _____
_____.

Review 1

Eric: Ms. Morris, I just can't _____ _____ _____ _____.
_____ _____ _____ _____?

Ms. Morris: Well, _____ _____ _____ _____ a special
program? When you _____ a time _____, the computer
_____ _____ at that time.

Eric: Oh, that's _____ _____ _____.

Ms. Morris: And _____ _____ _____ _____ _____ the
computer _____ _____ your room and _____ the
living room.

Eric: _____ _____ I _____. Thank you _____ _____
_____, Ms. Morris.

Communication

Solomon: Hello, you're _____ _____ _____.

Amy: Hi, Solomon. I'm Amy.

Solomon: Hi, Amy. _____ _____ _____?

Amy: I hate _____ my room _____ my little sister. She uses my
_____ _____ _____ me first. _____ _____ I
_____?

Solomon: Hmm.... I think you should _____ _____ _____
_____. And you should also _____ _____ _____
with your sister.

Amy: Oh, _____ _____ _____. _____ _____ the advice.

※ 다음 우리말에 맞도록 대화를 영어로 쓰시오.

Listen & Talk 1-A-1

M: _____

W: _____

M: _____

W: _____

M: 너 오늘은 별로 행복해 보이지가 않네. 무슨 일 있어?
W: 언니가 가장 좋아하는 티셔츠를 입었어. 그런데 거기에 포도 주스를 쏟았지 뭐야.
M: 오, 저런. 너희 언니에게 말했어?
W: 아니, 아직. 내가 뭘 해야 할지 모르겠어.

Listen & Talk 1-A-2

Sora: _____

David: _____

Sora: _____

David: _____

Sora: David, 너 오늘 침울해 보여. 무슨 일 있어?
David: 머리를 잘랐는데 너무 짧아. 우스꽝스럽게 보여.
Sora: 모자를 벗으면 내가 한 번 볼게. 오, 괜찮아 보이는데.
David: 정말? 난 아직 익숙해지지 않은 것 같아.

Listen & Talk 1-B

Jane: _____

Mike: _____

Jane: _____

Mike: _____

Jane: _____

Mike: _____

Jane: 너 피곤해 보인다. 무슨 일 있어?
Mike: 오늘 아침에 밥을 못 먹었어. 너무 배가 고파.
Jane: 오, 안됐다. 점심시간까지 아직 두 시간도 더 남았는데.
Mike: 우리 학교도 매점이 있어야 돼. 그러면 간단히 아침이나 간식을 먹을 수 있잖아.
Jane: 내 생각도 그래. 어떻게 하면 우리가 그 제안을 할 수 있을까?
Mike: 우리는 이걸 제안 게시판에 올릴 수 있어.

Listen & Talk 2 A-1

Sujin: _____

Jake: _____

Sujin: _____

Jake: _____

Sujin: 수학을 더 잘하는 방법을 모르겠어. 나에게 조언을 좀 해 줄래?
Jake: 시험을 목표로 어떻게 공부해?
Sujin: 난 그냥 많은 문제를 풀어 봐.
Jake: 글쎄, 전부 풀지 마. 내 생각엔 네가 틀린 문제들에 집중해야 할 것 같아.

Listen & Talk 2 A-2

Emily: _____

Tom: _____

Emily: _____

Tom: _____

Emily: 나 또 수업에 늦었어. 난 정말 아침에 못 일어나겠어.

Tom: 자명종은 맞춰 두는 거야?

Emily: 응, 그렇지만 자명종을 끄고 다시 잠들게 돼.

Tom: 내 생각엔 자명종을 침대에서 멀리 떨어진 곳에 두어야 할 것 같아. 그러면 침대에서 일어날 수밖에 없을 거야.

Review 1

Eric: _____

Ms. Morris: _____

_____

Eric: _____

Ms. Morris: _____

_____

Eric: _____

Eric: Morris 선생님, 저 컴퓨터 게임하는 것을 멈출 수가 없어요. 제가 어떻게 해야 할까요?

Mr. Morris: 음, 특별한 프로그램을 써 보는 게 어떨까? 네가 시간 제한을 정해 두면 컴퓨터가 그 시간에 맞춰 종료돼.

Eric: 오, 좋은 생각이네요.

Mr. Morris: 그리고 내 생각엔 컴퓨터를 네 방에서 거실로 옮겨 두어야 할 것 같아.

Eric: 제 생각에도 그래야 할 것 같아요. Morris 선생님, 조언해 주셔서 감사합니다.

Communication

Solomon: _____

Amy: _____

Solomon: _____

Amy: _____

_____

Solomon: _____

Amy: _____

Solomon: 안녕하세요, (방송에) 연결되었습니다.

Amy: 안녕하세요, Solomon. 전 Amy라고 해요.

Solomon: 안녕하세요, Amy. 무슨 일 있어요?

Amy: 전 여동생이랑 제 방을 같이 쓰는 게 싫어요. 그 애는 제게 먼저 물어보지도 않고 제 물건을 쓰거든요. 제가 어떻게 해야 할까요?

Solomon: 흠.... 제 생각엔 당신의 기분을 여동생에게 말해야 할 것 같아요. 그리고 여동생과 몇 가지 규칙을 만들어 봐요.

Amy: 오, 그렇게 할게요. 조언 감사해요.

※ 다음 우리말과 일치하도록 빈칸에 알맞은 것을 골라 쓰시오.

1 Bella is 15 years _____ this year and _____ days her feelings are _____ up and _____.

    A. these   B. down   C. old   D. going

2 Today, she _____ _____.

    A. down   B. looks

3 _____ listen to Bella's _____ and _____ out why.

    A. find   B. let's   C. feelings

Day 1

4 Anger: _____ a day! I can't believe Jenny _____ _____ Bella _____ the school play.

    A. at   B. what   C. after   D. yelled

5 Sadness: Well, that's _____ Bella _____ her _____ on stage.

    A. forgot   B. because   C. lines

6 Anger: Jenny pointed _____ the mistake _____ Bella _____.

    A. made   B. out   C. that

7 How _____ she do that _____ _____ of everyone?

    A. front   B. could   C. in

8 Joy: But I'm _____ Jenny did not _____ to _____ Bella.

    A. hurt   B. mean   C. sure

9 They _____ _____ best friends _____ elementary school. Remember?

    A. since   B. been   C. have

10 Anger: That's _____ I'm _____.

    A. saying   B. what

11 A true friend would _____ _____ Bella _____ like that.

    A. put   B. never   C. down

12 Fear: I'm worried _____ they are not _____ to _____ friends anymore.

    A. going   B. that   C. be

13 Joy: Come on, Fear. _____ go too _____. We'll _____.

    A. don't   B. far   C. see

Day 2

14 Anger: I can't _____ Jenny. She didn't _____ a _____ to Bella.

    A. word   B. forgive   C. say

15 Fear: Jenny didn't _____ _____ _____ her.

    A. at   B. even   C. look

---

1 Bella는 올해 15세이고 요즘 그 애의 기분은 좋다가 안 좋다가 한다.

2 오늘 그 애는 우울해 보인다.

3 Bella의 감정에 귀 기울여 보고 그 이유를 알아보자.

Day 1

4 Anger: 정말 끔찍한 하루야! 학교 연극이 끝난 후 Jenny가 Bella에게 소리를 지르다니 믿을 수가 없어.

5 Sadness: 글쎄, 그건 Bella가 무대에서 그녀의 대사를 잊어버렸기 때문이잖아.

6 Anger: Jenny는 Bella가 저지른 실수를 지적했잖아.

7 어떻게 모든 사람 앞에서 그렇게 할 수가 있니?

8 Joy: 하지만 난 Jenny가 Bella에게 상처를 주려고 했던 건 아니었다고 확신해.

9 그들은 초등학교 때부터 가장 친한 친구였잖아. 기억하지?

10 Anger: 내 말이 바로 그거야.

11 진정한 친구라면 절대로 그런 식으로 Bella를 깎아내리지 않을 거야.

12 Fear: 나는 그들이 더 이상 친구로 지내지 않을까봐 걱정돼.

13 Joy: 자, Fear. 너무 극단적으로 생각하지 마. 곧 알게 되겠지.

Day 2

14 Anger: 난 Jenny를 용서할 수 없어. 그 애는 Bella에게 한마디도 말을 안 했어.

15 Fear: Jenny는 심지어 Bella를 쳐다 보지도 않았어.

16 Jenny _____ _____ _____ this cold before.

    A. never   B. has   C. been

17 Sadness: Bella ate _____ _____ lunch today. Poor Bella!

    A. during   B. alone

18 Joy: Jenny is Bella's _____ _____.

    A. friend   B. best

19 I'm sure there is a _____ that we don't _____ _____.

    A. about   B. reason   C. know

20 Anger: I can't _____ this _____ _____.

    A. any   B. stand   C. longer

21 Bella should just _____ and _____ her _____ her feelings.

    A. about   B. tell   C. go

22 Fear: I don't _____ Bella _____ be _____ again.

    A. to   B. hurt   C. want

23 She should _____ it _____.

    A. go   B. let

24 Joy: They are good friends. They will _____ it _____.

    A. out   B. work

Day 3

25 Joy: Whew! I'm _____ happy _____ they are _____ again.

    A. that   B. talking   C. so

26 Anger: Yeah, Bella _____ to Jenny and _____ to _____ first.

    A. talked   B. went   C. her

27 Joy: Jenny didn't _____ Bella _____ _____.

    A. on   B. avoid   C. purpose

28 Sadness: Yeah, Jenny _____ know a _____ to _____ sorry.

    A. say   B. way   C. didn't

29 Fear: I hope Bella _____ have _____ _____ problems like this.

    A. any   B. doesn't   C. more

30 Joy: Me, _____. But problems are _____ of growing _____.

    A. part   B. too   C. up

31 Just _____ this time, Bella will _____ the problems, solve them, and become _____ in the _____.

    A. face   B. like   C. end   D. wiser

---

16 Jenny가 전에 이렇게 차가웠던 적이 없었어.

17 Sadness: Bella는 오늘 점심시간에 혼자 밥을 먹었잖아. 가엾은 Bella!

18 Joy: Jenny는 Bella의 가장 친한 친구야.

19 나는 우리가 모르는 어떤 이유가 있다고 확신해.

20 Anger: 나는 더 이상 이 상황을 못 참아.

21 Bella는 일단 가서 Jenny에게 자신의 감정을 말해야 해.

22 Fear: 나는 Bella가 또다시 상처받는 걸 원하지 않아.

23 그 애는 그냥 내버려 두어야 해.

24 Joy: 그 애들은 좋은 친구야. 그 애들이 잘 해낼 거야.

Day 3

25 Joy: 휴! 나는 그 애들이 다시 이야기하게 되어 무척 기뻐.

26 Anger: 그래, Bella가 Jenny에게 가서 그 애에게 먼저 말을 걸었지.

27 Joy: Jenny는 일부러 Bella를 피한 게 아니었어.

28 Sadness: 맞아, Jenny는 사과하는 방법을 몰랐던 거야.

29 Fear: 나는 Bella에게 이번과 같은 문제가 더 이상 없기를 바라.

30 Joy: 나도 그래. 하지만 문제들은 성장의 일부야.

31 이번과 꼭 마찬가지로 Bella는 문제들에 직면하게 될 거고, 그것들을 해결할 거고, 그리고 결국 더 현명해질 거야.

※ 다음 우리말과 일치하도록 빈칸에 알맞은 말을 쓰시오.

1 Bella is 15 _____ _____ this year and _____ _____ her feelings are _____ _____ _____ _____.

2 Today, she _____ _____.

3 _____ _____ _____ Bella's _____ and _____ _____ _____.

Day 1

4 Anger: _____ _____ _____ ! I can't believe Jenny _____ _____ Bella _____ the school play.

5 Sadness: Well, that's _____ Bella _____ her _____ _____ _____.

6 Anger: Jenny _____ _____ the mistake _____ _____.

7 How _____ she do that _____ _____ _____ everyone?

8 Joy: But I'm _____ Jenny _____ _____ _____ _____ Bella.

9 They _____ _____ best friends _____ _____ _____. Remember?

10 Anger: That's _____ I'm _____.

11 A true friend _____ _____ _____ Bella _____ like that.

12 Fear: I'm worried _____ they are _____ _____ _____ _____ _____ _____.

13 Joy: Come on, Fear. _____ _____ _____ _____ _____. We'll _____.

Day 2

14 Anger: I _____ _____ Jenny. She _____ _____ _____ _____ to Bella.

15 Fear: Jenny _____ _____ _____ _____ her.

1 Bella는 올해 15세이고 요즘 그 애의 기분은 좋다가 안 좋다가 한다.

2 오늘 그 애는 우울해 보인다.

3 Bella의 감정에 귀 기울여 보고 그 이유를 알아보자.

Day 1

4 Anger: 정말 끔찍한 하루야! 학교 연극이 끝난 후 Jenny가 Bella에게 소리를 지르다니 믿을 수가 없어.

5 Sadness: 글쎄, 그건 Bella가 무대에서 그녀의 대사를 잊어버렸기 때문이잖아.

6 Anger: Jenny는 Bella가 저지른 실수를 지적했잖아.

7 어떻게 모든 사람 앞에서 그렇게 할 수가 있니?

8 Joy: 하지만 난 Jenny가 Bella에게 상처를 주려고 했던 건 아니었다고 확신해.

9 그들은 초등학교 때부터 가장 친한 친구였잖아. 기억하지?

10 Anger: 내 말이 바로 그거야.

11 진정한 친구라면 절대로 그런 식으로 Bella를 깎아내리지 않을 거야.

12 Fear: 나는 그들이 더 이상 친구로 지내지 않을까봐 걱정돼.

13 Joy: 자, Fear. 너무 극단적으로 생각하지 마. 곧 알게 되겠지.

Day 2

14 Anger: 난 Jenny를 용서할 수 없어. 그 애는 Bella에게 한마디도 말을 안 했어.

15 Fear: Jenny는 심지어 Bella를 쳐다 보지도 않았어.

16 Jenny _____ _____ _____ this cold before.

17 Sadness: Bella _____ _____ _____ lunch today. Poor Bella!

18 Joy: Jenny is _____ _____ _____ .

19 I'm sure there is a _____ _____ _____ _____ _____ _____ .

20 Anger: I _____ _____ this _____ _____ .

21 Bella should just _____ and _____ her _____ her feelings.

22 Fear: I don't _____ Bella _____ _____ _____ again.

23 She _____ _____ _____ _____ _____ .

24 Joy: They are good friends. They will _____ _____ .

Day 3

25 Joy: Whew! I'm so happy _____ they _____ _____ again.

26 Anger: Yeah, Bella _____ _____ Jenny and _____ _____ _____ first.

27 Joy: Jenny _____ _____ Bella _____ _____ .

28 Sadness: Yeah, Jenny didn't know _____ _____ _____ _____ _____ .

29 Fear: I hope Bella doesn't have _____ _____ _____ _____ this.

30 Joy: _____ , _____ . But problems are _____ _____ _____ _____ .

31 _____ _____ this time, Bella will _____ the problems, _____ _____ , and become _____ in the _____ .

16 Jenny가 전에 이렇게 차가웠던 적이 없었어.

17 Sadness: Bella는 오늘 점심시간에 혼자 밥을 먹었잖아. 가엾은 Bella!

18 Joy: Jenny는 Bella의 가장 친한 친구야.

19 나는 우리가 모르는 어떤 이유가 있다고 확신해.

20 Anger: 나는 더 이상 이 상황을 못 참아.

21 Bella는 일단 가서 Jenny에게 자신의 감정을 말해야 해.

22 Fear: 나는 Bella가 또다시 상처 받는 걸 원하지 않아.

23 그 애는 그냥 내버려 두어야 해.

24 Joy: 그 애들은 좋은 친구야. 그 애들이 잘 해낼 거야.

Day 3

25 Joy: 휴! 나는 그 애들이 다시 이야기하게 되어 무척 기뻐.

26 Anger: 그래, Bella가 Jenny에게 가서 그 애에게 먼저 말을 걸었지.

27 Joy: Jenny는 일부러 Bella를 피한 게 아니었어.

28 Sadness: 맞아, Jenny는 사과하는 방법을 몰랐던 거야.

29 Fear: 나는 Bella에게 이번과 같은 문제가 더 이상 없기를 바라.

30 Joy: 나도 그래. 하지만 문제들은 성장의 일부야.

31 이번과 꼭 마찬가지로 Bella는 문제들에 직면하게 될 거고, 그것들을 해결할 거고, 그리고 결국 더 현명해질 거야.

※ 다음 문장을 우리말로 쓰시오.

1 Bella is 15 years old this year and these days her feelings are going up and down.

➡ _____

2 Today, she looks down.

➡ _____

3 Let's listen to Bella's feelings and find out why.

➡ _____

4 Anger: What a day! I can't believe Jenny yelled at Bella after the school play.

➡ _____

5 Sadness: Well, that's because Bella forgot her lines on stage.

➡ _____

6 Anger: Jenny pointed out the mistake that Bella made.

➡ _____

7 How could she do that in front of everyone?

➡ _____

8 Joy: But I'm sure Jenny did not mean to hurt Bella.

➡ _____

9 They have been best friends since elementary school. Remember?

➡ _____

10 Anger: That's what I'm saying.

➡ _____

11 A true friend would never put Bella down like that.

➡ _____

12 Fear: I'm worried that they are not going to be friends anymore.

➡ _____

13 Joy: Come on, Fear. Don't go too far. We'll see.

➡ _____

14 Anger: I can't forgive Jenny. She didn't say a word to Bella.

➡ _____

15 Fear: Jenny didn't even look at her.

➡ _____

16 Jenny has never been this cold before.

➡ _____

17 Sadness: Bella ate alone during lunch today. Poor Bella!

➡ _____

18 Joy: Jenny is Bella's best friend.

➡ _____

19 I'm sure there is a reason that we don't know about.

➡ _____

20 Anger: I can't stand this any longer.

➡ _____

21 Bella should just go and tell her about her feelings.

➡ _____

22 Fear: I don't want Bella to be hurt again.

➡ _____

23 She should let it go.

➡ _____

24 Joy: They are good friends. They will work it out.

➡ _____

25 Joy: Whew! I'm so happy that they are talking again.

➡ _____

26 Anger: Yeah, Bella went to Jenny and talked to her first.

➡ _____

27 Joy: Jenny didn't avoid Bella on purpose.

➡ _____

28 Sadness: Yeah, Jenny didn't know a way to say sorry.

➡ _____

29 Fear: I hope Bella doesn't have any more problems like this.

➡ _____

30 Joy: Me, too. But problems are part of growing up.

➡ _____

31 Just like this time, Bella will face the problems, solve them, and become wiser in the end.

➡ _____

※ 다음 괄호 안의 단어들을 우리말에 맞도록 바르게 배열하시오.

1 (is / Bella / years / 15 / old / year / this / and / days / these / feelings / her / going / are / down. / and / up)
➡ _____
_____

2 (she / today, / down. / looks)
➡ _____

3 (listen / let's / Bella's / to / and / feelings / why. / out / find)
➡ _____

4 (a / what / day! // can't / I / Jenny / believe / at / yelled / Bella / the / play. / school / after)
➡ Anger: _____
_____

5 (that's / well, / Bella / because / forgot / lines / her / stage. / on)
➡ Sadness: _____

6 (pointed / Jenny / the / out / that / mistake / made. / Bella)
➡ Anger: _____

7 (could / how / do / she / that / front / in / everyone? / of)
➡ _____

8 (I'm / but / Jenny / sure / not / did / to / mean / Bella. / hurt)
➡ Joy: _____

9 (have / they / been / friends / best / school. / elementary / since // remember?)
➡ _____

10 (what / that's / saying. / I'm)
➡ Anger: _____

11 (true / a / would / friend / put / never / Bella / that. / like / down)
➡ _____

12 (worried / I'm / they / that / not / are / to / going / anymore. / friends / be)
➡ Fear: _____

13 (on, / come / Fear. // go / don't / far. / too // see. / we'll)
➡ Joy: _____

14 (can't / I / Jenny. / forgive // didn't / she / word / a / say / Bella. / to)
➡ Anger: _____

15 (didn't / Jenny / look / even / her. / at)
➡ Fear: _____

1 Bella는 올해 15세이고 요즘 그 애의 기분은 좋다가 안 좋다가 한다.

2 오늘 그 애는 우울해 보인다.

3 Bella의 감정에 귀 기울여 보고 그 이유를 알아보자.

Day 1

4 Anger: 정말 끔찍한 하루야! 학교 연극이 끝난 후 Jenny가 Bella에게 소리를 지르다니 믿을 수가 없어.

5 Sadness: 글쎄, 그건 Bella가 무대에서 그녀의 대사를 잊어버렸기 때문이잖아.

6 Anger: Jenny는 Bella가 저지른 실수를 지적했잖아.

7 어떻게 모든 사람 앞에서 그렇게 할 수가 있니?

8 Joy: 하지만 난 Jenny가 Bella에게 상처를 주려고 했던 건 아니었다고 확신해.

9 그들은 초등학교 때부터 가장 친한 친구였잖아. 기억하지?

10 Anger: 내 말이 바로 그거야.

11 진정한 친구라면 절대로 그런 식으로 Bella를 깎아내리지 않을 거야.

12 Fear: 나는 그들이 더 이상 친구로 지내지 않을까봐 걱정돼.

13 Joy: 자, Fear. 너무 극단적으로 생각하지 마. 곧 알게 되겠지.

Day 2

14 Anger: 난 Jenny를 용서할 수 없어. 그 애는 Bella에게 한마디도 말을 안 했어.

15 Fear: Jenny는 심지어 Bella를 쳐다 보지도 않았어.

16 (has / Jenny / been / never / before. / cold / this)

➡ _____

17 (ate / Bella / during / alone / today. / lunch // Bella! / poor)

➡ Sadness: _____

18 (is / Jenny / friend. / best / Bella's)

➡ Joy: _____

19 (sure / I'm / is / there / reason / a / that / don't / we / about. / know)

➡ _____

20 (can't / I / this / stand / longer. / any)

➡ Anger: _____

21 (should / Bella / go / just / and / her / tell / about / feelings. / her)

➡ _____

22 (don't / I / want / to / Bella / again. / hurt / be)

➡ Fear: _____

23 (should / she / go. / it / let)

➡ _____

24 (are / they / friends. / good // will / they / out. / it / work)

➡ Joy: _____

25 (I'm / whew! / so / that / happy / they / again. / talking / are)

➡ Joy: _____

26 (Bella / yeah, / to / went / Jenny / and / first. / her / to / talked)

➡ Anger: _____

27 (didn't / Jenny / avoid / purpose. / on / Bella)

➡ Joy: _____

28 (Jenny / yeah, / know / didn't / way / a / sorry. / say / to)

➡ Sadness: _____

29 (hope / I / doesn't / Bella / any / have / problems / this. / like / more)

➡ Fear: _____

30 (too. / me, // problems / but / part / are / up. / growing / of)

➡ Joy: _____

31 (like / just / time, / this / Bella / face / will / problems, / the / them, / solve / become / and / wiser / end. / the / in)

➡ _____

_____

16 Jenny가 전에 이렇게 차가웠던 적이 없었어.

17 Sadness: Bella는 오늘 점심시간에 혼자 밥을 먹었잖아. 가엾은 Bella!

18 Joy: Jenny는 Bella의 가장 친한 친구야.

19 나는 우리가 모르는 어떤 이유가 있다고 확신해.

20 Anger: 나는 더 이상 이 상황을 못 참아.

21 Bella는 일단 가서 Jenny에게 자신의 감정을 말해야 해.

22 Fear: 나는 Bella가 또다시 상처받는 걸 원하지 않아.

23 그 애는 그냥 내버려 두어야 해.

24 Joy: 그 애들은 좋은 친구야. 그 애들이 잘 해낼 거야.

Day **3**

25 Joy: 휴! 나는 그 애들이 다시 이야기하게 되어 무척 기뻐.

26 Anger: 그래, Bella가 Jenny에게 가서 그 애에게 먼저 말을 걸었지.

27 Joy: Jenny는 일부러 Bella를 피한 게 아니었어.

28 Sadness: 맞아, Jenny는 사과하는 방법을 몰랐던 거야.

29 Fear: 나는 Bella에게 이번과 같은 문제가 더 이상 없기를 바라.

30 Joy: 나도 그래. 하지만 문제들은 성장의 일부야.

31 이번과 꼭 마찬가지로 Bella는 문제들에 직면하게 될 거고, 그것들을 해결할 거고, 그리고 결국 더 현명해질 거야.

※ 다음 우리말을 영어로 쓰시오.

1 ▶ Bella는 올해 15세이고 요즘 그 애의 기분은 좋다가 안 좋다가 한다.

➡ _____

2 ▶ 오늘 그 애는 우울해 보인다.

➡ _____

3 ▶ Bella의 감정에 귀 기울여 보고 그 이유를 알아보자.

➡ _____

4 ▶ Anger: 정말 끔찍한 하루야! 학교 연극이 끝난 후 Jenny가 Bella에게 소리를 지르다니 믿을 수가 없어.

➡ _____

5 ▶ Sadness: 글쎄, 그건 Bella가 무대에서 그녀의 대사를 잊어버렸기 때문이잖아.

➡ _____

6 ▶ Anger: Jenny는 Bella가 저지른 실수를 지적했잖아.

➡ _____

7 ▶ 어떻게 모든 사람 앞에서 그렇게 할 수가 있니?

➡ _____

8 ▶ Joy: 하지만 난 Jenny가 Bella에게 상처를 주려고 했던 건 아니었다고 확신해.

➡ _____

9 ▶ 그들은 초등학교 때부터 가장 친한 친구였잖아. 기억하지?

➡ _____

10 ▶ Anger: 내 말이 바로 그거야.

➡ _____

11 ▶ 진정한 친구라면 절대로 그런 식으로 Bella를 깎아내리지 않을 거야.

➡ _____

12 ▶ Fear: 나는 그들이 더 이상 친구로 지내지 않을까봐 걱정돼.

➡ _____

13 ▶ Joy: 자, Fear. 너무 극단적으로 생각하지 마. 곧 알게 되겠지.

➡ _____

14 ▶ Anger: 난 Jenny를 용서할 수 없어. 그 애는 Bella에게 한마디도 말을 안 했어.

➡ _____

15 ▶ Fear: Jenny는 심지어 Bella를 쳐다보지도 않았어.

➡ _____

16 Jenny가 전에 이렇게 차가웠던 적이 없었어.
⇨ _____

17 Sadness: Bella는 오늘 점심시간에 혼자 밥을 먹었잖아. 가엾은 Bella!
⇨ _____

18 Joy: Jenny는 Bella의 가장 친한 친구야.
⇨ _____

19 나는 우리가 모르는 어떤 이유가 있다고 확신해.
⇨ _____

20 Anger: 나는 더 이상 이 상황을 못 참아.
⇨ _____

21 Bella는 일단 가서 Jenny에게 자신의 감정을 말해야 해.
⇨ _____

22 Fear: 나는 Bella가 또다시 상처받는 걸 원하지 않아.
⇨ _____

23 그 애는 그냥 내버려 두어야 해.
⇨ _____

24 Joy: 그 애들은 좋은 친구야. 그 애들이 잘 해낼 거야.
⇨ _____

25 Joy: 휴! 나는 그 애들이 다시 이야기하게 되어 무척 기뻐.
⇨ _____

26 Anger: 그래, Bella가 Jenny에게 가서 그 애에게 먼저 말을 걸었지.
⇨ _____

27 Joy: Jenny는 일부러 Bella를 피한 게 아니었어.
⇨ _____

28 Sadness: 맞아, Jenny는 사과하는 방법을 몰랐던 거야.
⇨ _____

29 Fear: 나는 Bella에게 이번과 같은 문제가 더 이상 없기를 바라.
⇨ _____

30 Joy: 나도 그래. 하지만 문제들은 성장의 일부야.
⇨ _____

31 이번과 꼭 마찬가지로 Bella는 문제들에 직면하게 될 거고, 그것들을 해결할 거고, 그리고 결국 더 현명해질 거야.
⇨ _____

※ 다음 우리말과 일치하도록 빈칸에 알맞은 말을 쓰시오.

Wrap up 1

1. Mr. Jones: Daisy, you're _____ _____.

2. Daisy: I'm really sorry, Mr. Jones. I _____ _____ _____ again _____ _____.

3. Mr. Jones: Well, I think you _____ _____ _____ go to bed _____.

4. You _____ _____ _____ your bag the night before, so you can _____ _____ in the morning.

5. Daisy: Okay, Mr. Jones. I'll _____ _____ _____.

1. Mr. Jones: Daisy, 너 또 지각이구나.
2. Daisy: Jones 선생님, 정말 죄송해요. 어젯밤에 또 늦게까지 자지 않고 깨어 있었어요.
3. Mr. Jones: 음, 내 생각엔 넌 더 일찍 잠자리에 들려고 노력해야 할 것 같구나.
4. 또 전날 밤에 가방을 싸 둔다면 아침에 시간을 절약할 수 있어.
5. Daisy: 알겠어요, Jones 선생님. 조언해 주신 것을 해 볼게요.

Read & Think

1. Bella: Jenny, I was _____ _____ you _____ _____ my mistake _____ _____ _____ _____.

2. But I'm sure you didn't _____ _____ _____ my feelings.

3. Jenny: I'm so sorry, Bella. _____ _____ _____ _____ to me first.

1. Bella: Jenny야, 네가 다른 사람들 앞에서 내 잘못을 지적했을 때 화가 났어.
2. 그렇지만 난 네가 내게 상처를 주려고 일부러 그런 게 아니라고 믿어.
3. Jenny: Bella야, 미안해. 먼저 내게 와 줘서 고마워.

Think & Write

1. Dear _____ _____,

2. I _____ _____ _____ you a problem that I _____.

3. I'm _____ _____ my terrible _____ _____.

4. I _____ _____ this problem _____ _____ _____.

5. I want to _____ _____ in math.

6. But when I _____ _____ _____ math, I just _____ _____ _____ it.

7. I don't know _____ _____ _____.

8. I _____ _____ _____ a good night's sleep _____ _____ this worry.

9. Can you _____ my worries _____?

1. 걱정 인형에게,
2. 나는 너에게 내가 가진 문제를 말하고 싶어.
3. 나는 나의 끔찍한 수학 성적이 걱정돼.
4. 나는 작년부터 이 문제를 가지고 있어.
5. 나는 수학을 더 잘하고 싶어.
6. 하지만 내가 수학을 공부하려고 하면, 나는 단지 그것에 집중할 수 없어.
7. 나는 무엇을 해야 할지 모르겠어.
8. 이 걱정 때문에 밤에 잠도 잘 못자.
9. 내 걱정을 없애 줄 수 있겠니?

※ 다음 우리말을 영어로 쓰시오.

Wrap up 1

1. Mr. Jones: Daisy, 너 또 지각이구나.
   ➡ _____

2. Daisy: Jones 선생님, 정말 죄송해요. 어젯밤에 또 늦게까지 자지 않고 깨어 있었어요.
   ➡ _____

3. Mr. Jones: 음, 내 생각엔 넌 더 일찍 잠자리에 들려고 노력해야 할 것 같구나.
   ➡ _____

4. 또 전날 밤에 가방을 싸 둔다면 아침에 시간을 절약할 수 있어.
   ➡ _____

5. Daisy: 알겠어요, Jones 선생님. 조언해 주신 것을 해 볼게요.
   ➡ _____

Read & Think

1. Bella: Jenny야, 네가 다른 사람들 앞에서 내 잘못을 지적했을 때 화가 났었어.
   ➡ _____

2. 그렇지만 난 네가 내게 상처를 주려고 일부러 그런 게 아니라고 믿어.
   ➡ _____

3. Jenny: Bella야, 미안해. 먼저 내게 와 줘서 고마워.
   ➡ _____

Think & Write

1. 걱정 인형에게,
   ➡ _____

2. 나는 너에게 내가 가진 문제를 말하고 싶어.
   ➡ _____

3. 나는 나의 끔찍한 수학 성적이 걱정 돼.
   ➡ _____

4. 나는 작년부터 이 문제를 가지고 있어.
   ➡ _____

5. 나는 수학을 더 잘하고 싶어.
   ➡ _____

6. 하지만 내가 수학을 공부하려고 하면, 나는 단지 그것에 집중할 수 없어.
   ➡ _____

7. 나는 무엇을 해야 할지 모르겠어.
   ➡ _____

8. 이 걱정 때문에 밤에 잠도 잘 못자.
   ➡ _____

9. 내 걱정을 없애 줄 수 있겠니?
   ➡ _____

MEMO

MEMO

영어 기출 문제집

적중100

1학기

정답 및 해설

비상 | 김진완

중 2

영어 기출 문제집

1학기

정답 및 해설

비상 | 김진완

중 2

Lesson
3

I Wonder Why,
I Wonder How

시험대비 실력평가
p.08

01 impossible 02 weigh   03 ①   04 ②
05 (1) challenge (2) amusement (3) add (4) amount
06 ③   07 (A) of (B) up (C) up

01 주어진 관계는 반의어를 나타낸다. possible: 가능한, impossible 불가능한

02 주로 저울을 사용해서 어떤 사람이나 사물이 얼마나 무거운지 측정하다를 나타내는 말은 weigh(무게를 재다)이다.

03 ① experiment: 실험

04 lock은 동사로 '잠그다', 명사로는 '자물쇠'라는 의미를 나타낸다. lock ~ in one's arms는 '~를 꼭 껴안다, 끌어안다'를 의미한다.

05 challenge: 도전, amusement park: 놀이 공원, add: 더하다, amount: 양

06 주어진 문장에서 fair는 '박람회'를 뜻한다. 이와 같은 의미로 쓰인 것은 ③번이고 나머지는 모두 '공정한'을 의미한다.

07 take care of: ~을 돌보다, pick up: ~을 집다, light up: ~을 밝히다

서술형 시험대비
p.09

01 unlock   02 collector   03 hide
04 (1) Let's say that (2) pump up (3) light up
05 (1) car horn (2) unbelievable (3) scare
06 (A) possibility (B) amazingly (C) ability
07 (1) Let's paint evenly over the wall with yellow.
   (2) Have you heard about the special event at the science museum?
   (3) Let's say that potatoes produce electricity.

01 주어진 관계는 반의어를 나타낸다. lock: 잠그다, unlock: 자물쇠를 풀다

02 취미나 일로 무언가를 수집하는 사람을 가리키는 말은 collector(수집가)이다.

03 무언가를 보이지 않거나 찾을 수 없는 장소에 놓거나 보관하는 것은 hide(숨기다)이다.

04 let's say that ~라고 가정해 보자, pump up: 바람을 넣다, light up: ~을 환하게 밝히다, 점등하다

05 car horn: 자동차 경적, unbelievable: 믿을 수 없는, scare: 겁을 주다

06 possibility: 가능성, amazingly: 놀랍게도, ability: 능력

교과서

Conversation

핵심 Check
p.10~11

1 (1) Have you heard about (2) Yes, I have. Have you
  (3) No, I haven't
2 (1) What do you mean (2) What is it (3) tell, more

교과서 대화문 익히기

Check(√) True or False
p.12

1 T 2 F 3 T 4 F

교과서 확인학습
p.14~15

Listen & Talk 1 A-1
What show / Have you heard about it / science / interesting

Listen & Talk 1 A-2
No. I haven't / Let me show you / what a great application

Listen & Talk 1 B
Have you heard about / offers / how to control it

Listen & Talk 2 A-1
What do you mean / electricity

Listen & Talk 2 A-2
what did you do last weekend / put / in vinegar / turns into

Listen & Talk 2 B
What do you mean / hide / Mix / How can you read the card / appears

Communication
Have you heard about / Yes, I have / What do you mean / how to take care of it / useful

excited / experiments / looking forward to

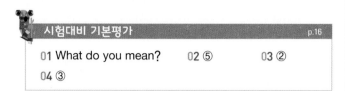

시험대비 기본평가 p.16

01 What do you mean?　　02 ⑤　　03 ②
04 ③

02 경험 여부를 묻는 질문에 대한 대답으로 'Yes, I have.' 또는 'No, I haven't.'가 적절하다.

03 주어진 문장은 경험 여부를 묻고 있으며 이에 대해 적절한 대답 (No, I haven't.)이 이어지므로 (B)가 적절하다.

04 Mike가 무엇에 관심이 있는지는 알 수 없다.

시험대비 실력평가 p.17~18

01 (B) – (A) – (E) – (D) – (C)　02 Have you heard about the DIY Drone Class?　03 ①　　04 We can make our own special drone and learn how to control it.　　05 No, I haven't.　　06 ①
07 ⑤　　08 ⑤　　09 ③　　10 달걀을 이틀 동안 식초에 담가 놓는다.　11 ②　　12 ④

01 (B) 경험 질문 - (A) 대답 및 구체적인 설명 요구 - (E) 구체적인 설명 및 시범 - (D) 질문에 대한 대답 - (C) 놀라움 표현

02 경험을 묻는 현재완료를 쓴다.

03 advertise: 홍보하다, apologize: 사과하다, appreciate: 고마워하다, celebrate: 축하하다, protest: 항의하다

04 DIY 드론 수업에서 당신만의 특별한 드론을 만들고 어떻게 이를 조종하는지 배울 수 있다.

06 문맥상 '설명하다'라는 뜻의 explain이 알맞다. produce: 생산하다, challenge: 도전하다, pump: 물을 퍼 올리다, decorate: 장식하다

07 나머지는 모두 흥미로움을 표현하지만 ⑤번은 관심이 없음을 이야기한다.

09 이어지는 문장에서 egg ball에 대한 자세한 설명이 이어져야 하므로 (C)가 적절하다.

11 (A)는 메시지를 숨길 수 있다는 의미가 되어야 하므로 hide, (B)는 베이킹 소다와 물을 섞으라는 의미가 되어야 하므로 Mix(섞다), (C)는 그러면 메시지가 보인다는 의미가 되어야 하므로 appears가 적절하다.

서술형 시험대비 p.19

01 Have you heard about the Sci-Magic show?

02 What do you mean?
03 ⓓ → to explain
04 It is about using science to explain magic tricks.
05 mean
06 (A) phone application　(B) any questions
　(C) the weather

02 이어지는 대화에서 BFF를 구체적으로 설명하고 있으므로 빈칸에 구체적인 정보를 요청하는 표현이 알맞다.

03 목적을 나타내는 to부정사 형태가 알맞다.

04 과학 마술 쇼는 마술 묘기를 설명하기 위해 과학을 사용하는 것에 관한 것이다.

05 potato clock이 무슨 의미냐고 묻는 표현이므로 mean이 적절하다.

06 오늘 나의 사랑스러운 아들 Tom이 새로운 휴대폰 어플리케이션 Chat Robot을 소개해 주었다. 이것은 어떠한 질문에도 대답할 수 있었다. Tom은 내게 어떻게 작동하는지 날씨에 대해 물어보며 보여주었다. 놀랍게도 이것은 우리에게 날씨에 대해 알려주었고 우리가 무엇이 필요할지 알려주었다. 나는 이 어플리케이션에 매우 놀랐다.

교과서
Grammar

핵심 Check p.20~21

1 (1) is covered with　(2) is run by
2 (1) to read　(2) to win　(3) to write on

시험대비 기본평가 p.22

01 (1) read about → read　(2) born → was born
　(3) choose → to choose　(4) for her → to her
02 (1) was invited　(2) to achieve　(3) are caused
　(4) to hurt　(5) were found
03 (1) I want something to eat.
　(2) We have a trip to plan.
　(3) The new highway was completed last month.
　(4) The ink is washed off easily with water.

01 (1) 'read a book'이 성립하므로 전치사 없이 수식하는 것이 옳다. (2) be born 태어나다 (3) options를 수식해야 하므로 to부정사 형태로 써야 한다. (4) 4형식 동사의 수동태가 직접목적어를 주어로 할 경우 간접목적어에 전치사를 붙이며, give는 전치사 to를 쓰는 동사이다. 단, 이때의 to는 생략하기도 한다.

02 (1) 주어가 회의에 초대받는 것이므로 수동태, (2) the goal을 수식해야 하므로 to부정사, (3) 사고가 야기되는 것이므로 수동태, (4) anything을 수식해야 하므로 to부정사, (5) 열쇠가 발견되는 것이며 이를 전의 일이므로 과거형 수동태를 쓰는 것이 옳다.

03 (1) '먹을 것'이므로 to eat이 something을 수식하게 한다. (2) '계획할 여행'이므로 to plan이 a trip을 수식하도록 만든다. (3) 고속도로가 '완공되는 것'이므로 수동태, (4) 잉크가 '지워지는 것'이므로 수동태를 쓰는 것이 옳다.

시험대비 실력평가
p.23~25

01 ④	02 ②	03 ④
04 something to play with	05 ④	06 ②, ⑤
07 ⑤	08 There is nothing to see here.	
09 borrow, to read	10 ③	11 ③
12 ④	13 ③	14 is expected 15 ④
16 ②	17 ④	18 I wasn't seen singing a song with my friends by anybody.
19 was discovered by	20 ③	21 ②
22 ②, ③	23 Do you have a story to tell?	
24 I was told to taste the food by Mom.		

01 'take care of twin sisters', 'ask many questions'라고 표현하므로 ④번이 옳다.

02 ① be filled with: ~으로 가득 차 있다 ③ 형용사와 to부정사가 동시에 명사를 수식할 때 '형용사+to부정사' 순서로 수식한다. ④ 5형식 동사의 목적격보어가 원형부정사인 경우 수동태를 만들 때 to부정사화한다. 따라서 made to do가 옳다. ⑤ make는 직접목적어를 주어로 한 수동태에서 간접목적어에 전치사 for를 붙이는 동사이므로 for me로 쓰는 것이 옳다.

03 모두 to부정사가 형용사로 사용되고 있으나 ④번은 목적을 나타내는 부사로 사용되었다.

04 play with something: 무언가를 가지고 놀다

05 ④ 구동사의 수동태에서 'by+행위자'를 생략하기 쉬우므로 이에 유의한다. was looked after by her라고 쓰는 것이 옳다.

06 주어진 문장은 4형식 동사의 과거 수동태이다. 따라서 능동태 시제를 과거로 고르는 것이 옳으며, 간접목적어가 주어로 쓰일 경우 별도로 전치사를 사용하지 않는다.

07 ①~④는 모두 수동태로 쓰여 made가 들어가는 것이 옳으며, ⑤번은 진행형으로 쓰여 making이 들어간다.

08 '볼만한 것'이므로 see를 to부정사로 만들어 nothing을 수식하게 만든다.

09 journey: 여행

10 by 이외의 다른 전치사를 쓰는 수동태 문제이다. be filled with: ~로 가득 차다 be pleased with: ~으로 기뻐하다

11 주어진 문장을 수동태로 바르게 만드는 문제이다. The child는 단수 주어이고, 시제가 saw로 과거형이므로 수동태를 만들 때 was seen으로 쓰고, 목적격보어 playing은 그대로 써주면 된다.

12 '백명의 손님을 대접할 점심'이므로 점심을 수식하면서 동시에 동사원형 serve를 취하기 위해서는 전치사 for가 아니라 to부정사를 쓰는 것이 옳다.

13 건물이 디자인된 것이냐고 묻고 있으므로 수동태를 써야 한다. 따라서 Did가 아닌 Was를 쓰는 것이 옳다.

14 정시에 도착하리라고 예상된다는 의미가 옳으므로 expect의 수동태를 써야 한다.

15 직접목적어를 주어로 할 때 간접목적어에 전치사 for를 붙이는 동사는 ④번이다. 나머지 동사들은 모두 to를 사용한다.

16 '친구에게 줄 어떤 것'이란 의미가 적절하므로 to give가 something을 수식하는 ②번이 옳다.

17 주어진 문장과 ④번은 형용사로 쓰인 to부정사이다. ① 부사적 용법, ②, ③, ⑤ 명사적 용법

18 주어진 문장의 의미는 '누구도 내가 내 친구들과 함께 노래 부르는 것을 보지 못했다.'는 의미이다.

19 누가 그 보물을 발견했는지를 묻고 있다. 수동태를 사용하여 Jackson 선장에 의해 발견되었다고 답할 수 있다.

20 deal with a problem이라고 쓰는 것이 옳으므로 to deal with가 정답이다. high blood pressure: 고혈압 deal with: ~을 다루다, ~을 대처하다

21 'play with friends'이므로 전치사 with를 쓰는 것이 옳다.

22 밑줄 친 offered는 4형식 동사로 직접목적어를 주어로 한 수동태에서는 간접목적어에 전치사 to를 붙이는 동사이다. 따라서 ②, ③번이 옳다.

23 '들려줄 이야기'이므로 to부정사가 a story를 수식하도록 문장을 만든다.

24 동사 told는 과거형이며 능동태의 목적어를 주어로 사용하여 수동태 문장을 만들어야 하므로 I에 수의 일치를 하여 was told를 쓴다.

서술형 시험대비
p.26~27

01 was written by

02 (1) to read (2) to study (3) to worry about

03 I was given the watch by my father a few years ago. / The watch was given (to) me by my father a few years ago.

04 was made to laugh a lot by Helen's brother

05 was built / was invented / was divided / is surrounded / were surprised

06 something to say to you

07 I don't have enough time to work out these days.

08 ⓐ to do ⓑ was thrown

09 ⓐ to walk ⓑ set ⓒ were taken ⓓwere brought

10 I have no reason to refuse his request.

11 (1) A tree was planted by the Emperor himself.

   (2) A French company made us this car.

   (3) The young girls look up to the man.

   (4) Honey is made by worker bees.

12 Do you have any samples to give out?

13 (1) to do (2) to eat (3) to talk about

   (4) to ride (5) to read

14 The brave young man caught the thief.

   The thief was caught by the brave young man.

01 햄릿은 누가 썼는지에 관한 질문이므로 셰익스피어에 의해 쓰여진 것이라고 답하면 된다.

02 (1) a magazine을 수식하는 to부정사가 와야 한다. (2) 공부할 많은 과목들'을 의미하므로 to부정사를 쓰는 것이 옳다. (3) '~에 관하여 걱정하다'는 'worry about ~'이므로 전치사 about을 써야 한다.

03 4형식 동사의 수동태를 묻는 문제이다. 동사 give는 직접목적어를 주어로 하는 수동태에서 간접목적어에 전치사 to를 붙인다. 이때의 to는 생략할 수 있다.

04 목적보어가 원형부정사인 경우 수동태를 만들 때 to부정사화한다.

05 건설 비용이 비싸지 않았기 때문에 한씨 가족이 새 기숙사를 지었다. / 야구 경기는 미국인들에 의해 만들어졌다. / 우리나라는 두 나라로 나뉘었다. / 한국은 삼면이 물로 둘러싸여 있다. / 우리는 그들이 회의에 오리라고 기대하지 않았지만 그들이 그곳에 있었다. 우리는 그들을 보고 놀랐다.

06 '말할 어떤 것'이라는 의미로 작문을 하는 것이 좋다. to부정사가 something을 꾸미도록 문장을 만든다.

07 '운동할 시간'이므로 time to work out의 어순이 옳다.

08 '해야 할 많은 것'이므로 to부정사 형태로 many things를 수식하는 것이 옳으며 throw a party는 '파티를 열다'는 의미이다.

09 ⓐ '달 위를 걸은 최초의 인간'이라는 의미이므로 to부정사로 만들어 the first man을 수식하게 한다. ⓑ Neil이 달에 발을 디딘 것이므로 능동태 과거시제로 쓴다. ⓒ 사진이 찍혀서 지구로 가져다진 것은 수동태를 쓰는 것이 옳다.

10 거절할 이유라고 하였으므로 refuse를 to부정사로 만들어 reason을 수식하게 만든다.

11 (1) Emperor: 황제 (2) 4형식으로 쓰인 make이다. 직접목적어를 주어로 사용하고 있으므로 간접목적어에 전치사 for를 붙인다. 능동태로 A French company made this car for us.로 써도 좋다. (3) look up to: ~을 존경하다 (4) worker bee: 일벌

12 나눠주는 샘플이 있나요? give out: 나눠주다

13 (1) many boring things를 수식하는 to부정사 가 와야 하며,

'지겨운 일을 하다'는 'do boring things'이므로 to do가 오는 것이 옳다. (2) '먹을 것'이므로 something을 수식하는 'to eat'을 쓰는 것이 옳다. (3) '~에 관하여 말하다'는 표현은 'talk about ~'이다. (4) a bicycle을 수식하는 to부정사를 써야 한다. (5) '읽을 시간'이므로 to read를 써서 time을 수식한다.

14 catch: ~을 붙잡다

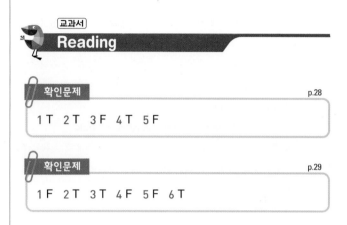

Reading

확인문제 p.28

1 T 2 T 3 F 4 T 5 F

확인문제 p.29

1 F 2 T 3 T 4 F 5 F 6 T

교과서 확인학습 A p.30~31

01 amazing things are possible

02 are they actually possible 03 Let Down

04 must lower, to let people in

05 could, hold up a person

06 hold up, has about

07 All those hairs, hold up

08 the ability to hold up

09 wrap her hair around

10 doesn't, will get, sore 11 Scare for

12 scare children to get, from 13 is powered by

14 produce electricity to light up, from

15 be changed into

16 helpful in, because the amount is, small

17 For example, from, produces

18 of the average, electricity

19 an unbelievable amount of screams, entire

20 Away 21 is lifted and flown by

22 actually work 23 weighs about

24 normal, an amusement park

25 about, to lift up

26 have to think about, themselves

27 add a few more thousand

28 challenge, pumping up all those

1 In animation movies, amazing things are possible.

2 But are they actually possible in real life?

3 Let Down Your Hair, Rapunzel!

4 In the animation, Rapunzel must lower her long hair to let people in her tower.

5 But could human hair really hold up a person?

6 Surprisingly, yes! A single hair can hold up 100g and an average head has about 120,000 hairs.

7 All those hairs could hold up a couple of elephants!

8 With her hair, Rapunzel has the ability to hold up a person.

9 But she should wrap her hair around something strong and heavy.

10 If she doesn't, she will get a very sore neck.

11 We Scare for Energy

12 In the animation, monsters scare children to get energy from their screams.

13 Amazingly, their city is powered by this sound!

14 But could we actually produce electricity to light up a city from sound?

15 Yes, sound can be changed into electricity.

16 But it would not be helpful in our everyday activities because the amount is too small.

17 For example, the sound from a car horn only produces 50mv.

18 That is only 1/4400 of the average 220v of electricity in our homes.

19 So, we would need an unbelievable amount of screams to light up an entire city.

20 Up, Up and Away!

21 The house is lifted and flown by thousands of balloons in the animation.

22 Could that actually work?

23 Let's say that a house weighs about 50,000kg.

24 A normal balloon at an amusement park can lift about 14g.

25 So we need about 3,570,000 balloons to lift up the house.

26 We also have to think about the weight of the balloons themselves and the strings.

27 Then, we need to add a few more thousand balloons.

28 Now, the biggest challenge is pumping up all those balloons!

01 amazing things	02 ④	03 ③
04 ③	05 is powered	06 ④	07 ③
08 ⑤	09 ①	10 animation	11 ③
12 The hardest part is pumping them up.	13 ③
14 ③	15 ⑤	16 doesn't wrap her hair around something strong and heavy	17 ④
18 We Scare for Energy	19 to light up	20 ③
21 ⑤	22 ⑤	23 is lifted and flown
24 ② → lift	25 ②

01 애니메이션 영화 속에서 벌어지는 놀라운 것들을 가리키는 대명사이다.

02 머리카락으로 코끼리도 들어 올릴 수 있다고 하였으므로 ④번은 글의 내용과 일치하지 않는다.

03 ③ Rapunzel의 머리카락으로 사람들을 들어 올릴 수 있는 것이므로 With라고 쓰는 것이 옳다.

04 '아픈 목'이라는 의미이므로 painful이 옳다.

05 소리에 의해서 동력 공급을 받는다는 의미가 자연스러우므로 수동태를 쓰는 것이 옳다.

06 소리가 전기로 바뀌는 양이 너무 적으므로 유용하지 않을 것이라는 말이 들어가는 것이 가장 적절하다. 따라서 ④번이 옳다. ①, ②: 감사하는 ③: 사려 깊은 ⑤: 훌륭한

07 소리로 전기를 만드는 것이 일상생활에 도움이 되지 않는 이유를 설명하기 위한 예를 들고 있다. 따라서 For example이 옳다.

08 ⑤번은 글에 나와 있지 않은 내용이다.

09 ⓐ에는 수동태에 쓰이는 전치사 by가 들어가고, ⓑ, ⓒ, ⓓ는 '대략'의 의미를 갖는 부사 about이 들어간다. ⓔ 전치사 about이 들어간다.

10 그림이 움직이는 것처럼 보이는 영화는 애니메이션이다.

11 ⓐ, ⓑ, ⓓ가 글의 내용과 일치한다. a piece of cake: 식은 죽 먹기

12 가장 큰 어려움은 모든 풍선에 바람을 넣는 것이라고 하였다.

13 (A)는 '~하는 것'이라고 해석되는 동명사이다. 따라서 ③번이 옳다.

14 주어진 문장의 All those hairs가 가리키는 것은 120,000 hairs이다.

15 밑줄 친 ⓐ는 '대략'이라는 의미로 쓰인 부사 about이다. 따라서 ⑤번이 정답이다. ①, ④ ~에 관한 ② 여기저기 ③ 지금 막 ~하려고 하여

16 앞 문장에서 언급한 것을 하지 않을 경우에 대하여 말하고 있다.

17 Rapunzel이 코끼리를 들어 올릴 수 있다는 말은 나와 있지 않다.

18 '우리는 에너지를 얻기 위해 겁준다.'는 의미이다.

19 도시를 밝혀주는 전기를 소리로부터 만들어 내는 것에 관한 글이다.

20 소리를 전기로 바꾸는 양이 매우 적기 때문에 전체 도시를 밝히기 위해서는 엄청난 양의 비명소리가 필요하다는 의미가 옳다. 따라서 ③번이 가장 적절하다. reasonable: 합리적인 incredible: 놀라운, 믿기 힘든

21 우리에게 전기가 필요한 이유는 글에 나와 있지 않다.

22 (A) 괴물들이 아이들을 겁주는 것이므로 능동태, (B) 괴물들의 도시를 지칭하는 것이므로 their, (C) 소리로부터 전기를 생산하는 것이므로 from이 옳다. into를 쓰면 전기를 소리로 바꾼다는 의미가 되므로 글의 내용상 옳지 않다.

23 수 천 개의 풍선이 집을 들어 올린 것이므로, 수동태를 쓰는 것이 옳다.

24 풍선이 대략 14g의 무게를 들어 올릴 수 있다는 의미이다. 따라서 수동태가 아닌 능동태로 쓰는 것이 옳다.

25 사람의 머리카락이 사람을 들어 올릴 수 있는지 물음 → (B) 머리카락 한 개가 들어 올릴 수 있는 무게와 사람의 평균 머리카락 개수 → (A) Rapunzel이 머리카락으로 사람을 들어 올릴 수 있음 → (C) 하지만 목이 아프지 않으려면 머리카락을 강하고 무거운 것에 감아야 함

서술형 시험대비
p.38~39

01 holding up a person with her hair **02** to allow people to enter her tower **03** is wrapped, strong and heavy **04** It can hold up 100g. **05** be held up **06** ⓐ 아이들의 ⓑ 괴물들의 **07** sound can be changed into electricity **08** Because the amount is too small. **09** is produced by the sound from a car horn **10** scared **11** The house is lifted and flown by thousands of balloons in the animation. **12** It can lift about 14g. **13** to lift a house / are needed, pumping up all those balloons

01 Rapunzel이 영화 속에서 하는 놀라는 일은 그녀의 머리카락으로 사람을 들어 올리는 것이다.

02 allow+목적어+to부정사: 목적어가 V하는 것을 허락하다. enter: ~로 들어가다

03 주어가 Rapunzel의 머리카락이므로 수동태를 써서 표현한다. Rapunzel의 머리카락이 강하고 무거운 것에 감겨 있지 않으면 그녀의 목이 아플 것이다.

04 질문: 한 올의 머리카락은 얼마만큼의 무게를 지탱할 수 있나요?

05 밑줄 친 문장 ⓑ를 수동태로 만드는 문제이다. 조동사 뒤에는 동사원형을 써야 하므로 be동사를 원형으로 바꿔 답을 쓰는 것에 유의한다.

06 아이들이 비명소리로부터 에너지를 얻어 괴물들의 도시에 전기를 공급받는다.

---

07 목적어가 sound이므로 sound를 주어로 하여 수동태를 만든다. 행위자가 중요한 대상이 아닐 경우 'by+행위자'는 생략해도 무방하다.

08 질문: 소리를 전기로 바꾸는 것이 우리들의 일상적인 활동에 왜 유용하지 않은지 그 이유를 쓰시오.

09 목적어를 주어로 두었으므로, 수동태 문장을 만든다. 50mv는 셀 수 없는 양이므로 be동사를 단수로 쓰는 것에 유의한다.

10 be scared: 겁먹다

11 목적어 the house를 주어로 하고, the house는 단수이므로 수의 일치에 유의하여 수동태를 만든다.

12 놀이공원에 있는 보통의 풍선은 몇 그램의 무게를 들어 올릴 수 있는지 묻고 있다.

13 풍선으로 집을 들어 올리는 것이 가능하냐는 질문에, 대략 357만개의 풍선이 필요하지만 그 모든 풍선에 바람을 넣는 것은 힘든 도전이라고 말한다. imagine은 동명사를 목적어로 취하는 동사이다.

영역별 핵심문제
p.41~45

01 surprisingly **02** (1) looking forward to (2) pump up (3) Let's say that (4) turn into **03** ④ **04** ④ **05** (1) May I pick your brain? (2) My mother asked me to light up the lamp. (3) I saw a couple of birds sitting on the bench. **06** Have you heard about the science festival? **07** ⓓ → show **08** ② **09** We put an egg in vinegar for two days. **10** the egg is changed into a ball **11** ⑤ **12** ⓔ appears **13** ⑤ **14** Yes, I have. **15** (A) a Pic Gardener App (B) how to take care of the plant (C) useful **16** ② **17** ② **18** ④ **19** Lamon's daughter was not allowed to go to the park alone by Lamon. **20** ③ **21** ④ **22** ④ **23** to read, to drink, to sit on[in] **24** ④ **25** are taken care of by him **26** ④ **27** ④ **28** her hair **29** ③, ④ **30** ⑤ **31** ⑤ **32** An unbelievable amount of screams

01 주어진 관계는 형용사와 부사의 관계를 나타낸다.

02 look forward to: ~을 기대하다, pump up: 바람을 넣다, let's say that: ~을 가정해 보자, turn into: ~가 되다

03 lower: 낮추다

04 주어진 문장에서 miss는 '놓치다'를 의미하며 이와 같은 의미로 쓰인 것은 '그들은 단 하나의 음도 놓치고 싶어 하지 않는다.'라는 의미로 쓰인 ④번이다. ①번은 '이해하지 못하다', ②, ③, ⑤번은 '그리워하다'를 의미한다.

05 pick one's brain: ~의 지혜를 빌리다

---

07 사역동사 let 뒤에 원형부정사 show가 적절하다.

08 엄마가 Tom의 시범을 통해 놀라움을 나타냈음을 알 수 있으므로 surprised(놀란)가 적절하다.

10 change를 사용하여 수동태로 바꾸어 쓸 수 있다. turn into: ~가 되다

11 왜 달걀이 공으로 변했는지는 알 수 없다.

12 동사가 오는 자리이므로 appears가 알맞다.

14 have 뒤에는 heard about it이 생략된 것이다.

15 나는 오늘 Minho와 함께 Smart App Contest에 대해 이야기하였다. 그는 거기에 참가할 것이라고 이야기하였다. 나는 a Pic Gardener App에 대한 그의 아이디어에 매우 인상 깊었다. 그것은 내가 식물 사진을 찍을 때 어떻게 식물을 관리해야 하는지 알려주는 앱이었다. 나는 이것이 유용할 것이라고 생각했다. 나는 그가 대회에서 잘할 것이라 믿는다.

16 Jin에 의하여 그림이 그려진 것이므로 ②번이 옳다.

17 ② disappear는 자동사로 수동태가 될 수 없다. was를 삭제한다.

18 의문문이므로 anything을 쓰는 것이 좋으며 -thing으로 끝나는 부정대명사는 '형용사+to부정사' 어순으로 수식을 받는다.

19 본동사가 과거이며 Lamon의 딸이 주어로 쓰이므로 3인칭 과거동사를 써서 수동태를 만든다.

20 ③ '함께 갈 친구'이므로 전치사 with와 함께 써야 한다.

21 ④ happen은 자동사이므로 수동태로 쓰일 수 없다.

22 ①번은 목적격보어가 원형부정사인 5형식 동사의 수동태이므로 to clean으로 고쳐야 하며, ②번은 친구들에 의해 강아지라고 불리는 것이므로 수동태인 was called, ③번은 방에 불들이 꺼졌는지를 물어보는 수동태 의문문이므로 주어 the lights에 맞추어 Were, ⑤번은 바이올린이 연주되는 것이므로 수동태를 쓰는 것이 옳다.

23 to부정사의 형용사 용법을 활용하여 빈칸을 채울 수 있다.

24 ④ discuss는 타동사이므로 전치사 없이 목적어를 취한다. 따라서 전치사 about을 삭제하는 것이 옳다.

25 목적어가 복수명사인 my sisters이므로 수동태 be동사를 복수동사로 쓴다. relieved: 안도한 take care of: ~을 돌보다

26 pick은 '(꽃)을 꺾다', '(과일)을 따다', '~을 고르다'의 의미이다. '~을 줍다'라는 의미로 사용될 때에는 pick up으로 표현한다.

27 ⓐ amazing ⓑ lower ⓒ let ⓓ wrap이 들어가는 것이 옳다.

28 Rapunzel은 그녀의 머리카락으로 사람을 들어 올리는 능력이 있다.

29 하나의 머리에 평균적으로 120,000개의 머리카락이 있다고 하였다. 코끼리 한 마리의 무게는 6톤이다. (0.1x120,000/2) ①, ②, ⑤번은 글을 읽고 답할 수 없다.

30 주어진 문장의 That이 지칭하는 것은 50mv이다. 따라서 ⑤번에 들어가는 것이 가장 적절하다.

31 ⓐ는 형용사로 쓰인 to부정사로 electricity를 수식하고 있다.

---

⑤번은 부사로 사용된 to부정사로 '~하기 위하여'라는 의미로 해석된다.

32 마지막 문장을 수동태로 만든 것이다. 주어 자리가 비어 있으므로 본래 문장의 목적어를 빈칸에 써준다.

단원별 예상문제 　　　　p.46~49

01 (1) take away　(2) turn on　(3) take care of　(4) light up　　02 experiment　　03 (1) turn into　(2) wrap, around　(3) a couple of　　04 ⑤ 05 (C) – (E) – (B) – (D) – (A)　　06 have you heard about the Chat Robot? 07 application 08 ⑤　　09 She made a potato clock yesterday.　　10 It can work because potatoes can produce electricity.　　11 ④ 12 ③　　13 ④　　14 ③　　15 Did he show the picture to you? / Was the picture shown to you by him?　　16 Practice is the only way to master English.　　17 ⑤　　18 ⑤ 19 ③　　20 ⑤　　21 They scare children. 22 ④　　23 Lifting up a house with thousands of balloons　24 the weight of the balloons, the strings

01 take away: ~을 가져가다, turn on: ~을 켜다, take care of: ~을 돌보다, light up: ~을 밝히다, 점등하다

02 무슨 일이 일어나는지 연구해서 새로운 과학적 지식을 얻기 위해 행해지는 과학적 검사

03 turn into: ~이 되다, wrap A around B: A를 B에 감싸다, a couple of: 한 쌍의, 둘의

04 lift: (동) 들어 올리다, (명) 승강기

05 (C) 무슨 쇼를 보고 있는지 질문 - (E) 대답 및 경험 질문 - (B) 대답 및 구체적인 설명 요구 - (D) 프로그램에 대한 구체적 설명 - (A) 흥미 표현

07 특정한 일을 하기 위해 고안된 프로그램을 가리키는 말은 application(응용 프로그램)이다.

08 Tom의 엄마가 밖에 비에 놀란다는 설명은 대화의 내용과 일치하지 않는다.

09 Mina는 어제 감자 시계를 만들었다.

10 Mina의 시계는 감자가 전기를 만들어 내기 때문에 작동할 수 있다.

11 전치사 at의 목적어 자리이므로 동명사로 만들고, '의지할 친구'이므로 to부정사로 a friend를 수식하게 만드는 것이 옳다.

12 ⓑ disappear는 자동사이므로 수동태로 쓸 수 없다. ④ 누군가와 결혼한 상태임을 표현할 때에는 'be married to'라고 쓰는 것이 옳다.

13 -thing으로 끝나는 부정대명사의 수식은 '형용사+to부정사' 어순이므로 ④번이 옳다.

14 ③ 능동태의 시제가 과거이므로 were canceled로 쓰는 것이 옳다.

16 practice: 연습 master: ~에 숙달[통달]하다

17 (A) let down: ~을 아래로 내리다 (B) the ability를 수식하는 to부정사 (C) 부정어를 포함하고 있으므로 Unless는 쓸 수 없다.

18 밑줄 친 ⓐ는 '목적'을 나타내는 부사로 사용된 to부정사이다. ① hope의 목적어로 쓰인 명사적 용법 ② 목적격 보어로 사용된 명사적 용법의 to부정사 ③ 진주어로 사용된 명사적 용법의 to부정사 ④ a chair를 수식하는 형용사적 용법의 to부정사 ⑤ '~하기 위해서'라는 의미의 목적을 나타내는 부사적 용법의 to부정사.

19 make는 produce를 대신하여 쓰일 수 있다. 따라서 밑줄 친 ⓐ를 수동태로 전환한 ③번이 같은 의미의 문장이다.

20 자동차 경적소리가 만들어 내는 소리의 양이 50mv라는 의미이므로 수동태가 아닌 능동태를 쓰는 것이 옳다.

21 괴물들은 에너지를 얻기 위하여 아이들을 겁준다고 하였다.

22 집 한 채를 들어 올리기 위해서는 약 3,570,000개의 풍선이 필요하다고 하였다.

23 that은 풍선으로 집을 들어 올리는 것을 의미한다.

24 집을 들어올릴 계획을 할 때, 집 무게뿐만 아니라 풍선의 무게와 실의 무게 역시 고려해야 한다고 하였다.

하는 것이 자연스럽다.

05 3, 4, 5형식으로 쓰일 수 있는 동사 make를 수동태로 만드는 문제이다. 첫 번째 문장은 3형식 동사로 쓰인 make이고, 두 번째 문장은 4형식 동사로 쓰인 make이다. 이때 사람을 주어로 하는 수동태는 쓸 수 없으므로 직접목적어를 주어로 한 수동태를 만들어 간접목적어에 for를 붙인다. 마지막 문장은 목적어가 목적격 보어의 주체가 되는 5형식으로 목적어인 us를 수동태 주어로 만들고, 목적격보어의 형태는 그대로 유지한다.

06 swim in a pool이므로 전치사 in을 쓰는 것이 옳다.

07 수동태의 주어가 복수명사인 the oranges이므로 복수동사 were를 써서 수동태를 만드는 것에 유의한다.

08 '결정할 시간'이므로 time to decide를 쓸 수 있다.

09 질문: 글에 따르면, 사람들이 탑에 들어가기 위해서 무엇이 내려져야 하나요?

10 사람이 머리카락에 의해 떠받쳐질 수 있는지를 묻는 문장이다. 밑줄 친 ⓐ에서 hold up의 목적어가 주어로 쓰이고 있으므로 수동태를 답으로 쓰면 된다.

11 해석: 나는 친구를 내 성으로 들이기 위해서 내 머리를 감을 무언가가 필요해. 나는 그것이 강하고 무겁길 원해. 그런 것 가지고 있니? to부정사의 형용사 용법을 활용하여 문장을 만든다.

12 질문: 애니메이션 영화에서 괴물들은 왜 아이들을 겁주나요?

13 A: 자동차 경적 소리에 의해 전기가 만들어질 수 있다는 걸 아니? B: 정말? 난 몰랐어. 얼마나 많은 전기가 만들어지는데? A: 겨우 50mv야.

🦉 서술형 실전문제 p.50~51

01 It is special because it can hide your message.

02 She needs a card, baking soda and water.

03 카드를 포도 주스로 칠하면 메시지를 볼 수 있다.

04 I have many things to plan

05 (1) Some mistakes were made by me.
　(2) A pretty doll was made for me by my friend.
　(3) We are always made bored by Jason.

06 swim → swim in

07 were not bought

08 You were given enough time to decide.

09 Her long hair must be lowered.

10 is held up

11 to wrap around, strong, heavy

12 They scare children to get energy from their screams.

13 can be produced

01 "Mystery Card"는 메시지를 숨길 수 있기 때문에 특별하다.

02 "Mystery Card"를 만들기 위해 카드, 베이킹 소다 그리고 물이 필요하다.

04 바빠 보인다며 무슨 일이냐고 묻는 말에 계획할 일이 많다고 답

🐰 창의사고력 서술형 문제 p.52

|모범답안|

01 (A) 3 p.m. every Wednesday in May
　(B) The Youth Community Center
　(C) make your own drone and learn how to control it

02 (1) The safe wasn't unlocked.
　(2) My closet was opened by my friend.
　(3) The sandwich was taken away by somebody.
　(4) I was hit by a flying ball.
　(5) Mom's vase was broken by us.
　(6) The flour is poured into a bowl.

03 (1) I have a book to borrow from you.
　(2) We have no money to spend.
　(3) You don't have a right to speak for them.
　(4) She has the reason to believe that.
　(5) There was no chance to win the race.
　(6) People have the desire to learn English.

01 I can't wait for it.   02 They can do different kinds of experiments.   03 ⑤   04 They should prepare some water, vinegar, baking soda, and beans.   05 (A) heard   (B) Make   (C) to control   06 (A) with   (B) in   (C) for   (D) into   07 ②   08 (A) Write a message on the card with it.   (B) Paint over the card with grape juice.   09 ②, ⑤   10 ⑤   11 Have you heard about the science fair?   12 ②   13 Give the other person a chance to talk.   14 was laughed at by Jason   15 ③   16 ⑤   17 ④   18 ④   19 ②   20 Wrap your hair around something strong and heavy   21 ②   22 ②   23 electricity from sound, it is helpful   24 ④

01 'look forward to ~ing'는 '~을 기대하다'라는 의미로 'can't wait for'와 바꾸어 쓸 수 있다.

02 Hojin과 Katy는 과학 박람회에서 다른 종류의 실험을 할 수 있다.

03 ⑤번을 제외한 나머지는 모두 제안을 나타낸다.

04 Dancing Beans를 만들기 위해 약간의 물, 식초, 베이킹 소다 그리고 콩을 준비해야 한다.

05 (A) 경험을 묻는 현재완료로 hear의 과거분사 heard가 알맞다. (B) 명령문에 해당하므로 Make가 알맞다. (C) 어떻게 이를 조절할 수 있는지를 배우라는 의미를 표현하므로 '의문사+to부정사' 형태인 to control이 알맞다.

06 (A) '~와 함께'를 나타내는 with, (B) '~에 넣다'는 의미가 되어야 하므로 in, (C) '이틀 동안'을 나타내므로 for, (D) turn into: ~가 되다

07 would like to: ~하고 싶다

09 enter는 '참가하다, 들어가다'라는 의미로 사용되었다. share: 공유하다 exit: 나가다; 출구

12 상대방이 한 말에 대해 '나도 그렇다'고 말할 때 'So do I.' 또는 'So am I.'를 사용할 수 있다. 상대방이 사용한 동사가 be동사이므로 'So am I.'로 바꾸어 쓸 수 있다.

13 '말할 기회'이므로 a chance를 to talk가 수식하도록 문장을 만든다.

14 laugh at: ~를 비웃다, 놀리다

15 주어진 문장의 to부정사는 rules를 수식하는 형용사로 사용되었다. ③은 something을 수식하는 형용사로 사용된 to부정사이다. make money 돈을 벌다

16 '먹을 것'이 아무것도 없었다는 의미이다. to eat이 nothing을 수식하도록 만드는 것이 옳은 문장이다.

17 ④ 주어가 복수명사인 The towels이므로 복수 동사를 쓰는 것

이 옳다. 따라서 were이다.

18 밑줄 친 ⓐ에는 '실제의 삶 속에서'라는 의미를 완성하는 전치사 in이 들어간다. ① worry about: ~에 대해 걱정하다 ② wait for: ~을 기다 리다 ③ be full of: ~으로 가득 차다 ⑤ be known for: ~으로 유명하다 ④ be interested in: ~에 흥미가 있다

19 ⓑ의 to부정사는 the ability를 수식하는 형용사로 사용되었으므로 ②번이 옳다.

20 강하고 무거운 것에 머리카락을 감아야 목이 아프지 않을 것이라고 하였다.

21 양이 너무 적기 때문에 일상의 활동에 유용하지 않다는 것이므로 이유를 나타내는 because가 옳다.

22 ② 괴물들의 도시는 아이들의 비명소리에 의해 동력을 공급 받는다고 하였다.

23 최신 기술로, 우리는 실제로 소리로부터 전기를 만들 수 있다. 그러나 그 양이 너무 적기 때문에 그것이 우리 일상생활에 도움이 된다고 말하기는 어렵다.

24 밑줄 친 ⓐ는 부사로 쓰인 to부정사로 '~하기 위하여'라고 해석된다. ④번은 형용사로 사용된 to부정사이다.

Lesson 4

Your Only Limit Is You

03 win a race: 경주에 이기다, miss a chance: 기회를 놓치다, be filled with: ~로 가득 차다

교과서 Conversation

핵심 Check   p.62~63

1 (1) Don't take it too hard
　(2) Don't be so hard on yourself
　(3) Cheer up, You can do it
2 (1) me help you
　(2) Do you need any help
　(3) deep / Don't worry, help you

시험대비 실력평가   p.60

01 ③　　　　02 ④　　　　03 ①
04 memorable　　　　　05 ③
06 (1) cheer up　(2) sit up　(3) satisfied with
　(4) gas pedal　(5) finish line

---

01 타자에게 공을 던지는 선수를 나타내는 말은 pitcher(투수)이다. catcher: 포수, coach: 코치, hitter: 타자, outfielder: 외야수

02 lap이 '무릎'이라는 뜻도 있지만 이 문장에서는 '한 바퀴'를 의미한다.

03 주어진 문장에서 count는 '중요하다'라는 의미로 사용되었으며 이와 같은 의미로 쓰인 것은 ①번이다. 나머지는 '(수를) 세다'를 의미한다.

04 주어진 관계는 반의어 관계이다. forgettable: 잊을 만한, memorable: 기억할 만한

05　complete: 완전한; 끝내다

06 gas pedal: 가속 페달, finish line: 결승선, cheer up: 기운을 내다, sit up: 바로 앉다, be satisfied with: ~에 만족하다

교과서 대화문 익히기

Check(√) True or False   p.64

1 T　2 F　3 F　4 T

서술형 시험대비   p.61

01 uncomfortable
02 (1) official　(2) hit　(3) lap　(4) balance
03 (1) win a[the] race　(2) miss a chance
　(3) were filled with
04 (1) I walked ahead of him.
　(2) I heard that my sister won (the) second place.
　(3) I didn't want to miss the chance to meet the famous singer.
05 (1) Why the long face?
　(2) You'll do better next time.
06 (1) The project should be completed in a week.
　(2) He pressed down hard on the gas pedal.
　(3) I was not satisfied with my pitching.

01 주어진 관계는 반의어 관계이다. comfortable: 편안한, uncomfortable: 불편한

02 official: 심판, hit: 부딪히다, lap: 바퀴, balance: 균형

교과서 확인학습   p.66~67

Listen & Talk 1 A-1
missed, chances, three, pointer / hard, You'll do better

Listen & Talk 1 A-2
volleyball match / close match, strong enough / you're a great player

Listen & Talk 1 B
won the match / Congratulations / pitching / you're a great pitcher, do better

Listen & Talk 2 A-1
first time / keep my balance / hold / Don't let / Sit up, look straight ahead

Listen & Talk 2 A-1
how to stand on my head / Let me help you, catch you

Listen & Talk 2 B
I'm still not comfortable with it / What problem / lift my leg high enough / Let me, side kick

Communication
worried about / Why are / catch high balls / gave away

11

/ let me help you / my skills get better / Don't worry

Wrap Up 1

Do you come / once a week / easy for me / how to swim / that'll help me a lot

시험대비 기본평가   p.68

01 You'll do better next time.

02 ⑤   03 (A) pitching   (B) pitcher 04 ③

02 ⑤번은 상대방에게 도움을 요청하는 표현이며 이를 제외한 나머지는 모두 상대방에게 도움을 제안하고 있다.

03 pitching: 투구, pitcher: 투수

시험대비 실력평가   p.69~70

01 (I'm) Sorry, but I can't help you now.

02 ⑤   03 ③   04 ⑤

05 It(=The score) was eight to seven.   06 ④

07 (B) – (D) – (C) – (A) – (E)

08 I gave away too many goals.   09 ②

10 He takes a swimming class once a week.

11 She teaches them how to swim.   12 ⑤

02 ⑤번을 제외한 나머지는 모두 격려하는 표현이다.

03 (A)close는 '아슬아슬한, 접전의'를 뜻하며 이와 같이 쓰인 것은 ③번이다. ①, ④번은 '닫다' ②번은 '가까운', ⑤번은 '친한'으로 쓰였다.

04 ⑤ Jack은 경기에 이겼다.

05 The Reds팀은 야구 경기에서 8대 7로 이겼다.

06 (A)는 과거시제이므로 won, (B)는 접전을 가리키는 말이므로 close game이다, (C) 이유를 묻고 있으므로 Why가 적절하다.

07 (B) 처음 자전거를 타보는지 여부 질문 - (D) 대답 및 어려움 설명 - (C) 도움 제공 - (A) 감사 표현 및 부탁 - (E) 안심 시키기 및 자전거 가르쳐주기

08 give away: 내주다

09 Megan은 지난 축구 경기에 대해 걱정하다가 James의 도움으로 자신의 실력이 나아지길 희망하고 있다.

10 Jake는 일주일에 한번 수영 수업을 듣는다.

11 Anna는 학교 동아리에서 아이들에게 수영하는 법을 가르친다.

12 ⑤번을 제외한 나머지는 모두 시무룩한 얼굴을 하고 있는 이유를 언급하고 있다.

서술형 시험대비   p.71

01 Can I give you a hand?

02 (A) stand   (B) Kick   (C) catch

03 stand on her head

04 She can't catch high balls.

05 He is going to kick high balls to her.

06 the taegwondo side kick / lift my leg high enough / the kick pad / my side kick

02 stand on one's head: 물구나무서다, kick: ~을 차다, catch: 잡다

03 Sarah는 물구나무서기를 시도하고 있다.

04 Megan이 가진 문제는 그녀가 높은 공을 잡을 수 없는 것이다.

05 James는 Megan의 축구 기술을 향상시키기 위해 그에게 높은 공을 차 줄 것이다.

06 나는 태권도 옆차기를 연습했을 때 실망스러움을 느꼈다. 내가 열심히 연습했음에도 불구하고 나는 편하게 잘 안 되었다. 특히, 나는 내 다리를 높이 들어올릴 수가 없었다. 그것은 나의 가장 큰 문제였다. 다행히, 나의 코치님이 킥 패드를 들고 나를 도와주었다. 나는 코치님에게 나의 옆차기를 보여주었고 그와 함께 많은 연습을 하였다. 나는 나를 도와준 코치님께 정말로 감사했다.

교과서

Grammar

핵심 Check   p.72~73

1 (1) who   (2) whose camera

2 (1) dancing(또는 dance)   (2) shaving(또는 shave)
  (3) watching(또는 watch)   (4) falling(또는 fall)
  (5) pouring(또는 pour)

시험대비 기본평가   p.74

01 (1) I have a friend who speaks English very well.
  (2) We stayed in a hotel which was located near the beach.
  (3) Do you want to see the pictures which I took?
  (4) Jenny took care of a dog whose tail was hurt.

02 (1) playing(또는 play)   (2) making (또는 make)
  (3) talking(또는 talk)   (4) crossing(또는 cross)

03 (1) Did you eat the cake that she bought for you?
  (2) Is there anything that you want to see?
  (3) Did you hear him cry[crying]?
  (4) Kelly sees a person wave[waving] a white flag.

01 (1) He가 사람이고 주격이므로 주격 관계대명사 who. (2) 선행사가 사물인 a hotel이고, 대명사 It이 주격으로 쓰였으므로 관계대명사 which. (3) them이 목적격으로 쓰인 사물이므로 관계대명사 which. (4) Its가 소유격으로 쓰이고 있고 개를 지칭하므로 관계대명사 whose를 쓴다.

02 (1)~(4) 모두 지각동사의 목적격보어의 형태를 묻는 문제이다. 지각동사의 목적격보어는 원형부정사나 현재분사를 쓴다.

03 (1) '그녀가 너에게 사준 케이크'이므로 관계절이 cake를 수식하도록 문장을 만든다. (2) 의문문이나 부정문에서는 anything을 쓴다. (3) 들은 주체는 you이고 '그가 우는 것'이므로 he를 목적격으로 만들고 cry를 목적격보어로 하여 문장을 만든다. (4) '어떤 사람이 깃발을 흔드는 것'이므로 a person을 목적어로, wave를 목적격보어로 하여 영작한다.

시험대비 실력평가   p.75~77

01 ②, ③, ⑤   02 ④   03 ③   04 I like the boy who wanted to come to the party yesterday.
05 ①, ⑤   06 ⑤   07 She heard water running(또는 run).
08 ④   09 ④
10 ②, ⑤   11 We heard a dog barking in the middle of the night.   12 ⑤   13 I know a girl who[that] really enjoys swimming.   14 ③   15 who [that], which[that], that   16 build[building]
17 ④   18 is the month that comes before
19 playing   20 ③   21 come(또는 coming), paint(ing), call(ing), climb(ing)

---

01 목적격 관계대명사 whom의 자리이다. 따라서 who가 가능하며 that이 쓰여도 무방하다.

02 watch는 지각동사이므로 목적격보어로 원형부정사나 현재분사를 취한다. want는 to부정사를 목적격보어로 취하는 동사이다.

03 ③번 문장은 'Jane has a sister whose hobby is running.'으로 쓰는 것이 우리말을 바르게 옮긴 문장이다.

04 who를 대신하여 that을 써도 무방하다.

05 목적격보어로 원형부정사를 사용하고 있으므로 빈칸에는 지각동사가 들어가는 것이 옳다.

06 모두 주격 혹은 목적격으로 사용된 관계대명사 who를 쓰지만 ⑤번은 소유격 관계대명사 whose의 자리이다.

07 'hear'는 지각동사이므로 목적격보어로 원형부정사나 분사를 사용하여 작문한다.

08 ①, ③, ⑤번은 지각동사로 fly(ing)를 목적격보어로 쓸 수 있으나, ④번은 'allow+목적어+to 부정사'가 수동태로 전환된 것이므로 to fly가 들어간다. ②는 현재진행형으로 쓰이고 있으며 '그 비행기는 관광객들을 집으로 실어 나르는 중이다'라는 의미로 해석 할 수 있다. ⑤ fly in: 날아 들어오다

09 ④번은 선행사가 사람이므로 who를 쓰는 것이 옳다.

10 'He has blond hair.' 혹은 'His hair is blond.'로 표현할 수 있다.

11 '개가 짖는 것'이므로 지각동사 hear의 구조를 이용하여 hear a dog barking을 기본 토대로 문장을 만들 수 있다.

12 소년이 괴롭힘당하는 것이므로 'being bullied'라고 쓰는 것이 옳다.

13 '수영하는 것을 정말로 즐기는'이 소녀를 수식하고 있으므로, 관계대명사를 이용하여 a girl을 수식하도록 한다. enjoy는 동명사를 목적어로 취하는 동사이다.

14 선행사가 사물인 the house이므로 관계대명사 which를 쓰는 것이 옳다.

15 첫 번째 문장은 사람을 선행사로 받는 주격 관계대명사 who 또는 that이 들어가야 한다. 두 번째 문장은 사물을 선행사로 받는 목적격 관계대명사 which 또는 that이 들어가야 하며, 마지막 문장에는 사람과 동물이 혼합되어 있는 선행사이므로 관계대명사 that을 쓰는 것이 옳다.

16 '나는 새로운 주차장이 그들에 의하여 지어지는 것을 보았다.'라고 하였으므로 '나는 그들이 새로운 주차장을 짓는 것을 보았다.'라고 쓰면 된다.

17 ④번은 명사절을 이끄는 접속사 that이다. 명사절을 이끄는 접속사 that은 완전한 문장을 이끈다. 관계대명사 that은 불완전한 문장을 이끈다.

18 8월은 9월 앞에 오는 달이다.

19 진행형을 만드는 Ving와 지각동사의 목적격보어는 모두 현재분사이며, enjoy의 목적어는 동명사이므로 playing이 공통으로 들어간다.

20 ③번은 주격 관계대명사 which로 생략이 불가능하다. 생략가능한 관계대명사는 목적격 관계대명사이다.

21 지각동사 see, hear, watch는 목적격보어로 원형부정사나 현재분사를 취한다. portrait: 초상화

서술형 시험대비   p.78~79

01 (1) Dan lectured on a topic. /
     The topic was very boring.
  (2) I know the woman. /
     Her necklace was stolen.
02 You will hear birds sing(ing) in the early morning.
03 that, smile(또는 smiling)
04 A fire fighter is someone who puts out fires. /
     The woman who was in the hospital is in her home now. /
     The bus which left an hour ago was the last bus. /
     A train has a number of cars which are all

connected together. /

Milk is the white liquid which is produced by cows, goats, and some other animals.

05 She felt her heart beat(ing) faster.

06 Is the chair which was made by you comfortable?

07 steal(ing) / stolen

08 (1) I don't like stories which(또는 that) have sad endings.

　(2) Jason works for a company which(또는 that) makes cars.

　(3) We live in a world which(또는 that) is changing all the time.

　(4) There are people who(또는 that) are cheering excitedly.

09 We watched a man try(ing) to get off the train.

10 whose / whom(또는 who, that) / who(또는 that)

11 Did you see the window locked?

12 I want to see your fish swim(ming) in a group.

13 that I can do for you

---

01 lecture: (대학에서) 강의하다 topic: 주제 (1) Dan은 아주 지루한 주제에 관하여 강의했다.

02 지각동사 hear는 목적어와 목적격보어를 이끈다. '새들이 지저귀는 것'이므로 hear birds sing(ing)을 토대로 작문한다.

03 사람과 사물 모두를 선행사로 받아줄 수 있는 관계대명사는 that이며, 지각동사 see는 목적격보어로 원형부정사나 현재분사를 쓴다.

04 which, who를 대신하여 that을 써도 무방하다. put out: ~을 끄다 a number of: 다수의 produce: ~을 생산하다

05 feel은 원형부정사와 현재분사를 목적격보어로 취하는 지각동사이다.

06 which 뿐만 아니라 that도 가능하다.

07 위 문장은 Tyler가 훔치는 주체이므로 빈칸에 원형부정사나 현재분사를 쓰고, 아래 문장은 목적어로 사물이 나와 있으므로 과거분사를 써서 수동 관계를 표현하는 것이 옳다.

08 (1) 나는 슬픈 결말을 가진 이야기를 좋아하지 않는다. (2) Jason은 차를 만드는 회사에서 일한다. (3) 우리는 항상 변화하는 세상에서 산다. (4) 흥분하여 응원하는 사람 들이 있다.

09 get off: ~에서 내리다 try to: ~하려고 애쓰다

10 첫 번째 문장은 빈칸 뒤에 명사가 있으며, 의미상 '남자의 아들'이므로 소유격 관계대명사가 들어가는 것이 옳다. 두 번째 문장은 선행사가 사람이며 이어 나오는 문장에 목적어가 빠져 있으므로 목적격 관계대명사를 쓰는 것이 옳다. 마지막 문장에는 사람을 선행사로 받아주는 주격 관계대명사가 들어가는 것이 옳다.

11 see는 지각동사로 'see+목적어+목적격보어'의 구조로 쓰이며 목적격보어로는 원형부정사와 분사를 사용한다. 창문이 '잠긴' 것이라고 하였으므로 목적어와 수동 관계를 이룬다고 볼 수 있다.

따라서 lock의 과거분사 형태를 쓴다.

12 want는 to부정사를 목적어로 취하는 동사이며, see는 지각동사이다.

13 that을 대신하여 which를 써도 무방하다.

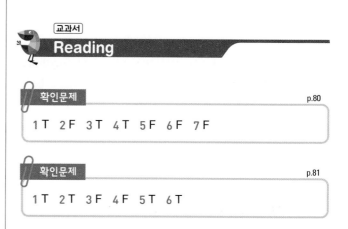

교과서 Reading

확인문제　　　　　　　　　　　　　　p.80

1 T　2 F　3 T　4 T　5 F　6 F　7 F

확인문제　　　　　　　　　　　　　　p.81

1 T　2 T　3 F　4 F　5 T　6 T

교과서 확인학습 A　　　　　　p.82~83

01 At, track, there are, who are cheering

02 that are, are waiting

03 waves, flag, starts

04 pushes, down hard, as, completes

05 On, pulls right beside

06 won many races, was coming in

07 chance to finish second

08 be satisfied with, place　　09 gets to meet

10 to miss, to meet

11 completes, to go

12 sees, ahead, out of

13 closer and closer

14 hits the back end

15 drive into, presses harder on

16 catch up　　17 waving a white flag, means

18 right behind

19 getting closer, from the crowd, getting louder

20 can do it　　21 feel, beating hard

22 rush across　　23 Who

24 filled with tears, finds out that

25 No need for tears　　26 can't believe

27 who is standing, is　　28 not the winner

29 a real close race

30 didn't win the race, did　　31 that counts

32 Did, do my best　　33 After, smiles

34 guess, did

1 At the go-kart race track, there are many people who are cheering excitedly.

2 The karts that are making loud engine noises are waiting.

3 An official waves a green flag and the race starts!

4 Max pushes his foot down hard on the gas pedal as he completes his sixth lap on the track.

5 On the straightaway, Max pulls right beside the race's leader, Simon.

6 Last year, Simon won many races, but Max's best result in a race was coming in fifth place.

7 This time, he has a chance to finish second.

8 But he isn't going to be satisfied with second place today.

9 The winner gets to meet the world famous racer L. J. Richards!

10 He doesn't want to miss the chance to meet his role model.

11 Max completes the tenth lap and now has five more laps to go.

12 Max sees Simon's kart ahead, just out of Max's reach.

13 Max's kart gets closer and closer to Simon's.

14 It almost hits the back end of Simon's kart.

15 They drive into the straightaway and Max presses harder on the gas pedal.

16 "I can catch up," says Max.

17 Max sees the official waving a white flag which means the last lap.

18 Max is right behind Simon.

19 The finish line is getting closer, and the cheering from the crowd is getting louder.

20 "I can do it!" Max says loudly.

21 He can feel his heart beating hard.

22 The karts rush across the finish line.

23 Who is the winner?

24 Max's eyes are filled with tears as he finds out that he came in second.

25 "No need for tears, kid," says a man's voice.

26 Max can't believe his eyes.

27 The man who is standing in front of him is L. J. Richards!

28 "Thank you, but I'm not the winner," says Max.

29 "It was a real close race.

30 Even though you didn't win the race, you did your best.

31 That's the thing that counts!" says L. J. Richards.

32 'Did I do my best?' thinks Max.

33 After a moment, he smiles.

34 "Yeah, I guess I did."

01 ⑤	02 that	03 ④	04 ④
05 ④	06 ③	07 ④	08 ⑤

09 (A) getting closer   (B) getting louder

10 beat[beating]   11 ③   12 who [that] are, getting closer and closer   13 ⑤

14 ⑤   15 The man who is standing in front of him is L. J. Richards!   16 ③   17 ③

18 I did my best.   19 ②   20 the winner has the chance to meet L. J. Richards.

21 whom(또는 that이나 who), the world famous racer

22 ④   23 ②   24 in front of   25 finish line   26 ⑤

01 (A) many people에 수의 일치를 해야 하므로 there are, (B) 주어가 The karts이므로 are, (C) 동사 자리이므로 waves가 옳다.

02 사물과 사람을 모두 받아주는 관계대명사는 that이다.

03 사람들은 신이 나서 응원하고 있다고 하였다. 따라서 ④번이 가장 적절하다.

04 현재 카트들은 기다리고 있는 중이라고 하였다.

05 2등을 할 기회가 있지만 2등으로 만족하지 않을 것이라는 내용이 이어지는 것이 적절하다.

06 내용상 '때'를 나타내는 의미로 쓰인 as라고 볼 수 있다.

07 Simon이 얼마나 많은 경기를 이겼는지는 글을 읽고 답할 수 없다.

08 각각 ① chance ② beside ③ famous ④ push의 유의어이며, lose는 win의 반의어이다.

09 결승선이 더 가까워질수록 관중의 응원 소리가 더 커진다고 할 수 있다. get+비교급: 더 ~하다

10 his heart와의 관계가 능동이므로 원형부정사나 현재분사로 써서 feel의 목적격보어를 만든다.

11 현재시제로 글을 쓰고 있으므로 hits라고 쓰는 것이 옳다.

12 응원하고 있는 사람들은 Max의 카트가 바로 앞에 있는 카트에 점점 가까워지고 있는 것을 본다.

13 (D)는 부사로 '세계'라는 의미로 쓰였다. ①, ④ 딱딱한 ② (이해하거나 답하기) 힘든, 어려운 ③ (육체적이나 정신적으로) 힘든 ⑤ 세계

14 글에는 승자가 나와 있지 않으므로, Max가 2등으로 들어온다는 것은 글의 내용과 일치하지 않는다.

15

15 '그 앞에 서 있는 남자는 L. J. Richards이다!'는 문장으로 만들어준다.

16 밑줄 친 ⓐ는 명사절을 이끄는 접속사로 쓰인 that이다. ③번은 관계대명사 that이다.

17 count, matter 모두 '중요하다'는 의미이다.

18 앞서 자문한 'Did I do my best?'에 대한 대답이므로 'I did my best.'라고 쓰면 된다.

19 모두 Max를 지칭하지만, ⓑ는 Simon을 지칭하는 대명사이다.

20 Max가 경기에서 이기기를 원하는 이유는 대회의 승자가 L. J. Richards를 만날 기회를 얻기 때문이다.

21 Max가 존경하는 L. J. Richards는 세계에서 유명한 레이서이다.

22 밑줄 친 (A)는 the chance를 수식하는 형용사구로 쓰인 to부정사이다. ① 목적격보어 ② 목적을 나타내는 부사구 ③ 진주어 ④ 형용사구 ⑤ 동사 hope의 목적어로 각각 쓰였다.

23 문장 ⓐ는 Max의 카트가 Simon의 카트를 바짝 추격하여 바로 뒤에 있다는 의미이다.

24 마지막 바퀴에서 Max는 Simon의 바로 뒤에 있다고 하였으므로, Simon은 Max의 바로 앞에 있다고 할 수 있다.

25 경기가 공식적으로 끝나는 트랙 위의 장소는 '결승선'이다.

26 (B)의 첫 문장에 나오는 he는 Simon을 가리키는 것이므로 Simon을 처음 언급하는 (C)가 (B) 앞에 오는 것이 옳다. 2등에 안주할 수 없는 이유를 설명하는 (A)가 (B)에 이어지는 것이 가장 자연스럽다.

서술형 시험대비 p.90~91

01 there are many people who are cheering excitedly
02 심판이 초록 깃발을 흔들 때
03 ⓐ won ⓑ to meet ⓒ to miss
04 who[that] won many races
05 be satisfied
06 in fifth place
07 He pulls right beside Simon.
08 result
09 Max sees Simon's kart going ahead
10 waving a white flag / It means, the last lap
11 closer, cheering, beating
12 stand(ing) in front of
13 He finished the race in (the) second place.
14 Doing our best is more important than being the best.

01 many people을 선행사로 하여 They가 이끄는 문장을 관계사절로 만든다. They가 주어이므로 주격 관계대명사를 사용한다. who 대신 that을 써도 좋다.

02 'An official waves a green flag and the race starts.'라고 하였다.

03 ⓐ: win의 과거형, ⓑ: get to V: ~하게 되다, ⓒ: want의 목적어로 to부정사

04 작년에 많은 경기에서 이긴 Simon은 경주의 선두이다.

05 satisfy는 '만족시키다'는 의미이다. '~에 만족하다'는 be satisfied with이다.

06 작년에, Max가 한 경주에서 5등으로 들어왔을 때 그것이 Max의 가장 좋은 결과였다.

08 결과는 대회의 마지막에 존재하는 상황이다.

09 Max는 Simon의 카트가 앞에 있는 것을 본다는 의미이므로 지각동사의 목적격보어를 적절히 이용하여 'Max는 Simon의 카트가 앞에 가고 있는 것을 본다.'는 문장으로 만든다.

10 흰색 깃발을 흔드는 것은 마지막 바퀴라는 의미이다.

11 내가 결승선에 더 가까워졌을 때, 나는 관중들이 응원하는 소리를 들을 수 있었다. 또한 내 심장이 매우 세게 뛰는 것을 느끼기 시작했다.

12 지각동사 see는 목적격보어로 원형부정사나 현재분사를 취한다. 남자가 Max 앞에 서 있는 것이므로 stand 혹은 standing을 쓴다.

13 그는 경주에서 2등을 차지했다.

14 최선을 다하는 것이 최고가 되는 것보다 더 중요하다.

영역별 핵심문제 p.93~97

01 ① 02 ⑤ 03 ② 04 ②
05 (1) keep up with (2) do their best / take a chance
   (3) is filled with 06 I'll give you a hand.
07 ④ 08 I learned how to stand on my head in PE class. 09 ⑤ 10 kick 11 ③
12 I teach children how to swim in the school club.
13 ⑤ 14 ⓑ → did 15 He was not satisfied with his serves. 16 ⑤ 17 ③
18 ③ 19 Did you hear your phone ring(ing)?
20 ④ 21 ③ 22 is a story which expresses traditional beliefs 23 ③
24 the plane take[taking] off / us fight(ing) / Jinna jump(ing) a rope 25 ④ 26 ⑤
27 ④ 28 the chance to meet his role model
29 ④ 30 He feels his heart beating hard.
31 ④

01 누군가를 위해 지지나 칭찬을 보여주기 위해, 또는 용기를 북돋아 주기 위해 크게 소리 지르는 것을 나타내는 말은 cheer(환호하다)이다.

02 volleyball: 배구, dodge ball: 피구

03 주어진 문장에서 official은 '심판'을 의미하며 이와 같은 의미로 쓰인 것은 ②번이다. 나머지는 모두 '공식적인'을 의미한다.

04 place는 명사로 '순위, 등위' 또는 '장소'를 나타내며 동사로는

'~을 놓다'를 나타낸다.

07 ④ Mina는 'Don't let go'라고 하며 자전거를 잡아주기를 부탁하고 있다.

09 ⑤번은 '포기하지 마'라는 의미이다.

10 당신의 발로 누군가나 또는 무언가를 치는 것을 나타내는 말은 kick(차다)이다.

11 (A) 대화의 흐름상 편하게 잘 안된다는 의미가 되어야 하므로 uncomfortable, (B) 다리를 들어 올릴 수 없다는 의미이므로 lift, (C) 킥 패드를 들어준다는 의미가 적절하므로 hold가 되어야 한다.

13 수영이 여전히 쉽지 않지만 수업이 만족스럽지 않다는 내용은 없다.

14 과거형 Did로 질문하고 있으므로 'Yes, I did.'가 알맞다.

15 Jack은 자신의 서브에 만족하지 않았다.

16 선행사가 사람과 동물이 함께 있을 때에는 관계대명사 that을 쓴다.

17 소년들이 서로에게 소리를 지르는 것이므로 현재분사나 원형부정사를 쓰는 것이 옳다.

18 feel은 지각동사이다. '누군가가 우리를 따라오는 것'이므로 목적어로 someone, 목적격보어로 following us를 써서 문장을 만든다.

19 지각동사 hear는 목적격보어로 원형부정사나 현재분사, 과거분사를 취하며, '전화기가 울리는' 것이므로 수동 관계가 성립하지 않는다. 따라서 원형부정사나 현재분사를 사용하여 문장을 만든다.

20 주어진 문장의 빈칸에는 주격 관계대명사 who나 that이 들어간다. ④번에는 소유격 관계대명사 whose가 들어가지만 ① which[that] ② which[that] ③ who(m)[that] ⑤ that이 들어간다.

21 위 문장은 목적격보어로 현재분사를, 아래 문장은 목적격 보어로 to부정사를 취하고 있으므로 각각 heard, would like를 쓰는 것이 적절하다.

22 신화란 전통적인 믿음을 표현하는 이야기이다.

23 ⓐ 주격 관계대명사가 빠져 있다. people who aren't interested in other people at all로 쓰는 것이 옳다. ⓑ 목적격 관계대명사가 생략되어 있으나 빠져도 무방하다. ⓒ which는 the tip을 선행사로 받아주는 주격 관계대명사이다. ⓓ 목적격 관계대명사로 두 문장이 이어지고 있으므로 대명사 it을 빼는 것이 옳다. ⓔ 주격 관계대명사 that을 사용하여 앞 문장과 연결되어 있다.

24 see, hear, watch는 모두 지각동사이다. 목적어와 목적격보어의 관계가 모두 능동이므로 현재분사나 원형부정사를 목적격보어로 사용하여 문장을 만든다.

25 페달 위를 밟거나 트랙 위를 달리는 것이므로, '~ 위'를 나타낼 때 쓰이는 전치사 on이 공통으로 들어간다.

26 빈칸 ⓒ에는 전치사 with가 들어간다. ① take care of: ~를

돌보다 ② be different from: ~와 다르다 ③ be interested in: ~에 흥미가 있다 ④ get used to: ~에 익숙해지다 ⑤ be filled with: ~으로 가득 차 있다

27 글의 내용으로 보아 2등으로 시작하는 것이 아니라 끝내는 것을 의미한다. 따라서 finish를 쓰는 것이 옳다.

28 '만날 기회'라고 하였으므로 meet을 to부정사로 만들어 chance를 수식하도록 한다.

29 '경주에서 이기지 못할 지라도 최선을 다했으면 됐다'는 의미가 가장 적절하다.

30 질문: 결승선에 가까이 올 때 Max는 무엇을 느끼나요?

31 결과를 본 순간 눈물이 가득 찼다고 하였으므로 ④번은 옳지 않다.

단원별 예상문제 p.98~101

01 ② 02 (1) Cheer up (2) out of babies' reach (3) close match 03 ⑤ 04 ②
05 ② 06 ⑤ 07 ③ 08 ride a bike[bicycle] 09 ⑤ 10 ⑤ 11 ③
12 ④ 13 Unfortunately we couldn't go to the wedding which[that] we were invited to. 14 ③
15 ③ 16 We watched a B-boy perform(ing) on the stage. 17 ① 18 ③ 19 making loud engine noises 20 Max sees the official waving a white flag which [that] means the last lap.
21 crowd 22 ① 23 ②, ⑤ 24 winner

01 사람이나 자동차 등이 경주하기 위해 특별한 표면을 가진 땅의 일부를 가리키는 말은 track(경주로)이다.

02 cheer up: 기운 내다, out of one's reach: ~에게 닿지 않는, close match: 접전, 아슬아슬한 경기

03 주어진 문장과 나머지 문장에서 tear는 '눈물'이라는 뜻이지만 ⑤번은 '찢어지다'는 뜻이다.

04 엄마의 위로에 대한 대답으로 '저도 그러길 바라요.'가 적절하다.

05 David는 많은 기회를 놓쳐서 낙담하고 있다.

06 David의 엄마가 자책하고 싶어 했다는 설명은 바르지 않다.

07 주어진 문장은 균형을 잡을 수 없다는 Mina의 말에 이어지는 것이 적절하므로 (C)가 알맞다.

08 Mina는 지금 자전거 타는 법을 배우고 있다.

09 Brain의 문제점에 대해 듣고 도와주겠다고 하는 내용이 이어져야 하므로 (E)가 적절하다.

10 코치가 Brain에게 태권도 옆차기를 보여주었다는 설명은 대화의 내용과 일치하지 않는다.

11 첫 번째 문장은 소년의 꿈이 비행기 조종사가 되는 것이므로 소유격 관계대명사가 들어가는 자리이다. 두 번째 문장의 빈칸은 동사를 이끌고 있으므로 주격 관계대명사 자리이다. sour: (맛이) 신

12 see, watch, hear는 모두 지각동사이다. 목적어와 목적격 보어

의 관계에 따라 목적격보어의 형태가 달라지는데, ④번은 음악이 '연주되는 것'이므로 과거분사 played가 들어가고, 나머지는 모두 목적어와 목적격보어의 관계가 능동이므로 원형부정사나 현재분사가 들어간다. play catch: 캐치 볼하다 stadium: 경기장

13 불행히도 우리는 초대받은 결혼식에 갈 수 없었다.

14 hear와 watch는 모두 지각동사이다. serve: 손님 시중을 들다

15 명사절 접속사 that은 완전한 문장을 이끌고, 관계대명사 that은 주어나 목적어가 빠진 불완전한 문장을 이끈다. ③번 문장에서는 전치사 about의 목적어가 비어 있으므로 관계대명사 that이고, 나머지는 모두 명사절을 이끄는 접속사 that이다.

16 watch는 지각동사이며 B-boy가 공연을 하는 것이므로 목적격보어로 원형부정사나 현재분사를 써서 문장을 만든다.

17 빈칸에는 사람을 선행사로 받아주는 주격 관계대명사 who가 들어간다. ① whose ② which ③ who ④ which ⑤ which가 들어간다. who나 which를 대신하여 that이 쓰일 수 있다.

18 ③ 심판이 흔드는 깃발의 색깔은 초록이라고 하였다.

19 지각동사 hear는 목적어와 목적격보어의 관계가 능동일 경우 원형부정사나 현재분사를 목적격보어로 취할 수 있다.

20 관계대명사 which를 대신하여 that을 써도 무방하다.

21 함께 모여 있는 한 무리의 사람들을 '군중'이라고 한다.

22 ④만 일치하는 문장이다. hold one's breath: 숨죽이다

23 빈칸 ⓐ는 동사를 바로 이끌고 있으므로 주격 관계대명사 자리이다.

24 win: 이기다 winner: 승자

02 사람들이나 팀들이 서로 경쟁하는 스포츠 행사를 가리키는 말은 match(경기)이다

03 John이 자신의 투구가 마음에 들지 않은 이유는 2개의 홈런을 허용해서이다.

04 who, which를 대신하여 that을 써도 무방하다.

05 see는 지각동사이며 꽃이 바람에 흔들려 춤추는 것이므로 현재분사나 원형부정사를 이용하여 문장을 만든다.

06 see는 지각동사이다. 목적어와 목적격보어의 관계가 능동인 경우 원형부정사나 현재분사가 목적격보어로 쓰일 수 있고, 수동 관계에 있는 경우 과거분사를 목적격보어로 사용한다.

07 냉장고 안에 넣어두었던 치즈가 어디 있는지를 묻는 문장으로 쓰면 된다.

08 (1) 선행사가 a custom이므로 관계대명사 that이나 which를 쓰는 것이 옳다. (2) 선행사가 사람이므로 목적격 관계대명사 whom이나 that을 써서 문장을 하나로 만든다. (3) 사람이 선행사이므로 관계대명사 who나 that을 이용한다.

09 지각동사 see는 목적어와 목적격보어의 관계가 능동일 경우 원형부정사나 현재분사를 목적격보어로 취할 수 있다.

10 관계사절 'that are making loud engine noises'를 독립된 문장으로 만들어 주면 된다.

11 우리는 카트들이 트랙 위에서 기다리고 있는 것을 볼 것이다. 심판이 초록 깃발을 흔들면 go-kart 경기는 시작된다.

12 Max는 처음에 2등으로 들어왔지만 경주의 결과에 만족하지 않았다.

13 질문: L. J. Richards에 따르면, Max에게 경주에서 무엇이 중요한가요?

서술형 실전문제　　　　　p.102~103

01 It was a close game.

02 match

03 Because he allowed two homeruns.

04 (1) who decides, acts　(2) dolls which have
　(3) whose eyes were

05 You can see flowers dance(또는 dancing) in the wind.

06 make[making] / made

07 Where is the cheese which(또는 that) I put in the refrigerator?

08 (1) that has existed for a long time
　(2) whom you saw driving a car
　(3) who don't feel sorry for other people

09 cheer(ing) excitedly

10 The karts are waiting. They are making loud engine noises.

11 wait(ing), waves a green flag, starts

12 satisfied, even though

13 Doing his best is important.

창의사고력 서술형 문제　　　　　p.104

|모범답안|

01 (A) our next soccer match　(B) catching high balls
　(C) a hand　(D) kicked high balls to her

02 (1) who teach math to students
　(2) who build buildings
　(3) that is made from coffee beans
　(4) which operates with an engine
　(5) who invented Hangeul

03 (1) I saw some kids splash(ing) around in water.
　(2) Can you hear someone knock(ing) at the door?
　(3) They watched us looking for the key.
　(4) I was listening to her talking[talk] nonsense.
　(5) He felt the phone vibrating[vibrate] in his bag.
　(6) Did you see the woman talk(ing) to herself?

01 (1) do my best　(2) is filled with　(3) keep up with
(4) was satisfied with　　02 ⑤　　03 ⓐ →
satisfied　　04 ①, ③　　05 ⑤　　06 She
learned how to stand on her head in PE class.
07 Tom told Sarah to kick her legs in the air again.
08 don't be so hard on yourself　　09 He lost
his game and missed too many chances for a three–
pointer.　　10 ⑤　　11 ④　　12 ②, ⑤
13 ⑤　　14 I saw Jason and Helen ride(또는
riding) a bike[bicycle] together.　　15 There
are a girl and a goat that are resting on the hill.
16 ①　　17 ③　　18 ④
19 meet(ing) my role model　20 are filled with
21 ④　　22 ⑤　　23 come, did his best
24 (B) → (D) → (C) → (A)　　25 (B)–(A)–(C)

01 be satisfied with: ~에 만족하다, be filled with: ~로 가득
　 차다, keep up with: ~을 따라잡다, ~에 뒤떨어지지 않다, do
　 one's best: 최선을 다하다

02 주어진 문장은 '너무 상심하지 마.'라는 뜻으로 Keine의 걱정에
　 대해 이어질 말로 적절하므로 (E)가 알맞다.

03 be satisfied with: ~에 만족하다

04 worried는 '걱정스러운'을 나타내며 concerned, anxious와
　 바꾸어 쓸 수 있다.

06 Sarah는 체육 시간에 물구나무서는 법을 배웠다.

07 Tom은 Sarah에게 공중에다 그녀의 다리를 한 번 더 차라고 말
　 했다.

09 그가 우울한 이유는 농구 경기에 졌고 3점슛을 위한 많은 기회
　 를 놓쳤기 때문이다.

10 주어진 표현은 홈런을 허용한 John을 격려하는 표현으로 적절
　 하므로 (E)가 적절하다.

11 빈칸 뒤로 관사가 없는 명사가 나오므로 소유격 관계대명사가
　 오는 것이 옳다.

12 '누군가가 내 이름을 부르는 소리'이므로 '내 이름이 불리는 소리'
　 와 의미가 같다.

13 위 문장은 '남자의 지갑이 도난당했다'는 의미이며, 아래 문장은
　 '모든 학생들에 의해 존경받는 사람'이라는 의미이다. 따라서 위
　 에는 소유격 관계대명사를, 아래에는 동사가 이어지고 있으므로
　 주격 관계대명사를 쓰면 된다.

14 see는 지각동사이다. Jason과 Helen은 자전거를 타는 주체가
　 되므로 현재분사나 원형부정사를 목적격보어로 사용한다.

15 선행사가 '사람+사물'일 때에는 관계대명사 that을 쓰는 것이 옳다.

16 hardly는 '거의 ~하지 않는'이라는 의미의 부사이다. '세게'라는
　 의미로 쓸 때에는 hard이며 이때 형용사와 부사의 형태가 같다.

17 ③ Simon이 작년에 얼마나 많은 경주에 이겼는지는 알 수 없다.

18 밑줄 친 (A)는 동명사이다. ④번은 지각동사의 목적격보어로
　 쓰인 현재분사이다.

19 L. J. Richards는 Max의 롤 모델이라고 하였다. 지각동사
　 see의 목적어로 Max가 왔으므로 목적격보어로 meet 혹은
　 meeting을 써서 빈칸을 완성한다.

20 be filled with: ~으로 가득 차다

21 ⓓ에서 사용된 close는 '아슬아슬한'이라는 의미로 사용되었다.

22 L. J. Richards는 최선을 다하는 것이 중요하다고 말하며
　 Max에게 용기를 주고 있다.

23 coming으로 써도 무방하다.

24 (B) 무엇을 하고 있는지 질문 → (D) 물구나무서기를 하고 있
　 음을 설명 → (C) 도움 제공 → (A) 감사 표현

25 다섯 바퀴가 남은 상황 → (B) Max의 카트가 Simon의 카트
　 와 점점 가까워짐 → (A) Max의 카트가 Simon의 카트 뒷부
　 분과 부딪힐 수 있을 정도로 가까워 짐 (첫 문장의 It이 지칭하는
　 것이 Max의 카트) → (C) 마 침내 마지막 바퀴에서 결승선이
　 더 가까워짐

Explore Your Feelings!

01 (h)ate   02 ⑤   03 (1) alone   (2) lines

    (3) limit   (4) since   04 ⑤

05 (1) I can't stand the cold very well.

   (2) They talked about the matter.

   (3) Give me some advice, please.

   (4) was upset because she used my stuff without

     asking me first.   06 ④

01 주어진 관계는 반의어 관계를 나타낸다. hate: 싫어하다

02 ⑤번 문장에서 line은 '대사'를 뜻한다. rude: 무례한

03 alone: 혼자, line: 대사, limit: 제한, since: ~ 이후로

04 '누군가가 특정한 상황에서 해야 하는 것에 대한 의견 또는 제안'
을 가리키는 말은 advice(조언)이다.

05 stand: 참다, matter: 문제, advice: 조언, stuff: 물건

06 주어진 문장에서 stand는 '참다, 견디다'를 의미하며 이와 같은 의
미로 쓰인 것은 ④번이다. 나머지는 모두 '서다, 서 있다'를 의미한
다. arrogant: 거만한

01 toothache

02 (1) lunch break(= lunch time)   (2) advice   (3) hurt

03 (1) on purpose   (2) gain weight   (3) focus on

    (4) In the end

04 (1) He sometimes puts people down.

   (2) She always points out my mistakes.

   (3) Set an alarm before you go to bed.

05 (1) Thank you for pointing out some mistakes in
     my report.

   (2) Here are your scripts, so practice your lines.

   (3) The reason I called was to ask about the
     plans for Saturday.

   (4) It is important to take measures to avoid the
     risk of fire.

01 치아의 아픔을 가리키는 말은 toothache(치통)이다.

02 lunch break: 점심시간, advice: 조언, hurt: 다치게 하다

03 on purpose: 고의로, gain weight: 체중이 늘다, focus on: ~
에 집중하다, in the end: 결국

04 put down: 깎아내리다, point out: 지적하다, set an alarm:
자명종을 맞추다

05 point out: 지적하다, script: 대본, reason: 이유, take
measures: 조치를 취하다

1 (1) nervous, What's the matter(= problem)

  (2) Why do you look so sad

  (3) wrong / What should I do

2 (1) I think you should

  (2) advise

  (3) Why don't you

Check(√) True or False   p.116

1 T   2 F   3 T   4 F

Listen & Talk 1-A-1

don't look, matter / wore, got / what to do

Listen & Talk 1-A-2

look down, What's the matter / haircut, funny / Take off
/ used to

Listen & Talk 1-B

tired / I didn't have breakfast this morning / too bad,
lunch break / snack bar / make, suggestion / post

Listen & Talk 2 A-1

how to do, advice / solve / solve, focus on / ones / got

Listen & Talk 2 A-2

late for, wake up / set an alarm / turn it off / far from,
That way

Listen & Talk 2 B

stop playing computer games. What should I do /
set, limit, shuts down / I think you should / out of,
into / advice

Communication

on the air / matter / sharing, with, stuff / feelings, make
some rules / I'll try that

01 (D) → (A) → (C) → (B)   02 ③   03 ②, ④
04 ②

01 (D) 자신의 고민을 이야기함 → (A) 자명종을 맞춰 두는지 질
문 → (C) 대답 → (B) 조언

02 이어지는 문장에서 매점이 있어야 하는 이유를 설명하고 있으므
로 (C)가 적절하다.

03 ⓐ는 상대방의 의견에 동의하는 표현이다.

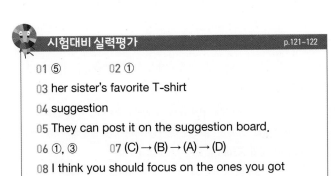

01 ⑤   02 ①
03 her sister's favorite T-shirt
04 suggestion
05 They can post it on the suggestion board.
06 ①, ③   07 (C) → (B) → (A) → (D)
08 I think you should focus on the ones you got
   wrong.   09 ⑤   10 ⓐ → playing
11 how about using a special program?   12 ④
13 She couldn't wake up in the morning.
14 Because she will have to get out of bed to turn it
   off.

01 (A)는 상대방의 기분이 언짢아 보일 때 무슨 일이 있는지 묻는
   표현이다. ⑤번은 직업을 묻는 표현이다.

02 언니의 티셔츠에 포도 주스를 쏟아 어찌할 바를 모르고 있는 여자
   의 심정으로 worried(걱정스러운)가 적절하다.

04 '다른 누군가가 그것에 관해 생각하도록 당신이 언급한 의견 또
   는 계획'을 가리키는 말은 suggestion(제안)이다.

05 Jane과 Tom은 제안 게시판에 그것을 게시할 수 있다.

06 (A)는 안타까움 또는 유감을 나타내는 표현으로 이와 바꾸어 쓸
   수 있는 표현은 ①, ③번이다.

07 (C) 무슨 일이 있는지 질문 → (B) 기분이 좋지 않은 이유 설명
   → (A) 모자를 벗고 보여줄 것을 요청 → (D) 반응

09 ⑤번을 제외한 (a)와 나머지 모두는 조언해 줄 것을 요청하는 표
   현이다.

10 stop+to부정사: ~하기 위해 멈추다, stop+~ing: ~하던 것을
   멈추다

11 why don't you ~?는 '~하는 게 어때?'라고 제안하는 표현으
   로 'how about ~?'과 바꾸어 쓸 수 있다.

13 Emily는 아침에 일어날 수 없어서 수업에 늦었다.

14 Tom이 자명종을 침대에서 멀리 놓으라고 조언한 이유는 그녀가
   그것을 끄기 위해 일어날 수밖에 없기 때문이다.

01 (방송에) 연결되었습니다.
02 Because her little sister uses Amy's stuff without
   asking her first.
03 tell her my feelings and make some rules with
   her
04 She doesn't know how to do better in math.
05 Sujin should focus on the math problems she got
   wrong.
06 (A) He can't stop playing computer games.
   (B) set a time limit, (C) his room, (D) the living room

01 be on the air: 전파를 타다

03 만약 내가 너라면 나는 그녀에게 내 기분에 대해 이야기하고 그
   녀와 함께 몇 가지 규칙을 정할 거야.

04 Sujin은 수학을 더 잘하는 법을 모른다.

05 Sujin은 그녀가 틀린 수학 문제에 집중해야 한다.

Grammar

1 (1) has studied   (2) has, arrived   (3) have done

2 (1) which(또는 that) you made
  (2) which(또는 that) he bought
  (3) who(m)(또는 that) Helen came with

01 (1) have you left → did you leave
   (2) teach → teaches
   (3) did → have done
   (4) whom → which[that]
02 (1) Have you found the pen that[which] you lost?
   (2) Did she take the class which[that] James
       taught?
   (3) I want to meet the boy whom[who/that] you
       speak highly of.
   (4) Molly likes the movie which[that] Tom Cruise
       starred in.
03 (1) I haven't finished my lunch yet.
   (2) She has been to the church two times.
   (3) I gave her all the money that I had.
   (4) Where is the report which we handed in?

01 (1) when이 있으므로 과거시제를 쓰는 것이 옳다. (2) Mr. Pang이 주어이므로 단수 동사를 쓴다. (3) 지금까지 오랫동안 이 일을 해 왔다는 것이므로 현재완료 시제를 쓴다. (4) 사물이 선행사이므로 which[that]를 쓰는 것이 옳다.

02 관계대명사 which, who(m)를 대신하여 that을 써도 무방하며, 목적격 관계대명사이므로 생략해도 좋다.

03 (2) '~에 가 보았다'라는 경험은 have been to로 표현한다.

시험대비 실력평가   p.127~129

01 ④　　02 ⑤　　03 ③

04 like the dress which you want to buy

05 ⑤　　06 ②　　07 ③

08 whom you invited　　09 ②　　10 ④

11 Tell me about the people who(m) you met in the hospital. 　12 ③　　13 ②　　14 ④

15 The letter that you sent to me has not arrived yet.

16 ④　　17 ⑤　　18 ③

19 Have you ever been to India before?　　20 ③

21 I have lost my cap.

22 The I-pad which[that] I got from my father was my birthday present.

23 that the children play with

01 ④ Have you ~?로 물을 때에는 Yes, I have. 혹은 No, I haven't.로 답한다.

02 'Jamie가 쓴 책'이므로 which Jamie wrote이 the book을 수식하도록 문장을 만든다.

03 현재완료가 쓰이고 있으므로 과거를 나타내는 어구는 빈칸에 쓰일 수 없다.

04 which를 대신하여 that을 써도 무방하다.

05 '~에 가 본 적이 있다'는 표현은 have been to를 쓴다. have gone to는 '~에 가고 없다'는 의미이다.

06 ② 과거를 나타내는 a few minutes ago는 현재완료 시제와 함께 쓸 수 없다.

07 현재완료 시제와 함께 쓰일 때 기간을 이끌 수 있는 전치사는 for이다. since는 특정 시점을 이끈다.

08 whom을 대신하여 who나 that을 써도 무방하다.

09 첫 번째 빈칸은 유명인을 만나본 적이 있느냐는 경험을 묻는 말이므로 현재완료 시제를 쓰는 것이 옳으며, 두 번째 빈칸에는 현재 그가 휴가를 즐기는 중이라는 말로 미루어 보아 '이탈리아에 가고 없다'는 표현이 들어가는 것이 옳다.

10 두 시간 전에 그 주제에 관하여 대화하기 시작하여 여전히 대화하고 있다는 것이므로 두 시간 동안 그 주제에 관하여 대화하고 있다는 것을 현재완료 시제로 나타낼 수 있다.

11 who(m)를 대신하여 that을 써도 무방하다.

12 모두 현재완료의 '완료' 용법이지만, ③번은 '계속'으로 쓰였다.

13 목적격 관계대명사나 '주격 관계대명사+be동사'를 생략할 수 있다.

14 사람과 동물이 함께 있는 선행사는 관계대명사 that으로 받는다.

15 '네가 나에게 보낸 그 편지'라고 하였으므로 관계대명사절 that you sent to me가 The letter를 수식하도록 문장을 쓴다.

16 (A) 특정 시점을 나타내고 있으므로 since, (B) 과거를 나타내는 last week은 현재완료와 함께 쓰일 수 없으며, (C) 지금까지 벽을 두 번 칠했다는 의미이므로 현재완료를 쓰는 것이 옳다.

17 ①~④는 주격 관계대명사로 쓰였으나 ⑤번은 목적격 관계대명사로 쓰인 that이다.

18 3년 전에 쓴 책이므로 과거시제를 쓰고 선행사가 사물이므로 which 혹은 that을 쓰는 것이 적절하다.

19 경험을 묻는 말이므로 현재완료 시제를 쓰는 것이 적절하다.

20 ③ 현재완료 시제는 명백한 과거를 나타내는 어구와 함께 쓰일 수 없다. 따라서 had로 쓰는 것이 옳다.

21 모자를 잃어버려 현재까지 그 상황이 이어지고 있으므로 현재완료 시제를 써서 한 문장으로 표현할 수 있다.

22 해석: 아버지로부터 받은 그 아이패드는 내 생일 선물이었다.

23 해석: 그 아이들이 가지고 노는 장난감은 더러워 보인다.

서술형 시험대비   p.130~131

01 It has been sunny since yesterday.

02 which you are drinking

03 since / for / ago / since

04 The missing boy whom people were looking for came home last night.

05 have you lived / ago, have lived, for

06 (1) What is the name of the man whom[who] you want to meet?
　(2) This is the car which my friend hopes to buy someday.
　(3) Where is the red sweater which I put in my drawer?

07 Have you seen an elephant before?
　No, I haven't.

08 (1) Did you throw a party for her yesterday?
　(2) I have been to Boston many times.
　(3) The sandwich which[that] he made for us is very delicious.

09 Kevin has lost his umbrella.

10 (1) isn't much information which you can get
　(2) gave Tim the pants which he always liked
　(3) he the man whom you respect very much

11 This is the desk which[that] my father made.

12 (1) The tennis game he played yesterday was great.

(2) Do you know the boy talking with your sister?

(3) The subject Jane is interested in is history and Korean.

13 that[which]she doesn't like

14 have lost

15 which you attended

01 현재완료 시제를 이용하여 어제 이후로 계속 맑다는 문장을 쓸 수 있다.

02 which 대신에 that을 써도 좋다. 또, drinking 대신에 having 을 써도 좋다.

03 특정 시점 앞에는 전치사나 접속사 since, 기간 앞에는 전치사 for 를 쓰며, ago는 과거동사와 함께 어울리는 부사이다.

04 '사람들이 찾던 그 실종 소년'이므로 The missing boy whom people were looking for라고 쓰는 것이 옳다.

05 이 집에서 얼마나 오랫동안 살았는지를 묻는 말이다. 현재완료 의 '계속' 용법을 이용하여 문장을 완성할 수 있다. 기간을 이끄 는 전치사는 for이다.

06 (1) 네가 만나기를 원하는 그 남자의 이름이 뭐야? (2) 이것이 내 친구가 언젠가 사기를 원하는 차야. (3) 내가 옷장에 넣어둔 빨간 색 스웨터는 어디에 있어?

07 경험을 묻는 말을 현재완료 시제를 사용하여 쓸 수 있다.

08 (1) 과거를 나타내는 yesterday는 현재완료 시제와 함께 쓸 수 없다. (2) '~에 가고 없다'는 의미의 have gone to는 3인 칭 주어에만 쓸 수 있다. (3) 선행사가 사물이므로 관계대명사는 which[that]를 쓰는 것이 옳다.

09 Kevin이 우산을 잃어버린 상황이 과거부터 현재까지 이어지므 로 현재완료 시제를 써서 한 문장으로 표현할 수 있다.

10 which를 대신하여 that을 써도 무방하며, whom을 대신하여 who나 that을 써도 좋다. (1) 네가 얻을 수 있는 많은 정보가 없어. (2) 나는 Tim이 항상 좋아하는 바지를 그에게 줬다. (3) 그가 네가 아주 존경하는 그 남자니?

11 '우리 아빠가 만드신 책상'이므로 관계사절이 the desk를 수식 하도록 문장을 만든다.

12 목적격 관계대명사와 '주격 관계대명사+be동사'를 생략할 수 있 다.

13 '그녀가 좋아하지 않는 음식'이므로 that[which] she doesn't like라고 쓰는 것이 옳다.

14 신발을 잃어버렸다는 결과를 나타내는 것이므로 현재완료 시제 를 이용한다.

15 which를 대신하여 that을 써도 좋다. attend a party: 파티에 참석하다, 파티에 가다

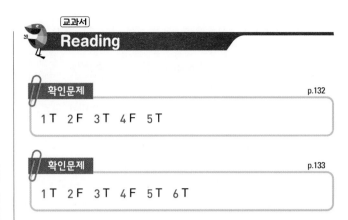

Reading

확인문제   p.132

1 T 2 F 3 T 4 F 5 T

확인문제   p.133

1 T 2 F 3 T 4 F 5 T 6 T

교과서 확인학습 A   p.134~135

01 years old, these days, going up and down

02 looks down

03 feelings, find out why

04 What a day, yelled at, after

05 because, forgot, lines

06 that Bella made

07 could, in front of

08 did not mean to hurt

09 have been, since

10 what, saying

11 would never put

12 that, not going to be friends   13 too far, see

14 forgive, say a word   15 even look at

16 has never been

17 ate alone during   18 best friend

19 that we don't know about

20 stand, any longer   21 go, tell, about

22 to be hurt   23 let it go   24 work it out

25 that, are talking   26 talked to her

27 avoid, on purpose

28 a way to say   29 any more problems

30 part of growing up

31 Just like, face, solve them, wiser

교과서 확인학습 B   p.136~137

1 Bella is 15 years old this year and these days her feelings are going up and down.

2 Today, she looks down.

3 Let's listen to Bella's feelings and find out why.

4 What a day! I can't believe Jenny yelled at Bella after the school play.

5 Well, that's because Bella forgot her lines on stage.

23

6 Jenny pointed out the mistake that Bella made.

7 How could she do that in front of everyone?

8 But I'm sure Jenny did not mean to hurt Bella.

9 They have been best friends since elementary school. Remember?

10 That's what I'm saying.

11 A true friend would never put Bella down like that.

12 I'm worried that they are not going to be friends anymore.

13 Come on, Fear. Don't go too far. We'll see.

14 I can't forgive Jenny. She didn't say a word to Bella.

15 Jenny didn't even look at her.

16 Jenny has never been this cold before.

17 Bella ate alone during lunch today. Poor Bella!

18 Jenny is Bella's best friend.

19 I'm sure there is a reason that we don't know about.

20 I can't stand this any longer.

21 Bella should just go and tell her about her feelings.

22 I don't want Bella to be hurt again.

23 She should let it go.

24 They are good friends. They will work it out.

25 Whew! I'm so happy that they are talking again.

26 Yeah, Bella went to Jenny and talked to her first.

27 Jenny didn't avoid Bella on purpose.

28 Yeah, Jenny didn't know a way to say sorry.

29 I hope Bella doesn't have any more problems like this.

30 Me, too. But problems are part of growing up.

31 Just like this time, Bella will face the problems, solve them, and become wiser in the end.

시험대비 실력평가
p.138~141

01 down　　02 ①, ②　　03 실수를 지적하는 것

04 ③　　05 ④

06 That's because Bella forgot her lines on stage.

07 ③　　08 ③　　09 ④　　10 forgive

11 ⑤　　12 part of growing up　　13 ①

14 Bella and Jenny are talking again　　15 ④

16 She feels up and down.

17 Fear is worried that Bella and Jenny are not going to be friends anymore.　　18 ②　　19 ③

20 ⑤　　21 she ate alone during lunch today

22 Anger wants Bella to go and tell Jenny about her

feelings.　　23 ②　　24 ④　　25 ②

26 wiser　　27 have not talked

01 오늘 있었던 일로 미루어 보아 Bella의 기분이 안 좋아 보인다고 하는 것이 옳다. down: 우울한

02 사물을 선행사로 취하는 목적격 관계대명사 which 혹은 that이 들어갈 수 있다.

03 Jenny가 Bella의 실수를 지적한 것을 의미한다.

04 현재완료에서 since는 특정 시점을 이끌고, for는 기간을 이끈다. 따라서 ③번에는 for가 들어간다.

05 Bella가 무대에서 왜 대사를 잊어버렸는지는 글을 읽고 알 수 없다.

06 Jenny가 Bella에게 소리를 지른 이유는 Bella가 무대에서 그녀의 대사를 잊어버렸기 때문이라고 하였다.

07 밑줄 친 (A)는 현재완료의 '경험'을 나타내는 말이다. 따라서 ③번이 옳다.

08 ⓒ는 Jenny를, 나머지는 모두 Bella를 가리키는 말이다.

09 Fear가 말하는 let it go는 '상황을 내버려 두다'는 의미로 Bella가 Jenny를 가게 해야만 한다는 것이 아니다.

10 누군가에게 화를 내거나 비난하는 것을 멈추는 것은 '용서하다(forgive)'이다.

11 on purpose: 일부러, 고의로 ① be satisfied with: ~에 만족하다 ② give up: 포기하다 ③ take part in: ~에 참가하다 ④ come up with: (생각을) 떠올리다 ⑤ turn on: ~을 켜다

12 전치사 of의 목적어로 동명사구를 쓰는 것에 유의한다.

13 in the end는 '결국, 마침내'라는 의미이다. 따라서 ①번이 옳다.

14 Joy가 행복한 이유는 'Bella와 Jenny가 다시 이야기하게 되어서'라고 하였다.

15 (A) listen은 자동사이므로 전치사 to와 함께 쓰일 때 목적어를 받음 (B) Jenny가 Bella에게 소리를 지른 이유를 설명하고 있으므로 that's because, (C) 초등학교 때부터 현재까지 가장 친한 친구라는 의미이므로 현재완료.

16 그녀의 기분은 좋다가 안 좋다가 한다고 하였다.

17 Fear는 Bella와 Jenny가 더 이상 친구로 지내지 않을까 봐 걱정된다고 하였다.

18 ⓔ는 '(연극, 영화의) 대사'라는 의미로 쓰인 line이다. 모두 line을 풀이한 말이며 ① (표면에 그어진) 선, 줄 ② 대사 ③ 주름살 ④ 윤곽선 ⑤ 줄, 열을 의미한다.

19 ③ Joy는 Jenny가 Bella에게 상처를 주려고 했던 것은 아니라고 확신한다. intend to: ~을 의도하다

20 밑줄 친 (A)는 불완전한 문장을 이끄는 관계대명사이다. ⑤는 접속사로 완전한 문장을 이끌고 있다.

21 Sadness가 Bella를 가엾어 하는 이유는 Bella가 오늘 점심시

간에 혼자 밥을 먹어서이다.

22 Anger는 Bella가 Jenny에게 가서 자신의 감정을 말하기를 원한다.

23 ② Fear는 Bella가 다시 상처받는 것을 원치 않는다고 하였다.

24 이번처럼 Bella는 문제를 피하는 것이 아니라 직면하게 될 것이다. avoid → face

25 Joy의 첫 번째 말로 미루어 보아 두 사람은 서로 이야기를 하지 않고 있다가 다시 이야기하게 되었으므로 ②번이 가장 적절하다.

26 문제를 해결하면서 Bella는 결국 더 현명해질 것이라 하였다.

27 이틀 동안 서로 대화를 하지 않았다는 의미로 현재완료 시제를 써서 나타낼 수 있다.

간에 혼자 밥을 먹었기 때문이다.

09 Bella가 Jenny에게 먼저 말을 걸어서 화해를 하게 되었다.

10 관계대명사 that을 대신하여 which를 써도 무방하다. 해석: Joy에 따르면 우리가 직면하는 문제들은 우리가 더 현명해지도록 돕는다.

11 Jenny는 사과하는 방법을 몰랐기 때문에 Bella를 피한 것이라고 하였다.

12 'I have a problem that I want to tell you.'라고 써도 좋다. that을 대신하여 which를 써도 무방하다.

13 since를 쓰며 현재의 문제를 이야기하고 있으므로 현재완료 시제를 쓰는 것이 가장 적절하다.

14 what to do: 무엇을 해야 할지

15 형편없는 수학 점수를 의미한다.

서술형 시험대비   p.142~143

01 why she looks down today
02 Bella made the mistake.
   Jenny pointed out the mistake.
03 They have been best friends since elementary school.
04 She forgot her lines on stage.
05 She yelled at Bella.
06 Jenny didn't say a word to Bella and she didn't even look at her.
07 I have forgiven my best friend before.
08 It's because she ate alone during lunch today.
09 She went to Jenny and talked to her first
10 that we face
11 she didn'tknow a way to say sorry
12 I want to tell you a problem that I have.
13 have had   14 I don't know what to do.
15 my terrible math grades

01 Bella의 감정에 귀 기울여 보고 기분이 안 좋은 이유를 알아보자는 의미이다.

02 the mistake를 선행사로 하여 만든 문장이므로 다른 하나의 문장은 Bella made the mistake.로 쓸 수 있다.

03 초등학교 때부터 가장 친한 친구였다는 의미이므로 현재완료 시제를 써서 표현할 수 있다.

04 Bella가 저지른 실수는 무대에서 대사를 잊어버린 것이다.

05 Jenny는 Bella에게 학교 연극이 끝난 후 소리를 질렀다고 하였다.

06 Jenny는 Bella에게 한마디도 말을 안 했고 심지어 Bella를 쳐다보지도 않았다고 하였다.

07 현재완료의 '경험'을 나타내는 말로 위 글의 표현을 이용하여 영어로 쓸 수 있다.

08 Sadness가 "가엾은 Bella"라고 말한 것은 그녀가 오늘 점심시

영역별 핵심문제   p.145~149

01 ②   02 ④
03 (1) You should focus on the problem at hand.
   (2) We can face a problem again.
   (3) Children grow up so fast these days.
04 elementary   05 ②   06 ②
07 ②   08 ③
09 (A) share my room with her, (B) advice, (C) tell my little sister my feelings and make some rules with her
10 (C) → (D) → (B) → (A)
11 ②   12 ②
13 Because he got a haircut but it's too short.
14 She thought it looked fine.   15 ①
16 ⑤   17 ②, ③
18 whom I care about most 19 ②, ⑤   20 ③
21 ⑤   22 she has gone to   23 ③
24 I will read the book which I borrowed from the library.   25 ③   26 ④
27 She forgot her lines on stage.   28 ⑤
29 ③
30 Bella and Jenny finally made up with each other.
31 ④

01 '당신에게 해롭게 하거나 화나게 하거나 또는 불안하게 하는 무언가를 한 사람에게 화내는 감정을 그만두다'를 나타내는 말은 forgive(용서하다)이다.

02 on purpose는 '고의로'를 의미한다.

03 at hand: 가까이에 (있는), face a problem: 문제에 직면하다, grow up: 성장하다

04 주어진 관계는 반의어 관계를 나타낸다. advanced: 상급의, 고등의, elementary: 초급의, 초보의

05 주어진 문장에서 lines는 '대사'를 나타내며 이와 같은 의미로

쓰인 것은 ②번이다. 나머지는 모두 '선'을 뜻한다.

06 mean은 동사로 '의미하다', 형용사로 '비열한, 인색한', means는 명사로 '수단, 방법'을 뜻한다.

07 (A) late: 늦은, lately: 최근에, (B) turn on: ~을 켜다 turn off: ~을 끄다, (C) close to: ~에 가까이, far from: ~에서 멀리

09 나는 오늘도 화가 났었다. 왜냐하면 내 여동생이 내게 먼저 물어보지도 않고 내 물건을 사용했기 때문이다. 나는 그녀와 더 이상 방을 같이 쓰고 싶지 않았다. 이 문제를 해결하기 위해, 나는 Solomon에게 전화를 해서 내게 조언을 해 줄 것을 요청하였다. 그는 내게 내 기분을 그녀에게 이야기하고 나의 여동생과 몇 가지 규칙을 정해볼 것을 조언하였다. 이것은 내게 훌륭한 조언이었으며 그것을 해 보기로 결정했다.

10 (C) 무슨 일이 있는지 질문 → (D) 기분이 좋지 않은 이유 설명 → (B) 반응 및 질문 → (A) 대답

11 이어서 특별한 프로그램의 기능을 설명하고 있으므로 (B)가 알맞다.

12 ② 위 대화를 통해 왜 Eric이 컴퓨터 게임을 멈출 수 없는지는 알 수 없다.

13 David는 머리를 잘랐는데 너무 짧아 침울하다.

14 Sora는 David의 머리가 괜찮아 보인다고 생각했다.

15 목적격 관계대명사가 생략된 문장이다. 선행사인 The watch 뒤에 위치하는 것이 옳다.

16 Mr. Kim taught the students English에서 온 문장이므로 ⑤번은 옳지 않다.

17 사물을 선행사로 취하는 목적격 관계대명사이므로 that이나 which를 쓰는 것이 옳다.

18 about whom I care most라고 써도 무방하다.

19 주어진 문장은 Jason이 여행에서 집으로 돌아왔다는 것으로 Jason이 과거에 여행을 떠났다가 현재 돌아와 집에 있다는 것을 말하는 문장이다.

20 우산을 잃어버렸지만 지금은 그것을 가지고 있다는 것이므로 '우산을 잃어버리고 있다'라는 두 번째 문장과 의미가 같지 않다.

21 주어진 문장의 현재완료는 '경험'을 나타낸다. ①, ④ 완료 ②, ③ 계속을 나타내는 현재완료이다.

22 Sally가 집에 가서 없다는 의미이므로 has gone to를 쓴다.

23 ③ yesterday는 과거를 나타내는 어구이므로 현재완료 시제와 함께 쓸 수 없다.

24 목적격 관계대명사 which를 대신하여 that을 쓰거나 생략해도 무방하다.

25 밑줄 친 (A)는 관계대명사 that으로 불완전한 문장을 이끈다. 따라서 ③번이 답이다.

26 Bella와 Jenny가 더 이상 친구가 되지 않을 것이라는 생각을 하지 말라는 의미이다.

27 Bella는 무대에서 그녀의 대사를 잊어버렸다고 하였다.

28 학교 연극의 이름이 무엇인지는 알 수 없다.

29 on purpose, intentionally: 고의로

30 두 사람은 마침내 화해하였다. make up with: 화해하다

31 Bella가 이러한 문제들에 직면하게 되지 않기를 바라는 것은 Fear의 희망이지, Bella가 원치 않는 것이 아니다.

단원별 예상문제 p.150~153

01 ④ 02 ⑤
03 Because he didn't have breakfast this morning.
04 They should wait for two more hours.
05 They can have a quick breakfast or snacks.
06 I think you should tell her your feelings. 07 ⑤
08 ③ 09 ②, ④
10 (B) → (D) → (C) → (A) 11 ④
12 (1) Where is the man? You cheered for him.
  (2) The car is very expensive. Tony Stark drives
    the car in the movie.
13 ⑤ 14 ③ 15 ⑤
16 I have lost my cell phone.
17 have seen, for 18 ③
19 I'm sure there is a reason.
  We don't know about the reason.
20 ③ 21 Fear wants her not to be hurt again.
22 ⑤
23 Fear hopes that Bella doesn't have any more
  problems like this. 24 ③ 25 ①, ④
26 I have had this problem since last year.

01 나머지는 모두 조언을 요청하는 표현이지만 ④번은 도움을 제안하는 표현이다.

02 ⑤번을 제외한 (A)와 나머지는 모두 조언을 하는 표현이다.

03 Mike는 오늘 아침에 아침을 먹지 않아 피곤해 보인다.

04 Jane과 Mike는 점심시간까지 두 시간 이상 기다려야 한다.

05 Jane과 Mike는 학교에 매점이 있다면 간단한 아침이나 간식을 먹을 수 있다.

07 Amy가 그녀의 여동생과 어떻게 화해할지는 알 수 없다.

08 Kevin은 엄마의 새 안경을 깨뜨려 걱정하고 있다.

09 빈칸 (A)는 유감이나 동정을 나타내는 표현이 적절하므로 ②, ④번이 적절하다.

10 (B) Daisy에게 지각함을 알림 → (D) 사과 및 지각한 이유 설명 → (C) 조언 → (A) 반응

11 주어진 문장은 현재완료의 '완료'를 나타내고 있다. ④번은 경험을 나타내는 현재완료이다.

12 (1) 네가 응원했던 그 남자는 어디에 있니? (2) 그 영화에서 Tony Stark가 운전하는 차는 아주 비싸다.

13 사람과 사물을 모두 선행사로 취할 수 있는 관계대명사는 that이다.

14 ③ 관계대명사로 이어진 문장이므로 it을 쓰지 않아야 한다.

15 목적격 관계대명사 혹은 '주격 관계대명사+be동사'를 생략할 수 있다.

16 휴대전화기를 잃어버린 상황이 현재까지 지속되고 있으므로 현재완료 시제를 써서 한 문장으로 표현할 수 있다.

17 '우리는 두 시간 동안 그 영화를 보고 있다'라고 쓸 수 있다.

18 (A) Jenny가 Bella를 쳐다보지도 않았다는 의미가 적절하므로 at, (B) 명사를 이끌고 있으므로 전치사 during, (C) 타동사는 대명사 목적어를 부사 앞에 위치시키므로 work it out이 옳다.

19 a reason이 선행사임에 유의하여 문장을 둘로 나눈다.

20 Bella가 혼자 점심을 먹었다고 하였으므로 ③번은 옳지 않다.

21 Fear는 Bella가 다시는 상처받지 않기를 원한다고 하였다.

22 밑줄 친 (A)는 앞의 명사를 수식하는 형용사로 쓰인 to부정사이다. 따라서 ⑤번이 답이다.

23 Fear는 Bella에게 이번과 같은 문제가 더 이상 없기를 바란다고 하였다.

24 Jenny가 Bella를 의도적으로 피한 것이 아니라고 하였으므로 ③번은 글의 내용과 일치하지 않는다.

25 선행사가 사물이므로 that이나 which를 써서 관계사절을 만든다.

26 작년 이래로 계속 이 문제를 가지고 있다는 것이므로 현재완료 시제로 표현할 수 있다.

01 What should I do?

02 The computer shuts down at the set time.

03 She advises him to move it out of his room and into the living room.

04 (1) Have you ever been to Busan?
(2) She has gone to Busan.

05 The box which she is lifting is not that heavy.
The restaurant which Paul runs is crowded with people.
The children whom I take care of are very noisy.

06 How long have you known each other?

07 The girl whom Tom is looking at is Danny's friend.

08 which[that] Jimmy is wearing

09 A: has, played　　B: when, has played, for

10 Jenny yelled at Bella after the school play.

11 A true friend would never put Bella down like that.

12 Jenny pointed out my mistake in front of everyone

13 ⓒ-ⓐ-ⓑ

14 whom I have known since elementary school

02 Eric이 특별한 프로그램을 사용하여 시간 제한을 설정하면 정해진 시간에 컴퓨터가 종료된다.

03 Ms. Morris는 Eric에게 컴퓨터를 그의 방에서 거실로 옮길 것을 조언하였다.

04 (1) 현재완료 시제를 이용하여 경험을 묻는 말을 쓸 수 있고, (2) '~에 가고 없다'는 결과 역시 현재완료 시제로 표현할 수 있다.

05 which를 대신하여 that을 쓸 수 있으며 whom 대신 who나 that을 써도 좋다. 모두 목적격 관계대명사이므로 생략해도 무방하다.

06 대답으로 미루어 보아 서로를 얼마나 오랫동안 알아왔는지를 묻는 말이 들어가는 것이 옳다.

07 'Tom이 바라보고 있는 그 소녀'이므로 관계사절 whom Tom is looking at이 명사 the girl을 수식하도록 문장을 쓸 수 있다.

08 wear a helmet: 헬멧을 쓰다

09 남동생이 얼마나 오랫동안 골프를 쳐 왔는지를 묻는 말에, 일곱 살 때 골프를 배워 지금까지 5년 동안 골프를 쳐 오고 있다는 대답을 하고 있다.

10 Jenny가 Bella에게 소리를 지른 것을 가리키는 말이다.

11 never는 빈도부사로 일반동사 앞, 조동사 뒤에 위치하는 것에 유의한다. put A down: A를 깎아내리다

12 Jenny는 모든 사람 앞에서 Bella의 실수를 지적하였다. in front of: ~ 앞에서

13 Bella가 자신의 대사를 잊어버리자 이를 지적하며 Jenny가 Bella에게 소리를 질렀고 Bella는 그것 때문에 슬펐다는 것이 사건의 순서이다.

14 whom을 대신하여 who 또는 that을 써도 무방하다.

|모범답안|

01 (A) I didn't have breakfast
(B) two more hours
(C) our school should have a snack bar
(D) the suggestion board

02 (1) I have argued with my best friend several times.
(2) My friends have visited my house once.
(3) I have never had a snow fight with my friend.
(4) I have known Sumin since 2015.
(5) I have been to a concert with my friends before.

03 (1) has lived in New York
(2) has been to Spain
(3) has raised Cooper since
(4) and John have known each other since

01 나는 늦게 일어나 버스를 거의 놓칠 번했다. 다행히, 학교에 지각하지 않았다. 하지만 나는 너무 피곤하고 배고팠다. 왜냐하면 아침을 먹지 않았기 때문이다. 심지어, 나는 점심시간을 위해 두 시간 이상을 기다려야 했다. 나는 우리학교가 배고픈 학생들을 위해 매점이 있어야 한다고 생각했다. 내가 이것에 대해 Jane과 이야기 했을 때 그녀는 내 생각에 동의했다. 나는 곧 내 생각을 제안 게시판에 게시할 계획을 세웠다.

단원별 모의고사　　　　　　　　　　p.157~160

01 (1) suggestion　(2) repeat　(3) forgive　　02 ⑤

03 (1) stay up late　(2) up and down　(3) wake up
　　(4) work out

04 (1) explain　(2) yell　(3) worry　(4) pack　(5) fight

05 ②　　　　　06 ④　　　　07 ③　　　　08 ①

09 (A) breakfast, (B) hungry, (C) have a snack barin
　　our school

10 Because she stayed up late again last night.

11 She should pack her bag the night before.

12 (1) I can't stand working with him any more.
　　(2) Minho has to memorize his lines in English.
　　(3) I was embarrassed when he pointed out my
　　　　mistakes.　　　13 ③　　　　14 ⑤

15 ④

16 I have just eaten the cake that you bought for me.

17 I have not found my gold necklace yet.　18 ④

19 No, she didn't. She pointed out my mistake in
　　front of everyone　　20 ④　　　　21 stand

22 ③　　　　23 they aregood friends

---

01 suggestion: 제안, repeat: 반복하다, forgive: 용서하다

02 since는 전치사로 '~부터, ~ 이래로', 접속사로 '~한 이래로, ~이기 때문에'를 의미한다.

03 stay up late: 늦게까지 자지 않고 있다, up and down: 좋다가 나쁘다가 하는, wake up: 잠에서 깨다, work out: 해결하다

04 explain: 설명하다, yell: 소리치다, worry: 걱정하다, pack: (짐을) 싸다, fight like cat and dog: 싸우다, 격렬하게 서로 으르렁거리다

05 위 대화에서 ⓐdown은 '우울한'을 의미하며 이와 같은 의미로 쓰인 것은 ②번이다.

06 David는 새로운 그의 머리 스타일 때문에 기분이 좋지 않다.

07 이어서 Amy가 그녀의 여동생과 방을 같이 쓰기 싫은 이유를 설명하고 있으므로 (C)가 적절하다.

08 Amy와 Solomon은 직접 마주하여 이야기를 하는 것이 아니라 통화하고 있다.

09 몇몇 학생들이 아침을 먹지 않아 배고픔을 느낀다. 우리 학교에

매점이 있어야 한다.

10 Daisy는 지난밤에 또 늦게까지 자지 않고 깨어 있었기 때문에 지각하였다.

11 Daisy는 아침에 시간을 절약하기 위해 전날 밤에 가방을 싸야 한다.

13 현재완료에서 'since+시점', 'for+기간'으로 쓰이는 것에 유의하자.

14 관계대명사가 전치사의 목적어로 쓰인 경우에 유의하자. talk about: ~에 대하여 말하다

15 어제 이후로 아무것도 먹지 않았다는 의미이므로 have eaten을 쓰는 것이 옳다.

16 '네가 나에게 사 주었던 그 케이크'이므로 the cake that you bought for me라고 쓰는 것이 옳다.

17 현재완료 시제를 이용하여 나는 아직 내 금목걸이를 찾지 못했다는 의미로 쓸 수 있다.

18 연극이 끝난 후에 Jenny가 Bella에게 소리를 질렀다고 하였다.

19 Jenny는 모든 사람들 앞에서 Bella의 실수를 지적하였다.

20 우울해 보이는 것은 Jenny가 아니라 Bella이다.

21 어려운 상황을 받아들이거나 잘 다룰 수 있는 것은 'stand(참다, 견디다)'이다.

22 Bella가 자신의 감정을 Jenny에게 말해야 한다고 Anger가 말했을 뿐, 실제로 Bella가 Jenny에게 먼저 말을 걸지는 않았다.

23 Joy는 Bella와 Jenny가 좋은 친구이므로 잘 해낼 것이라고 생각한다.

교과서 파헤치기

Lesson 3

1 weigh, 무게를 재다　2 collector, 수집가
3 average, 평균　4 challenge, 도전　5 possible, 가능한
6 scare, 무서워하다　7 add, 더하다　8 experiment, 실험
9 scream, 비명　10 hide, 숨기다　11 drone, 무인 비행기
12 battery, 건전지　13 lift, 들어 올리다
14 lower, 내리다, 낮추다　15 amusement, 재미, 즐거움
16 fair, 박람회

01 생산하다, 제작하다	02 유용한
03 식초	04 나타나다　05 풍선
06 콩	07 자동차 경적
08 무인 비행기, 무인 항공기	09 전체의
10 실험　11 평균	12 숨기다, 숨다
13 믿을 수 없는　14 불가능한	15 내리다, 낮추다
16 응용 프로그램, 적용	17 능력
18 괴물, 요괴　19 기록하다, 녹음하다	
20 보통의, 평범한　21 수집가	
22 겁주다, 겁먹게 하다	23 단 하나의
24 비명, 외침(소리)　25 전기, 전류	26 재미, 놀이, 오락
27 설명하다　28 자물쇠를 열다	29 전체의
30 놓치다, 그리워하다	31 접다
32 활동　33 아픈	34 실
35 둘의, 몇 개의　36 ~을 떠받치다	37 ~라고 하자
38 덧칠하다　39 주입하다, 채워 넣다	
40 ~을 돌보다　41 ~을 제거하다, ~을 치우다	
42 게다가, 더구나　43 ~을 두르다, ~을 감다	

01 amazingly	02 entire	03 weigh
04 amount	05 balloon	06 electricity
07 average	08 activity	09 fair
10 amusement	11 fold	12 however
13 advice	14 lift	15 miss
16 sore	17 explain	18 possible
19 battery	20 string	21 add
22 pick	23 challenge	24 unlock
25 ring	26 unbelievable	27 appear
28 lower	29 record	30 normal
31 monster	32 ability	33 useful
34 scream	35 take away	36 for example
37 turn off	38 light up	39 pump up
40 pick one's brain		41 turn into
42 in front of	43 take care of	

Listen & Talk 1 A-1

What show watching / watching, Have you heard about it / haven't, about / science to explain / sounds interesting

Listen & Talk 1 A-2

have, heard about / No, I haven't / phone application, can ask / Let me show you, what's, like / going to rain, need / what a great application

Listen & Talk 1 B

Have you heard about, own drone, class, offers, every Wednesday, Make, special drone, how to control it, Don't miss

Listen & Talk 2 A-1

what, made / What do you mean / works with, not with / electricity, interesting

Listen & Talk 2 A-2

what did you do last weekend / made, with / What, mean / put, in vinegar for / turns into / want to, too

Listen & Talk 2 B

let's, science experiment / What do you mean / special, hide your message / How, make / Mix, on the card with / How can you read the card / Paint over, with, and then, appears

Communication

Have you heard about / Yes, I have, going to / going to send, about / What do you mean / take a picutre of, tells, how to take care of it / sounds like, useful

Wrap Up 1

Have, heard about / going to go / too, excited, kinds of experiments / looking forward to

Listen & Talk 1 A-1

Mike: What show are you watching, Sally?

Sally: I'm watching the Sci-Magic show. It's a new program. Have you heard about it?

Mike: No, I haven't. What's it about?

Sally: The program uses science to explain magic tricks.

Mike: Oh, it sounds interesting.

Listen & Talk 1 A-2

Tom: Mom, have you heard about the Chat Robot?

Mom: No, I haven't. What is it?

Tom: It's a phone application. You can ask any questions and it will answer. Let me show you. "Emily, what's the weather like today?"

Emily: "It's going to rain, so you'll need an umbrella."

Mom: Wow, what a great application!

Listen & Talk 1 B

W: Hello, students. Have you heard about the DIY Drone Class? You can make your own drone in the class. The Youth Community Center offers the class at 3 p.m. every Wednesday in May. Make your special drone and learn how to control it. Don't miss this great chance!

Listen & Talk 2 A-1

Mina: You know what? I made a potato clock yesterday!

Jack: A potato clock? What do you mean?

Mina: My clock works with potatoes, not with batteries. Potatoes can produce electricity.

Jack: That's interesting!

Listen & Talk 2 A-2

Jimmy: Lisa, what did you do last weekend?

Lisa: I made an egg ball with my brother.

Jimmy: An egg ball? What do you mean?

Lisa: We put an egg in vinegar for two days. Then, the egg turns into a ball.

Jimmy: Wow, I want to make one, too!

Listen & Talk 2 B

Minho: Anna, let's make a "Mystery Card" for the science experiment.

Anna: A "Mystery Card?" What do you mean?

Minho: It's a special card. It can hide your message.

Anna: How do you make it?

Minho: Mix baking soda and water. Then, write a message on the card with it.

Anna: How can you read the card?

Minho: Paint over the card with grape juice, and then the message appears.

Communication

Jane: Have you heard about the Smart App Contest?

Minho: Yes, I have. Are you going to enter it?

Jane: Yeah, I'm going to send my idea about a Pic Gardener App.

Minho: A Pic Gardener App? What do you mean?

Jane: When you take a picture of a plant, the app tells you how to take care of it.

Minho: It sounds like a very useful app.

Wrap Up 1

Hojin: Hey, Katy. Have you heard about the science fair?

Katy: Yeah, I'm going to go there.

Hojin: Me, too! I'm excited about doing different kinds of experiments.

Katy: Yeah, I'm also looking forward to it!

본문 TEST Step 1   p.09~10

01 animation, amazing, possible

02 actually, real   03 Let Down

04 must lower, let, in

05 human, hold, person

06 single, average, about

07 All those, couple of

08 With, ability, up

09 wrap, around, heavy

10 doesn't, will, sore   11 Scare for

12 scare, to get, from

13 Amazingly, powered by

14 produce, light up, from

15 be changed into

16 helpful, because, amount, small

17 For example, from, produces

18 only, average, electricity

19 unbelievable, screams, entire

20 Up, Away   21 lifted, flown, thousands

22 Could, actually

23 Let's, weighs about

24 normal, amusement, lift

25 about, to lift up

26 have, about, themselves, strings

27 need, add, few

28 challenge, pumping, all those

본문 TEST Step 2   p.11~12

01 animation, amazing things are possible

02 actually possible, real life   03 Let Down

04 In, must lower, to let people in

05 could, hold up a person

06 Surprisingly, single, hold up average, has about

07 All those hairs, hold up

08 With her hair, the ability to hold up

09 wrap her hair around, strong, heavy

10 doesn't, will get, sore neck　　　11 Scare for

12 scare children to get, from their screams

13 Amazingly, is powered by

14 could, produce electricity to light up, from

15 be changed into electricity

16 would not, helpful in, because the amount is, small

17 For example, from, car horn, produces

18 of the average, electricity, in our homes

19 an unbelievable amount of screams, light up , entire

20 Up, Up, Away

21 is lifted and flown, thousands of balloons

22 Could, actually work

23 Let's say, weighs about

24 normal, an amusement park, lift about

25 need about, to lift up

26 have to think about, weight, themselves, strings

27 add a few more thousand

28 biggest challenge, pumping up all those

14 하지만 정말 소리로부터 도시를 밝히는 전기를 만들 수 있을까?

15 그렇다. 소리는 전기로 바뀔 수 있다.

16 그렇지만 그 양이 너무 적기 때문에 그것은 우리의 일상 활동에서는 도움이 되지 않을 것이다.

17 예를 들어, 자동차 경적 소리는 겨우 50밀리볼트를 만들어 낸다.

18 그것은 우리 가정에서 사용하는 일반적인 220볼트 전기의 1/4400밖에 되지 않는다.

19 그래서 도시 전체를 밝히기 위해서는 믿기 어려운 정도로 많은 양의 비명이 필요할 것이다.

20 높이, 높이 그리고 멀리!

21 만화 영화에서 집은 수천 개의 풍선에 의해 들려 올라가고 날아간다.

22 이게 실제로 가능할까?

23 집 한 채의 무게가 5만 킬로그램 정도라고 가정해 보자.

24 놀이공원에 있는 보통의 풍선은 대략 14그램을 들어 올릴 수 있다.

25 그래서 집을 들어 올리기 위해 우리는 약 3,570,000개의 풍선이 필요하다.

26 우리는 또한 풍선 자체와 줄의 무게에 대해서도 생각해야 한다.

27 그렇게 되면, 수천 개의 풍선을 더 추가할 필요가 있다.

28 이제 가장 큰 어려움은 그 모든 풍선에 바람을 넣는 일이다!

본문 TEST Step 3　　　　　　　　　　　　　p.13~14

1 만화 영화에서는 놀라운 일들이 가능하다.

2 하지만 그런 일들이 실생활에서 정말 가능할까?

3 라푼젤, 네 머리카락을 내려!

4 만화 영화에서 라푼젤은 사람들이 탑에 들어오게 하기 위해서 그녀의 긴 머리카락을 내려야 한다.

5 하지만 인간의 머리카락이 정말로 사람을 들어 올릴 수 있을까?

6 놀랍게도 그렇다! 머리카락 한 가닥은 100그램의 무게를 들어 올릴 수 있고 보통 머리에는 12만 개 정도의 머리카락이 있다.

7 그 모든 머리카락은 코끼리 두 마리를 들어 올릴 수 있다!

8 라푼젤에게는 머리카락으로 사람을 들어 올릴 수 있는 능력이 있다.

9 하지만 그녀는 머리카락을 어떤 강하고 무거운 것에 감아야 한다.

10 만약 그렇게 하지 않으면 그녀는 목이 많이 아플 것이다.

11 우리는 에너지를 얻기 위해 겁을 준다

12 만화 영화에서 괴물들은 아이들의 비명에서 에너지를 얻기 위해 아이들을 겁준다.

13 놀랍게도 그들의 도시는 이 소리로 동력을 공급받는다!

본문 TEST Step 4 · Step 5　　　　　　　　　p.15~18

1 In animation movies, amazing things are possible.

2 But are they actually possible in real life?

3 Let Down Your Hair, Rapunzel!

4 In the animation, Rapunzel must lower her long hair to let people in her tower.

5 But could human hair really hold up a person?

6 Surprisingly, yes! A single hair can hold up 100g and an average head has about 120,000 hairs.

7 All those hairs could hold up a couple of elephants!

8 With her hair, Rapunzel has the ability to hold up a person.

9 But she should wrap her hair around something strong and heavy.

10 If she doesn't, she will get a very sore neck.

11 We Scare for Energy

12 In the animation, monsters scare children to get energy from their screams.

13 Amazingly, their city is powered by this sound!

14 But could we actually produce electricity to light

up a city from sound?

15 Yes, sound can be changed into electricity.

16 But it would not be helpful in our everyday activities because the amount is too small.

17 For example, the sound from a car horn only produces 50mv.

18 That is only 1/4400 of the average 220v of electricity in our homes.

19 So, we would need an unbelievable amount of screams to light up an entire city.

20 Up, Up and Away!

21 The house is lifted and flown by thousands of balloons in the animation.

22 Could that actually work?

23 Let's say that a house weighs about 50,000kg.

24 A normal balloon at an amusement park can lift about 14g.

25 So we need about 3,570,000 balloons to lift up the house.

26 We also have to think about the weight of the balloons themselves and the strings.

27 Then, we need to add a few more thousand balloons.

28 Now, the biggest challenge is pumping up all those balloons!

구석구석지문 TEST Step 1 p.19

Grammar in Real Life

1. plan for
2. a lot of
3. to go, on
4. to borrow
5. science homework, by, foreign
6. On, talent show,
7. practice performing, talents show

Think & Write

1. my name
2. I'd like, talk about, wearable
3. helpful to take
4. show me a map
5. Try it out

Wrap Up 3

1. Have you heard, special, science museum
2. haven't
3. There are, during, only for

4. thank, for, there

구석구석지문 TEST Step 2 p.20

Grammar in Real Life

1. This is Jack's plan for this week.
2. There is a lot of work to do.
3. He needs to go to the library on Monday.
4. He has two books to borrow from the library.
5. Also he has science homework to finish by Thursday.
6. On Friday, he will be in the school talent show.
7. So, he will practice performing the songs at the talents show all this week.

Think & Write

1. Hello, my name is June.
2. Today I'd like to talk about my new wearable technology, SuperEye.
3. It is helpful to take pictures and video-record.
4. It is also useful to show me a map .
5. Try it out and experience a new world!

Wrap Up 3

1. Amy: Have you heard about the special event at the science museum?
2. Brian: No, I haven't. What's the event?
3. Amy: There are science magic shows during the weekend, but only for this month.
4. Brian: Oh, thank you for the information. I'll visit there this weekend.

Lesson 4

단어 TEST Step 1   p.21

01 놀랄 정도의, 굉장한	02 무서운, 심한
03 목소리	04 (경주, 대회 등의) 등위, 장소
05 엔진, 기관	06 막다, 방해하다 07 흥분하여, 기를 쓰고
08 갈채를 보내다, 환성을 지르다	
09 아슬아슬한 승부, 접전	10 지방의
11 (자동차의) 가속 페달	12 부딪치다
13 (경주에서 트랙의) 한 바퀴, 무릎	
14 시끄러운, (소리가) 큰	
15 (운동 경기의) 심판; 공식의	16 타격
17 매달다, 걸다 18 일직선의, 즉시의	19 3점슛
20 차다, 걷어차다 21 중요하다, (수를) 세다	
22 깊은	23 복잡한, 붐비는 24 기억할 만한
25 해산물	26 돌진하다 27 뛰다, 치다, 두드리다
28 완성하다, 달성하다; 완전한	29 결승선
30 군중, 관객 31 투수	
32 수리하다, 고정시키다	33 앞에, 앞선
34 누르다, 밀어붙이다	
35 (모험 삼아) 해 보다	
36 자세를 바로 하다, 바로 앉다	37 기회를 놓치다
38 ~에 만족하다 39 기운을 내다	40 ~로 가득 차다
41 최선을 다하다 42 ~에 뒤떨어지지 않다	
43 ~에게 닿지 않는, ~의 힘이 미치지 않는	

단어 TEST Step 2   p.22

01 beat	02 count	03 ahead
04 volleyball	05 track	06 pitching
07 finish line	08 flag	09 seafood
10 deep	11 complete	12 fix
13 crowded	14 memorable	15 kart
16 crowd	17 rush	18 pitcher
19 tear	20 press	21 terrible
22 cheer	23 excitedly	24 voice
25 close match	26 block	27 three-pointer
28 hang	29 punch	30 loud
31 amazing	32 straightaway	33 local
34 place	35 be satisfied with	
36 cheer up	37 do one's best	38 win a race
39 be filled with	40 keep up with	41 miss a chance
42 sit up	43 take a chance	

단어 TEST Step 3   p.23

1 kart, 소형 경주용 자동차   2 count, 중요하다, 가치가 있다
3 complete, 완성하다   4 kick, 차다   5 pitcher, 투수
6 tear, 눈물   7 track, 경주로, 트랙   8 seafood, 해산물
9 voice, 목소리   10 engine, 엔진   11 volleyball, 배구
12 memorable, 기억할 만한   13 cheer, 응원하다, 갈채를
보내다   14 block, 막다, 방해하다   15 crowd, 관객, 관중
16 finish line, 결승선

대화문 TEST Step 1   p.24~25

Listen & Talk 1 A-1

how, basketball game / lost, missed, chances, three, pointer / don't be so hard, You'll do better, hope so

Listen & Talk 1 A-2

volleyball match / You were great / but, were not strong enough / you're a great player, do better

Listen & Talk 1 B

heard, won the match, Eight to seven, Congratulations / a close game, not happy with, pitching / Why, say / allowed two homeruns / you're a great pitcher, do better

Listen & Talk 2 A-1

first time riding / can't keep my balance / Let me help, hold / Don't let / Sit up, look straight ahead

Listen & Talk 2 A-1

are, doing / how to stand on my head, trying, not easy / Let me help you, Kick, catch you / try again

Listen & Talk 2 B

Did, practice / I'm still not comfortable with it / What problem, having / can't lift my leg high enough / Let me, hold, Show, side kick

Communication

worried about our / Why are, worried / couldn't catch high balls / gave away / let me help you, kick high balls / my skills get better / Don't worry, do better

Wrap Up 1

Do you come to / take a swimming class, once a week / When, start the class / Last month, easy for me / let me help, how to swim / that'll help me a lot

대화문 TEST Step 2   p.26~27

Listen & Talk 1 A-1

Mom: David, how was your basketball game today?
David: We lost, Mom. I missed too many chances for a

three-pointer.

Mom: Oh, don't be so hard on yourself. You'll do better next time.

David: I hope so.

Jack: Did you come and watch my volleyball match yesterday?

Irene: Yeah, I did. That was a great volleyball match. You were great!

Jack: Thanks, but it was a close match. My serves were not strong enough.

Irene: Oh, you're a great player. You'll do better next time.

Emily: I heard your baseball team, the Reds, won the match. Eight to seven, right? Congratulations, John!

John: Thanks. It was a close game. I'm not happy with my pitching.

Emily: Why do you say that?

John: I allowed two homeruns.

Emily: Oh, you're a great pitcher. You'll do better next time.

Mike: Is it your first time riding a bike, Mina?

Mina: Yes, it is. I just can't keep my balance.

Mike: Let me help you. I'll hold your bike.

Mina: Thanks, Mike. Don't let go, okay?

Mike: Don't worry. Sit up and look straight ahead.

Tom: What are you doing, Sarah?

Sarah: I learned how to stand on my head in PE class. So I'm trying it now but it's not easy.

Tom: Let me help you. Kick your legs in the air again. I'll catch you.

Sarah: Oh, thanks. I'll try again.

Coach: Hey, Brian. Did you practice the *taegwondo* side kick?

Brian: Yes, Coach. But I'm still not comfortable with it.

Coach: What problem are you having?

Brian: Well, I can't lift my leg high enough.

Coach: I see. Let me help you. I'll hold this kick pad for you. Show me your side kick.

Megan: I'm worried about our next soccer match, James.

James: Why are you worried, Megan?

Megan: Well, I couldn't catch high balls in the last soccer match. I gave away too many goals.

James: I see. Here, let me help you . I'll kick high balls to you.

Megan: Oh, that'll really help. I hope my skills get better.

James: Don't worry. You'll do better next time.

Anna: Hi, Jake. Do you come to the pool often?

Jake: Oh, hi, Anna. I take a swimming class here once a week.

Anna: When did you start the class?

Jake: Last month. But swimming is still not easy for me.

Anna: Oh, let me help you. I teach children how to swim in the school club.

Jake: Oh, that'll help me a lot. Thanks.

01 At, there, who, cheering
02 that, making, are, waiting
03 waves, flag, starts
04 pushes, down as, completes
05 On, pulls, beside
06 won, result, coming, place
07 chance, finish second
08 going, satisfied, place
09 gets, meet, famous
10 miss, chance, role
11 completes, tenth, laps
12 ahead, out, reach   13 gets, closer
14 almost hits, end
15 drive into, presses harder   16 catch up
17 official waving, means
18 right behind   19 getting, cheering, crowd, louder
20 can do, loudly 21 feel, beating hard
22 rush across, finish   23 Who, winner
24 filled with, out
25 need, tears, voice   26 can't believe
27 standing, front, is
28 but, not, winner   29 real close race
30 Even, win, best   31 that counts
32 Did, best   33 After, smiles   34 guess, did

01 At, track, there are, who are cheering excitedly

02 that are making loud, are waiting

03 official waves, flag, starts

04 pushes, down hard, as, completes, sixth lap

05 On the straightaway, pulls right beside

06 won many races, was coming in fifth place

07 chance to finish second

08 be satisfied with second place   09 gets to meet

10 to miss, to meet his role model

11 completes the tenth lap, to go

12 sees, ahead, out of

13 gets closer and closer

14 hits the back end

15 drive into, presses harder on the gas pedal

16 can catch up

17 waving a white flag, means the last lap

18 right behind

19 getting closer, cheering from the crowd, getting louder

20 can do it, says loudly

21 can feel, beating hard

22 rush across the finish line   23 Who, winner

24 filled with tears, finds out that, in second

25 No need for tears

26 can't believe his eyes

27 who is standing in front of, is   28 not the winner

29 a real close race

30 Even though, didn't win the race, did

31 that counts   32 Did, do my best, thinks

33 After a moment, smiles   34 guess, did

---

10 그는 그의 역할 모델을 만날 수 있는 기회를 놓치길 원하지 않는다.

11 Max는 10바퀴를 다 돌고 이제 5바퀴를 더 돌아야 한다.

12 Max는 앞에 바로 닿을 듯한 거리에 있는 Simon의 카트를 본다.

13 Max의 카트는 Simon의 카트에 점점 더 가까워진다.

14 Max의 카트는 Simon의 카트의 뒷부분에 거의 닿을 것 같다.

15 그들은 직선 구간을 운전해가고, Max는 가속 페달을 더 세게 밟는다.

16 "나는 따라잡을 수 있어." Max가 말한다.

17 Max는 심판이 마지막 바퀴라는 것을 알려주는 흰색 깃발을 흔드는 것을 본다.

18 Max는 Simon 바로 뒤에 있다.

19 결승점이 점점 가까워지고, 관중으로부터 들리는 환호성이 점점 커진다.

20 "나는 할 수 있어!" Max는 큰 소리로 말한다.

21 그는 그의 심장이 세게 뛰는 것을 느낄 수 있다.

22 카트들이 돌진해 결승점을 지난다.

23 누가 승자인가?

24 Max는 자신이 2등으로 들어왔다는 것을 알았을 때, 눈에 눈물이 가득 찬다.

25 "울 필요 없단다, 얘야." 어떤 남자의 목소리가 말한다.

26 Max는 그의 눈을 믿을 수 없다.

27 그 앞에 서 있는 남자는 L. J. Richards이다!

28 "고마워요, 하지만 저는 일등이 아니에요." Max가 말한다.

29 "정말 아슬아슬한 경기였어.

30 네가 비록 경기를 이기지 못했지만, 너는 최선을 다했어.

31 중요한 것은 바로 그거란다!" L. J. Richards가 말한다.

32 '나는 최선을 다했을까?' Max는 생각한다.

33 잠시 후에, 그는 미소를 짓는다.

34 "네, 저는 최선을 다한 것 같아요."

---

1 고카트 경기 트랙에 신이 나서 응원하고 있는 많은 사람들이 있다.

2 시끄러운 엔진 소음을 내고 있는 카트들이 기다리고 있다.

3 심판이 초록 깃발을 흔들고, 경기가 시작된다!

4 Max는 트랙을 여섯 바퀴 돌았을 때, 발로 가속 페달을 힘껏 누른다.

5 직선 구간에서 Max는 경기에서 선두를 달리고 있는 Simon의 바로 옆까지 다가간다.

6 작년에 Simon은 경기에서 여러 번 이겼지만 Max의 최고 경기 성적은 5등으로 들어온 것이었다.

7 이번에 그는 2등으로 끝낼 수 있는 기회를 잡았다.

8 그러나 그는 오늘 2등으로 만족하지 않을 것이다.

9 우승자는 세계적으로 유명한 경주 선수인 L. J. Richards를 만나게 된다!

---

1 At the go-kart race track, there are many people who are cheering excitedly.

2 The karts that are making loud engine noises are waiting.

3 An official waves a green flag and the race starts!

4 Max pushes his foot down hard on the gas pedal as he completes his sixth lap on the track.

5 On the straightaway, Max pulls right beside the race's leader, Simon.

6 Last year, Simon won many races, but Max's best result in a race was coming in fifth place.

7 This time, he has a chance to finish second.

8 But he isn't going to be satisfied with second

---

place today.

9 The winner gets to meet the world famous racer L. J. Richards!

10 He doesn't want to miss the chance to meet his role model.

11 Max completes the tenth lap and now has five more laps to go.

12 Max sees Simon's kart ahead, just out of Max's reach.

13 Max's kart gets closer and closer to Simon's.

14 It almost hits the back end of Simon's kart.

15 They drive into the straightaway and Max presses harder on the gas pedal.

16 "I can catch up," says Max.

17 Max sees the official waving a white flag which means the last lap.

18 Max is right behind Simon.

19 The finish line is getting closer, and the cheering from the crowd is getting louder.

20 "I can do it!" Max says loudly.

21 He can feel his heart beating hard.

22 The karts rush across the finish line.

23 Who is the winner?

24 Max's eyes are filled with tears as he finds out that he came in second.

25 "No need for tears, kid," says a man's voice.

26 Max can't believe his eyes.

27 The man who is standing in front of him is L. J. Richards!

28 "Thank you, but I'm not the winner," says Max.

29 "It was a real close race.

30 Even though you didn't win the race, you did your best.

31 That's the thing that counts!" says L. J. Richards.

32 'Did I do my best?' thinks Max.

33 After a moment, he smiles.

34 "Yeah, I guess I did."

구석구석지문 TEST Step 1
p.38

Listen & Talk C

1. why the long face

2. couldn't block, other player

3. Don't worry, do better

Grammar in Real Life

1. cook who cooks delicious

2. always goes, which, fresh

3. is always crowded with, who

4. want you to try, most popular

Think & Write

1. between, and, was held, on

2. won, by a score

3. memorable players

4. One of, was

5. made a basket, the end of

6. great match

7. are looking forward

구석구석지문 TEST Step 2
p.39

Listen & Talk C

1. Amy: Michael, why the long face?

2. Michael: I couldn't block the other player.

3. Amy: Don't worry, Michael. You'll do better next time.

Grammar in Real Life

1. Ms. Green is a good cook who cooks delicious Italian food.

2. She always goes to the local store which has many fresh vegetables.

3. Her restaurant is always crowded with people who like to eat her food.

4. I want you to try her seafood pizza which is the most popular.

Think & Write

1. A basketball match between Class 1 and Class 2 was held at school on Friday.

2. Class 1 won the game by a score.

3. There are some memorable players.

4. One of them was Sarah.

5. She was the player who made a basket one second before the end of the game.

6. It was a great match.

7. We are looking forward to the next match.

단어 TEST Step 1 · p.40

01 피하다	02 제안	03 속상한, 마음이 상한
04 걱정하다; 걱정	05 접촉, 닿음	06 조언
07 싸우다	08 이발, 머리 깎기	09 홀로, 혼자
10 물건	11 다치게 하다, 아프게 하다	
12 어질러진, 더러운	13 현명한	14 공유하다, 나누다
15 점심시간	16 반복하다	17 문제
18 소리치다, 소리 지르다	19 ~부터, ~ 이후	
20 의도하다, 작정하다	21 싫어하다	
22 참다, 견디다	23 한계, 제한	24 설명하다
25 조언하다, 충고하다	26 아직	
27 싸다, 꾸리다	28 어려운	29 용서하다
30 초보의, 초급의	31 두려움, 공포	32 이유, 까닭
33 풀다, 해결하다	34 (연극, 영화의) 대사	
35 ~에 집중하다	36 잠에서 깨다	
37 늦게까지 자지 않고 있다	38 체중이 늘다	
39 고의로, 일부러	40 (기계가) 멈추다, 정지하다	
41 해결하다	42 결국, 마침내	43 지적하다

단어 TEST Step 2 · p.41

01 mirror	02 elementary	03 share
04 difficult	05 repeat	06 yell
07 contact	08 advise	09 matter
10 pack	11 fight	12 lunch break
13 haircut	14 stuff	15 hurt
16 stand	17 avoid	18 limit
19 yet	20 toothache	21 suggestion
22 alone	23 worry	24 messy
25 upset	26 reason	27 hate
28 line	29 advice	30 forgive
31 explain	32 fear	33 wise
34 solve	35 in the end	36 focus on
37 shut down	38 gain weight	39 up and down
40 stay up late	41 on purpose	42 set an alarm
43 wake up		

단어 TEST Step 3 · p.42

1 messy, 어질러진, 더러운 2 hate, 싫어하다

3 toothache, 치통 4 contact, 접촉

5 haircut, 이발, 머리 깎기 6 line, 대사 7 repeat, 반복하다

8 share, 공유하다 9 suggestion, 제안 10 fear, 두려움,공포

11 avoid, 피하다 12 elementary, 초급의

13 hurt, 다치게 하다 14 yell, 소리 지르다

15 advice, 조언 16 forgive, 용서하다

대화문 TEST Step 1 · p.43~44

Listen & Talk 1-A-1

look, happy, matter / wore, sister's favorite, got / Did, tell / not yet, what to do

Listen & Talk 1-A-2

look down, What's the matter / got a haircut, funny / Take off, let me see, looks fine / not used to

Listen & Talk 1-B

look tired, the matter / I didn't have breakfast this morning / too bad, until lunch break / snack bar, could have / think so, too, How, make, suggestion / can post, suggestion

Listen & Talk 2 A-1

how to do better, give me some advice / solve a lot of / solve, should focus on, ones, got wrong

Listen & Talk 2 A-2

was late for class, wake up / set an alarm / turn it off / think you should , far from, That way, get out of bed

Review 1

stop playing computer games, What should I do / why don't you use, set, limit, shuts down / a good idea / I think you should move, out of, into / I think, should, for the advice

Communication

on the air / What's the matter / sharing, with, stuff without asking, What should, do / tell her your feelings, make some rules / I'll try that, Thanks for

대화문 TEST Step 2 · p.45~46

Listen & Talk 1-A-1

M: You don't look so happy today. What's the matter?

W: I wore my sister's favorite T-shirt. But I got grape juice on it.

M: Oh, no. Did you tell your sister?

W: No, not yet. I don't know what to do .

Listen & Talk 1-A-2

Sora: David, you look down today. What's the matter?

David: I got a haircut but it's too short. I look funny.

Sora: Take off your hat and let me see. (*pause*) Oh, it looks fine.

David: Really? I guess I'm just not used to it yet.

37

Jane: You look tired. What's the matter?

Mike: I didn't have breakfast this morning. I'm so hungry.

Jane: Oh, that's too bad. We still have two more hours until lunch break.

Mike: Our school should have a snack bar. Then, we could have a quick breakfast or snacks.

Jane: I think so, too. How can we make that suggestion?

Mike: We can post it on the suggestion board.

Listen & Talk 2 A-1

Sujin: I don't know how to do better in math. Can you give me some advice?

Jake: How do you study for tests?

Sujin: I just solve a lot of problems.

Jake: Well, don't solve everything. I think you should focus on the ones you got wrong.

Listen & Talk 2 A-2

Emily: I was late for class again. I just can't wake up in the morning.

Tom: Do you set an alarm?

Emily: Yeah, but I turn it off and go back to sleep.

Tom: I think you should put it far from your bed. That way, you'll have to get out of bed.

Review 1

Eric: Ms. Morris, I just can't stop playing computer games. What should I do?

Ms. Morris: Well, why don't you use a special program? When you set a time limit, the computer shuts down at that time.

Eric: Oh, that's a good idea.

Ms. Morris: And I think you should move the computer out of your room and into the living room.

Eric: I think I should. Thank you for the advice, Ms. Morris.

Communication

Solomon: Hello, you're on the air.

Amy: Hi, Solomon. I'm Amy.

Solomon: Hi, Amy. What's the matter?

Amy: I hate sharing my room with my little sister. She uses my stuff without asking me first. What should I do?

Solomon: Hmm.... I think you should tell her your feelings. And you should also make some rules with your sister.

Amy: Oh, I'll try that. Thanks for the advice.

본문 TEST Step 1   p.47~48

01 old, these, going, down   02 looks down

03 Let's, feelings, find

04 What, yelled at, after

05 because, forgot, lines   06 out, that, made

07 could, in front

08 sure, mean, hurt

09 have been, since   10 what, saying

11 never put, down

12 that, going, be   13 Don't, far, see

14 forgive, say, word   15 even look at

16 has never been

17 alone during   18 best friend

19 reason, know about

20 stand, any longer   21 go, tell, about

22 want, to, hurt   23 let, go   24 work, out

25 so, that, talking

26 went, talked, her

27 avoid, on purpose

28 didn't, way, say

29 doesn't, any more

30 too, part, up   31 like, face, wiser, end

본문 TEST Step 2   p.49~50

01 years old, these days, going up and down

02 looks down

03 Let's listen to, feelings, find out why

04 What a day, yelled at, after

05 because, forgot, lines on stage

06 pointed out, that Bella made

07 could, in front of

08 sure, did not mean to hurt

09 have been, since elementary school

10 what, saying

11 would never put, down

12 that, not going to be friends anymore

13 Don't go too far, see

14 can't forgive, didn't say a word

15 didn't even look at

16 has never been

17 ate alone during

18 Bella's best friend

19 reason that we don't know about

20 can't stand, any longer   21 go, tell, about

22 want, to be hurt

23 should let it go   24 work it out

25 that, are talking

26 went to, talked to her

27 didn't avoid, on purpose

28 a way to say sorry

29 any more problems like

30 Me, too, part of growing up

31 Just like, face, solve them, wiser, end

1 Bella는 올해 15세이고 요즘 그 애의 기분은 좋다가 안 좋다가 한다.

2 오늘 그 애는 우울해 보인다.

3 Bella의 감정에 귀 기울여 보고 그 이유를 알아보자.

4 정말 끔찍한 하루야! 학교 연극이 끝난 후 Jenny가 Bella에게 소리를 지르다니 믿을 수가 없어.

5 글쎄, 그건 Bella가 무대에서 그녀의 대사를 잊어버렸기 때문이잖아.

6 Jenny는 Bella가 저지른 실수를 지적했잖아.

7 어떻게 모든 사람 앞에서 그렇게 할 수가 있니?

8 하지만 난 Jenny가 Bella에게 상처를 주려고 했던 건 아니었다고 확신해.

9 그들은 초등학교 때부터 가장 친한 친구였잖아. 기억하지?

10 내 말이 바로 그거야.

11 진정한 친구라면 절대로 그런 식으로 Bella를 깎아내리지 않을 거야.

12 나는 그들이 더 이상 친구로 지내지 않을까봐 걱정돼.

13 자, Fear. 너무 극단적으로 생각하지 마. 곧 알게 되겠지.

14 난 Jenny를 용서할 수 없어. 그 애는 Bella에게 한마디도 말을 안 했어.

15 Jenny는 심지어 Bella를 쳐다보지도 않았어.

16 Jenny가 전에 이렇게 차가웠던 적이 없었어.

17 Bella는 오늘 점심시간에 혼자 밥을 먹었잖아. 가엾은 Bella!

18 Jenny는 Bella의 가장 친한 친구야.

19 나는 우리가 모르는 어떤 이유가 있다고 확신해.

20 나는 더 이상 이 상황을 못 참아.

21 Bella는 일단 가서 Jenny에게 자신의 감정을 말해야 해.

22 나는 Bella가 또다시 상처받는 걸 원하지 않아.

23 그 애는 그냥 내버려 두어야 해.

24 그 애들은 좋은 친구야. 그 애들이 잘 해낼 거야.

25 휴! 나는 그 애들이 다시 이야기하게 되어 무척 기뻐.

26 그래, Bella가 Jenny에게 가서 그 애에게 먼저 말을 걸었지.

27 Jenny는 일부러 Bella를 피한 게 아니었어.

28 맞아, Jenny는 사과하는 방법을 몰랐던 거야.

29 나는 Bella에게 이번과 같은 문제가 더 이상 없기를 바라.

30 나도 그래. 하지만 문제들은 성장의 일부야.

31 이번과 꼭 마찬가지로 Bella는 문제들에 직면하게 될 거고, 그것들을 해결할 거고, 그리고 결국 더 현명해질 거야.

1 Bella is 15 years old this year and these days her feelings are going up and down.

2 Today, she looks down.

3 Let's listen to Bella's feelings and find out why.

4 What a day! I can't believe Jenny yelled at Bella after the school play.

5 Well, that's because Bella forgot her lines on stage.

6 Jenny pointed out the mistake that Bella made.

7 How could she do that in front of everyone?

8 But I'm sure Jenny did not mean to hurt Bella.

9 They have been best friends since elementary school. Remember?

10 That's what I'm saying.

11 A true friend would never put Bella down like that.

12 I'm worried that they are not going to be friends anymore.

13 Come on, Fear. Don't go too far. We'll see.

14 I can't forgive Jenny. She didn't say a word to Bella.

15 Jenny didn't even look at her.

16 Jenny has never been this cold before.

17 Bella ate alone during lunch today. Poor Bella!

18 Jenny is Bella's best friend.

19 I'm sure there is a reason that we don't know about.

20 I can't stand this any longer.

21 Bella should just go and tell her about her feelings.

22 I don't want Bella to be hurt again.

23 She should let it go.

24 They are good friends. They will work it out.

25 Whew! I'm so happy that they are talking again.

26 Yeah, Bella went to Jenny and talked to her first.

27 Jenny didn't avoid Bella on purpose.

28 Yeah, Jenny didn't know a way to say sorry.

29 I hope Bella doesn't have any more problems like this.

30 Me, too. But problems are part of growing up.

31 Just like this time, Bella will face the problems, solve them, and become wiser in the end.

Wrap up 1

1. late again

2. stayed up late, last night

3. should try to, earlier

4. should also pack, save time

5. try your advice

1. upset when, pointed out, in front of others

2. mean to hurt

3. Thanks for coming up

Think & Write

1. Worry Doll

2. want to tell, have

3. worried about, math grades

4. have had, since last year

5. do better

6. try to study, can't focus on

7. what to do

8. have not had, because of

9. take, away

구석구석지문 TEST Step 2   p.58

Wrap up 1

1. Mr. Jones: Daisy, you're late again.

2. Daisy: I'm really sorry, Mr. Jones. I stayed up late again last night.

3. Mr. Jones: Well, I think you should try to go to bed earlier.

4. You should also pack your bag the night before, so you can save time in the morning.

5. Daisy: Okay, Mr. Jones. I'll try your advice.

Read & Think

1. Bella: Jenny, I was upset when you pointed out my mistake in front of others.

2. But I'm sure you didn't mean to hurt my feelings.

3. Jenny: I'm so sorry, Bella. Thanks for coming up to me first.

Think & Write

1. Dear Worry Doll,

2. I want to tell you a problem that I have.

3. I'm worried about my terrible math grades.

4. I have had this problem since last year.

5. I want to do better in math.

6. But when I try to study math, I just can't focus on it.

7. I don't know what to do.

8. I have not had a good night's sleep because of this worry.

9. Can you take my worries away?

적중100

영어 기출 문제집

정답 및 해설

비상 | 김진완